MATHEMATICS

IN THE

MIDDLE

edited by Larry Leutzinger

University of Northern Iowa
Cedar Falls, Iowa

National Council of
Teachers of Mathematics

&

National Middle School
Association

Library of Congress Cataloging-in-Publication Data:

Printed in the United States of America

CONTENTS

**PART TWO
DEVELOPING
MIDDLE SCHOOL
CURRICULA**

**PART THREE
IMPLEMENTING
CHANGE IN
THE CLASSROOM**

PREFACE

This book is aptly named. It is most appropriate to have a publication devoted to the middle grades, since those years form the bridge between the elementary school and the high school. How well children acquire important mathematical concepts, processes, and skills during the middle years greatly affects the curriculum in secondary school and beyond. Programs that appeal to the adolescent must be implemented if students are to develop the proper attitude toward mathematics and an inclination toward mathematics-based careers.

Young people go through a significant period of life as they leave childhood and move toward early adolescence. They experience not only physical changes but significant and enduring social, emotional, and moral changes, as well. The young adolescent does not just become a more mature and bigger child; the person leaving the middle-level years is, quite literally, a new person. The personality, attitudes, and values that are formed during these years are, for the most part, the ones that will direct an individual's behavior throughout life.

A feature of this developmental stage that makes it especially difficult for educators is that every individual follows his or her own timetable of development. Some start the maturation process early, others late. Some move through the period rapidly, others slowly. The need to deal with diversity is a defining reality of middle-level education, as every middle school teacher knows.

Young adolescents are a wondrous, adventuresome, and eager lot engaged in discovering, exploring, and finding themselves. During these years most young people acquire the capacity to think hypothetically, to reason, to comprehend cause and effect, and to think about thinking. The importance of these formative years should never be diminished by the outward flightiness, silliness, and less-than-genteel behavior that also may characterize them. Decisions that lead to significant choices and consequences—about alcohol, drugs, and sex, for example—have lifelong implications.

As this new understanding of the age of early adolescence has become more widely shared and as the importance of the educational experiences youth undergo during this crucial period has been recognized, middle-level education has come to the forefront. The demand for content and methodology that reflect the nature of young adolescents and challenge them intellectually has been heard—although all too often it is couched excessively in terms of test scores.

Mathematics itself is in the middle—of a massive reform effort only now beginning to pay extensive dividends. With the advent of NCTM's (National Council of Teachers of Mathematics) three landmark *Standards* documents, middle schools throughout the nation started to rethink their curriculum, instructional methods, and assessment. The results of the implementation of *Standards*-based programs, reflected throughout this book, need to be shared with parents, teachers, and administrators. Many voices speak eloquently on important aspects of reform. They are speaking loudly and clearly on the issues facing middle-grades classes in particular and all mathematics classrooms in general.

Most of the articles are either written by middle-grades teachers or reverberate with their thoughts and feelings. And the voices of middle-grades students are present in a majority of the chapters.

This publication consists of three sections: Part One (articles 1–11) describes some important issues for middle-grades students, schools, and programs. Gary Tsuruda leads off with a powerful chapter that contrasts student-centered and content-centered classrooms.

Part Two (articles 12–18) is the centerpiece of the book. Each of five middle-grades *Standards*-based curricula is presented in detail by the program's director. The lead article in Part Two clearly outlines the levels at which teachers may enter reform in their classrooms, with the ultimate level that of implementing a *Standards*-based curriculum, perhaps one of the five that follow in Part Two. This part closes with an article that traces one teacher's journey in search of a curriculum that captivates her students.

Part Three (articles 19–28) presents projects, activities, and programs that are actively implementing some of NCTM's recommendations for middle-grades classrooms. All content strands are presented with rich connections or creative uses of technology.

This publication represents many hours of hard work by the authors of the articles. In addition, the members of the editorial panel spent long sessions selecting and editing articles. The panel represents a variety of backgrounds and experiences, all of which added important perspectives to the final product. Dan Dolan and Robert Hamada have served NCTM with distinction in many capacities. Dan is currently the director of the Project to Increase Mastery of Mathematics, and Bob is the mathematics coordinator of the Los Angeles Unified School District. Stephanie Z. Smith was a contributing author of *Mathematics in Context* and is a mathematics educator at Brigham Young University. Kathy Vielhaber teaches eighth grade at Parkway Middle School in Saint Louis, Missouri.

Those associated with the editing process at NCTM need also to be recognized. Jack Price had the insight to initiate this important publication. Marianne Weber and Eric Hart, chairs of the Educational Materials Committee, and Cynthia Rosso and Harry Tunis, of NCTM, provided guidelines and support. Charles Clements and his crew refined raw material into the finished product. Sue Swaim, executive director of the National Middle School Association (NMSA), provided poignant additions to this preface and NMSA support for *Mathematics in the Middle*. And special thanks goes to Jane Ericson, Nan Sash, and Mary Friedrich, who handled much of the communication between the panel and the authors.

PART ONE

ISSUES IN
MIDDLE SCHOOL
MATHEMATICS

1

Middle School Mathematics Reform: Form versus Spirit

GARY TSURUDA

How hard is it to implement mathematics reform at the middle school level? At a recent meeting of parents at a local middle school, one parent bemoaned the lack of a textbook aligned with the NCTM (National Council of Teachers of Mathematics) (1989) *Curriculum and Evaluation Standards for School Mathematics*. "After all," he said, "creating this kind of curriculum isn't rocket science." Another parent, a mathematician at Lockheed Martin Missiles and Space Company, a *real* rocket scientist, responded, "No, it's much harder than rocket science!" Therein lies the problem with middle school mathematics reform.

Good teaching has always been complex, frustrating, and demanding. It has required subject-matter knowledge along with management and organizational skills. In addition, good teachers need patience, curiosity, compassion, trust, imagination, and a well-developed sense of humor. It is a tribute to our profession that so many middle school mathematics teachers embody and maintain these qualities. Changing from a content-centered curriculum to one that is more in alignment with the *Standards* places a premium on these qualities of good teaching. The student-centered curriculum envisioned in the *Standards* requires a major change in the role of the teacher. This shift is at the heart of reform in mathematics education, and each teacher's personal resources will be challenged to meet the needs of the new curriculum.

Some teachers have been trying to implement mathematics reform for several years. Many others have only recently begun to try some of the new ideas in their classrooms. For others, the vision of *Standards* is far from reality in any form. This range of teacher's acceptance and implementation of new ideas is neither surprising nor disappointing. Change is difficult, especially in a large institution as tied to tradition as the educational system. Asking teachers to challenge belief systems that are rooted in generations of tradition is a huge challenge.

Many of the mathematics reform efforts in recent years have focused on the middle school. Perhaps this is because the character of the students in this age group demands the kind of curriculum advocated by the *Standards*. Traditional content-centered curricula dominated by skills instruction is very difficult to "sell" to students who are intensely curious, egocentric, social, and active. Telling middle school students how to perform a particular procedure without giving it a personal context and then requiring them to sit quietly by themselves to practice the procedure goes against their very nature. More than any other age group, middle school students need a curriculum that challenges them to think, discuss, and solve problems related to their lives.

Middle school is ripe for reform because the traditional middle school curriculum has been little more than a review of previous learning. This content-centered curriculum as defined by most traditional textbooks has used the middle school years as an opportunity to consolidate the skills covered over the previous several years in final preparation for the abstract concepts of high school mathematics.

We are starting to view the middle school in another way: as an opportunity to introduce students to a curriculum that takes advantage of their curiosity, energy, and social concerns. We can now do more than review skills. We can introduce students to mathematical thinking and problem solving through activities that are both engaging and rigorous. The move toward a more student-centered curriculum is essential. It is a major challenge for educators and an exciting opportunity to bring out the best in teachers and students.

Content-Centered Curriculum

How does a content-centered curriculum differ from a student-centered curriculum? Is there more content and less interest in the individual student in the former? Is there a lack of content and an emphasis on students' feelings in the latter? We need to be clear about the fact that mathematics reform is *not* about the transition from a bad curriculum to a good one. This is not an either-or situation, a mistake often made by critics of mathematics reform who assume that a change in emphasis is an abandonment of the parts of the curriculum they feel are important. In fact, reform is more about philosophy than it is about any particular curriculum. The difference between a content-centered curriculum and a student-centered curriculum is one of emphasis. Both include familiar mathematical content and both consider the needs of the student.

The traditional content-centered curriculum evolved because there was a need for students to know how to perform certain procedural skills. The pretechnological workplace demanded these skills, so the schools taught them. The teacher was viewed as a dispenser and the students as passive receptacles of knowledge in the form of facts, skills, and procedures. Textbooks supported this model by providing lessons that covered isolated skills algorithmically. Unfortunately, this traditional approach has been ineffective, as illustrated by the results of the National Assessment of Educational Progress and the Third International Mathematics and Science Study (TIMSS). Both of these assessments have shown that the traditional curriculum offered in the United States is producing students who cannot compute and cannot compete internationally. Only six of ten high school seniors can compute

with decimals, fractions, and percents, and fewer than one in ten can use beginning algebra. In the TIMSS eighth-grade data, the United States ranked twenty-first of forty-one countries studied.

In reality, there is no one right way to implement reform, no recipe for instant success. Instead, there is a set of the teacher's beliefs about how students learn and about what is important to know.

The move away from a curriculum dominated by procedures is also driven by recent advances in technology and learning research. Because of the rapid adoption of calculators and computers, the need for pencil-and-paper computational skills in the workplace is virtually nonexistent. Recent research indicates the need for students to construct their own knowledge from complex situations rather than have the information "fed" to them in small doses. This view is fundamental in helping to redefine the role of the teacher.

In summary, curricular change is necessary for three primary reasons: the current curriculum has been shown to be ineffective; new theories about how students learn call for a different instructional approach; and technological advancements have eliminated the need for some pencil-and-paper skills and have given us new tools for using mathematics to solve problems. For these compelling reasons we have an obligation to take another look at the way we provide mathematics instruction to our students.

Student-Centered Curriculum

A student-centered curriculum is not short on content. In fact, the opposite is true: the *Standards* calls for a curriculum that is more comprehensive and richer than traditional skills-based programs. One of the problems with characterizing traditional curricula as content-centered is the implicit assumption that content is not important in the new curriculum. Changing the focus of a curriculum does not necessarily mean throwing out content. If anything, mathematics curriculum reform involves trying to reorganize the essential elements of content into units of study that provide *more* depth of analysis of individual topics.

Critics of mathematics reform say that a student-centered curriculum waters down the content by eliminating arithmetic skills. In reality, arithmetic is as important now as it ever was. Some aspects of arithmetic are *more* important now, whereas others will receive less emphasis. For example, number sense has been made more important because of technology. It is essential that students be able to judge the reasonableness of answers through estimation and mental mathematics techniques. It is, however, much less important that students learn to find answers to computation problems using standard algorithms. Mental arithmetic and "back of the envelope" calculations are much more important than the ability to find exact answers to complex computation problems using pencil and paper.

A student-centered curriculum focuses on students' needs. Students, particularly at the middle school level, need to be actively engaged in learning. They need to be able to verbalize their ideas and share them with their classmates; to be given opportunities to build their understanding of mathematical concepts by "doing" mathematics; and to be actively involved in activities designed for collaboration, discussion, thinking, and reflecting. Further, they need to be engaged through a variety of materials, approaches, and strategies. Yes, this *is* harder than rocket science!

Contrasts: Form versus Spirit

Many people have tried to draw sharp distinctions between traditional and reform curricula by pointing out the differences in the outward appearances of traditional and reform classrooms. Such superficial comparisons are misleading because they focus on the form rather than the spirit of the two curricula. In reality, the differences are significant because the philosophies of learning that underlie them are antithetical. If we believe that students learn best by being told exactly what steps to follow, then a traditional curriculum makes sense. If, however, we believe that students learn best by constructing their own knowledge based on previous understandings, then a student-centered curriculum makes sense.

This is not an either-or situation. Most educators do not think in such black-and-white terms and are, therefore, aligned along a continuum of philosophical beliefs from very traditional to very reform oriented. It is doubtful that anyone believes that computational skills should be taught to the exclusion of all other mathematics topics, just as it is doubtful that anyone believes that students should never be allowed to practice any computational skill.

Most teachers do not think of themselves as researchers or curriculum experts or program designers, but they do fill these roles every day in their classrooms.

Consider a classroom on the cutting edge of mathematics reform: the desks are arranged in groups of four, manipulative materials are readily available for student use, students are involved in problem-solving activities, and calculators are available for every student to use. Outwardly this classroom manifests all the trappings of a student-centered curriculum. However, it *may* be that the desk groupings are nothing more than a different seating arrangement; the students may never be allowed to work together in their groups. The manipulatives may be used only to illustrate standard computational algorithms. Problem-solving activities may be nothing more than routine word problems that are never discussed in class. Calculators may be used only to check the answers to pencil-and-paper computations. This "cutting edge" classroom does not represent the spirit of mathematics reform. It is the result of a superficial understanding of the philosophy and goals of a student-centered curriculum. In fact, it is quite possible that a classroom that has desks arranged in rows, no weekly problem-solving activities, and no calculators might better exemplify the beliefs underlying mathematics reform. In reality, there is no one right way to implement reform, no recipe for instant success. Instead, there is a set of the teacher's beliefs about how students learn and about what is important to know. These beliefs, combined with hard work, dedication, patience, and common sense, are the hallmarks of successful mathematics curriculum reform.

Major change in education is a complex, difficult, and slow process. As teachers, we need to approach change with enthusiasm tempered by common sense. Trying out new ideas is part of growing and improving as a teacher, but implementing wholesale changes without careful consideration and planning can turn into a disaster. Administrators need to be careful about mandating change without proper support. Most teachers are excited about new ideas if they are given the time and support to incorporate them into their own classrooms. We need to concentrate on the beliefs underlying mathematics reform. A focus on form without the philosophical underpinnings can result in classrooms that do a disservice to students, to teachers, and to mathematics education.

A Real Constructivist Classroom

Underlying the appearance of the following classroom is a rationale that defines a student-centered curriculum. The desks are arranged in groups in order to allow students to work together, collaborate on mathematical tasks, make conjectures, and discuss strategies for solving problems, as well as to share and build on one another's ideas. These are the activities that help students construct their own mathematical knowledge; the desk arrangement is merely a way of encouraging the collaboration and discourse. Of course, there is nothing magical about arranging desks in groups of four. Students do not automatically begin to work well together, sharing ideas and debating issues. Without direction, most middle school students use groups for social interaction. It takes time, experience, good materials, and hard work to make group work effective, but it is well worth the effort. A classroom in which students are engaged and involved in constructing their own learning is a beautiful thing to see and experience; it shows mathematics reform in action.

Manipulative materials are tools to help students explore mathematical ideas. As such, they should be available to students at all times, and their broadest possible use should be encouraged. Manipulatives should not be limited to single applications. Pattern blocks should not be limited to exploring geometric relationships, two-color chips should not be used just for learning integer operations, and the use of color cubes should extend beyond building three-dimensional structures. Middle school students are *not* too old to use manipulative materials in mathematics. In fact, manipulatives are essential in helping students understand some of the most important concepts in the middle school curriculum. We need to impress on students the idea that manipulative materials, like rulers, scissors, and calculators, are their tools. When given a problem to solve or a situation to investigate, they should, on their own, use any available materials that will assist them.

Many middle school teachers use a variation of a problem-solving program in which students are given an extended time to solve a nonroutine problem and are asked to describe their solutions in written form. This frequently used idea is easy to incorporate into any classroom structure. Having students solve this type of problem is a worthwhile activity, and solving a variety of problems is an excellent way to learn how and when to apply mathematical ideas in new situations. A good problem is accessible to students who are struggling with mathematics and challenging to those who catch on more quickly. It is engaging to a large range of students and has more than one solution

method or more than one correct answer. However, an effective problem-solving program does much more than expose students to many problems. Helping students learn to solve problems involves providing models of good problem solving and clear explanations of solutions. Students' discussions during the problem-solving process and after solutions have been found are indispensible for internalizing both techniques and attitudes. We want students to look forward to the challenge of problems with enthusiasm and confidence throughout their lifetimes.

Ultimately, however, mathematics reform does not take place in specific curriculum materials, research papers, textbooks, or administrative offices; it takes place in classrooms.

At the middle school level, problems need to be sequenced to provide more complexity and a greater degree of abstraction as the student progresses in problem-solving ability. For example, early in the sixth grade, students might be asked to solve the "handshake" problem. At this level, students might solve the problem by simulation or by making a table and extending a pattern. A solution to the same type of problem at the seventh-grade level might involve a discovery of "Gauss's method" of adding a sequence of consecutive numbers. At the eighth-grade level, students might solve a similar problem by generalizing the pattern using correct algebraic notation.

An effective problem-solving program requires interaction between students both during and after a solution has been found. Collaboration can be a very effective method for helping students gain confidence in their problem-solving abilities, especially when group discussions are used as a springboard to individual thinking about a problem. Many students benefit from a short brainstorming session within their groups before attempting to solve a problem. Having a safe forum for sharing their ideas and interacting with others is essential to the development of a positive mindset about problem solving. Once students have been given time to solve a problem and describe their solution processes, they need to be given an opportunity to share their solutions with one another. This activity not only gives students recognition for their efforts but also provides other students with valuable ideas for solving future problems. Teachers who assign problems must be willing to invest the time to read and provide feedback on students' solutions. This is a time-consuming but necessary commitment if we want students to become good mathematical problem solvers; teachers who are not willing to provide students with helpful feedback on their problem-solving efforts should not assign problems for students to solve. This is another example of the form rather than the spirit of mathematics reform.

Another important consideration facing teachers in construtivist classrooms relates to assessment and technology. For many years, mathematics teachers have resisted allowing their students to use calculators for anything more than checking their answers to pencil-and-paper calculations, or they have allowed calculators only after students have demonstrated the ability to perform calculations manually. The seeming hypocrisy of this practice originates in the dilemma that confronts most middle school teachers of mathematics. Even if we believe that many—perhaps even most—pencil-and-paper calculations are unnecessary because of the availability of calculators, our students and our programs are assessed using standardized tests that require extensive pencil-and-paper skills. For teachers, this is a no-win situation. We are forced to compromise either our students' test scores or our beliefs about what is important for students to learn.

More than any other age group, middle school students need a curriculum that challenges them to think, discuss, and solve problems related to their lives.

Teachers, schools, and districts need to discuss the issue of computational skills openly and agree on standards. They need to address the issue of balance among mental estimation and calculation, pencil-and-paper algorithms, and calculator and computer computation. A new view of curriculum will result from a reasoned examination of what students will need in the workplace of their future. Most people will probably agree on the importance of mental arithmetic and number sense, and the availability of calculators and computers will reduce the importance of some but not all pencil-and-paper computation.

Teachers cannot sit back and wait for decisions to be made about external forms of assessment. We have an obligation to provide meaningful internal assessments of our students' progress that match our beliefs about

what students need to know. For most of us, a balance will be reached among computational skills, essential concepts, and problem solving. Our assessments are no longer limited to simple teacher-made tests. We now include open-ended questions, projects, portfolios, and performance tasks among our methods of assessment. Such variety gives us a better picture of our students' understanding about the mathematical ideas we value.

Perhaps the real spirit of a student-centered curriculum can best be seen through the eyes of students. Instead of a set routine in which the teacher presents and explains procedures, the students experience a wide range of activities, from whole-class presentations by students to small-group discussions to individual thinking and writing. Instead of passively trying to absorb knowledge, students are actively involved in exploring ideas and trying to solve problems. Instead of being asked on tests to replicate procedures, students' learning is assessed in a variety of ways directly linked to learning activities.

In a traditional content-based curriculum, students might learn to find the area of a trapezoid by first being shown the formula. The formula would be explained with well-labeled drawings and several examples. The students would then be given problems to practice on their own to ensure that they could use the formula correctly, and then would start on the homework, fifteen to twenty exercises like the examples they had just seen. This whole process would probably take one or two class periods.

The same topic might be approached in a student-centered curriculum by having students discuss their understandings of prerequisites such as the concept of area, the use of formulas for simpler shapes like rectangles and triangles, and the properties of trapezoids. Students would then examine the areas of many different trapezoids using dot paper. By sharing data in small groups, they could look for patterns and develop a formula for finding the area of any trapezoid. Different equivalent formulas would be shared and discussed, including the "standard" formula. This whole process would also take one or two class periods.

The students in the first example would probably be able to apply the formula in simple exercises but would have gained little else from the lesson. The students who discovered a formula of their own would also be able to apply the formula, and in addition, they would have learned or reviewed problem-solving techniques, pattern identification and generalization, algebraic formulas, and group collaboration processes and would have engaged in reflective thinking about previous learning. Isn't this the richness we want for our students?

We need to rethink our role as teachers in order to

make this type of curriculum work. Simply providing students with clear, concise explanations of procedures in a sequenced, manageable way is not enough. Teachers need to assess the needs of students and plan classroom activities that are sequenced to meet those needs, bringing in as many resources as necessary to make the activities engaging, rich, and challenging. Teachers must also create a climate in the classroom that encourages free thinking and supports risk taking while maintaining a focus on the important mathematical ideas. Establishing an environment that promotes positive interactions among students about mathematics is no easy task, but it is an essential component of a student-centered classroom.

Teachers, schools, and districts need to discuss the issue of computational skills openly and agree on standards.

The ways we assess students' understanding must change along with our ways of helping students learn. We need to find ways of matching our assessments and our learning activities that blur the lines of distinction so that learning and assessing learning "feel" the same to students. Perhaps this involves little more than seeing assessment in broader terms. Certainly, it means changing our beliefs that assessment is a rather narrow set of things we do to students after we think we have taught them what they need to know.

Teachers need to find a balance between the successful ideas that have worked with students in the past and the new ideas we think hold promise for the future. Balance in a mathematics curriculum means different things to different people; some antireform groups say that balance means more computational skills, whereas some proreform groups say it means more problem solving. In reality, balance is about common sense. We in education have been guilty for too long of jumping on bandwagons in search of the simple solution to all our problems. The result has been major swings in our approaches to instruction. Unfortunately, a panacea doesn't exist; there are no magic answers. We need to reach a consensus, if only in our own districts and schools, about what makes sense for our students in light of what we have done in the past, how students learn, and what resources we have available to us. Dividing into proreform and antireform groups will not help us find that balance.

Overcoming Barriers to Change

How can we find a way to create learning environments in which students are challenged to think mathematically while striking a balance between what we have been doing well and what we need to do better?

To start, we need to be realistic about the barriers to change that we are facing. Change is difficult under the best of circumstances. It is a slow, painstaking process that begins with the acceptance of the need to change. Teachers don't just suddenly decide to teach differently. Most of us have a great deal of ourselves invested in our teaching, and giving up on some of these long-held beliefs, even those we have not consciously considered for many years, is tough. Even if we clearly see the need to change, it is not easy to do; there is a great deal to unlearn.

There is also a great deal to learn; and what we need to learn is not simple. Very few exemplars exist, and there is no "one right way," no set of steps to follow, to become a "reform" teacher. To be consistent with the philosophy of constructivism, teachers need to think about ideas in light of their previous experiences, try them out in their classrooms, and decide what works for their students. For some teachers, "problems of the week" are a good way to start this process. For others, group activities, one or two days a week, make the transition easier. No matter how we choose to start, the shift will not be easy. For each teacher, the move to a more student-centered curriculum is dependent on time and support.

Teachers need time to consider the ideas of others, time to discuss these ideas with colleagues and to reflect on the ideas within the context of their own classrooms. If change is to occur on a large scale, the educational establishment will have to find ways to create this time. In addition, we will need to establish ongoing collegial support. Without this time and continued support, the student-centered classroom will exist only in a few classrooms.

An Invitation to Middle School Mathematics Teachers

Reforming mathematics education at the middle school level is a huge challenge for everyone involved. Curriculum developers, university researchers, textbook publishers, and school administrators are all key players in this undertaking; but ultimately, the real mathematics education reformers are teachers in classrooms. Most teachers do not think of themselves as researchers or curriculum experts or program designers, but they do fill these roles every day in their classrooms. We need to acknowledge our importance in the overall picture of mathematics education reform and begin to take responsibility for the important decisions affecting our students. Those we consider experts in mathematics education reform are our most important allies, and we should enlist all the support and ideas they have to offer. Ultimately, however, mathematics reform does not take place in specific curriculum materials, research papers, textbooks, or administrative offices; it takes place in classrooms.

Middle school students are not too old to use manipulative materials in mathematics.

Middle school mathematics teachers are invited to take part in an exciting new venture: to take on a task that is harder than rocket science, for which there is no blueprint and few exemplars, in an atmosphere of political resistance to change. Sound like fun?

The answer is "yes!" Middle school mathematics teachers are a special breed of people. Like the students they teach, they are energetic, inquisitive, competitive, and daring. But they would also have to be crazy to want to take on such a challenge, wouldn't they? Perhaps not, because there are many compelling reasons to accept this challenge, not the least of which is the understanding and belief that our current approach to teaching mathematics simply does not work for most of our students. Teachers who take part in this effort to improve mathematics education will experience new highs in excitement and exhilaration. They will experience increases in students' achievement and improvements in students' attitudes toward mathematics. And they will see excitement in their students.

When you think about it, isn't this why most of us are teachers?

For Further Reading

Acquarelli, Kris, and Judith Mumme. "A Renaissance in Mathematics Education Reform." *Phi Delta Kappan* (March 1996): 478–84.

Ball, Deborah L. "Teacher Learning and the Mathematics Reforms." *Phi Delta Kappan* (March 1996): 500–508.

Elmore, Richard F., and Susan H. Fuhrman, eds. *The Governance of Curriculum.* Alexandria, Va.: Association for Supervision and Curriculum Development, 1994.

Fiske, Edward B. *Smart Schools, Smart Kids.* New York: Simon & Schuster, 1991.

Mathematical Sciences Education Board. *Reshaping School Mathematics.* Washington, D.C.: National Academy Press, 1990.

Middle Grade Task Force. *Caught in the Middle.* Sacramento, Calif.: California State Department of Education, 1987.

National Center for Education Statistics. *Pursuing Excellence.* Washington, D.C.: U.S. Government Printing Office, 1996.

National Council of Teachers of Mathematics. *Assessment in the Mathematics Classroom.* 1993 Yearbook of the National Council of Teachers of Mathematics, edited by Norman L. Webb. Reston, Va.: National Council of Teachers of Mathematics, 1993.

———. *Assessment Standards for School Mathematics.* Reston, Va.: National Council of Teachers of Mathematics, 1995.

———. *Curriculum and Evaluation Standards for School Mathematics.* Reston, Va.: National Council of Teachers of Mathematics, 1989.

———. *Professional Standards for Teaching Mathematics.* Reston, Va.: National Council of Teachers of Mathematics, 1991.

Resnick, Lauren B. *Education and Learning to Think.* Washington, D.C.: National Academy Press, 1987.

Sarason, Seymour B. *The Predictable Failure of Educational Reform.* San Francisco, Calif.: Jossey-Bass, 1990.

Gary Tsuruda, *Jordan Middle School, Palo Alto, California*

2

Algebra: The First Gate

ELIZABETH PHILLIPS AND
GLENDA LAPPAN

One of the basic tenets of the current reform effort in mathematics education is *inclusion*—to help *every* student develop his or her full mathematical potential. This means that we must become smarter about how to make algebra—the first "gate"—challenging but accessible to all students. The development of algebraic skills and reasoning is too complex and important to be consigned to one or two separate and narrowly defined courses at the high school level. Experiences with algebra and algebraic reasoning must begin in early elementary school and extend throughout secondary school. The basic issue facing curriculum writers and mathematics teachers is how to develop a focused, coherent grades K–12 algebra strand. In this paper we provide examples of rich algebraic experiences in the middle grades, show their potential as part of a coherent and focused grades K–12 algebra curriculum, and raise concerns about some of the obstacles to developing such a curriculum.

A Course Called Algebra

Courses called algebra have been the centerpiece of standard secondary school mathematics curricula for

The authors wish to thank Linda Walker of Tallahassee, Fla., for providing students' reflections on the Who Wins the Race? and Crossing the Line problems featured in this article.

decades. The foremost goal of algebra instruction in the traditional curricula has always been to develop students' proficiency in using symbolic expressions to represent and reason about numerical situations—in other words, to solve equations and inequalities and to manipulate symbolic expressions into their "simplest" equivalent forms. The successful completion of algebra is seen as a "gateway" to future success in scientific and other postsecondary studies (Silver 1997; Moses 1993).

Getting through the algebra gate is so important that it has given rise to prealgebra courses, usually a combination of arithmetic drills and simple equation solving. However, merely taking more prealgebra and algebra courses has not proved successful for many students. Approximately one-third of the entering freshman population at Michigan State University are placed in a beginning (no-credit) algebra course—a common trend that is reflected in colleges and universities throughout the United States. The recent Third International Mathematics and Science Study (TIMSS) (Babcock 1996) confirms that the United States is falling short in the goal of improving algebraic understanding by all students. The TIMSS curriculum analysis suggests that the mathematics curriculum in the United States lacks coherence and focus (Schmidt et al. 1996). Nowhere is this lack of focus and coherence more noticeable than in the area of algebra. Grades K–8 mathematics programs fail to build a platform of understanding for the study of algebra; then, suddenly, in grade 8 or 9, students are thrust into a symbolic world with particular rules governing the ways that symbols are manipulated. Many students fail to thrive in this symbolic environment, and others learn to move the symbols around but have very little insight into why these skills are useful. This is reflected in a statement released by the Board of Directors of the National Council of Teachers of Mathematics (NCTM):

> First-year algebra in its present form is not the algebra for everyone. In fact, it is not the algebra for most high school graduates today. (NCTM 1994, p. 3)

The continued demonstration of students' lack of basic skills in spite of decades of a skill-and-drill curriculum must convince us to look for new ways of bringing students and algebra together. Clearly, a program that uses all the years of a student's mathematics education to develop algebraic thinking, skill, and understanding has the potential to be successful with more students.

Developing a Coherent Algebra Curriculum

If algebra is to be a strand across grades K–12, then it makes sense to use unifying themes to guide the development. One promising theme is suggested below:

> It is essential for students to learn algebra both as a style of mathematical thinking, involving the formalization of patterns, function, and generalizations, and as a set of competencies involving the representations of quantitative relationships. (Silver 1997)

Algebra can be viewed as the study of patterns and regularities and of ways to represent and communicate these patterns, themes that have the potential to bring coherence to the grades K–12 algebra curriculum. Similar organizing themes have been proposed by the NCTM Algebra Working Group (1997). Many of the recently funded National Science Foundation (NSF) curriculum projects have used such themes as guides to develop challenging, coherent mathematics projects for grades K–12. These curriculum projects have sought to analyze what is important for students to know and be able to do in algebra and to study how these important ideas can be developed over time. Many of these projects include embedding important mathematical ideas within the context of interesting problems—real applications, whimsical settings, or mathematics-problem situations. In solving the problems, students observe, generalize, and formalize patterns, developing the appropriate skills along the way.

These problem-based curricula put quantitative reasoning in the forefront and thereby provide the basis from which to investigate patterns of regularity among rates of change between the variables.

Examples of Algebraic Reasoning in the Middle Grades

Taken altogether, the intuitive uses of algebraic thinking in a problem-based curriculum plus the specific development of the concepts of variables and relationships among variables constitute a powerful, sense-making approach to algebra in the grades K–12 curriculum. To illustrate, we turn to examples of situations from one of the NSF-funded curricula, the Connected Mathematics Project (CMP) (Lappan et al. 1995). The first two examples involve problems from a seventh-grade unit that looks at linear relationships in many different situations. The third example includes a problem from an eighth-grade unit exploring reasoning with symbols. The discussions that follow each problem are short summaries of the reasoning and the mathematics that students find in the problem. These summaries, however, do not capture the rich discussion that occurs as students share strategies and ideas and as the teacher continues to probe their understandings.

Example 1: Patterns and Representations

PROBLEM: WHO WINS THE RACE?

Amel used a stopwatch to time his brother, Bonne, walking 100 meters and found Bonne's walking rate to be 1 meter per second. Bonne then challenged Amel to a walking race. Amel—who knows his own rate to be 2.5 meters per second—accepted the challenge and gave Bonne a head start of 45 meters.

Amel knows his brother would enjoy winning the race, but he does not want to make the race so short that Bonne would feel insulted. What would be a good distance for the race if Amel wants his brother to win but wants it to appear to be a close race? Describe your strategy and what evidence you would use to support your answer. What would be a good distance to choose if Amel wants to beat his brother but wants it to appear to be a close race? Explain.

Reflecting on Students' Reasoning

A teacher in Florida, Linda Walker, posed the Who Wins the Race? problem at the beginning of the linearity unit to assess what knowledge her students were bringing to the unit. The following comments and graphs taken from the students' work represent how this group of students reasoned about the problem:

- "When I first got this problem I had no clue how to solve it. When I did the chart and graph, it was much easier to understand."

- "At first I thought, 'how could someone walk 2.5 meters per second???' Then we stepped outside and each student walked to the end of the meter sticks and found out how fast they walked. To my surprise, my speed was pretty similar to that of Amel's."

- "On my graph [figure 2.1] I think I should have done a smaller scale because I would rather show when Amel and Bonne tie. You can tell they will, but I'd rather show it."

- "In the beginning . . . I had no idea. . . . I started with 45, gave Bonne a good winning feel and jumped to 75 m. Testing that, I realized Amel would win. So going up instead of down I kept guessing and Amel always won. It didn't occur to me to go down until everyone's answers were a lot lower."

- "First I figured out that Amel could go 5 m in 2 sec. And that Bonne could go 2 m in 2 sec. Using

that, I found that in 18 sec. Amel would be where Bonne started and that Bonne would be at the 63 m mark."

- "I used 2.5t to find Amel's distance and 45 + t to find Bonne's distance. At the beginning of this class I didn't know why you would put letters into math, but when I did this problem I realized why. It's just to make the math easier."

Reflecting on the Mathematics

These comments reveal that the students are somewhat comfortable with tables and graphs but that scale and interpretation still pose some problems. One student is beginning to see the constant rate that underlies all linear relationships; that is, if Amel walks at 2.5 m/s, then he walks 2.5 m in one second, 5 m in 2 seconds, 7.5 m in 3 seconds, and so on. Another student feels comfortable enough with symbols to use them efficiently in exploring the problem.

The purpose of Who Wins the Race? and other problems in this investigation is to gradually stimulate students to recognize the salient features of linearity and how these features show up in various representations. The next problem builds on the students' use of various representations to help them focus more explicitly on linearity.

Example 2: Rates of Change—a Key to Linearity

PROBLEM: CROSSING THE LINE

For both Bonne and Amel—

- make a table to show the distances walked every 2 seconds, up to the distance walked in the first 40 seconds;
- make graphs on the same axes to show how the distance walked changes as time passes for Amel and for Bonne;
- write an equation for each brother that shows the relationship between the distance walked and the time passed.

1. Explain how you can use the table and the graph to answer the following questions:

   (*a*) How far from the starting line does Amel overtake Bonne?

   (*b*) How many seconds does it take Amel to overtake Bonne?

2. (*a*) After 3 seconds who is ahead? By how much?

   (*b*) How far has Bonne walked from the starting line when Amel has walked 10 meters?

3. Explain how you can use the table, the graph, and the equation to answer the following question: How far from the starting line is each person after 5 minutes?

4. (*a*) Which graph is steeper?

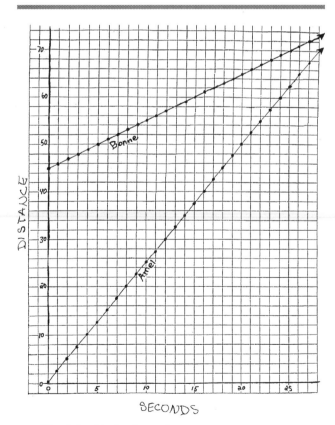

Fig. 2.1. *Student graph*

(b) How can you determine the steepness of the line from the table? From the equation?

5. (a) At which points do Amel's and Bonne's graphs cross the y-axis? What does this mean in terms of the race?

(b) How can you predict from a table where a graph will cross the y-axis? From an equation?

6. Suppose Amel's brother has a head start of h meters and walks at 2 meters per second.

(a) Make a table for 0 to 10 seconds.

(b) Write an equation that represents the distance Bonne has covered from the starting line.

Reflecting on the Mathematics

Crossing the Line is intended to help the teacher and students focus more closely on the underlying mathematics in the Bonne and Amel problem. The questions elicit several important concepts. Questions 1–3 serve as a preliminary introduction to solving equations, but at this stage students solve them using a table, graph, or reasoning about the situation. Question 4 refers to the "steepness" of a line. Amel's graph is steeper, and his faster walking rate affects the steepness of the line. This question opens students' minds to the salient feature of linearity: as one variable changes by a constant amount, the second variable also changes by a constant amount.

Table 2.1 shows, second by second, how far from the starting line Bonne and Amel have walked. From the table, notice how much the dependent d (distance) variable is changing in relation to the independent t (time) variable. The constant rate of change can be observed in the pattern of change between time and distance traveled:

For Amel, as t increases from 0 to 1 second, Amel's distance increases by 2.5 meters. As t increases from 1 to 2 seconds, Amel's distance increases by 2.5 meters. As t increases from 2 to 3 seconds, Amel's distance increases by 2.5 meters.

For each walker, the rate of change between the two variables is a constant. From the equation, many students begin to realize that the constant rate is the coefficient of the independent variable:

$$\text{Distance for Amel} = 2.5t$$
$$\text{Distance for Bonne} = 45 + t$$

In the graph of the data (figure 2.2), the constant rate of change between the two variables is represented by a straight line. The greater the constant rate of change, the steeper the graph. Later in the unit this constant rate of change is called the *slope* of the line.

Question 5 examines the y-intercept. The line representing Amel crosses the vertical axis when the value is zero. The line representing Bonne crosses the vertical axis when the value is 45. These values are connected to their starting places. You can find the value from a table when the independent variable is zero (the start of the race). From an equation, it will be the constant term. Slope and intercepts represent important information about a situation; they are also important "benchmarks" for writing equations and determining graphs of linear situations.

Reflecting on Students' Reasoning

Linda Walker continued to write about the development of her students' algebraic understanding as they moved through the unit on linear relationships:

By the time I reached the unit on linearity, the enthusiasm of my students was impressive. The notion of rate had begun in Variables and Patterns and continued in Comparing and Scaling, and we now seemed to be getting comfortable and confident.

I paid attention to their preference for the head start in the race or the startup costs to be written before the variable—the old $y = mx + b$ became $y = b + mx$, but we didn't talk in terms of m and b and they didn't have to ask why m, why b? We are telling a real story with symbols rather than words, but it was a real story!

I noted the intuitive development of the concept of slope and found that the students' language was "as x increases this amount, y increases this amount." Their visualization was tremendous and they confidently communicated in terms of steepness of the line.

An important part of students' learning is to stand back and look for patterns, ideas, or generalizations that emerge from a set of problems. Such perspectives

TABLE 2.1.

	0	1	2	3	4	5	6	7	8	9	10	11	12	13	14	...	30	31
							Time in seconds											
Bonne	45	46	47	48	49	50	51	52	53	54	55	56	57	58	59	...	75	76
Amel	0	2.5	5	7.5	10	12.5	15	17.5	20	22.5	25	27.5	30	32.5	35	...	75	77.5

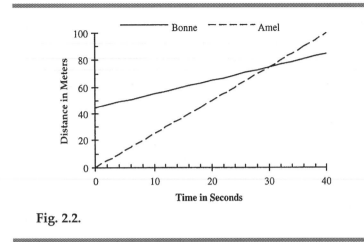

Bonne: $d = t + 45$

Amel: $d = 2.5t$

A. Amel meets and passes Bonne at 75 meters.

B. Amel meets and passes Bonne at 30 seconds.

Fig. 2.2.

help students refine strategies into efficient, problem-solving techniques, deepen their knowledge of mathematical ideas and concepts embedded in the set of problems, and make connections to other mathematics. At the end of the investigation containing the problems about Bonne and Amel, the following questions were used to guide students' reflections:

- "What have you learned about patterns in tables and equations that could help you decide if a situation is linear or not?"

- "In general, how can you compare rates of change by looking at two tables or two graphs or two equations?"

- "What are some advantages and disadvantages of using a graph, table, or equation to answer a question?"

  Think about these questions; discuss your ideas with the whole class; then write a summary of your ideas in your journal.

Examining the rate of change between the two variables becomes a tool for recognizing linearity. Studying patterns of change in related variables becomes a mathematical way of thinking for students moving on to study other families of functions in the eighth grade and high school. It is the concept of "rate of change" that helps students identify, represent, and reason about families of linear, quadratic, and exponential functions.

Example 3: Generalizations and Formalizations— Reasoning with Symbols

In this example students are presented with a situation in which contextual clues can be interpreted in different ways to produce different symbolic expressions representing the relationship between the two vari-

ables. Students are asked to justify, in informal ways, the equivalence of the expressions that represent different geometric analyses of the situation.

PROBLEM: TILING POOLS

Many people enjoy amusement parks in the summer. But swimming, diving, and lazy soaking go on year-round in pools and hot tubs of many shapes and sizes in recreation centers, schools, and homes. It is typical for such a pool or tub to have a border of tiles. How many 1-foot-square tiles will be needed for the border of a square pool that has an edge length of s feet? [See figure 2.3.]

1. Write an equation relating side length s and number of tiles N for any pool.

2. See if you can come up with more than one way to express the pattern relating s and N. Then find a way to convince your classmates that the two rules are *equivalent*.

Reflecting on Students' Reasoning

Students usually come up with several different ways to think about the relationship between the two variables: the side length of the pool and the number of border tiles. For example, some students will use pictures

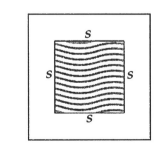

Fig. 2.3.

14

or verbal descriptions to assist them in writing symbolic expressions to represent their strategies. Teachers may have asked different groups of students to write their expressions on the chalkboard. The rest of the class then tries to figure out how that group reasoned about the problem. The following are different ways students in one classroom thought about the problem:

- "$4s + 4 = N$. There are 4 sides of the square of length s, so you need a total of $4s$ border tiles to match these 4 sides. Then you need to add the 4 corner border tiles."

Another group claimed that they had the same equation. They made a table and observed that the pattern in the table was linear. Next they determined that the slope is 4 and the y-intercept is 4, so the number of border tiles is $4s + 4$. (See figure 2.4.)

- "$N = 4(s + 1)$. The border has four strips of equal lengths, $s + 1$. So, the number of border tiles is $4(s + 1)$."

Another group claimed they had the same equation, but they saw a different pattern. We made a table. The pattern in the table of values suggests that you add 1 to the length and then multiply by 4 to get the number in the border. So the number of border tiles is $4(s + 1)$. (See figure 2.5.)

- "$N = 2(s + 2) + 2s$. The border has four strips—two of length $s + 2$ and two of length s, so the number of border tiles is $2(s + 2) + 2s$." (See figure 2.6.)
- "$N = 4(s + 2) - 4$. The length of the four outer edges of the border is $s + 2$. But the sum of these lengths includes counting the corner tiles twice, so the number of border tiles is $4(s + 2) - 4$."
- "$N = (s + 2)^2 - s^2$. The number of border tiles is the difference between the area of the larger

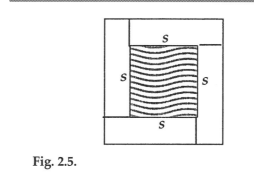

Fig. 2.5.

square (pool plus border) and the area of the pool. So the number of border tiles is $(s + 2)^2 - s^2$.

- "$N = s + s + s + s + 4$. The number of border tiles is the sum of the tiles around the four sides of the pool plus four corner tiles, so $N = s + s + s + s + 4$."
- "$N = 8 + 4(s - 1)$."

This group also used a table, but they found that if the pool has an edge length of 1 foot, then there are 8 border tiles. They also noticed that the table is increasing by 4 each time and that the number of 4s that have to be added to the first pool to find any larger pool is 1 less than the length of the side of the pool. Hence the number of border tiles is $8 + 4(s - 1)$.

Reflecting on the Mathematics

These students believe that the justification of an answer is important and that there is often more than one way to solve a problem. In the Tiling Pools problem students have the opportunity, without excessive formalization, to justify the equivalence of two or more symbolic expressions given as the answer to the same problem. At this informal stage, to show equivalence

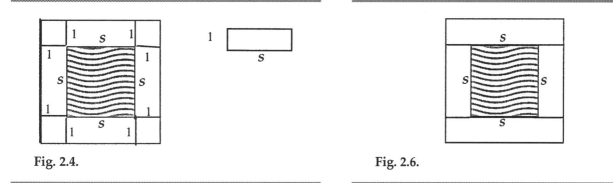

Fig. 2.4.

Fig. 2.6.

students use pictures to decide on the reasonableness of the argument put forth. They also use graphing calculators to find that equivalent expressions have the same tables and graphs.

The problems have been chosen to make it likely that important properties of numbers and operations will have to be articulated and used. These include the distributive and commutative properties, as well as order of operations. Students subsequently use these properties to show that the various algebraic expressions in the pool problem are equivalent.

Connecting Elementary, Middle, and High Schools

The examples of student reasoning in the preceding problems reflect a variety of middle school classes. Collectively, they provide evidence that more students can be successful with algebra if given an opportunity to a engage in, and make sense of, interesting mathematical situations. Given these examples of students' algebraic reasoning in the middle grades, what are some similar experiences from the elementary grades that might facilitate and enhance these experiences? What are the appropriate areas of study as students move to the high school?

An adaptation of the Tiling Pools problem has been used in grades K–6 (Ferrini-Mundy, Lappan, and Phillips 1997). In the early grades students can be asked to build square pools with borders, using white tiles to represent the border and blue tiles to represent the pool as in figure 2.7.

At first they investigate the number of tiles needed to build the pool and its border. Then they build the next biggest pool, looking for patterns in the number of tiles, or in the shape of the pool. In the upper elementary grades, students can use their patterns to generate a table (see table 2.2) and look for patterns that describe the relationship between the two variables—the number of border tiles and the number of pool tiles.

A fifth-grade student claimed that the number of border tiles (white) is always a multiple of 4 and used a geometric picture (figure 2.8) to convince his classmates.

Students also describe the patterns of change in each type of tile and represent this pattern in pictures, tables, or graphs, thus laying the foundation for middle-grades students to probe more deeply into these two patterns of change. The number of border tiles is a linear function, whereas the number of pool tiles is a quadratic function.

The collection of related problems for the elementary grades, together with the Tiling Pools problem for the middle grades, provides a glimpse into how quantitative reasoning can be developed across grades K–8. In high school, students can generalize the pool problem to one that has a border with more than one row of border tiles or to one that includes a rectangular or even a circular pool.

The preceding problems illustrate that reasoning with symbols is still important, but they also illustrate a shift in emphasis. Traditional curricula have usually focused on finding the "simplest" form of an expression. However, when using symbols to represent the patterns within a situation, such as in the Tiling Pools problem, it is not always the simplest form that is important—rather what is important is what information about the patterns is gleaned from different, but equivalent, expressions of the pattern. Showing that these expressions are equivalent is important, but students now have a variety of methods with which to reason about this equivalence.

Collectively, the mathematics embedded in these problems represent important steps in the development of students' algebraic understanding and reasoning. Throughout the elementary grades students are observing patterns in number, shape, and data; noting regularities; and developing ways to represent and

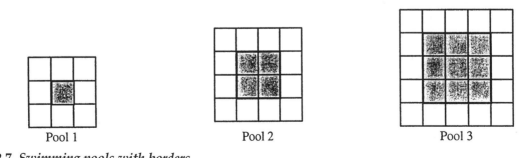

Pool 1   Pool 2   Pool 3

Fig. 2.7. *Swimming pools with borders*

TABLE 2.2.
Organizing the data

Pool number	Number of blue tiles	Number of white tiles	Total number of blue and white tiles

reason about these patterns. From such experiences in elementary school and those described for middle school, students move to solving more-complex problems, including more-formal representations and reasoning, in high school.

Teachers who are involved with these problem-centered curricula also comment on students' perseverance in pursuing new problems and their flexibility in choosing or moving among representations to express their reasoning and generalizations. Most important, teachers talk about the "habits of mind" that their students are developing. Students learn important questions, such as the following, to ask themselves about any situation that can be represented and modeled mathematically:

What are the variables? How are they changing in relation to each other?

How is an increase in the independent variable related to a change in the dependent variable?

Where is the dependent value changing the most? The least?

How can this change be seen in a table? Detected in a story? Observed in a graph? Read from symbolic representations?

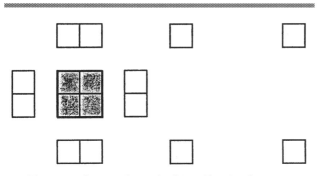

Fig. 2.8. *The number of white tiles is always a multiple of 4.*

Where does the graph cross the *x*-axis and the *y*-axis, and what is the significance of each of these intersections?

Where does the dependent variable reach its greatest value and its least value, and what is the significance of each?

What effects does a change in a parameter have on the situation?

These questions reflect the power and potential of using observation and formalization of patterns as a unifying theme for algebra across grades K–12.

Obstacles to Building a Coherent Curriculum

A course called algebra has been in existence for a long time, but many students fail to thrive in that traditional algebra course. Those who fail either repeat the course or take a watered-down version in a later year; this usually indicates the student will be relegated to nonrigorous mathematics courses for the college bound. At the same time parents put pressure on schools to allow their children to take an algebra course as early as possible, usually in eighth grade, so they can take calculus in high school. However, only a small number of students who take algebra in eighth grade go on to take calculus in high school, and many who take algebra in eighth grade end up repeating algebra in the ninth grade or as a remedial course in college. Furthermore, if many students take algebra in eighth grade, some parents lobby for their child to take algebra in seventh grade. An algebra course has become a status symbol, and it will remain so only if large numbers of students continue to fail the course or are denied access to it. No parents want their child to fail, but the evidence on national, international, and college-placement examinations reveals that large numbers of students leave high school with a weak foundation in mathematics.

Even though evidence is emerging that problem-centered curricula offer exciting promise for all students, there is a strong resistance to change. If a course called algebra disappears and is replaced by an integrated curriculum, it is often difficult for a school district to convince parents that algebra is still in the curriculum. Some states are mandating an algebra course for graduation from high school. Whether these states will accept algebra from an integrated program is under debate. Many people fear change and are suspicious of any kind of reform, particularly in mathematics.

What happens to students who have experiences similar to those described in this paper? Preliminary reports from school districts that use problem-centered curricula in both middle and high school suggest that students have little difficulty making the transition from one level to the next. However, concern is voiced when no coherent curriculum is in place. Students who are used to exploring interesting problems—by conjecturing, explaining, and generalizing using a variety of rich representative tools—may have a difficult time moving into an environment where the emphasis is on manipulating symbols with little understanding of the rules. A major question is, Will high school teachers of a traditional algebra course recognize and appreciate the power of algebraic reasoning that middle school students bring to their classrooms?

Problem-centered curriculum materials look quite different from traditional materials. Sometimes it is difficult for teachers and parents to thumb through these materials and see the mathematics, particularly if they are looking for symbol manipulation, rules, and drill. These kinds of materials do not conform to the conventional two-page format. The problem situations should dictate the length of the lessons. In a problem-centered curriculum, projects are selected to embody important concepts and procedures and to allow students to develop a deep understanding of the embedded mathematics and mathematical reasoning in the process of solving the problems. Skills are developed and practiced in the context of problems. Therefore, it may be difficult to see the development of skills at a glance, and this could also provide an obstacle to change. These are difficult times. We need to come together as a community of professionals and honestly examine the evidence on both sides of the issue of a "course called algebra."

Summary

Problem-centered curricula focus on relationships between variables in a situation, and the emphasis is on functions or relationships and their use in modeling patterns of quantitative change. Although symbols are used early in the curricula to represent patterns, training in routine symbolic manipulations is delayed until students have the deep understandings of the concepts needed to write equivalent symbolic expressions. The emphasis is not on simplest form but rather on what information or reasoning each expression reveals about the pattern. These practices are a radical departure from the traditional algebra curriculum that focused almost exclusively on manipulating expressions and solving symbolic equations.

> The curriculum students encounter in schools—the specific topics that are taught and how these topics are presented and developed—fundamentally shapes what students learn and are able to do. Unless the U.S. vision of mathematics and science changes, classrooms will not change. (Babcock 1996, p. 9)

Grades K–12 teachers are essential players in the improvement of students' learning of algebra. Any efforts to reform the algebra curriculum or methods of teaching must help teachers see the potential for developing mathematical power in their students and help them communicate this idea to parents. This is the key to student growth and performance. Parents and administrators will and should judge whether such efforts are worthwhile by looking at students' achievement. However, the message must be heard: Improvement does not happen overnight and does not happen without support for teachers. With a focused, coherent curriculum, time, and support, teachers implementing problem-centered curricula are producing the kinds and magnitude of student growth that indicate that the effort pays off.

References

Babcock, Jacqueline E., ed. *Third International Mathematics and Science Study.* U.S. National Research Center report no. 7. East Lansing, Mich.: Michigan State University, 1996.

Ferrini-Mundy, Joan, Glenda Lappan, and Elizabeth Phillips. "Experiences with Patterning." *Teaching Children Mathematics* 3, no. 6 (1997): 282–88.

Lappan, Glenda, James Fey, Susan Friel, William Fitzgerald, and Elizabeth Phillips. *The Connected Mathematics Project.* Palo Alto, Calif.: Dale Seymour Publications, 1995.

Moses, Bob. "Algebra, the New Civil Right." Paper presented at the SUMMA (Strengthening Underrepresented Minority Mathematics Achievement) II Conference, Cambridge, Mass., 6 November 1993.

National Council of Teachers of Mathematics. "Board Approves Statement on Algebra." *NCTM News Bulletin* 30 (May 1994): 1, 3, 6.

National Council of Teachers of Mathematics Algebra Working Group. *Algebra in the K–12 Curriculum; Dilemmas and Possibilities*. Final report to the Board of Directors. East Lansing, Mich.: Michigan State University, 1997.

Schmidt, William H., Doris Jorde, Leland S. Cogan, Emilie Barrier, Ignacio Gonzalo, Urs Moser, Katsuhiko Shimizu, Toshio Sawada, Gilbert A. Valverde, Curtis McKnight, Richard S. Prawat, David E. Wiley, Senta A.

Raizen, Edward D. Britton, and Richard G. Wolfe. *Characterizing Pedagogical Flow, an Investigation of Mathematics and Science Teaching in Six Countries*. Dordrecht, Netherlands: Kluwer Academic Publishers, 1996.

Silver, Edward. "'Algebra for All': Increasing Students' Access to Algebraic Ideas, Not Just Algebra Courses." *Mathematics Teaching in the Middle School* 2, no. 4 (1997): 204–7.

Elizabeth Phillips and Glenda Lappan, *Michigan State University, East Lansing, Michigan*

3

A Multiple-Intelligence Approach
to Middle School Mathematics

DEAN A. MURPHY

In 1983 Howard Gardner set out his novel approach to human intelligence in his book *Frames of Mind*, in which the theory of multiple intelligence (MI) was delineated for the first time. As Gardner later wrote,

> [W]e are not all the same; we do not all have the same kind of minds; education works most effectively for most individuals if these differences in mentation and strengths are taken into account rather than denied or ignored. . . . [A]ny uniform educational approach is likely to serve only a minority of children. (Gardner 1995, p. 208)

Following the publication of *Frames of Mind*, volumes of research in education, prompted by the desire to put forth a superior product, led directly to the publication in 1989 of the *Curriculum and Evaluation Standards for School Mathematics* by the National Council of Teachers of Mathematics (NCTM). From these seemingly unconnected and diverse writings springs the main point of this article—that successful middle school mathematics reform should rely on the recognition that there is a close relationship between the major tenets of the *Standards* and the seven intelligences of Gardner.

When Howard Gardner was conducting the research that would lead to MI theory, he disengaged himself from the traditional assumptions about human intelligence that view cognition as a unitary entity that can be quantified. Instead, his view was that people possess a spectrum of intelligences and use them in unique fashions. In brief, the seven intelligences that Gardner proposed in 1983 are as follows:

- *Linguistic intelligence*, which is concerned with the ability to use language
- *Logical-mathematical intelligence*, which makes it possible to calculate, consider hypotheses, and carry out complex mathematical operations
- *Bodily-kinesthetic intelligence*, which enables a person to unite the body and mind in physical performances
- *Visual-spatial intelligence*, which involves the capacity to think three dimensionally
- *Interpersonal intelligence*, which allows effective communication with others
- *Intrapersonal intelligence*, which includes the talent to understand oneself and to plan and solve problems in one's imagination
- *Musical intelligence*, which is evident in people with a sensitivity to the elements of music (Campbell, Campbell, and Dickinson 1992)

Gardner presented his new theory to the world of the psychologists, but he did not speak up about the applicability of MI to the world of education. In 1995, although he did not mention mathematics specifically, he noted that one of the positive ways that MI theory can be used in education is by

> approaching a concept, subject matter or *discipline* [italics added] in a variety of ways . . . ranging from the telling of a story, to a formal argument, to an artistic exploration, to some kind of hands-on experiment or simulation. Such pluralistic approaches should be encouraged. (Gardner 1995, p. 208)

If mathematics instruction and learning are approached with this fundamental understanding, there should be at least three noticeable and desirable outcomes. First and foremost, the excitement and wonder of mathematics will be appreciated by many more students, and all children will be better able to deal with challenging topics. Middle schoolers will look forward to mathematics class and will go to high school believing that they can succeed in rigorous mathematics. Perhaps, as adults, they will not go to their children's conferences and say, "I never was any good at mathematics"—a phrase heard from at least one parent at many parent-teacher conferences.

. . . the excitement and wonder of mathematics will be appreciated by many more students, and all children will be better able to deal with challenging topics.

Second, if a menu of mathematical activities that spans the intelligences is the norm in the mathematics classroom, all students will find areas of mathematics in which they are the expert. Middle school students are at a crucial stage in the development of their self-image and their feelings of self-esteem, and being perceived by peers and oneself as competent is of vital importance. Leadership skills begin to emerge at this age, and the members of the cooperative groups in which each student works will look to one another for leadership on the tasks in which each is viewed as the expert.

Finally, the *Standards*-MI connection should go a long way toward helping teachers begin to use and meet the *Standards*. For some teachers, the implementation of the *Standards* is viewed as an impossible stretch and so becomes more threatening than it is comfortable. Yet MI theory is more familiar to many teachers, and some educators have years of experience in teaching using MI. Comfort with the use of MI in the class-

room could assist teachers, who may have been "math phobics" themselves in their earlier lives, in beginning to implement *Standards*-based activities.

The four groups that were charged with writing the *Standards* seem to have had the concepts of MI theory in the back of their minds. For example, the following quotation from the conclusion of the grades 5–8 section reveals several MI influences:

> The spirit and vision of the *Standards* cannot be achieved if instruction is inconsistent with its underlying philosophy. . . . Thus, the elaboration of each standard . . . includes expectations about teachers' actions, such as the use of a *variety of sequences, grouping procedures, instructional strategies, and techniques for evaluation* [emphasis added]. (NCTM 1989, p. 252)

Conversely, one can see this consistency in Gardner's definition of the concept of intelligence and see the inherent connection of his MI theory to the *Standards*. In 1983, Gardner gave an entirely new twist to human "smartness" by defining intelligence as "the ability to solve problems that one encounters in real life [and] the ability to generate new problems to solve" (Campbell, Campbell, and Dickinson 1992, p. xv). Thus, what the NCTM generated in 1989 for the discipline of mathematics, with its problem-solving focus, was a mirror image of what Gardner had conceived of concerning cognition in 1983.

How this philosophical similarity would translate into an MI-centered approach in the mathematics classroom can be clearly illustrated by citing several examples, beginning with one from the section on problem solving in the grades 5–8 *Standards*. The following sample problem is given in the discussion section:

> **How many handshakes will occur at a party if every one of the 15 guests shakes hands with each of the others?**

Immediately thereafter is a list of possible approaches students might take. "Some students will choose to act out the problem. Some might draw a picture of a simpler case to approximate the situation. . . . Other students might start with a simpler problem and look for a pattern" (NCTM 1989, p. 77). Without having said so explicitly, the writers were recognizing that the first students cited would be using their kinesthetic intelligence, the second ones would be displaying their visual-spatial intelligence, and the last group would be using their logical-mathematical intelligence. In fact, it is likely that there would be as many approaches as there would be groups. Other kinesthetically oriented learners would head for the manipulatives and move chips around on the table top. Graph or chart making would occupy the thoughts of other logical-mathematical or visual-spatial types, and the interpersonally intelligent would collaborate to brainstorm ideas. Thus, in the problem-centered classroom that the *Standards* embraces, MI theory would flourish.

Although this MI approach to mathematics education allows each child the opportunity to enhance his or her learning, a greater burden falls on the teacher to assess adequately what learning has taken place. No longer is a paper-and-pencil mathematics test (especially one on which the student fills in the bubbles) acceptable or appropriate. In fact, the information gleaned from such instruments could lead to inaccurate judgments because they provide little or no opportunity to show the thinking taking place. Instead, teachers need to observe the students as they work, provide chances to work on problems over long periods of time, and allow students to use the range of their intelligences.

One example of this assessment process can be seen in the creation of formal portfolios of written responses to problems (which can and should include charts, graphs, sketches, and diagrams). Another example would be to use oral presentations that might include the acting out of a problem's solution. The most important component of such assessment is that the correct answer to the problem is just one small part of the student's learning.

A second quote from the *Standards* again illustrates the connection to Gardner's work:

> Learning should engage students *both intellectually and physically*. They must become *active learners*, challenged to apply their prior knowledge and experience in new and increasingly more difficult situations. Instructional approaches should *engage students in the process of learning* rather than transmit information for them to receive. *Middle grade students are especially responsive to hands-on activities in tactile, auditory, and visual instructional modes* [emphasis added]. (NCTM 1989, p. 67)

If the *Standards* had been written with references to Gardner's MI work interspersed, the last sentence might instead have read, "Middle grade students are especially responsive to kinesthetic activities, a linguistic intelligence approach, and visual-spatial modes." Such a notion is not in harmony with the traditional manner in which mathematical knowledge has been imparted through the years—the "broadcast" approach, which is based solely on the authority of the teacher and denies any and all opportunities for discovery and exploration.

As Gardner's theory has come to be applied by others in educational settings, this active learning concept has typically been embodied in two different ways: through the use of cooperative groups and through the inclusion of activities specifically geared toward students with a highly developed kinesthetic intelligence.

> [M]any children and adults find visual and auditory modes insufficient sensory channels for understanding and remembering information. Such individuals rely on tactile or kinesthetic processes and must manipulate or experience what they learn in order to understand and retain it. (Campbell, Campbell, and Dickinson 1992, p. 8)

A classic problem-solving situation that can be used at the beginning of the school year to set the stage is the Foxes and Geese Dilemma. Although this problem has many variations, the common factor in them is to get a group of three foxes and three geese across a river using a boat that can hold at most three at a time (the ability to row is assumed) while never letting the foxes outnumber the geese anywhere (since they would eat them for lunch). When students begin work on this problem, MI theory is at work. Some kinesthetic learners may use manipulatives and move two-colored discs across a riverbed drawn on papers, whereas others may get up and move themselves back and forth across an imaginary river in the classroom. In the meantime, linguistic students begin writing out their ideas while the visual-spatial learners draw sophisticated sketches with detailed boats and rivers. Allowed to use the most comfortable approach to build their own understanding, the students bring their unique spectrum of intelligences to bear in solving the task. If the students are allowed to share their thinking and learn from one another's approaches, the result can be deeply ingrained learning.

. . . teachers need to observe the students as they work, provide chances to work on problems over long periods of time, and allow students to use the range of their intelligences.

As students progress through the middle school years, fundamental changes occur in their cognitive development: The young middle schooler may still think concretely, whereas the middle school graduate reasons more abstractly. Each then approaches and deals with problem-solving situations in different ways, which again makes the case for an MI approach in the mathematics classroom.

An example of another classic problem that would demonstrate the changes that occur as children mature is the Locker Problem. Although this problem also has many variations, the common element involves the opening and closing of a series of numbered doors (perhaps as many as 500). All the lockers begin closed, and student number 1 goes down the line and opens each one. Student number 2 then goes to every second locker and closes it. Student number 3 then proceeds down the row and changes every third locker (opening it if it is closed or closing it if it is open). Student number 4 changes every fourth locker, and so on, until student number 500 changes only the 500th door. The question asks, Which lockers end up open? Just as in the Foxes and Geese problem, students will be up and about the room approaching the problem using their preferred intelligence. But a distinction ought to be observed between the concrete thinkers (who likely will be doing or drawing the entire opening-and-closing process in some form) and the abstract reasoners (who may discover the underlying pattern involving square numbers and why only those lockers end up open). How students approach such a problem should tell a great deal about their stage of maturation.

It would come as no shock to anyone who deals with middle school–aged children that "middle schoolers are social!" They thrive on peer interactions. If one accepts the fundamental tenets of Gardner's theory, it is small wonder that the mathematics education of today's parents failed for so many because those with a strongly developed interpersonal intelligence, who tend to excel at group work and team efforts, were never reached. For "interpersonal intelligence is so closely connected to interaction with others that most educators claim they couldn't teach without pairing or grouping students" (Campbell, Campbell, and Dickinson 1992, p. 104). If the goals of the cooperative groups align with the rationale expressed in the *Standards*, with each group playing its part in the piecing together of the jigsaw puzzle of problem solving, then the result is a climate of acceptance and teamwork.

MI theory and the *Standards* come together on two different levels in the use of small cooperative groups. On the one hand, there is the obvious connection of the interpersonal intelligence as noted. On the other hand, there is a significant connection to all the other intelligences that justifies the proper use of small groups. Small groups thrive on the cultivation of a variety of approaches to solve the same problem—a variety that is engendered by allowing students to use the full spectrum of their intelligences and is enhanced by grouping students heterogeneously. If the groups are then presented with a weekly or monthly menu of activities that require the use of all the intelligences, the success of the group will depend on each member's contribution in his or her area of strength.

The young middle schooler may still think concretely, whereas the middle school graduate reasons more abstractly.

The MI connection to cooperative groups also underscores a rationale for using heterogeneous rather than traditional homogeneous groupings within mathematics classes. Simply stated, an MI approach and traditional homogeneous groups are mutually incompatible! Clearly, the entire notion of what constitutes a homogeneous group becomes somewhat of a paradox in light of Gardner's work. In traditional classes, the usual determinant for grouping homogeneously is a student's computational proficiency. Yet groups formed homogeneously in that context still are anything but homogeneous because each student has a unique array of mathematics skills if all intelligences are considered. According to MI theory, any small group must be heterogeneous and take advantage of all intelligences. The idea that an entire classroom can be homogeneous is a myth! Only if the first-period class were composed of kinesthetic learners and the second-period class were made up of visual-spatial learners, and so on, would homogeneity of the intelligences be approached. But how boring it would be, and most of the rationales for using small groups cited in the paragraphs above would be rendered irrelevant. So why even try to justify classroom lists drawn up on the basis of computational ability alone? Mathematics classrooms need to be heterogeneous in order to support an MI approach and embrace the vision of the *Standards*.

The transformations that have been evolving since the landmark events of the 1980s are promoting the beginning of a new wave of education reform. I do not mean to imply no more changes should occur. The implication rather is that education may be endorsing substantive change, based on a better understanding of how children learn, that will be effective, universally embraced, and long lasting. Part of that substantive change should be the recognition of the symbiotic relationship between the NCTM Standards and Gardner's MI theory. Finally, as expressed by Howard Gardner,

[I]f as a result of these discussions, a more personalized education is the outcome, I feel that the heart of MI theory has been embodied. And if this personalization is fused with a commitment to the achievement of worthwhile (and attainable) educational understanding for all children, then the basis for a powerful education has indeed been laid. (Gardner 1995, p. 209)

Bibliography

Burns, Marilyn. *About Teaching Mathematics: A K–8 Resource.* White Plains, N.Y.: Math Solutions Publications, 1992.

Campbell, Linda, Bruce Campbell, and Dee Dickinson. *Teaching and Learning through Multiple Intelligences.* Seattle, Wash.: New Horizons for Learning, 1992.

Carnegie Task Force on Education of Young Adolescents. *Turning Points: Preparing American Youth for the Twenty-First Century.* New York: Carnegie Council on Adolescent Development of the Carnegie Corporation, 1989.

Crosswhite, F. Joe, John A. Dossey, and Shirley M. Fry. "NCTM Standards for School Mathematics: Visions for Implementation." *Arithmetic Teacher* 37 (November 1989): 55–60.

Davidson, Neil. "Small-Group Cooperative Learning in Mathematics." In *Teaching and Learning Mathematics in the 1990s,* 1990 Yearbook of the National Council of Teachers of Mathematics, edited by Thomas J. Cooney, pp. 52–61. Reston, Va.: National Council of Teachers of Mathematics, 1990.

Gardner, Howard. *Frames of Mind.* New York: Basic Books, 1983.

———. *Multiple Intelligences: The Theory in Practice.* New York: Basic Books, 1993.

———. "Reflections on Multiple Intelligences: Myths and Messages." *Phi Delta Kappan* 77 (November 1995): 200–209.

National Council of Teachers of Mathematics. *Curriculum and Evaluation Standards for School Mathematics.* Reston, Va.: National Council of Teachers of Mathematics, 1989.

———. *Teaching and Learning Mathematics in the 1990s.* 1990 Yearbook of the National Council of Teachers of Mathematics, edited by Thomas J. Cooney. Reston, Va.: National Council of Teachers of Mathematics, 1990.

National Research Council. Mathematical Sciences Education Board. *Everybody Counts: A Report to the Nation on the Future of Mathematics Education.* Washington, D.C.: National Academy Press, 1989.

National Research Council. *Moving beyond Myths: Revitalizing Undergraduate Mathematics.* Washington, D.C.: National Academy Press, 1991.

Secada, Walter G. "The Challenges of a Changing World for Mathematics Education." In *Teaching and Learning Mathematics in the 1990s,* 1990 Yearbook of the National Council of Teachers of Mathematics, edited by Thomas J. Cooney, pp. 135–43. Reston, Va.: National Council of Teachers of Mathematics, 1990.

Thompson, Alba G., and Diane J. Briars. "Assessing Students' Learning to Inform Teaching: The Message in NCTM's Evaluation Standards." In *Implementing the K–8 Curriculum and Evaluation Standards: Readings from the 'Arithmetic Teacher,'* edited by Thomas E. Rowan and Lorna J. Morrow, pp. 19–23. Reston, Va.: National Council of Teachers of Mathematics, 1993.

Dean A. Murphy, *Solomon Schechter Day School, Worcester, Massachusetts*

4

Conceptual and Procedural Understanding in Middle School Mathematics

ANTHONY RICKARD

A major goal of mathematics education reform involves helping students develop deep and connected understandings of mathematical concepts and procedures with less emphasis on teaching students rote algorithms. In the *Professional Standards for Teaching Mathematics,* the National Council of Teachers of Mathematics (NCTM) stresses that teaching and learning school mathematics should move "away from merely memorizing procedures [and] toward connecting mathematics, its ideas, and its applications" (NCTM 1991, p. 3). Middle school students should be able to use formulas to find the areas of rectangles, triangles, or circles, but they should also know how the formula for calculating areas of triangles can be understood through geometric relationships between parallelograms and triangles (*procedural understanding*). Moreover, students should be able to explain and interpret area as the number of square units needed to cover a shape and perimeter as the linear distance around a shape (*conceptual understanding*). Students who understand area and perimeter conceptually and procedurally can use appropriate formulas to find areas of triangles and parallelograms; can recognize that no formula is appropriate for finding the area of a blob; and can also estimate the area of that figure by covering the figure with a transparent grid. Students who view area and perimeter only as rote algorithms

may think of area as "length times width" or "one-half base times height" and be unable to interpret solutions or solve problems that involve more than plugging numbers into formulas (NCTM 1989, 1991, 1995; Rickard 1993; Shroyer and Fitzgerald 1986).

This article examines how a sixth-grade mathematics teacher taught her students about area, perimeter, and circumference. She initially adhered closely to an innovative mathematics unit that helped her students develop conceptual and procedural understanding of area and perimeter of rectangles, triangles, and hexagons; however, she then deviated sharply from the unit and taught circumference of circles as a rote algorithm. These examples of teaching will illustrate that among the challenges of implementing the NCTM *Standards* is helping teachers shift their practice from developing students' proficiency with rote algorithms to consistently teaching for conceptual and procedural understanding.

Teaching Area, Perimeter, and Circumference

Karen is a sixth-grade teacher with more than twenty years of teaching experience. She has taught a variety of subjects in grades K–8 but has taught primarily mathematics and social studies over the past ten years. She teaches in a large middle school (grades 6–8) with a racially and socioeconomically diverse student population. Because she is a teacher who wants to address problem solving and emphasize conceptual and procedural understanding in her teaching, Karen was recommended by her district's mathematics coordinator as someone interested in piloting a unit developed by the Connected Mathematics Project (CMP).

The pilot unit, Covering and Surrounding (CMP 1992a, 1992b, 1996a, 1996b), focuses on teaching students about the area and perimeter of two-dimensional shapes and the connections between these concepts. The unit develops students' conceptual understanding of area as the number of square units needed to *cover* a figure and perimeter as the number of linear units required to *surround* a figure. Throughout the unit, students use square tiles and transparent grids to cover figures as they determine the area. Students also develop strategies for estimating the area and perimeter of irregular shapes (e.g., blobs, lakes), make connections between shapes and their angles, and experiment with patterns and shapes to develop formulas for finding the areas and perimeters of rectangles, triangles, parallelograms, and circles.

Teaching Area and Perimeter for Conceptual and Procedural Understanding

Karen's interest in teaching the unit stemmed from her belief that problem solving and hands-on opportunities are important for the development of middle school students' understanding of mathematical concepts. Prior to teaching the unit, Karen said, "Problem-solving skills will help my students in real life; they need to be able to reason through situations." She felt she needed to do more with problem solving, saying, "We're going more and more toward problem solving, but I'm not spending that much time on it." Karen stressed the use of formulas in teaching mathematics, but she had become aware that her students needed "hands-on activities before they can use the formulas."

The opening activity of Covering and Surrounding introduces students to area and perimeter by physically covering figures (all of which have straight edges and right angles) with one-inch square tiles where the number of tiles is the area and the number of tile edges is the perimeter. Karen had her students find the area and perimeter of a variety of figures with square tiles and then design a figure having an area of twelve square units and a perimeter of at least fourteen units. Students first needed to make their figures with tiles and then draw diagrams on grid paper, explaining how their figures met the problem conditions (i.e., area of 12

square units and perimeter of at least 14). Throughout three class periods, Karen worked with her students on this activity; she stressed the conceptual representations of area as covering with square units and perimeter as surrounding with linear units.

One week into the unit, and three class periods after finishing the opening activity, each of the twenty-four students in Karen's class described what they thought "covering and surrounding" meant in terms of area and perimeter. The following two students' comments are representative of those of the class:

AUTHOR: Could you tell me what the relationship is between covering and surrounding and area and perimeter?

ELLEN: I guess [pause]. Covering is like area and surrounding is, like, perimeter. You cover things with area and, sort of like, surround them with the perimeter.

Another student initially confused area and perimeter but was able to use the covering and surrounding representation to correct himself:

AUTHOR: Has covering and surrounding helped you to think about perimeter and area?

AARON: Yea—covering and surrounding is finding the perimeter and area, just about. 'Cause the perimeter is the covering [student pauses and traces a triangle in the air with two fingers]—I mean, the surrounding is the perimeter and the covering is the area. Surrounding, or like, perimeter, are straight [traces a straight line segment in the air with one finger] and covering you use [pause] flat square units for the area [traces a square in the air with one finger].

Ellen and Aaron developed conceptual understanding of area and perimeter in ways typical for Karen's students—through the covering and surrounding representation. Instead of trying to remember a formula, Ellen drew on her conceptual understanding of area and perimeter to distinguish between the measures. Aaron used his conceptual understanding to check his description of what area and perimeter measure.

Karen's students also developed procedural understanding of area and perimeter. About two weeks into the unit, Karen helped students, working in groups, develop the area formula for triangles by studying parallelograms, rectangles, and triangles. The first group to develop the formula showed how to divide a rectangle into two triangular halves by drawing a diagonal. Three students reasoned that the area of each of the two congruent triangles was "one-half the base times the height" because, as one of the students explained, "The area of the whole rectangle is base times height, and we want just half because the triangle is, like, half the rectangle." This example of procedural understanding shows how students can connect a formula for the area of a particular figure to the formula for the area of a related figure.

. . . innovative curricula are intended to serve as vehicles for change in the classroom, not to provide temporary diversions from teaching old mathematics. . . .

Another example of how Karen's students developed procedural understanding occurred when students had to explain strategies for finding the area and perimeter of regular hexagons. One student, Carlos, explained how he subdivided a hexagon into "a rectangle and two triangles that are the same—and I just found out the area of each one and added them up." Another student, Amanda, subdivided her hexagon into six congruent triangles and then said, "I just used my [transparent] grid to find the area of one and then multiplied that by 6 because there're six triangles." Both Carlos and Amanda found the perimeter of hexagons by measuring the length of one edge and multiplying that measure by 6 because "all the sides are the same and there're six of those" (Amanda's words). Like their classmates, Carlos and Amanda demonstrated their procedural understanding of area and perimeter by successfully developing and explaining, as well as applying, valid procedures for finding the area and perimeter of a figure for which no formulas were known.

Teaching Circumference as a Rote Algorithm

Karen was pleased with her students' work in Covering and Surrounding. However, after teaching four of the seven sections of the unit, she decided to teach her students about circumference of circles without doing "hands-on activities" (Karen's words). Karen explained,

> They [i.e., her students] have a good handle on perimeter and area now, so I don't have to go through more of these activities—we can go to the formula and they'll understand like they do for rectangles and triangles [pause] but without having to go through the hands-on.

The unit does perimeter and area for circles with hands-on, but I'm going to go right to the formulas—that's what I want them to know.

Karen added that she had already spent about four weeks on the unit and typically taught her students formulas for the area and perimeter of rectangles, triangles, and circles in much less time. She described how she was feeling pressured to complete area and perimeter and move on to other topics. Karen also commented, "It's much easier and faster to teach kids formulas" and "hands-on activities are good, but they take so long!"

Karen felt that using formulas, together with computational drill exercises (e.g., 342×19.9), was good "skill maintenance" (Karen's words) for her students. Karen's concerns about spending too much time on area and perimeter and not enough on computational drill exercises were connected to wanting her students to be prepared for an upcoming standardized test. Karen explained that the test was administered to all sixth-grade students and that a student's score on the test determined which of the district's three mathematics tracks her students would follow in seventh and eighth grade. Since the test was largely composed of computational drill exercises, Karen reasoned that learning and practicing rote algorithms was the best way to prepare her students.

Karen taught her students perimeter of circles (i.e., circumference) by drilling them on the formulas $C = 2\pi r$ and $C = \pi d$ and on the value of π as 22/7, or 3.14. After calling on several of her students to recite the two formulas and expressions for the value of π, Karen worked on several examples using the $C = \pi d$ and $C = 2\pi r$ formulas. Two typical examples were, "What is the circumference of a circle with $r = 9$ cm?" and "What is the circumference of a circle with a diameter of 2 1/2 inches?" Karen concluded the lesson by assigning fifteen similar exercises for homework.

Aaron, who shared his thinking earlier about how covering and surrounding connected to area and perimeter, expressed what he thought about the circumference lesson:

AUTHOR: What do you think about your work on circumference today?

AARON: It's really easy.

AUTHOR: You think so?

AARON: Yea. It's kinda hard once you learn it, but once you got it down, it's easy.

AUTHOR: Why is it easy?

AARON: Well, alls you do is multiply by two and then three point one four.

Comparing Aaron's comments about circumference to his earlier remarks about covering and surrounding further emphasized the difference between teaching rote algorithms and teaching for conceptual and procedural understanding.

Moving between Conceptual and Procedural Understanding and Rote Algorithms

Although it might seem unusual to teach closely related topics so differently, other teachers share Karen's approach—teaching some topics for conceptual and procedural understanding and others as rote algorithms (cf. Ball 1990b; Lambdin and Preston 1995; Lappan and Briars 1995; Putnam et al. 1992; Rickard 1993, 1995a, 1995b; Thompson 1985; Wiemers 1990). This method of teaching raises questions about how to consistently emphasize conceptual and procedural understanding in the classroom as part of implementing the *Standards*. Teachers' personal teaching goals can be shaped not only by recognition of the importance of problem solving and the motivation to help students develop conceptual and procedural understandings but also by factors such as perceived time constraints and demands of standardized evaluation instruments. Karen's decision to teach some area and perimeter topics for conceptual and procedural understanding and others as rote algorithms can arguably be viewed as a pragmatic one. But the result of Karen's teaching may be a disconnected approach and will likely leave her students with gaps in their conceptual and procedural understanding.

One thought that might help Karen and other teachers implement the *Standards* more consistently is to note that learning mathematics for conceptual and procedural understanding includes being able to successfully apply computational algorithms. For example, the area and perimeter unit provided exercises requiring students to determine the area and perimeter of triangles; Karen assigned these problems to her students, who completed them successfully (see Rickard 1993). However, developing fluency with formulas was only one thing they learned about the area of triangles. Her students' comments illustrate how they were also solving problems, communicating, reasoning, and making connections. Contrasting the shallow understanding students typically acquire through learning mathematics as rote algorithms with the deep and connected understandings Karen's students developed by learning through conceptual and procedural understanding may help teachers like Karen align their teaching goals more closely with the *Standards*. Clearly, knowing and applying formulas and algo-

rithms are only a part of what students can and should learn. This realization is especially important for teachers who are skeptical of implementing the *Standards* because they think students will lack proficiency with formulas and computation.

A second implication of Karen's teaching is that her use of Covering and Surrounding and teaching circumference as a rote algorithm demonstrates that innovative curricula alone may be viewed as insufficient by some teachers. However, innovative curricula are intended to serve as vehicles for change in the classroom, not to provide temporary diversions from teaching old mathematics (CMP 1996c; NCTM 1989, 1991, 1995). How can innovative mathematics curricula be used in effective ways, both by and for teachers, to help implement the *Standards*? Teaching with innovative curricula for a longer period of time might well help teachers make changes. (Karen taught only part of one unit; if she had taught with the innovative curriculum for the entire year, she would have had more time to emphasized conceptual and procedural understanding.) Even informed and motivated teachers use innovative mathematics curricula in different ways that reflect the *Standards* and the goals of the curriculum to varying degrees (cf. Ball 1990a, 1990b; Lambdin and Preston 1995; Rickard 1995b, 1996; Simon 1995; Thompson 1985; Wiemers 1990).

Although Karen's teaching suggests that innovative curricula can play a role in implementing the *Standards* as demonstrated by her students' conceptual and procedural understanding of area and perimeter, her practice also indicates that curricula can interact with teachers' beliefs about constraints (e.g., time needed to prepare for computational standardized tests and concern that students will not develop proficiency with formulas) to shape teaching goals. Using innovative mathematics curricula as vehicles for classroom change, therefore, may imply the need to simultaneously help teachers face and overcome perceived constraints in order for them to align their teaching more closely with the *Standards*. For example, although Karen had attended in-service training in innovative mathematics materials similar to the area and perimeter unit, she did not have the benefit of colleagues also teaching from the same innovative curriculum. Support for Karen and other teachers to address and overcome constraints might include funding for additional in-service training, release time for extra planning for teaching with innovative materials, or collaboration with other teachers and administrators to develop implementation strategies (e.g., working toward aligning standardized tests with innovative mathematics curricula and the *Standards*).

References

Ball, Deborah L. *Halves, Pieces, and Twoths: Constructing Representational Contexts in Teaching Fractions* (Craft Paper 90-2). East Lansing, Mich.: National Center for Research on Teacher Education, Michigan State University, 1990a.

———. "Reflections and Deflections of Policy: The Case of Carol Turner." *Educational Evaluations and Policy Analysis* 12 (1990b): 263–76.

Connected Mathematics Project. *Covering and Surrounding* (Student Edition—working draft). East Lansing, Mich.: Department of Mathematics, Michigan State University, 1992a.

———. *Covering and Surrounding* (Teacher Edition—working draft). East Lansing, Mich.: Department of Mathematics, Michigan State University, 1992b.

———. *Covering and Surrounding: Two-Dimensional Measurement* (Student Edition). Palo Alto, Calif.: Dale Seymour Publications, 1996a.

———. *Covering and Surrounding: Two-Dimensional Measurement* (Teacher Edition). Palo Alto, Calif.: Dale Seymour Publications, 1996b.

———. *Getting to Know CMP: An Introduction to the Connected Mathematics Project.* East Lansing, Mich.: Department of Mathematics, Michigan State University, 1996c.

Lambdin, D. V., and R. V. Preston. "Caricatures in Innovation: Teacher Adaptation to an Investigation-Oriented Middle School Mathematics Curriculum." *Journal of Teacher Education* 46 (March–April 1995): 130–40.

Lappan, Glenda, and Diane Briars. "How Should Mathematics Be Taught?" In *Seventy-five Years of Progress: Prospects for School Mathematics*, edited by Iris M. Carl, pp. 131–56. Reston, Va.: National Council of Teachers of Mathematics, 1995.

National Council of Teachers of Mathematics. *Curriculum and Evaluation Standards for School Mathematics.* Reston, Va.: National Council of Teachers of Mathematics, 1989.

———. *Professional Standards for Teaching Mathematics.* Reston, Va.: National Council of Teachers of Mathematics, 1991.

———. *Assessment Standards for School Mathematics.* Reston, Va.: National Council of Teachers of Mathematics, 1995.

Putnam, R. L., R. M. Heaton, R. S. Prawat, and J. Remillard. "Teaching Mathematics for Understanding: Discussing Case Studies of Four Fifth-Grade Teachers." *Elementary School Journal* 93 (1992): 213–28.

Remillard, J. *Abdicating Authority for Knowing: A Teacher's Use of an Innovative Mathematics Curriculum.* Elementary Subjects Center Series no. 42. East Lansing, Mich.: Center for the Teaching and Learning of Elementary Subjects, Michigan State University, 1991.

Rickard, A. *Teachers' Use of a Problem-Solving Oriented Sixth-Grade Mathematics Unit: Two Case Studies.* East Lansing, Mich.: Unpublished doctoral dissertation, Michigan State University, 1993.

———. "Problem Solving and Computation in School Mathematics: Tensions between Reforms and Practice." *National Forum of Applied Educational Research Journal* 8, no. 2 (1995a): 41–51.

———. "Teaching with Problem-Oriented Curricula: A Case Study of Middle School Mathematics Instruction." *Journal of Experimental Education* 64, no. 1 (1995b): 5–26.

———. "Connections and Confusion: Teaching Perimeter and Area with a Problem-Solving Oriented Unit." *Journal of Mathematical Behavior* 15, no. 3 (1996): 303–27.

Shroyer, J. L., and W. M. Fitzgerald. *Mouse and Elephant: Measuring Growth.* Middle Grades Mathematics Project series. Reading, Mass.: Addison-Wesley Publishing Co., 1986.

Simon, M. A. "Reconstructing Mathematics Pedagogy from a Constructivist Perspective." *Journal for Research in Mathematics Education* 26, no. 2 (1995): 114–45.

Thompson, A. G. "Teachers' Conceptions of Mathematics and Teaching Problem Solving." In *Teaching and Learning Mathematical Problem Solving: Multiple Research Perspectives*, edited by E. Silver. Hillsdale, N.J.: Lawrence Erlbaum, 1985.

Wiemers, N. J. "Transformation and Accommodation: A Case Study of Joe Scott." *Educational Evaluation and Policy Analysis* 12 (1990): 297–308.

Anthony Rickard, *Alma College, Alma, Michigan*

5

Transforming Middle School Mathematics through Teacher Empowerment

AZITA MANOUCHEHRI
AND CAROL SIPES

Recommendations for reform in mathematics education uniformly call for an increased emphasis on meaningful experiences in school mathematics and a decreased emphasis on repeated practice of computational algorithms (National Council of Teachers of Mathematics [NCTM] 1989), a major restructuring of traditional mathematics curricula. In recent years, in an attempt to design curriculum models that support the visions for reform of middle school mathematics, several *Standards*-based textbooks have been developed and are now being used.

In this article, we describe the activities of sixteen middle school mathematics teachers from one school district in Saint Louis, Missouri, as they enacted *Standards*-based curricula in their classrooms over a two-year period. We offer an overview of the challenges these teachers have faced and the professional development initiative that has taken place to assist them in dealing with those challenges. Moreover, we report on what we have observed of teachers' growth in the process and the key elements that still need attention.

The Kirkwood School District is located in the city of Saint Louis. The district contains five elementary schools, two middle schools, and one high school. The combined middle school enrollment in the district is 1226 students, including a 26.2 percent minority population. The sixteen middle school mathematics teachers

represent a range, from beginning teachers to several with advanced degrees and more than twenty years of teaching experience. Because of the differences in background and training, the teaching styles range from very traditional to innovative and student centered.

Phase I: Induction and Evaluation

During the school year 1995–1996, a group of sixty middle school teachers and administrators from twenty Missouri school districts were invited to participate in a curriculum review project (Missouri Middle School Mathematics Project [M³]) funded by the National Science Foundation. This project involved the participating middle school teachers in the review and evaluation of four innovative middle school curriculum materials (Mathematics in Context, Connected Mathematics Project, Seeing and Thinking Mathematically, Six through Eight Mathematics [STEM] [now known as Middle Grades Math Thematics]), and it provided teachers with knowledge and experience using curriculum materials as they implemented several units from each program. Participating school districts received a two-day in-service training on each of the programs. Student and teacher editions were provided for the teachers to use in their classrooms.

Four teachers from the two middle schools in the Kirkwood School District were encouraged by their principals to join the project. Two of these teachers taught sixth-grade mathematics and two taught eighth-grade mathematics. This group participated in the curriculum workshops sponsored by the project and began implementing units from each program in their classrooms.

The programs under evaluation were significantly different from traditional textbooks in that they were heavily student centered and problem based. Cooperative group activities, self-evaluation and peer evaluation, and reading and writing were required in the materials. The topic explorations were not sequential (as is the norm in traditional textbooks), and much time was needed for students' concept development. Mathematical ideas were not presented in an explicit and isolated fashion but embedded in various activities. This required the teachers to have not only an understanding of the concepts presented in the units and how those concepts were linked but also the ability to assist students in making connections among the ideas explored in the different investigations. The natural consequence of such content organization was the need for a radical change in the role of the teacher in the learning environment. The design and nature of the activities in nearly all the programs placed greater emphasis on the role of the teacher as facilitator of knowledge. Each program also demanded more work from both students and teachers. The students were expected to read problem contexts in the units, define the conditions of the problems, form arguments, make conjectures, and convince others of their reasoning both orally and in writing. The teacher was expected to attend to the individual needs of students, individualize instruction while promoting cooperative group dynamics, assist students in reading the materials, and review their written work. The teachers learned about using new instructional tools such as manipulatives and graphing calculators because many such tools were used in the units. In addition, the teachers learned strategies for facilitating group activities and assessment techniques for measuring students' mathematical understanding.

Many teachers were not experienced in these new demands. Thus, planning and instruction became increasingly time-consuming for them. However, in spite of the tremendous amount of time and energy required of teachers for planning and teaching these materials, there was evidence of students' growth in mathematical thinking and improvement in their problem-solving and reasoning skills. Teachers were excited to see their students eager about learning mathematics; many "learning disabled" and "slow achievers" demonstrated success. The teachers noticed that the new curriculum materials had the potential for improving learning in *all* students. Indeed, because of these student outcomes, three other teachers in the district decided to use the materials in their classrooms.

The programs under evaluation were significantly different from traditional textbooks in that they were heavily student centered and problem based.

As teachers used the programs, they repeatedly identified the issues of students' mastery of "basic skills" and "assessment" as essential with the new curricula. Teachers felt there was a lack of an adequate amount of "practice of the basic skills" in the programs. Moreover, teachers claimed that the number and quality of group quizzes and self-evaluation tools were insufficient for measuring student progress. In order to compensate for what they considered shortcomings of the programs, teachers began using supplementary materials in their classrooms—standard worksheets and tests previously used. Some teachers were using the investigations as enrichment activities rather than as core instructional materials. This practice was due to a lack of knowledge of mathematics and appropriate teaching strategies for the implementation of the programs. Moreover, teachers avoided some activities or entire units because they were not confident with the mathematics involved.

After these observations, we realized more than ever that teachers needed time for learning, communicating with their peers, exchanging ideas, and planning teaching strategies that reflected the underlying constructivist framework of the *Standards*-based curricula. Access to innovative curriculum materials was a necessary condition for altering the mathematics curriculum presented to students, but it was not sufficient for radically changing the nature of mathematics learning and instruction in classrooms. To implement reform mathematics curricula, teachers needed assistance in developing new teaching strategies and required more training in the use of new instructional tools. They also needed time for planning their instruction and opportunities for reflecting on the outcomes of their activities. In other words, the use of the "new" materials highlighted the need for establishing a "new" classroom culture and a better understanding of how to create and sustain that culture within the learning environment.

Phase II: Adoption

At the end of the 1995–1996 school year and after implementing units from each of the four curricula over a period of one year, the teachers recommended adopting one of the programs, STEM, as the district's new textbook series. There were several factors that contributed to the teachers' selection of this particular program: teachers felt the content of the program was most compatible with the district's curriculum guidelines; they appreciated the interdisciplinary nature of the curriculum; and teacher guides seemed more detailed and useful.

The teachers noticed that the new curriculum materials had the potential for improving learning in all *students.*

Because the STEM materials were only in field-test form and not ready for publication, all sixth-grade teachers in the district decided to pilot the program during the 1996–1997 school year, whereas the seventh- and eighth-grade teachers selected appropriate modules for their grade levels and used them in their classrooms. The school district accepted the copying cost for student editions despite the fact that it was two years before the next textbook adoption.

At this point, there was the need and context for expanding the professional development experiences of the teachers in the district. Thus, the mathematics facilitator of the school district, with assistance from a university professor, wrote and submitted a Missouri state incentive grant (Making Middle School Mathematics Meaningful [M⁴]), which proposed to support a one-year, districtwide professional development initiative designed specifically for the middle school mathematics teachers. The main goals of the M⁴ project included—

- providing teachers with ongoing, relevant professional development opportunities. Monthly workshops on emerging issues concerning middle school mathematics reform were offered. The central focus was to provide teachers with occasions to grow both mathematically and pedagogically;
- providing teachers adequate time for reflection on their practice and for sharing of ideas. Teachers were given the opportunity to come together regularly and engage in a systematic dialogue about the events taking place in their classrooms; and

- providing teachers with the resources they needed to productively implement the new program. Classroom sets of graphing calculators, computer utilities, and software were purchased.

Some of the workshop topics were chosen in collaboration with teachers and based on the issues that had emerged in the previous year. In particular, teachers expressed a need to learn about authentic assessment, working with "diverse ability" students, and the use of technology in the classroom. Teachers needed to learn in greater depth about problem solving as a method of instruction. The proposal was supported by the district administration as well as the schools' principals and was funded by the state of Missouri in July of 1996. The activities of the M⁴ project were begun in August of 1996 (prior to the beginning of the 1996–1997 school year). Since then, the M⁴ project has served as a vehicle for teachers' reexamination of their practices and as a professional forum for the exchange of ideas about improving the teaching and learning of middle school mathematics.

New Perspectives

We watched carefully as teachers began efforts to implement the new program in their classrooms. In addition to observing their instruction as they tried out new instructional strategies, we engaged in team-teaching sessions with them in situations wherein they were uncomfortable with new tools and methods of instruction. Teachers continued to seek reasonable solutions as they struggled with the problem of how to create a balance between "telling" and "facilitating" ideas in the classrooms, and as they questioned their own decisions and the impact of those decisions on students' learning. We watched our teachers celebrate as they learned to trust that children can learn and succeed in ways they had never experienced as learners themselves. Although the evolution of teachers' instructional practices was slow, we saw growth among them as pedagogical problem solvers and as professionals.

A significant dimension of the growth of our teachers was their realization of the need for creating a professional community in which issues concerning learning and teaching mathematics are shared and discussed. The issue of time was the determining factor in the development of such collaborative spirit. Teachers found it easier to rely on one another's insight and knowledge rather than explore everything alone. Although all seventh- and eighth-grade teachers were not directly involved in the implementation process, they supported sixth-grade teachers by exchanging teaching strategies and participating in collaborative efforts to deal with problems of content and pedagogy. Teachers relied on one another for ideas and capitalized on the others' strengths while planning instruction. In particular, those teachers most proficient with technology assumed leadership roles in conducting modeling sessions on the use of technology in other teachers' classrooms. Assessment instruments developed by teachers were shared with all grade levels in both schools. Teachers engaged in team efforts to prepare guidelines for evaluation of students' writing assignments and portfolios. In addition, those teachers with stronger mathematics backgrounds provided others with insights on how to synthesize mathematical discussions in class and how to link mathematical concepts embedded in different activities. This professional socialization allowed even those skeptical of the goals of the reform to become more active and willing to try out new ideas in their classrooms.

The primary reason for creation of this cooperative spirit was that teachers themselves were the decision makers in the process of adoption of the mathematics program and experienced many of the short- and long-term outcomes of the new materials firsthand. Unlike the traditional top-down model of imposing change on teachers, reform has been the result of the teachers' professional leadership. In addition, districtwide efforts to facilitate their work has provided teachers with evidence that district administrations support and value their decisions.

A significant dimension of the growth of our teachers was their realization of the need for creating a professional community in which issues concerning learning and teaching mathematics are shared and discussed.

We repeatedly hear from teachers that they need more opportunities to reflect on what is occurring in their classrooms and to learn about the outcomes of using certain activities in different groups. Many teachers have initiated team planning and sharing of teaching ideas on their own time. Many of them have engaged in collaborative troubleshooting as they offer each other alternative strategies for dealing with learning diversity that exists among students. We hear teachers discuss methods for facilitating students' learning and progress and discuss learners' cognitive difficulties as they encounter certain mathematical topics. Resource personnel work closely with the mathematics fa-

culty in designing strategies for assisting those students who need additional help as they work with the new materials. In fact, several of these resource personnel volunteered to participate in the monthly M[4] project meetings along with mathematics faculty in order to broaden their own understanding of content and to best serve students. The use of the *Standards*-based curriculum has brought together many community professionals. In this sense, the efforts are no longer episodic and isolated but collaborative and systematic.

Challenges

The adoption and implementation of the new curriculum materials created questions and challenges for teachers. These related not only to the new skills required of learners and knowledge required of teachers but also to the acceptance of the community at large, particularly parents, of the goals of the mathematics reform.

Parents

At the beginning of the school year, the goals of the reform movement were shared with parents. Moreover, detailed rationale for the changes that our teachers were making was discussed with parents. However, the reality of these changes did not materialize until later in the school year. Unlike in the past, worksheets were not being sent home. Instead, the students were working on explorations that did not resemble what parents had seen in the course of their own mathematics education. Parents indicated they were unhappy with changes in the mathematics education of their children. Because of the nature of the assignments, they felt unable to assist their children at home.

It was apparent that in order to facilitate change in the district, parents needed to become educated more systematically about what teachers hoped to accomplish in their classrooms. Parents needed to be convinced of the value and rationale for change. Teachers organized family mathematics evening sessions during which they engaged the parents in solving the same types of problems that their children were experiencing. They invited parents to their classrooms in order to provide them the opportunity to observe the quality of the mathematical discourse that was taking place throughout the day. Changing the perspectives of all parents is an ongoing process. Many parents have extended their support of the changes, but some remain skeptical and seek constant reassurance.

New Demands

Another challenge relates to teachers' and students' lack of experience with the demands placed on them in light of the new materials. For instance, writing about mathematics is a new endeavor for many students. In addition, learning to read about mathematics is an unfamiliar task for them—especially for those who read below grade level. The need for students' acquisition of new skills has created new responsibilities for teachers. Teachers must constantly assist students to read mathematics for understanding and help them write about their mathematical solutions in ways that go beyond simply stating answers. Although teachers have taken great strides in helping students in these areas and students have demonstrated remarkable progress in how they read and write, the process has been slow and time-consuming. Some teachers have experienced frustration because this challenge is ongoing. Many of the teachers are now beginning to realize other alternatives for assisting students in these areas. For example, volunteer parents are invited to help children with their reading and writing in the mathematics classrooms. In this way parents not only are becoming more involved in the education of their children but are also taking part in achieving goals of the reform movement.

Conceptual versus Algorithmic Knowledge

One of the major challenges that our teachers are currently facing is seeking out ways for creating a balance between students' "practice of basic skills" as traditionally perceived and teaching for understanding of mathematical concepts. This challenge is closely affiliated with the varying levels of mathematical backgrounds children bring to the learning environment.

Although theoretically many of our teachers are in agreement with the mathematics reform recommendations that these two domains are not necessarily dichotomous, they struggle to find productive means for improving their students' mastery of basic skills without bombarding them with worksheets. This issue continues to be a point of discussion among the teachers and derives from a lack of knowledge on the part of the teachers about the long-range content goals of the curriculum materials, the way the units are organized, and the extent to which different ideas and topics are addressed in various units and grade levels. Teachers find it difficult to adjust to the fact that the curricular approaches to the teaching of mathematics do not assume that concepts or skills introduced in a unit will be mastered within that unit. The programs are designed so that the concepts are built up slowly and completely; this gradual procedure is new to many teachers. Conse-

quently, teachers feel the need to supplement or to bring closure to a unit by discussing an algorithm and using traditional worksheets to establish mastery of those algorithms.

Teachers' Content Knowledge

Because the nature of *Standards*-based programs is such that ideas and algorithms are not presented in an explicit fashion and concepts are developed through the use of a number of interrelated activities and investigations, teachers need broad and contextual mathematics knowledge. This, however, is not the case for many of the teachers in our district. Teachers vary greatly in their mathematical knowledge. Many of our teachers need to learn and relearn mathematical topics from a conceptual standpoint. They also need to learn better mathematics and become better mathematical problem solvers. This fact, however, is not always recognized by teachers themselves. Too often their preoccupation with immediate classroom needs serves as an obstacle to this facet of their professional knowledge. Some teachers have begun to carefully reexamine their own level of understanding of mathematics. Some have already enrolled in mathematics and mathematics education courses offered at local universities, whereas others are reluctant to address this issue.

Some teachers have begun to carefully reexamine their own level of understanding of mathematics.

Through the M⁴ activities, we have attempted, both implicitly and explicitly, to provide teachers with opportunities to learn more mathematics. However, teachers need much more systematic and intense mathematical training. The need for this training becomes even more serious as students learn to ask important "why" questions and demand deeper explanations and more significant mathematical reasoning from their teachers.

Final Comments

Recent research on teachers has provided evidence that successful accomplishment of the goals of mathematics reform requires sustained and ongoing professional development for teachers and time for them to reflect. The use of *Standards*-based curricula also highlights this need.

Using *Standards*-based curricula requires careful enculturation of both the learners and teachers into the new demands of the programs. Teachers need to be carefully oriented to the potential of the materials; they also need support as they learn about the new instructional demands. Teachers need assistance as they think about the content, the possibilities for connections, and the pedagogical practices conducive to effective implementation of the curricula. This is a time-consuming process. The most crucial components of reform are teachers' willingness to take risks, experiment with ideas, critically evaluate the results of their actions, and plan and replan their instruction in light of those evaluations. These qualities are nurtured when adequate time for training is provided for teachers and when their work conditions are supportive of their efforts. Teachers face many difficulties as they struggle to make sense of both the content and context of mathematics reform. They struggle as they try to examine their own personal theories about learning and teaching and adopt a new educational paradigm. This process demands commitment to quality teaching and ongoing efforts toward improving the conditions of learning. Imperative to the success of these efforts is the district's support of its mathematics teachers and of professional development opportunities for them. This support is also fundamental in motivating teachers to sustain commitment to the missions and goals of mathematics reform.

Reference

National Council of Teachers of Mathematics. *Curriculum and Evaluation Standards for School Mathematics.* Reston, Va.: National Council of Teachers of Mathematics, 1989.

Azita Manouchehri, *Maryville University of Saint Louis, Saint Louis, Missouri,* and Carol Sipes, *Kirkwood School District, Kirkwood, Missouri*

6

The Role of Technology in the Middle Grades

GARY G. BITTER AND
MARY M. HATFIELD

The growth in the use and application of technology in the world continues to increase and indeed permeates communities. Announcements of technology breakthroughs are common news. In the early 1980s, a typically challenging student assignment was to list all the ways that technology affects our lives—today, the challenge would be to describe ways in which technology does *not* affect us all. There seems to be no limit to technological change—especially with regard to computers.

In 1965, Gordon Moore [a cofounder of Intel] . . . made a memorable observation. When he started to graph data about the growth in memory chip performance, he realized there was a striking trend. Each new chip contained roughly twice as much capacity as its predecessor, and each chip was released within 18–24 months of the previous chip. If this trend continued, he reasoned, computing power would rise exponentially over relatively brief periods of time. Moore's observation now known as Moore's Law, described a trend [that] . . . is still remarkably accurate. It is the basis for many planners' performance forecasts. In 25 years, as Moore's Law predicted, the number of transistors on a chip has increased more than 2,300 times, from 2,300 on the 4004 in 1971 to 5.5 million on the Pentium Pro processor. The Intel Co-founder predicted transistor density on microprocessors would double every two years. This predic-

tion, so far, has proven amazingly accurate. If it continues, Intel processors should contain between 50-to-100 million transistors by the turn of the century and execute 2 billion instructions per second. (www.intel.com)

Predictions such as Moore's law imply that technology will continue to affect our life and education. Exploring Moore's law would be an excellent middle school mathematics project that would include large numbers, graphing, probability, prediction, gathering data, and hypothesizing.

Technology in Education

Technology is an important tool and resource in the teaching and learning of middle school mathematics. Projects involving technology—calculators, computers, and the World Wide Web (WWW)—can extend over several days and make connections with other school subjects. (See article 22, "Mathematics by E-Mail.") For example, in the preparation of this article, the fluid nature of the Web allowed access to the Moore's law information; then a quick "copy and paste" command put the quotation into this article. In addition the Web site provided other WWW links and additional information on the topic. Not only does the Web offer digital information, but students can explore ways to search and link information from the Web that combines text, graphics, sound, and video. Web sites on many mathematics topics are available and provide unlimited resources for students and teachers (see the references at the end of this article). Currently, 1.3 million pages of information are added to the Web each month, which means that an unending supply of current databases of information can be used as problem-solving and research tools.

Rapid advancements have been made in calculator use in many middle schools. Although the calculator has been available for use since the late seventies, extensive application did not occur until the solar calculator became available. Then the cost decreased and capabilities increased. The fraction calculator and, of late, the graphing calculator have become available to most middle school mathematics classes. Most calculator applications are created and directed by the teachers.

An important use of technology in the teaching of middle school mathematics is to make mathematics into a study of highly motivational real-world problems. No longer does mathematics need to be applied to problems with contrived situations and answers. Research indicates that school mathematics is not often integrated with out-of-school learning. Through the use of computer technology, real-world problems can now be an integral part of daily mathematics. Students can focus on researching and problem solving rather than memorizing and applying fabricated projects.

Technology can play a role in enhancing mathematical thinking, student and teacher discourse, and higher-order thinking by providing the tools for exploration and discovery. (See article 25, "Technology-Based Geometric Explorations for the Middle Grades.") Using the tools of technology provides opportunities for students to reflect on their activities and to promote metacognitive processes in their problem solving. Middle-grades students can learn to persist in considering paths to alternative solutions and make connections to past mathematical experiences. Intrinsic motivation builds when students struggle with a problem. Research indicates that middle-grades students prefer curriculum material that goes beyond the surface level (Hart and Walker 1993) and comes from the real world. (See article 17, "Engaging Middle Schoolers in and through Real-World Mathematics.") Technology applications fit such needs to the personalities of adolescent students.

Teachers who use calculators with their middle-grades students can elicit higher levels of active student thinking and encourage problem solving. Students can perform mathematical computations quickly and efficiently, freeing them to explore the data and note resulting changes. With the capabilities of graphing calculators and careful planning by teachers, students learn to plot a variety of equations. The meaning of constants and equations can be analyzed. Exploring concepts of transformational geometry along with notions of size changes (enlargements or reductions) promotes deeper understandings than merely learning definitions. Such explorations allow students to synthesize and generalize ideas that connect algebra and geometry. New mathematics curricula provide a seamless use of the calculator (such as described in "Algebra: The First Gate," article 2).

An important use of technology in the teaching of middle school mathematics is to make mathematics into a study of highly motivational real-world problems.

The computer provides many options for the integration of technology into the mathematics curriculum. Computer software exists with many different objectives. Geometry construction tools allow for exploration of geometry and trigonometry concepts. Teaching approaches may vary but emphases on constructions and mathematical explorations provide students with opportunities to develop and refine their own theories of geometric shapes and measure. Simulation software allows students to explore realistic situations, and the integration of science, social studies, and other disciplines with mathematics is becoming a reality. Technology-based laboratory devices have been available for computers and now are popular with graphing calculators. These devices have the capacity to collect and analyze data, including comparison graphing. Mathematical theories can be conjectured, tested, and hypothesized using Calculator-Based Laboratory (CBL) and Microcomputer-Based Laboratory (MBL) (www.vernier.com). The integration of mathematics and science is emphasized in CBL and MBL projects.

Microworlds also have the potential for exploring mathematical theories. Logo is a popular microworld having extensive geometric exploration possibilities. Microworlds combine text, graphics, music, and animation and allow teachers and students to link mathematics content to other curriculum areas. Computer algebra systems including symbolic, graphical, and numerical representations have potential to explore algebra topics with different approaches and to match different learning styles. "Intelligent tutors" (i.e., tutorial software) exist in middle school mathematics and are slowly becoming available as a learning option. Modeling software is used in many disciplines and is showing potential for learning and understanding mathematics. Interactive multimedia provide the user learning experiences with video graphics and sound. Characteristics of interactive multimedia technology to enhance learning are listed in figure 6.1.

The World Wide Web brings a new technological capability to mathematics classrooms. Soon interactive lessons will be accessible to students for research and mathematical problem solving. The Investigations in Math series, developed by TERC, fosters communication among students (at http://www.wkbradford.com, see the following TIMS units under Middle School titles: Connectany, Koetke's Challenge, and Triangle Chaos). The software includes activities for students to directly explore science and mathematics. Research data report students involved in this project appreciated the importance of *understanding* answers rather than just obtaining correct answers (Hatfield and Bitter 1991). Teaching methods should offer students the opportunity to observe, discover, and use a variety of resources in the social and physical environment.

Educational Issues in Technology

The use of technology in the teaching and learning of middle school mathematics provokes several concerns. Financial concerns for purchasing and updating the technology are a major issue. The rapidly changing technological scene calls for continued upgrading of existing equipment with additional memory, wiring buildings for Internet access, and purchasing new software and hardware. The future holds new types of media offering exciting features that promise to be bigger, better, and faster, but maintenance of a technology-based education requires a formal, comprehensive technology plan that establishes standards appropriate for the demands of the twenty-first century. An often overlooked aspect of that plan is the technical staffing that the new equipment requires. Administrators and school boards must accept the notion that continued funding to support a technological environment is a necessary part of the annual budget.

Access difficulties follow from lack of finances. Surveys report that almost every school in America has at least one computer; many teachers have at least one computer in their classroom. Although the student-to-computer ratio has decreased, few schools provide adequate numbers of computers per classroom to ensure their appropriate use for integrated instructional purposes. Typically students have access to computers for only a limited period of time each week.

Another issue concerns the attitudes and beliefs of students, teachers, administrators, and the general public about technology's role in education. For some of them, the new technological approach to learning presents a frightening threat; this attitude persists despite several decades of use. In one study of middle school students, students favored the presence of calculators during mathematics activities, but some (37 percent) remained concerned that calculator use might hinder understanding of basic computational skills (Bitter and Hatfield 1993).

The appropriate use of technology in education is another considerable issue. The use of computers to support constructivist approaches to instruction, to allow independent exploration and problem solving, and to provide interactive databases of information can produce positive educational benefits. Computers are often an add-on when time permits at scheduled periods during which students go to the computer or media center. In the development of national standards, little mention is made of engaging students in a computer environment structured to enhance the learning process.

In many cases wherein the technology is present, the lack of appropriate professional development for teachers limits its use. Plans must be made to help teachers acquire the knowledge and self-confidence to use technology to enhance students' learning. Time and experiences are needed for teachers to build new definitions of the nature of their classrooms and the kind of teaching practices envisioned. "Integrating technology into classroom practice is a complex process of profes-

---

1. Promotes active versus passive learning
2. Offers models or examples of exemplary and nonexemplary instruction
3. Is illustrative and interactive
4. Facilitates the development of decision making and problem solving
5. Provides user control and multiple pathways for accessing information
6. Provides motivation and allows for variability of learning styles
7. Facilitates the development of perceptual and interpretational abilities
8. Offers efficient management of time for learning and less instructional training time
9. Allows for numerous data types
10. Offers multilingual presentation

Fig. 6.1. *Characteristics of interactive multimedia (Hatfield and Bitter 1994, p. 106)*

sional development. Teachers must gain confidence with the equipment, find techniques for using the technology in meaningful experiences, investigate learner competencies, and plan new forms of classroom organization" (Hatfield and Bitter 1994, p. 108). Multimedia approaches to professional development can provide experienced teachers with opportunities to engage in reflective teaching, to focus on ways of presenting particular content in a range of representations, and to monitor learner outcomes. Districts must establish a technology-resources committee to shape a formal technology plan that includes professional development and technical staffing needs for their schools.

Technology can play a role in enhancing mathematical thinking, student and teacher discourse, and higher-order thinking by providing the tools for exploration and discovery.

Although technology is changing many aspects of our culture, some universities are slow to incorporate technology thoroughly in their teacher preparation program (Bitter and Hatfield 1994). Certainly, some professors use technology in their own classroom teaching, but many fail to link technology to integrated instructional models. Teacher education programs need to provide leadership in developing models of classroom instruction using new technologies (National Council for Accreditation of Teacher Education [NCATE] 1997). Some new multimedia applications target the National Council of Teachers of Mathematics (NCTM) *Curriculum and Evaluation Standards* and the *Professional Standards for Teaching Mathematics* (http://tblr.ed.asu.edu/utindex.html, http://mathedology.ed.asu.edu/). Such possibilities for applications allow users to regulate their own learning experiences, gain confidence in understanding the content and intent of the NCTM's mathematics standards, and practice in simulated settings.

Changing existing school cultures and structures calls for a commitment to systemic reform. Strategies described as networking, reculturing, and restructuring become important components of changing the nature of learning and teaching (Fullan 1996). If change is to be successful, teachers' beliefs, values, attitudes, and pedagogical knowledge must be considered (Hatfield 1996). The public must also be persuaded and convinced of the instructional value of technology. Morton warns, "[T]he skills that graduating students take with

them into the world must be a major focus of any serious effort to reform schools, and such computer-based skills as the ability to access and manipulate current information, the ability to communicate globally, the ability to expand creativity, and the ability to test new knowledge through sharing and rebuilding can only be developed in a supportive computer-based environment" (Morton 1996, p. 419).

Looking to the Future

Technological environments in schools should be part of a structured learning environment. The technology-integrated classroom would include computers, calculators, a computer projection system, MBL and CBL probes with related software, simulation and application software, computer-assisted mathematics programs, and supportive curriculum materials. Access to the computers and calculators is imperative. The technology should be available to students at any time for their mathematical problem-solving activities. Finally, at least one computer should have Internet access and browsing capability.

In such an environment, the teacher becomes a facilitator encouraging student investigation, conjecture, and discourse. A significant teacher challenge is to provide meaningful mathematical experiences and foster discussions among students about the images generated by the technology. Technology's primary role is to support instruction. The teacher's concern is to insure that the intriguing nature of the technology does not impede the understanding of mathematics.

To develop a vision of technology in our classrooms, curriculum development, professional development, and sustained support are needed. The computer environment has great potential to stimulate learning when it is used as the foundation of an integrated learning environment. As Morton claims, "It is difficult to understand why curriculum planners exclude computer-based learning environments from curriculum development. Instead of being integral to curriculum development and completely integrated into it, the computer environment remains peripheral, an 'add-on' in space and time that many teachers and administrators can reject" (Morton 1996, p. 417).

Interestingly, with the American public school educational systems being challenged by home schooling, charter schools, corporate-financed schools, and a proliferation of private schools, the value of technology may be more fully realized by these groups. The expedient use of data from the Web and the easy access to entire libraries of information may find the Web as the equalizer for such alternative educational choices.

The future seems to be leading to a "palm top" type

of computer for every student. We have seen the evolution of the calculator to the level of the TI-92, which exhibits many computer characteristics. Currently, cost prohibits each student from having his or her own computer, but experience indicates that costs will decrease. The future school computer "palm top" will have Internet access, word processing, and many mathematical capabilities. These devices will provide a calculator, graphing capabilities, spreadsheets, geometry construction tools, simulations, algebra systems, and "intelligent tutor" capabilities. It will adapt to the user's interests and abilities—and it may even talk back.

An interactive environment that promotes exploration, problem solving, communication, and mathematical reasoning is ideal for middle-grades students. Small-group discussions followed by classroom sharing help students debate the issues and solutions. Such discourse helps students understand the central ideas in personal and meaningful ways. As video images are integrated with worldwide databases, students can work collaboratively with their counterparts in other countries and can simultaneously view them. Multicultural activities will no longer be trite and contrived by the teacher but will be outcomes of collaborative work.

As we explore ideas about future technological environments, educational change must be linked to cultural change. According to Sheingold, "The successful transformation of student learning and accomplishment in the next decade requires effectively bringing together three agendas: an emerging consensus about learning and teaching, well-integrated uses of technology, and restructuring. Each agenda alone presents possibilities for educational redesign of a very powerful sort. Yet none is likely to realize its potential in the absence of the other two" (Sheingold 1990, p. 402). The progress of technology in our schools may not be as rapid as some supporters wish; however, it is inevitable. Through technology the challenges and opportunities to enhance the teaching and learning of mathematics in the middle grades are endless.

References

Bitter, Gary G., and Mary M. Hatfield. "Integration of the Math Explorer™ Calculator in the Mathematics Classroom: The Calculator Project Report." *Journal of Computers in Mathematics and Science Teaching* 12 (January 1993): 59–81.

———. "Training Elementary Mathematics Teachers Using Multimedia." *Educational Studies in Mathematics* 26 (1994): 405–9.

Bitter, Gary G., and Jerald L. Mikesell. *Using the Explorer Plus™ Calculator.* Menlo Park, Calif.: Dale Seymour Publications, 1998.

Fullan, Michael G. "Turning Systemic Thinking on Its Head." *Phi Delta Kappan* (February 1996): 420–23.

Hart, Laurie E., and Jamie Walker. "The Role of Affect in Teaching and Learning Mathematics." In *Research Ideas for the Classroom: Middle Grades Mathematics*, edited by Douglas T. Owens, pp. 22–38. Reston, Va.: National Council of Teachers of Mathematics, 1993.

Hatfield, Mary M. "Using Multimedia in Preservice Education." *Journal of Teaching Education* 47 (May–June 1996): 223–28.

Hatfield, Mary M., and Gary G. Bitter. "Communicating Mathematics." *Mathematics Teacher* 84 (November 1991): 615–21.

———. "A Multimedia Approach to the Professional Development of Teachers: A Virtual Classroom." In *Professional Development for Teachers of Mathematics*, 1994 Yearbook of the National Council of Teachers of Mathematics, edited by Douglas B. Aichele, pp. 102–15. Reston, Va.: National Council of Teachers of Mathematics, 1994.

Morton, Chris. "The Modern Land of Laputa: Where Computers are Used in Education." *Phi Delta Kappan* 77 (February 1996): 416–19.

National Council for Accreditation of Teacher Education. *Technology and the New Professional Teacher: Preparing for the Twenty-first Century Classroom.* Washington, D.C.: 1997. http://www.ncate.org/specfoc/techrpt.html

National Council of Teachers of Mathematics. *Curriculum and Evaluation Standards for School Mathematics.* Reston, Va.: National Council of Teachers of Mathematics, 1989.

———. *Professional Standards for Teaching Mathematics.* Reston, Va.: National Council of Teachers of Mathematics, 1991.

Sheingold, Karen. "Restructuring for Learning with Technology: The Potential for Synergy." In *Restructuring for Learning with Technology*, edited by Karen Sheingold and Marc Turner, pp. 7–12. New York: Center for Technology in Education and National Center on Education and the Economy, 1990.

World Wide Web References

Appetizers and Lessons for Math and Reason
http://www.cam.org/~aselby/lesson.html

Ask Dr. Math: a searchable archive of math questions arranged by grade level.
http://forum.swarthmore.edu/dr.math/dr-math.html

Authors' Project Site
http://tblr.ed.asu.edu
http://tblr.ed.asu.edu/projects.html

Authors' Site
http://tblr.ed.asu.edu/bitter.html
http://seamonkey.ed.asu.edu/~hatfield

Calculator-Based Laboratory (CBL) and Microcomputer-Based Laboratory (MBL): resources
www.vernier.com

Calculator Resources
www.casio.com

www.ti.com/calc
listserve@lists.ppp.ti.com

Eisenhower National Clearinghouse
http://www.enc.org/

The Fractory: teaches about fractals.
http://tqd.advanced.org/3288/

The Geometry Center
http://www.geom.umn.edu/welcome.html

The Geometry Center at the University of Minnesota: contains multimedia exhibits about geometric structures.
http://freeabel.geom.umn.edu/

High School Math Lessons: list of links to textual lesson plans.
http://www.col-ed.org/cur/math.html#math3

History of Mathematics: includes mathematician biographies, chronologies and more.
http://www-groups.dcs.st-and.ac.uk:80/~history/

Intel Corporation
www.intel.com

Interactive Mathematics Online
http://tqd.advanced.org/2647/index.html

Interactive Physics and Math with JAVA: a set of more than 20 scientifically accurate, easily understandable, user-friendly educational applets.
http://www.lightlink.com/sergey/java

K–5 List of Math Lessons: list of links to textual lesson plans.
http://www.col-ed.org/cur/math.html#math1

K-12 Acceptable Use Policies
http://www.erehwon.com/k12aup/index.html

Learning about Education through Statistics
http://nces.ed.gov/pubs/96871.html

Mathematical Quotations: provides a collection of mathematical quotations from famous mathematicians.
http://math.furman.edu/~mwoodard/mquot.html

Mathematics Archives K–12: long list of mathematics education Web links.
http://archives.math.utk.edu/k12.html

Mathematics Dictionary: a dictionary of math terms.
http://www.mathpro.com/math/glossary/glossary.html

Mathematics Education Projects
http://forum.swarthmore.edu/mathed/curriculum.dev.html

Mathematics in Ancient Greece: an exhibition (primarily a textual presentation).
http://sunsite.unc.edu/expo/vatican.exhibit/exhibit/d-mathematics/Mathematics.html

The Math Forum Student Center: site contains student activities.
http://forum.swarthmore.edu/students/

Mathematics Software
http://www.venturaes.com/

MathMania: knots, graphs.
http://csr.uvic.ca/~mmania/

MegaMath: presents unusual and important mathematical ideas.
http://www.c3.lanl.gov/mega-math/welcome.html

National Council of Teachers of Mathematics (NCTM)
http://www.nctm.org

National Science Foundation (NSF)
http://www.nsf.gov/

National Science Foundation (NSF): professional development projects
http://tblr.ed.asu.edu/projects.html
http://tblr.ed.asu.edu/utindex.html
http://mathedology.ed.asu.edu/

Plane Math Features: ideas about math and aeronautics.
http://www.planemath.com/

Project ARISE: math taught in real-world context.
http://www.napanet.net/~jlege/

Public Broadcasting Service (PBS) Mathline
http://www.pbs.org/learn/mathline/

6–8 List of Math Lessons: list of links to textual lesson plans.
http://www.col-ed.org/cur/math.html#math2

The Spanky Fractal Database: provides resources for fractal images.
http://spanky.triumf.ca/

Stories and Activities for K–12 Students, presented by Los Alamos National Laboratory
http://www.c3.lanl.gov/mega-math/

TIMS: TERC Investigations in Math
http://www.wkbradford.com

U.S. Department of Education
http://www.ed.gov/

Gary G. Bitter and Mary M. Hatfield, *Technology Based Learning and Research,*
Arizona State University, Tempe, Arizona

7

Parents: A Critical Piece of the Mathematics Reform Puzzle

MARY L. DELAGARDELLE AND
MATTHEW A. LUDWIG

Educational reform, like a favorite jigsaw puzzle, has many distinctly different pieces that must connect to complete the puzzle and hold the vision together. Converting these fragmented puzzle pieces into a meaningful whole is a complex process that requires time, resources, expertise, persistence, and patience; however, each time the puzzle is assembled, the experience itself can improve future efforts. Thirty-five years after the "new math" reform efforts of the 1960s, educators know more about change than ever before. Using the lessons learned along the way, we should be able to assemble the pieces of reform in a manner that improves the mathematics education of our young people and builds the confidence of our various publics.

An essential piece of the mathematics reform puzzle is the role that parents can and should play in improving the educational experience for their children. Parents want the best for their children and, in many cases, are motivated by the fear that any change will jeopardize their children's success in the future (National Council of Supervisors of Mathematics [NCSM] 1997). Just as parents care deeply about their children, so must the schools care deeply about the questions, concerns, and involvement of parents in any change effort. In this article, we attempt to share some of what we have learned about the questions and concerns of parents during the implementation of a *Standards*-based, middle-grades mathematics program as well as what we have learned about involving parents in a meaningful way in the reform effort.

Parents' Questions

Educators should anticipate and prepare to address questions that parents have regarding change efforts in mathematics. However, educators typically address the questions *they* believe parents *should* ask rather than deal with the issues that are most important from a parental perspective. Through various forums designed to communicate with parents, teachers and administrators in the Ames Community School District informally recorded parents' questions in an effort to be better prepared for future communications. Although answers to the questions may vary among communities, the questions themselves were not different from those posed by parent groups across the country. The concerns that surfaced repeatedly within the district were related to the following topics:

- The emphasis placed on basic facts and computation skills
- A consideration of what is "basic" at specific ages
- The importance of speed in computation

42

- Parents helping their children at home
- Homework
- The credibility of the people behind all levels of the change effort
- The amount of time devoted to mathematics during the school day
- Meeting the needs of mathematically talented students
- Grading performance-based measures of students' achievement
- Students' ability to compete on standardized achievement tests
- The "experimental nature" of the change effort, instructional strategies, and instructional materials
- What is being de-emphasized in the curriculum in order to add emphasis in areas such as algebra, statistics, probability, geometry, logic, and discrete mathematics
- The appropriate use of calculators and other technological tools
- The training and preparation of teachers as well as their mathematical expertise (particularly at the elementary level)
- The belief that children need to learn basic facts and computation skills before applying them in problem-solving situations
- The need for repeated practice of skills in isolation
- How parents will receive information about their childrens' progress on a regular basis
- The mathematical expertise of the district curriculum and instruction leadership
- The need for all students to learn more mathematics

The answers to these concerns are not easily constructed, nor can they be answered with a scripted response. They must come from a deep understanding of the questions as well as a deep understanding of the purpose for the change. These understandings, more than the questions or the answers, will help educators elicit the support of parents for improvements in mathematics education for their children.

Five Categories of Concerns

The development and implementation of a *Standards*-based mathematics curriculum framework and participation in the field-testing of innovative curriculum materials in grades 5 through 8 provided leaders in the Ames School District an opportunity to better understand parent concerns related to mathematics reform. The questions and concerns that surfaced appeared to be based on different assumptions about the reasons for the change effort, the nature of mathematics, the role of public education, and the ways in which teachers and the district were viewed by the community. From the various community forums, five distinctly different categories of concerns became evident, along with the realization of the need to differentiate the response on the basis of the source of the concern.

Support

The first category of concerns was based on parents' support of the changes in the mathematics program. These concerns were from parents who had observed their children thinking differently about mathematics and who appreciated the complex tasks and meaningful contexts used in the program. Parents expressed needs for evening classes, additional information more specific to the mathematics content, and opportunities to "relearn" mathematics for themselves. Such needs are extremely important for strengthening support from this group of parents but place additional demands on district personnel who may already be consumed in their attempt to facilitate the change effort. Finding the expertise, both within and external to the district, to support these needs not only will help these parents work more effectively with their children but can also build a larger voice of support within the community.

Misinformation

Misinformation or lack of information created a second category of concerns. Parents who voiced these concerns may have misunderstood the philosophy behind the problem-solving focus, received misinformation about the importance of basic facts and computation skills, or may not have been able to see the mathematics being developed within a problem-solving scenario. To properly respond, administrators and teachers need to be prepared to listen carefully, answer questions, organize various formats for sharing information (seminars, informational meetings, newsletters, videos, conferences, workshops, etc.), share examples of student work, and help parents see how the mathematical content is embedded in the problem-solving process. The ability to remedy misinformation and provide new information without becoming defensive is important for maintaining open communication with concerned parents.

Implementation

Another category of concerns was based on issues related to implementation. These were valid concerns caused by errors that can occur when implementing a new program. One example of an implementation error was observed in a classroom where a teacher repeatedly responded to students' questions by saying, "Try to figure this out for yourself. Please go back to

---

Just as parents care deeply about their children, so must the schools care deeply about the questions, concerns, and involvement of parents in any change effort.

---

your desk and think about it a little longer." This teacher had mistakenly interpreted the focus on students *constructing their own strategies* for solving problems and the *teacher's role as a facilitator* to mean the teacher should not offer *any* help or support. The parents became concerned because their children were feeling frustrated when their teacher wouldn't help them. Clearly, this situation provided evidence of a need for more in-service education related to questioning skills, student-teacher discourse, and the role of a facilitator of learning. To respond to concerns related to implementation, it is important for parents to understand the complexity of the change effort and realize that the initiative is being approached in a thoughtful and systematic manner. It is also important to be candid with parents about the needs of teachers as they learn to teach in new ways, about staff development plans to address those needs, and about where teachers are in their own "learning curve" as professionals. It is sometimes difficult to understand that teachers, like their students, must be actively engaged in "doing" while they are "learning." It is very important to be able to provide evidence of both students' and teachers' progress during the implementation process.

Trust

Issues of trust formed the basis of another category of concerns. Parents indicated they believed philosophically in the recommended program changes but didn't trust that teachers could pull it off or that the school had the capacity to sustain this type of change effort. Parents expressed concern that educators were "exper-

imenting" with their children and were not convinced that the instructional methods or materials had been proved successful. Their concerns were intensified when teachers, backed into a corner by questions they were not prepared to address, reacted with disparaging comments about the curriculum materials, the staff development efforts, or the district's expectations. An important strategy for building and maintaining trust is to avoid putting classroom teachers in a position of defending a program or philosophy when they have not had enough experience and training to be comfortable in this role. As programs are being implemented, teachers often are expected to be able to explain and defend an innovation they do not yet fully understand; this compromises the integrity of the teacher and contributes to misinformation disseminated to the parents and the public. Enthusiasm and commitment to a new program are not enough to address the concerns of parents and develop trust in the change effort, nor will they develop confidence in the school's ability to implement the change effectively. School districts must be prepared to provide "expert" support (people with a solid knowledge base regarding the research supporting the initiative, the philosophy on which the initiative is based, and considerable implementation experience at the classroom level) to principals and teachers as they communicate with parents about an innovation in the early stages of its implementation.

Traditional Views of Schooling

The final category of concerns was based on a more traditional view of schools, the approach to curriculum and content, and the role of schooling in our society. These closely held beliefs were based on a different view of schooling than expressed in the philosophy and beliefs of the school district. Parents expressed concerns about the focus on the development of critical-thinking skills, cooperative learning, encouraging students to construct their understanding of mathematical concepts, the role of the teacher as a facilitator of learning, and equitable access to more mathematics for all students. Many of these parents expressed a preference for traditional arithmetic taught by traditional methods and practiced in a rote and repetitive manner. Attempts to meet the needs of these parents should not focus on persistent efforts to convince them to change their beliefs. We must learn to recognize and value these beliefs, attempt to arrive at a compromise focused on meeting the needs of the child, and ensure that the child does not get caught in the middle of a disagreement between home and school.

Involving Parents in a Meaningful Way

Informing parents about a change effort is not the same as *involving* them in the decision to make the change. "Many educators and parents view decision making as the most empowering and productive type of parent involvement. It is also considered the most difficult and challenging type to organize and implement" (Peressini 1997, p. 227). Too often, efforts to involve parents in reform initiatives have stopped at the level of telling them what is intended rather than including them in development, implementation, and evaluation of the curriculum. If we want to build strong partnerships with parents, then parents must be empowered to participate in—

- the study of the current research and best thinking in the field of mathematics;
- the study of the current status of mathematics education within the district;
- setting goals for mathematics education;
- developing curriculum expectations to address the goals;
- determining the best instructional strategies to support the curriculum expectations;
- monitoring the implementation of the curriculum; and
- evaluating the effectiveness of the curriculum on the basis of student achievement.

Token involvement of parents or one-way conversations that are not focused on parent input into the decision-making process will only heighten the breakdown of communication between schools and homes. Authentic parent involvement at a level that influences decision making can link the classroom to the community and create a network of support to enhance all students' learning of mathematics.

Unfortunately, the pieces of the mathematics reform puzzle do not go together in a sequenced or predictable way. Change is always difficult and problems abound; however, understanding the questions of concern to the parents, improving the ability to respond to divergent parent concerns, and connecting parents as a critical piece of the change process can increase a school district's capacity to improve mathematics instruction at the classroom level.

References

Ames Community School District. "Mathematics: Problems and Answers." *A Parent Connection: A Newsletter for Parents and Guardians of Students in the Ames Community School District* 6, no. 1 (April 1995): 1–4.

California Mathematics Council. "High Expectations." *They're Counting on Us: A Parent's Guide to Mathematics Education* (Fall 1995): 1.

Meyer, Margaret R., Mary L. Delagardelle, and James A. Middleton. "Addressing Parents' Concerns over Curriculum Reform." *Educational Leadership* 53, no. 7 (April 1996): 54–57.

National Council of Supervisors of Mathematics. *Supporting Improvement in Mathematics Education: A Public Relations Source Book.* Golden, Colo.: National Council of Supervisors of Mathematics, 1997.

Ohanian, Susan. *Garbage Pizza, Patchwork Quilts, and Math Magic: Stories about Teachers Who Love to Teach and Children Who Love to Learn.* New York: W. H. Freeman & Co., 1992.

Peressini, Dominic. "Building Bridges between Diverse Families and the Classroom: Involving Parents in School Mathematics." In *Multicultural and Gender Equity in the Mathematics Classroom: The Gift of Diversity,* 1997 Yearbook of the National Council of Teachers of Mathematics, edited by Janet Trentacosta, pp. 222–29. Reston, Va.: National Council of Teachers of Mathematics, 1997.

Mary L. Delagardelle, *Iowa Association of School Boards, Des Moines, Iowa,* and
Matthew A. Ludwig, *Iowa Department of Education, Des Moines, Iowa*

8

Implementing Recommended Reforms in Middle School Mathematics Education: Perceptions of Preservice Teachers

TODD JOHNSON

Recommended reforms in middle school education (Carnegie Council on Adolescent Development 1990; National Council of Teachers of Mathematics 1991) call for teachers to—

- guide individual, cooperative group, and whole-class activities;

- use technology in ways that promote learning;

- help students make connections between previous and developing knowledge;

- select motivating tasks that deepen students' understanding of mathematics and its application; and

- develop in all students the ability to communicate using mathematics, to make connections between mathematical ideas and other disciplines, to reason mathematically in a variety of problem-solving situations, and to live and work productively in a multicultural society.

Properly preparing preservice teachers to implement these reforms requires addressing their conceptions of the situations in which they will implement them.

To assess their conceptions, students enrolled in a middle school mathematics methods course were asked to read and interpret Plato's *Allegory of the Cave*.

This course is taken after the students have completed twenty-seven credits of mathematics but before they begin student teaching. The enrollment ranges from twenty-five to thirty students, with women composing more than 75 percent of every class. Returning adult students and minority students each account for approximately 10 percent of the students. The following summary was written by a student who was asked to interpret the allegory.

> The *Allegory of the Cave* is a story about men living as prisoners in an underground cave believing that shadows are reality. One day, one of the men is released up into the light and is told that in fact the world outside the cave is reality. At first he disbelieves, then gradually his eyes adjust to light and he believes the world outside the cave to be the true reality. In an attempt to enlighten his friends still in the cave, the man returns. As he goes back into the darkness, the man's vision becomes blurred, and he cannot see the reality that his friends see. Because of this, the man's friends mock him and say that he was foolish to go up into the light only to loose his sight. Now, after seeing one man's mistake, none of the cave-dwellers wish to go to the surface.

The initial reading and interpretation of Plato's *Allegory of the Cave* occurred at the beginning of a semester in preparation for a discussion about what is knowable.

46

However, after reading the allegory, rather than discuss what is knowable the class began discussing problems they would face if they taught in a way compatible with recommended reforms. The following is one student's interpretation of the allegory; it is representative of the interpretations of the students in the class.

> As I see it, this fable describes people's tendency to be very narrow-minded and closed off to new ideas. The implication of this greatly impacts education in many ways. There is the issue of the man who was made to "see the light." I see this man as representing all the graduating seniors who went into education thinking they would teach using traditional methods that had been ingrained in their minds since kindergarten who now see that style of teaching as ineffective. These young men and women will soon be attempting with their own classrooms to implement the new techniques and share the latest views on education that they have learned. This all sounds fine and good, but these future teachers have the same problem that the man in the cave had. When the man tried to share his new ideas with the cave dwellers, he was made fun of and told that his experiences outside the cave had distorted his perceptions of reality. Much in the same way, I fear these new teachers (I am one myself) will be shunned to some extent and asked to conform to traditional methods.

To address concerns about implementing recommended reforms, the class was asked to identify barriers to implementation, possible responses to these barriers, and what others could do to aid in the implementation of reforms. The barriers identified by the majority of the students in the class were (a) conflicting expectations of other teachers, school administrators, students, parents, and the community; (b) insufficient money and materials; and (c) insufficient time to plan lessons. Experienced teachers identified these same barriers in teaching mathematics (Philipp et al. 1994).

Teachers who try to change things will face obstacles and suffer the consequences no matter how much sense the changes make.

In response to these barriers, students in the methods class determined they could (a) talk with teachers, administrators, and parents about what they intend to do in their classes; (b) invite teachers, administrators, and parents to observe their classes; (c) apply for grants to get needed materials; (d) continue to improve their teaching by attending conferences and workshops;

(e) implement change slowly; and (f) manage their time to adequately plan for each class.

Moreover, these students indicated that implementation of recommended reforms could be assisted by (a) other teachers willing to discuss their instructional practices; (b) parents willing to assist in classrooms; (c) supportive school administrators; and (d) university faculty who conduct informative workshops and aid in acquiring grants.

It was the consensus that the point of the allegory was, Teachers who try to change things will face many obstacles and suffer the consequences no matter how much sense the changes make. However, one student identified a second theme in the allegory; her summary and interpretation follow:

> There is a section at the end of the parable where the narrator tells his friend, "You must go down . . . to live with the rest and let your eyes grow accustomed to the darkness. You will then see a thousand times better than those who live there always; you will recognize every image for what it is and what it represents." I think that the narrator's words should be taken to heart by future teachers. The point here is that we should not abandon our ideas and views and stop sharing them simply because many of our colleagues and students' parents may disagree, but instead continue to try helping the disbelievers "see the light" and see the value in our new styles of teaching. I also believe that we need to continue to go outside ourselves in an attempt to understand others' points of view so that we are not kept "in the dark" about techniques and philosophies that may help make our teaching more effective. Also, if we open our eyes to the ways other people understand, we become more understanding of their views, and we now have a place to introduce our beliefs in a context to which they can relate.

This interpretation of the second part of the allegory is encouraging. In addition to recognizing that the implementation of educational reforms may be met with resistance and require perseverance, the student recognized the moral obligation of those with insight to work toward improving the profession. Moreover, she identified the importance of educational reformers, understanding the views of others in order to "introduce our beliefs in a context to which they can relate."

The next two methods classes did not respond with a uniform interpretation. However, in each class, approximately half the students interpreted the allegory as the first class did—a story about teachers. The following is one such interpretation:

> The cave members could be seen as teachers. These teachers are ones that have been teaching the same way for many years and do not vary their lessons, styles, or viewpoints of teaching over many years. They are stuck

in a rut and are not adapting to their students' needs and changes as they should be. The cave member who gets out is the teacher who is not afraid to try or learn something new and is willing to adapt to their students' changing needs and change their own perceptions. As teachers, we need to constantly adapt to the changing environment and be willing to learn new things and keep up-to-date with new technology and teaching ideas. We also need to listen to the teachers who have new ideas and not condemn them for being different.

Another interpretation offered by several students in recent classes describes the allegory in terms of the education of middle school students:

Plato really was not writing this for middle school students. However, Plato's statement makes sense when teaching middle school. He was saying that the people who live in the caves see shadows and think those shadows are the real thing. People need to come out of the caves to see the real light. This philosophy pertains to teachers and students. The teachers need to bring the students out of their shells. Students are scared to learn and see the realities of education. Once they go to school and realize that their life is not like everyone else's life they open their eyes to reality. What they perceive changes when they experience something new.

One unique interpretation of the allegory came from a student who completed the summary at the end of the semester. This interpretation may indicate the mood of others at the end of the semester—tired of course work and ready to begin student teaching:

I believe that this myth is very close to the way that I feel currently. I feel that the prisoners are other college students and myself. We are like the prisoners because we are tied down by our teachers and are only learning from the fire light what our teachers want us to learn. Our teachers have prepared us and taught us for teaching to a point where the only way we can learn more is to experience teaching firsthand. We have also been taught content and ideas so many times that we are hearing them over and over again. This is just like the prisoners who are seeing the light over and over again. I believe that the prisoner who left the cave was a student who had graduated or began their student teaching and was learning more from the outside world. I believe that once I am out of the cave, I will begin my most valuable learning.

Reading and interpreting the *Allegory of the Cave* offers the opportunity to build a classroom climate that supports discussion and to gain insight into the students' perceptions of teaching. However, as the last interpretation of the allegory points out, reading and discussing is not sufficient to prepare teachers to implement recommended reforms in middle school mathematics. Future teachers need to learn how to teach in ways compatible with recommended reforms in real classrooms, teaching real students. Moreover, teacher education programs need to address the future teachers' perceptions of these classrooms. Just as ignoring the situated nature of knowledge in mathematics education may result in the production of unusable knowledge of mathematics (Brown et al. 1989), ignoring the situated nature of knowledge in teacher education may result in the production of unusable knowledge of teaching.

References

Brown, John S., Allan Collins, and Paul Duguid. "Situated Cognition and the Culture of Learning." *Educational Researcher* (January 1989): 32–41.

Carnegie Council on Adolescent Development. *Turning Points: Preparing American Youth for the Twenty-first Century.* Washington, D.C.: Carnegie Council on Adolescent Development, 1990.

National Council of Teachers of Mathematics. *Professional Standards for Teaching Mathematics.* Reston, Va.: National Council of Teachers of Mathematics, 1991.

Philipp, Randolph A., Alfinio Flores, Judith T. Sowder, and Bonnie P. Schappelle. "Conceptions and Practices of Extraordinary Mathematics Teachers." *Journal of Mathematical Behavior* 13 (1994): 155–80.

Todd Johnson, *Illinois State University, Normal, Illinois*

9

Rethinking Professional Development: Supporting Reform in Middle-Grades Mathematics through the Cultivation of Teaching Dispositions

RON RITCHHART

Professional development has traditionally focused on providing teachers with information and training in current innovations related to curriculum and instruction. In this article, a shift from this "how to" model of professional development to a model focused on the development of "teaching dispositions" is advocated. In proposing such a model, some of the problems associated with the current "how to" paradigm are first examined, the concept of "teaching dispositions" is developed, and a short list of particularly powerful dispositions is offered. Finally, an example of a professional development program aimed at fostering professional dispositions through the examination of student work is discussed.

An Alternative to "How to" Training

What's wrong with a "how to" approach to professional development for teachers? After all, it fills a real and legitimate need of teachers to develop their curricular and instructional repertoire. Reasonable objec-

tions can be raised about the actual implementation, long-term effectiveness, and dominance of the "how to" model.

With its focus on techniques, materials, and logistics, "how to" training is often stripped of its philosophical and epistemological roots and implemented as "activities for" training. However, knowing what to do may not translate into effective classroom practice. Preece (1994) found that preservice teachers instructed in effective teaching practices were actually less effective teachers in the classroom than those not receiving this explicit instruction. It may be that engaging in, and reflecting on, the process of teaching and learning is more likely to influence practice than learning a set of specific practices. Without philosophical grounding, teachers struggle to adapt techniques to specific populations, make effective adjustments while maintaining the integrity of the innovation, or diagnose and respond to students' unexpected responses.

While many "how to" and even "activities for" opportunities provide teachers with rich occasions for sharing and gathering ideas for teaching, they fall short as opportunities to confront one's teaching practices, develop greater subject-matter knowledge, and probe issues of student learning. Counterbalancing this dominant culture of "how to" professional development are the advocates of a richer professional life for teachers

This work was supported by Harvard PACE, a research center directed by Dennie Palmer Wolf and sponsored in part by the Rockefeller Foundation and the Annie E. Casey Foundation. A version of this paper was presented at the annual meeting of the American Educational Research Association in Chicago, Illinois, 1997.

who place a premium on the importance of teachers' being students of the learning process (Brown 1991; Meier 1996; Sarason 1982). Within such a context, professional development places less emphasis on the development of techniques than on the enculturation of a set of teaching dispositions.

Which Dispositions?

What exactly are dispositions? In contrast to skills, which may or may not be exercised, and habits, which are triggered automatically, dispositions describe abiding behavioral tendencies or ways of operating that are under the control of the individual. Dispositions are recognized in the patterns of our frequently exhibited, voluntary behavior. They are learnable by nature and represent internalized characteristics that act to animate, shape, and assemble our abilities into action. Dispositions capture ability, motivation, sensitivity, and action (Tishman, Perkins, and Jay 1995).

Proposing a single set of dispositions for thinking, for teaching, or for any endeavor is both a good exercise and a dangerous endeavor. Thinking about a list of dispositions forces one to clarify what is really important, to examine exemplary models, to identify what can exert real influence, and to consider what behaviors are learnable. At the same time, any proposed list is likely to have gaps, to reflect a cultural bias, and to need adaptation to individual circumstances—and not to find consensus among the proposed constituency. With those caveats in place, the following set of five dispositions with rich potential are proposed. These five build on a previous discussion of the role of dispositions in teacher education by Lilian Katz and James Rath (1985):

1. *The disposition to grant students reason* entails the ability to suspend judgment about children's work and behavior while considering interpretations that assume that children, like adults, usually have some reason behind what they do. This involves looking for patterns among cases that appear to be unique, talking with students about their work, and listening to what they have to say.

2. *The disposition to learn from students* involves the activation of one's ability to look for connections between one's teaching practices and students' performance, assuming most of the responsibility for failure and being appropriately skeptical of one's role in success. In learning from students, teachers must be open to what students can teach them about planning meaningful and responsive instruction.

3. *The disposition to grapple with the pedagogy* calls on teachers to acknowledge that the "how" is as important as the "what." Teachers must also be willing to take risks and experiment with alternative methods, examine the effect of those methods, and modify instruction accordingly.

4. *The disposition to focus on the big ideas* addresses the need for coherence in a curriculum often dominated by facts and skills. Being clear about the big picture and what we want students to understand is helpful in making connections and distinguishing the forest from the trees.

5. *The disposition to seek and offer collegiality* involves considering points of view other than one's own and recognizing one's own biases. Only by trying to see what is good in others' teaching and withholding judgment can teachers collectively establish a safe environment where they can learn from others.

The Conversations About Student Work Project

The Conversations About Student Work (CASW) project was a collaborative, international research project involving teachers in grades 6 to 10 at sites in Massachusetts, Connecticut, and Israel that took place during the 1996–1997 school year. It was an outgrowth of previous work with middle school teachers done at PACE (Performance Assessment Collaboratives for Education). The CASW project was conceived as a modest, low-budget, and highly transportable intervention. The project sought to investigate the potential implications or "consequential validity" of teachers' engaging in regular conversations about student work on a shared topic—in this case functions and graphs. Such conversations are an institutionalized component of teachers' planning time in many schools in other countries, such as Japan and Germany, but are a less common feature in American schools (Stevenson and Stigler 1992). The CASW project studied the potential influence such conversations might have on the way teachers thought about planning and teaching. How might these conversations influence teachers' interaction with their students? Would these conversations have an impact on students' learning?

Four components of a conversation—reciprocity, equality, responsibility, and the construction of understanding—make conversations a good vehicle for developing professional dispositions. By its very nature, a conversation implies reciprocity. In the CASW project, we made it clear to teachers that each of them had something to say, both to us and to each other. In addition, participants are generally on an equal footing in a real conversation. (Without this component, the conversation becomes tense, formal, and inauthentic.) Accordingly, we made it clear to teachers that, as facilitators, we were learners, too. Participation in a conversation also implies the responsibility to listen to, and build on, the ideas of others. Finally, conversations are more than pleasantries and small talk; they are about issues, ideas, opinions, decisions, and questions. In a good conversation, the whole is more than the sum of its parts and some new understanding is created.

Structure and substance are also crucial to a good conversation. Substance came from the student work itself; structure was provided through the development and use of a specific protocol for our conversations. In our protocol, there are three principal roles: the facilitator, the presenting teacher, and the respondents. The facilitator guides the transition of the conversation from one aspect to another and reinforces the norms of the conversation. The presenting teacher introduces a collection of work to be discussed. During the conversation, the presenting teacher takes notes on the comments being made and summarizes what she has learned at the end of the conversation. The respondents actively discuss the work and build on the comments of others to collectively achieve a better understanding of the work.

Although admittedly a high-risk, time-intensive, and sensitive venture, mathematics reform will not progress without directly confronting and building teachers' understanding of mathematics.

The protocol itself consists of four parts: overviewing, analyzing, drawing implications, and summing up. During the overview, the presenting teacher briefly describes the context in which the work was done (e.g., by individuals or groups, at the beginning of a unit, independently). The respondents "read" the work and become more familiar with it by initially describing all noticeable aspects of the work. In this phase of the protocol, attention focuses on "noticing" rather than evaluating, inferring, or making judgments. Next, respondents analyze the work, looking for evidence of understanding and possible alternative conceptions. Inferences are made on the basis of evidence. Then, respondents draw implications for future teaching. Finally, the presenting teacher summarizes what she has gained by listening to the conversation.

By using a protocol we set norms and explicitly conveyed to teachers the kinds of dispositions we valued—for example, the disposition to grant students reason. In addition, by focusing on learning to use the protocol, we were able to provide teachers with clear and nonthreatening feedback about their behavior in the conversation—something that would have been both difficult and inappropriate if we were not operating under a set of explicit conventions. Through such modeling and subsequent practice, new behaviors and ways of operating are learned.

Attention to the five teaching dispositions occurred simultaneously throughout the course of the project. At times, our conversations focused on a particular disposition, and at other times, a disposition was developed more implicitly. In the remainder of this section, each disposition is discussed and evidence that teachers were developing each disposition is presented.

The Disposition to Grant Students Reason

Initially, teachers wanted to tell their colleagues about their students rather than learn how others characterized the students on the basis of their work. By focusing first on describing the work, teachers were forced to look at the work closely and to delay judgment and evaluation. Although they initially found pure description difficult, teachers soon began to monitor themselves and one another during this phase of the protocol. In addition, presenting teachers often commented that others were able to notice more and different aspects of the work. For example, Paul, a fifth- and sixth-grade teacher, commented, "The conversations are just eye-opening. I think I see quite a bit, but other people point out things and I am, like, 'Oh, yeah, I didn't see that.'" Even when the protocol was not being used, teachers began to engage spontaneously in the description phase. The analyzing phase of the protocol helped to further focus teachers' attention on students' reasoning. Gradually, teachers showed a greater interest in why students did what they did and reported asking students to explain more of their reasoning during class discussions.

In addition to the use of the protocol, specific attention was paid to identifying students' alternative conceptions—for example, the notion that a variable is a fixed but unknown quantity or the idea that graphs are a type of map. Teachers began to identify these alternative conceptions in their students' work. Although many teachers simply view these inaccuracies as mistakes, their identification as alternative conceptions helped teachers take them more seriously and not brush them aside as the result of students' carelessness or lack of understanding.

The Disposition to Learn from Students

At our first meeting, we asked teachers to predict what their students would do prior to instruction when asked to graph the relationship between the grades of four fictitious girls and the time they spent studying (with more time spent studying, Sara's grades improve, Jennifer's decline, Marcia's stay the same, and Brenda's improve with up to three hours of studying but then decline). In her work with Israeli students, Zemira Mevarech (1997) found, contrary to teachers' predictions, that even high-ability students in algebra courses exhibit a variety of predictable alternative conceptions about the graphing of these functional relationships. Furthermore, these conceptions are often quite stable under traditional instruction. For example, two common conceptions involve either constructing an entire graph as a single point or as a series of graphs, each representing one factor from the relevant data.

It may be that engaging in, and reflecting on, the process of teaching and learning is more likely to influence practice than learning a set of specific practices.

For the most part, the project teachers predicted that their students would create fairly accurate line graphs in response to the studying task. In examining the results of this preassessment, teachers were amazed at the actual variety of responses. Several students created a different type of graph for each scenario—a circle graph, a bar graph, and a line graph. Teachers recognized that this response represented the way they frequently assigned graphing tasks—by asking students to use several different methods, thus causing students to internalize the message that all graphs are interchangeable. This preassessment demonstrated to teachers the value of embedded assessment and how much they could learn from their students. The expectation that the student work was informative and useful for making decisions was also emphasized in the implications phase of the conversation protocol.

In addition, teachers' willingness and desire to learn from students carried over into teachers' classroom practice. Rick, a seventh- and eighth-grade teacher, said,

"What I have started to do is to have these conversations with the students about their work. I mean not every assignment that comes down the pike—but on some. Every once in a while, we stop and I say, 'What do you guys think is important here?'" Rick also talked with his students about the differences between learning from the text and learning from performance tasks. He used this as a vehicle to engage students in reflecting on their own thinking while learning more about their reactions to his teaching.

The Disposition to Grapple with the Pedagogy

Throughout the project, teachers were willing to ask questions, share what they did not understand, and admit to making mistakes. Implicitly, teachers recognized that rich discussions of student work were dependent on equally rich assignments, and they became more willing to take risks in their teaching. At our fourth meeting, Mike left the results of the day's lesson—a graph of "the Wave"—on the overhead projector for the group to discuss. The first words out of his mouth as we entered his room were, "We did this today, but I think I told the kids wrong. I said that time is usually on the *x*-axis. Is that right? We had a discussion about it in class with this problem, and some of the kids thought it should be the other way around. I told them that I wasn't really sure but that we were having this meeting today, and I would talk to this group about it." Mike's willingness to admit he did not know provided powerful opportunities for discussion. As he stated, "You know, when you begin something new, you don't really understand things as much as you would like to. You feel a little tenderness, and the best thing to do is to just take a risk and do it."

In the same spirit, Paul, a teacher who joined the group midway through the project and participated mostly as a discussant, commented that he really wanted to bring work to the last meeting. This led to an interesting discussion about entry points and the best way to begin the teaching of functions and graphs at different grade levels.

The Disposition to Focus on Big Ideas

By asking teachers to identify the "big ideas" involved in the teaching of functions and offering support to grapple with this challenge, we provided teachers with a rich opportunity to develop disciplinary understanding. Although admittedly a high-risk, time-intensive, and sensitive venture, mathematics reform will not progress without directly confronting and building teachers' understanding of mathematics. In his case study of an Australian teacher implementing a "function approach" to algebra, David Haimes (1996) showed that a teacher's conception of the discipline of mathematics guides her instruction and overrides the particular materials used. Thus, promoting reform through the prescription of both method and content, although seemingly efficient, may have less impact than we might expect. The need to grapple with both content and pedagogy is a recurring theme in interventions aimed at fostering greater understanding in students (Wiske 1997).

Our list of big ideas proved to be a powerful force for directing teachers' work. Although our conversations at times dealt with "how to" and "activities for" questions, they were always embedded in the larger issue of what was really important, such as (*a*) What types of graphs are important for kids to know—not just for next year but in order to really understand and be able to use mathematics? (*b*) How do you deal with the confusion about independent and dependent variables? (*c*) When are you teaching conventions and when are you teaching mathematics?

The Disposition to Seek and Offer Collegiality

Collegiality—an explicit focus of the protocol—was evidenced in the way teachers sought the advice of their colleagues. While using the protocol, teachers seldom told other teachers what they should do. Comments were generally framed in terms of questions: "I wonder if it would help to . . . ?" or "What do you think your students' responses would be to . . . ?" Such comments helped set a collegial tone.

In discussing the value of our mixed group of teachers from different schools and grade levels, Rick commented, "This kind of a conversation gives me a broader perspective than I could get from people in the school. The people in the school can help me in a week-to-week, day-to-day basis, looking at what is going on. They [teachers from the school and those not from the school] serve two different purposes, both of which are important." Mike added, "If we are going to do this, if we are going to use embedded assessment, we have to talk across grades."

Looking Ahead

Our particular focus on teacher conversations has shown promise. Through substantive conversations about teaching and learning, our teachers developed new patterns of behavior both in and out of the classroom and experienced changes in their curriculum, pedagogy, and sense of professionalism. Specifically, we saw greater comfort and facility with the use of embedded assessment. Teachers became more adept at diagnosing students' difficulties and designing responsive instruction. Teachers' interaction with their students changed as teachers probed more deeply into their students' reasoning. In addition, as teachers reported becoming more comfortable with the use of performance tasks, there was a greater emphasis on teaching for understanding than on teaching for coverage.

With regard to curriculum, the conversations proved to be an effective way to support teachers as they tried something new—the teaching of functions at the middle school level. Others may find the use of such conversations equally helpful in implementing new project-based or performance-oriented curricula. By focusing on student work, we were able to ground the implementation of a new curriculum in issues of teaching and learning rather than technique. Of equal importance to the teachers was the sense of professionalism and personal agency that they developed. All teachers reported feeling less isolated professionally, and new teachers indicated that the conversations were particularly useful in helping them feel more comfortable as teachers.

Although all teachers in the project commented on its value, some teachers dropped out or missed meetings because of scheduling conflicts. All commented about feeling that they had no time to engage in these kinds of conversations within the school day. In looking to foster these types of conversations in new settings, the support of administration in providing time for these types of conversations will be crucial to their success. It is important to send the clear message that professional dialogue is valued. Collectively, teachers and administrators need to explore creative scheduling possibilities to support teachers' conversations about student work.

Our teachers were all volunteers and eager to teach mathematics in a more meaningful way; further, each group was small. In starting new groups, it may be wise to follow those guidelines. Working initially only with interested teachers gives the group an opportunity to take risks and develop at its own pace. In the Massachusetts group, new members were recruited by enthusiastic participants sharing positive experiences with their colleagues. We have learned that four to six teachers are needed to get a conversation rolling but that groups as large as twelve were still effective.

Our initial work in the CASW project has shown us that a new direction for teachers' professional development is indeed possible. We *can* provide professional development opportunities that cultivate teaching dispositions, not just teaching skills. In doing so, we raise the standard for professional development by seeking a substantive rather than a superficial level of change. Well-chosen dispositions are ultimately more empowering than discrete skills. Furthermore, a dispositional focus for professional development is more authentic to the act of teaching. Ask anyone what makes someone a good teacher and you are likely to get a list of dispositional traits. We know that skills and knowledge alone are insufficient. Finally, a focus on cultivating dispositions helps to establish a learning community and contribute to the intellectual ethos of a school, enhancing the lives of both teachers and students.

References

Brown, Rexford G. *Schools of Thought: How the Politics of Literacy Shape Thinking in the Classroom.* San Francisco: Jossey-Bass, 1991.

Haimes, David H. "The Implementation of a 'Function' Approach to Introductory Algebra: A Case Study of Teacher Cognition, Teacher Actions, and the Intended Curriculum." *Journal for Research in Mathematics Education* 27, no. 5 (1996): 582–602.

Katz, Lilian G., and James D. Raths. "Dispositions as Goals for Teacher Education." *Teaching and Teacher Education* 1, no. 4 (1985): 301–7.

Meier, Deborah. *The Power of Their Ideas.* Boston: Beacon Press, 1996.

Mevarech, Zemira R. "Stability and Change in Students' Alternative Conceptions." Paper presented at the annual meeting of the American Educational Research Association, Chicago, Ill., 1997.

Preece, Peter F. W. "'Knowing That' and 'Knowing How': General Pedagogical Knowledge and Teaching Competence." *Research in Education* 52 (1994): 42–49.

Sarason, Seymour Bernard. *The Culture of the School and the Problem of Change.* Boston: Allyn & Bacon, 1982.

Stevenson, Harold W., and James W. Stigler. *The Learning Gap: Why Our Schools Are Failing and What We Can Learn from Japanese and Chinese Education.* New York: Summit Books, 1992.

Tishman, Shari, David N. Perkins, and Eileen Jay. *The Thinking Classroom: Learning and Teaching in a Culture of Thinking.* Boston: Allyn & Bacon, 1995.

Wiske, Martha Stone, ed. *Teaching for Understanding: Linking Research with Practice.* San Francisco: Jossey-Bass, 1997.

Ron Richhart, *Performance Assessment Collaboratives for Education, Harvard University, Cambridge, Massachusetts*

10

Accomplishing New Goals for Instruction and Assessment through Classroom-Embedded Professional Development

NANCY KATIMS AND CLARA F. TOLBERT

The [previous] training meeting was helpful because it gave me a chance to work through the problem and see where and what additional work I would have to do with my students. . . . It didn't completely prepare me for the teaching/facilitating of it. I think that will come from debriefing during this session—listening to other teachers' experiences and how they . . . dealt with the issues that arose as the class progressed.

The statement above, made by a middle school mathematics teacher from the Philadelphia Public Schools, describes her reaction to an innovative approach to professional development that supports and promotes the implementation of classroom practices integral to the recommendations for mathematics education reform. The approach is intended to optimize the teachers' real-time experiences in implementing new classroom practices with their students. As the quote indicates, this professional development in-

cludes the traditional "training meeting," coupled with some rather nontraditional features such as "working through the problem," "debriefing," and "listening to other teachers' experiences" in dealing with issues arising from their students.

The teacher made this comment as part of a collaborative effort between the Urban Systemic Initiative (USI) of the Philadelphia Public Schools and the Educational Testing Service (ETS). The effort, involving about one hundred middle school mathematics teachers in a year-long classroom-embedded professional development experience, focuses on teachers' learning to effectively integrate assessment and instruction. The purpose of this article is to describe how classroom-embedded professional development can foster the implementation of effective classroom practices in middle school mathematics.

Classroom-Embedded Professional Development

Guidelines for effective professional development have been well articulated (Corcoran 1995; National Staff Development Council 1994). Lee Shulman (1989) summarized these principles particularly well: "Do not do unto teachers what you would not have teachers do unto students." Because good teaching allows opportunities for students to be active learners, with an emphasis on

The authors would like to thank Alice Alston, Miriam Amit, and Roberta Schorr, consultants to the PACKETS program; Jacqueline Jones, Educational Testing Service researcher; and Mary Coe-Collins, M. Diane Conyers, Charlotte Foreman, Alwina Green, Katherine Hebert, Bonnie Jamison-Berry, Catherine Schrader, Wayne Watson, and Hope Yursa, of the Philadelphia schools for their invaluable assistance in planning, delivering, and documenting this professional development project and to thank Karen Sloan El of the PACKETS program for her dedicated preparation of materials for each workshop session.

hands-on, experiential learning, the same applies to effective teacher education.

Raizen and Loucks-Horsley (1994), in their list of components of effective teacher development, expressed this as modeling teaching principles and strategies that can be transferred to the classroom and allowing teachers to actively construct knowledge through hands-on activities. Other important components include linking teachers to resources, providing actual or simulated problems or real-world challenges, designing activities for teachers to learn cooperatively in small groups, and allowing opportunities for teachers to practice new classroom strategies.

Coupled with the need to provide teachers with meaningful professional development is the need to use precious time more efficiently and effectively. One way to increase teachers' time for professional development is to combine professional development with teachers' immediate classroom experiences and to use some of the time spent in the classroom implementing activities that promote teacher growth and learning. Sparks and Hirsh (1997) call this "job-embedded learning," a concept they apply to any educator learning on the job, and they predict a large increase in this form of professional development for the future. Classroom-embedded professional development focuses on this kind of learning, defined as "planned activities intended to further professional development which can be incorporated within one's normal teaching responsibilities" (Collins and Sinatra 1976, p. 19).

Loucks-Horsley (1994) points out that on-the-job training, although long considered legitimate in other areas, is just recently emerging in schools as a form of professional development. Along with addressing the problem of lack of time for staff development, classroom-embedded approaches can benefit teachers as they explore questions about learning with their students, experiment with new approaches, and work with other teachers to develop new and different strategies.

The Philadelphia Project

Figure 10.1 depicts how the Philadelphia USI implemented classroom-embedded professional development. Essentially, the approach is cyclical, with teachers trying out new approaches with their students, meeting with colleagues to reflect on and share their classroom experiences, and modifying their approaches according to their self-reflection and input from colleagues—then moving into a new cycle (as in an upward spiral) by applying their new understandings in their classrooms with students. The focus for the yearlong classroom-embedded professional development project was the implementation of a set of supplementary middle

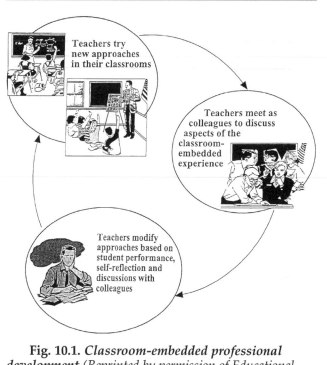

Fig. 10.1. *Classroom-embedded professional development* *(Reprinted by permission of Educational Testing Service, the copyright owner.)*

school mathematics materials (Katims et al. 1995) based on years of research in mathematics education (Lesh and Lamon 1992). The staff development model works as follows (Katims and Lesh 1995).

Teachers are first introduced to the materials and practices in a workshop setting. They collaborate in small groups, in a simulated class situation, solving a complex, nonroutine problem, using the same tools and resources available to students. They present their solutions to the group and discuss the various solution approaches used. Following the class simulation, the teachers reflect on the experience from their professional perspective, discussing issues relevant to implementation, assessment, and teaching practices.

The teachers subsequently implement with their students the same problem they solved in the class simulation. After the class implementation, teachers meet with colleagues to share successes, frustrations, and strategies that did and did not work and to delve more deeply into issues of local interest.

Activities of Participants

Each participating middle school teacher received a class set of materials from the PACKETS® Program for Middle School Mathematics and sixteen hours of workshop time outside the classroom. The overall time was far greater when one factors in the amount of time teachers spent implementing four different projects with their students, examining student work, and talking about the experience with colleagues at their schools.

The workshop training, interspersed with teachers' classroom-embedded experiences, proceeded as follows:

WORKSHOP SESSION 1

- Participants learned about the program and solved project 1 together as colleagues in a class simulation.

Classroom Experience 1

- Participants implemented project 1 with their students.

WORKSHOP SESSION 2

- Participants discussed issues and examined student work from classroom experience 1.

- Participants solved project 2 with colleagues in a class simulation.

Classroom Experience 2

- Participants implemented project 2 with their students.

WORKSHOP SESSION 3

- Participants discussed issues and examined student work from classroom experience 2.

- Participants solved project 3 with colleagues in a class simulation.

The sessions continued in a similar way, with participants implementing four projects with students and meeting with colleagues in five Saturday morning sessions during the school year. (The specific projects implemented are listed and briefly described in table 10.1.) All teachers, regardless of grade level, started with the same project. The other three projects for each grade level were chosen to fit contexts of interest to

TABLE 10.1.
PACKETS projects implemented in Philadelphia Professional Development Initiative

Grade level	Sequence	Project name	Philadelphia mathematics content standards addressed*	Brief description of project
6, 7, 8	1	Million Dollar Getaway	Number Systems; Measurement; Geometry	Evaluate the possibility of one person carrying $1 million in small bills.
6	2	Making Money	Patterns, Algebra, and Functions; Using Data, Statistics, and Probability	Given specific data, evaluate and predict the sales performance of vendors at an amusement park.
6	3	Bike-A-Thon	Measurement; Geometry	Design three bicycle routes that meet specified criteria.
6	4	Walkabouts	Number Systems; Using Data, Statistics, and Probability	Given different types of data, develop a rating system that can rate any walkabout.
7	2	Arranging Booths	Number Systems; Measurement; Geometry	Given explicit data, develop a method for arranging fair booths and paths on a field.
7	3	You Count	Number Systems; Using Data, Statistics, and Probability	Given an aerial photo of a wildlife area, develop a procedure for estimating the number of trees.
7	4	Snakes Alive!	Patterns, Algebra, and Functions; Using Data, Statistics, and Probability	Given data, identify predictors for a certain snake behavior and the best time for snake sightings.
8	2	Fast Track	Patterns, Algebra, and Functions; Using Data, Statistics, and Probability	Predict running speeds for the next 50 Olympic Games and conclude whether women's running times will surpass those of men.
8	3	Better Bouillon Boxes	Number Systems; Measurement; Geometry	Design a box pattern for bouillon cubes that makes efficient use of 24 × 36 inch sheets of cardboard.
8	4	Easy Does It	Number Systems; Patterns, Algebra, and Functions; Using Data, Statistics, and Probability	Construct a method for estimating the blood alcohol concentration for people of different sizes.

*All PACKETS projects address the Philadelphia standards of (1) Problem Solving and Reasoning, (2) Applications and Connections, (3) Mathematical Communication, and (4) Use of Tools and Technology.

Philadelphia students as well as important topics in the mathematics curriculum. Although more projects might be implemented in a school year, four seemed an appropriate number for the first year of the program. External consultants and internal staff collaborated on the design and delivery of the training, pairing external and internal presenters to maximize resources and build internal district capacity for the future.

Program Expectations

The decision to implement the professional development experience using the PACKETS program was based on several needs of the Philadelphia USI and the school district.

1. *Leaders in the Philadelphia schools want to help their teachers achieve important standards in their classrooms.*

The Philadelphia schools have a set of mathematics content standards (School District of Philadelphia 1996) reflecting the vision of the *Curriculum and Evaluation Standards for School Mathematics* (National Council of Teachers of Mathematics 1989). In addition to specific content standards, each grade level has standards on (*a*) problem solving and reasoning, (*b*) applications and connections, (*c*) mathematical communication, and (*d*) use of tools and technology.

Because good teaching allows opportunities for students to be active learners, with an emphasis on hands-on, experiential learning, the same applies to effective teacher education.

Using any of the twenty-four units from the PACKETS Program for Middle School Mathematics meets all four of the standards above. Each unit begins with a mathematics-rich newspaper article that sets the context and links the mathematical ideas to other disciplines. After students read the article, they solve the Focus Project, a multiday task requiring the use of reasoning, logic, problem solving, and higher-level thinking, coupled with basic mathematical knowledge and skills. Students may use any available resources, tools, and technologies. Each project is carefully constructed according to six principles (Lesh, Hoover, and Kelly 1992), the most significant being that an effective solution to each project requires the construction of a mathematical model—a new and useful (generalizable) concept relating two or more variables. Creating oppor-

tunities for students to integrate several mathematical topics is strongly encouraged in the *Standards* (National Council of Teachers of Mathematics 1989, p. 84), but the traditional organization of mathematics curricula with each topic presented in isolation rarely produces such experiences for students.

In addition, because each project connects several big ideas in mathematics, implementing a project covers one or more of Philadelphia's specific content standards (e.g., number systems; measurement; geometry; patterns, algebra, and functions; using data, statistics, and probability).

To illustrate how the PACKETS program helps teachers implement both district and national standards, an example of a newspaper article and Focus Project (model-eliciting activity) appears in figure 10.2. In this sample project, Better Bouillon Boxes, students use a wide variety of mathematical ideas involving concepts in geometry and measurement (weight, volume, surface area, scale) as well as whole numbers and computation and fractions and decimals. In creating their box design, students must address several issues simultaneously, including dealing with weight constraints, the number of cubes, and the dimensions of the box, while trying to maximize the surface area. Additionally, they must make mathematical sense out of imprecise real-life economic and environmental concerns, another challenge not usually posed in textbook exercises.

2. *Because Philadelphia middle schools use a wide variety of mathematics textbooks, the administrators need a program that not only addresses the standards but is compatible with any middle school mathematics curriculum and addresses the district's cross-cutting competencies.*

Being supplementary in nature, PACKETS projects can be used in conjunction with any mathematics curriculum. The units are basically independent and unsequenced, but because of the many connections in each, they can serve a variety of purposes for teachers. Teachers can select a unit that meets their purpose at any time in the school year. For example, they might choose to use a PACKETS activity at the beginning of a new mathematics topic to ascertain their students' intuitive understanding of it or at the end of several topics to see how students apply and integrate their basic knowledge and skills to solve a complex nonroutine problem. Regardless of the textbook series used, teachers see their students' mathematical thinking revealed in new and different ways.

3. *Philadelphia administrators want to encourage an increased use of the team approach among middle school teachers.*

Because of their thematic interdisciplinary links (e.g., the environment, geography, economics, biology), the projects adapt well to the middle school team approach, with extensions possible in science and social studies. In addition, every unit includes links to English or language arts—reading a newspaper article, making an oral presentation, and writing and revising the final product to make it useful for the client.

4. *According to local surveys, Philadelphia students want to see how they will be able to use the skills they learn when they are out in the real world* (Lelyveld 1997).

Each "big ideas" project involves a client (a person or group in some everyday role) who is requesting a product to meet a specific purpose. For example, in Better Bouillon Boxes, the client is the Better Foods Company, asking for a report describing a box design and specifications for the purpose of making a box for bouillon cubes that will keep costs down and be environmentally friendly. The "client" feature helps students see how mathematics can be purposeful and how people in the workforce use their basic mathematics knowledge and skills to solve real-life problems. One Philadelphia teacher described the client feature as giving students the idea of an "audience" for their work, helping them stay more focused. Additionally, the client aspect helps students engage in meaningful self-assessment. By playing the role of the client, students can ascertain on their own whether their product meets the needs of the client, instead of always thinking in terms of what will please the teacher.

5. *Philadelphia educators want their students to perform well on high-stakes assessments.*

The Philadelphia schools administer two high-stakes assessments that include measures of students' abilities to deal with open-ended mathematics performance tasks—the Pennsylvania state assessment and the district achievement test.

Providing new kinds of learning opportunities that allow students to demonstrate their mathematical talent in broad and meaningful ways can very positively affect the expectations of teachers and students about what constitutes mathematical ability.

The projects engage students in thinking mathematically and processing information in ways similar to what is expected on the high-stakes assessments. For example, students have to read and interpret complex material; they must answer open-ended questions re-

quiring them to determine what steps and operations to follow, what information to use, and what to ignore. By implementing the projects as classroom-based assessment integrated with instruction, Philadelphia teachers give their students learning opportunities to prepare them for the assessments used to measure academic progress.

Goals of the Professional Development Initiative

The main objective of the Philadelphia project was to increase teachers' use of effective classroom practices in mathematics education and, in turn, to increase students' abilities to develop and use effective strategies to solve challenging real-life problems. Crosscutting this main objective was one relating to equity—both for teachers and for students. Providing new kinds of learning opportunities that allow students to demonstrate their mathematical talent in broad and meaningful ways can very positively affect the expectations of teachers and students about what constitutes mathematical ability. And when participants become better teachers, all students of these teachers benefit from the improved classroom practices.

"Effective classroom practices" are defined in the *Curriculum and Evaluation Standards* (National Council of Teachers of Mathematics 1989) and the *Professional Standards for Teaching Mathematics* (National Council of Teachers of Mathematics [NCTM] 1991). Although not all education standards could be explicitly addressed in this project, the unified vision of the NCTM *Standards* served as the foundation for the professional development activities undertaken. By using PACKETS materials in their classrooms, teachers created opportunities for their students to integrate mathematical topics, connect their mathematical thinking to other subjects and real life, communicate mathematics orally and in writing, and develop and apply a variety of strategies to solve multi-step and nonroutine problems. Similarly, these materials provided teachers opportunities to observe, listen to, and gather information about what their students were learning in situations that elicited mathematical abilities not usually assessed.

However, using new approaches like these also illuminates mathematics teaching as the very complex endeavor it is. When teachers who have used traditional teaching methods throughout their careers are faced with the changing teaching role outlined in the *Professional Teaching Standards*, numerous questions, difficulties, and challenges arise that teachers have not previously faced. The workshop sessions that brought

Ridge Earth Defenders to study packaging policy

Everyone wants to put planet Earth first, but this is not as simple as it sounds. This Saturday, Earth Defenders at Ridge Middle School will take another step toward "Earth First," an effort aimed at improving the environment and keeping it safe for future generations. They are sponsoring a community-wide workshop to discuss whether their school cafeteria should buy milk in plastic bottles or in waxed paper cartons.

Earth Defenders is a group of inner-city students who work to help our planet, starting in their own back yard. Ridge Middle School lies in one of the poorest sections of the city.

The students will meet with leaders from the plastics and paper industries. In addition to the milk carton issue, they will study proposals to routinely recycle paper, glass, and aluminum refuse generated by the school.

Some schools in other areas have recently switched to recyclable plastic bottles and have increased other recycling efforts. Students from these schools will describe their experiences.

"Making a decision like this is not easy," explains Ricardo Tomas, president of Ridge Middle School's chapter of Earth Defenders. "Each type of container has its pros and cons."

Eighth grader Muna Dixwell thinks plastic is best. "We

resource. We can always plant more trees. Plastic is made from petroleum. Once the supply of oil is used up, there won't be any more plastic."

Americans already use about 5.5 million tons of paper each year just for packaging. One way to reduce this is to have more efficient paper packaging. Another way is to use plastic.

Each day Americans throw out about 1.6 pounds of paper per person. This is a big increase over thirty years ago. In 1960, the average person produced about 0.91 pound of paper trash each day.

Americans are also disposing of more plastic than ever before. In 1960, the daily average was 0.01 pound per person. Today the average is 0.32 pound per person.

Ridge Middle School principal Les Turner says, "Student efforts to improve the environment should pay off. I'm expecting our Earth Defenders to make a report at next month's School Board meeting."

Tomas notes, "Everyone says kids in a neighborhood like ours can't help the environment. They think we have too many other problems. Well, they're wrong."

Tomas says the public is invited to attend the workshop and join in the discussions. He hopes many adults will come. "This is important to all of us. Green is more than the color of money. It's a color of life."

should save trees," she says. "Most paper is made from wood pulp. Making paper milk cartons means cutting more trees," Muna warns. "The less paper we use, the fewer trees we need to cut down."

Kemal Jackson disagrees. "At least lumber is a renewable

> "A tree is like a house for the animals. They tore down 3 buildings on our block last year. We planted 72 trees."
>
> **Kemal Jackson**

> "Our recycling campaigns are awesome. So far, we've held a Trash Bash, a Can Scan, and a Glass Pass. They're totally fun and they help the environment."
>
> **Muna Dixwell**

LOCAL NEWS

Garbage Made Daily by Americans

Pounds per person per day:

	Paper	Metal	Plastic	Glass
	1.6 lb	.34 lb	.32 lb	.28 lb

Fig. 10.2. *Reprinted by permission of Educational Testing Service, the copyright owner.*

PACKETS PROJECT
Better Bouillon Boxes

Better Foods Company needs your help designing a box for "Souper Cubes," the company's new bouillon cubes. They want a box design that keeps costs down and is environmentally friendly.

The company wants to use a "tuck-top" box like the one shown in the pattern. A tuck-top box is reclosable at the top. Tabs on the bottom and sides are glued. The tabs on the top are folded. The result is a strong, durable box with no cracks.

A box should hold between 150 g and 200 g of bouillon cubes. The company thinks customers prefer this amount. Each Souper Cube measures $\frac{1}{2}$ in. by $\frac{1}{2}$ in. by $\frac{1}{2}$ in. and weighs 3.68 grams.

Better Foods has a large supply of cardboard sheets, each measuring 24 in. by 36 in. They want to use this cardboard to make the tuck-top boxes. You can cut several tuck-top boxes from each piece of cardboard. Since cardboard comes from trees, an important natural resource, the company wants to use it efficiently. So, they want the boxes to fit well on their 24-in. by 36-in. pieces of cardboard.

Determine the width, depth, and height of a box that would make good use of the cardboard and would hold 150 g to 200 g of the Souper Cubes.

Write a report to the company about your design. In your report include:

1. the number of cubes in your box and their total weight,
2. a pattern for cutting out your tuck-top box,
3. a layout plan for cutting the boxes from each cardboard sheet, and
4. a justification that explains why your design is a good use of cardboard.

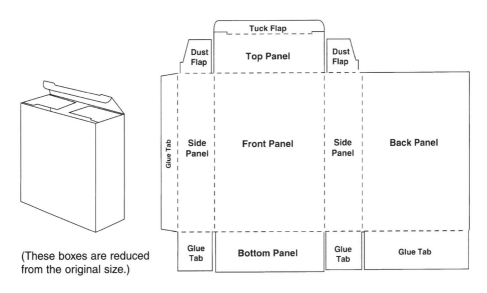

(These boxes are reduced from the original size.)

Fig. 10.2. *(continued)*

the teachers together as colleagues to discuss their classroom-based experiences were designed to deepen their understanding of their roles as facilitators and guides of students' learning.

For example, helping the teachers to effectively implement Standard 2, the Teacher's Role in Discourse, from the *Professional Teaching Standards*, was an important part of the project. According to this standard, the mathematics teacher should orchestrate discourse by—

- posing questions and tasks that elicit, engage, and challenge each student's thinking;
- listening carefully to students' ideas;
- asking students to clarify and justify their ideas orally and in writing;
- deciding what to pursue in depth from among the ideas that students bring up during a discussion;
- deciding when and how to attach mathematical notation and language to students' ideas;
- deciding when to provide information, when to clarify an issue, when to model, when to lead, and when to let a student struggle with a difficulty. (NCTM 1991, p. 35)

Since PACKETS projects can be solved in a variety of ways, one cannot predict all the ideas that students might generate. To successfully orchestrate the discourse standard, teachers need an in-depth understanding of content and students and the ability to make judgments at a moment's notice about what ideas to pursue and how to pursue them most productively.

Decisions about letting students struggle when they are dealing with a novel and challenging task, when and how to ask guiding questions, and when to tell students something directly are central to creating effective mathematical discourse. Students must plan what steps to follow in a situation with both too much and too little information. They must make assumptions about the data, recognize these assumptions, and build their products with the implications of these assumptions in mind.

Lacking experience with such challenges, students invariably seek assistance from their teacher rather than struggle with these concepts. In fact, American teachers tend to be uncomfortable with letting their students struggle with difficult material. Videotapes from the recent Third International Mathematics and Science Study (TIMSS) (U.S. Department of Education 1997) indicate that U.S. teachers assist their students at the first sign of struggling, whereas teachers in the high-achieving countries of Japan and Germany let their students struggle through difficult material, resulting in the students' gaining confidence and deeper understanding of the concepts.

Therefore, the Philadelphia professional develop-

ment project was designed to help teachers not only implement new approaches that embody the *Standards* but also analyze the resulting teaching and learning and deal with the difficult issues that inherently arise.

Outcomes of the Program

At the first workshop session, teachers completed the opening exercise shown in figure 10.3. Participants' answers to this exercise included sets of numbers such as prime and not prime, odd and even, one and two digits, multiples of 3 and nonmultiples of 3. After sharing a variety of answers, the teachers reflected on questions of whether the activity—

- has more than one acceptable solution;
- requires documentation of one's answer;
- provides criteria (that can be used by teachers, students, parents) for judging the adequacy of an answer;
- offers a complex, nonroutine problem to solve;
- connects several math topics;
- connects math to other disciplines; and
- connects math to real life.

The presenters' objective was to contrast a rather small but potentially interesting activity with the complex "big ideas" problem that would follow. In addition, the exercise offered insight into how the teachers interpreted some important concepts in the *Standards*. The presenters' perspective attached "yes" answers to

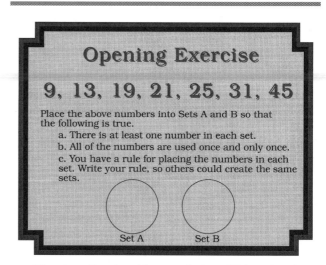

Fig. 10.3. *Reprinted by permission of Educational Testing Service, the copyright owner.*

only the first three of the questions above. To their surprise, all the questions above received "yes" answers from at least some participants, who explained their answers in some interesting ways. For example, participants perceived connections among topics as a function of having shared different mathematics used to create the sets. Participants saw connections to other subjects and to real life as a result of a few of their more creative sets referring to real-life topics. Participants saw the problem as "nonroutine" because many did not usually give problems like this to their students.

Documentation of the workshop discussions (Bruschi and Courtney 1997) indicated changes in teachers' thinking over the course of the year. At the beginning of the year, teachers were most likely to focus on questions about implementation, such as the materials and amount of class time needed. Later in the year teachers' concerns focused more on the mathematics used by students, asking questions such as, "Why did my students use only one type of approach in solving this problem?" In a conversation about student work from Better Bouillon Boxes, teachers heatedly discussed how much wasted box space is "acceptable."

As teachers interacted they realized the variety of teacher approaches used in orchestrating discourse. For example, one teacher asked, "Do I help students develop the scale or have the kids develop them and then deal with the consequences?" Comparing student products from different classes within the same district was also enlightening to the teachers. For example, one student product that implicitly developed a concept of scale without using a ruler received criticism from some teachers but applause from others when a teacher said, "If my class gave these products, I'd be jumping for joy!"

Self-reported survey data from teachers indicated changes in their classroom practices. For example, about 64 percent of the respondents across grade levels indicated they interacted differently with students as a result of this project and learned how to be more of a facilitator and guide. About 76 percent of the respondents indicated they thought differently about their students' mathematics performance as a result of this project, with comments such as, "Students proved they can do more mathematical thinking than I thought they could do!" and "Students are able to ask questions maybe I didn't think of." About 63 percent indicated changes in how they teach mathematics and reported an increased use of, and comfort with, open-ended problem solving. Many who reported no changes in their teaching practices had already been using these kinds of teaching methods.

Teachers' reports of students' reactions at the beginning of the year ranged from frustration to excitement. A typical comment from the first classroom experience was, "The kids really enjoyed the change of pace. But they had a difficult time staying on task and trying out different solutions." Later in the year, the comments about students focused more on the mathematics, such as, "Their questions centered on how to figure out what the box dimensions should be."

The following percents of responding teachers indicated noticing increases in —

- students using effective problem-solving strategies (88);
- students being willing to work through difficult problems without giving up (73);
- students working well in groups (72);
- students showing interest and motivation to do mathematics (69); and
- students exhibiting a higher level of mathematics performance than expected by the teacher (59).

Some of the most interesting observations dealt with changing expectations about different populations of students. For example:

"Top students did not come out on top."

"Lower students became interested and outspoken."

"Students not normally interested in math became vocal and involved."

"My children have learning disabilities. This project was very inspiring and challenging for the class. . . . The children were constantly and expeditiously involved in all different concepts . . . place value, addition, subtraction, division, money, measurement, counting, decimals and fractions. . . ."

The majority of teachers across grades indicated they felt their students were better prepared for high-stakes assessments. Prior to the project, students were given open-ended mathematics tasks on the district achievement test. Many middle school teachers reported that their students simply closed their test booklets in frustration without even attempting the tasks. Teachers reported that PACKETS activities provided opportunities for students to be involved in similar problem-solving tasks and that their students were less apprehensive about the tests. One sixth-grade teacher commented, "Like [the district achievement

63

test], the PACKETS activities require students to be able to synthesize their math knowledge to solve a problem. They require students to . . . make sense of what they read and use the information for a purpose." In the spring of the Philadelphia project, some teachers reported their students opened up the mathematics performance section of the achievement test booklet, said, "Oh, PACKETS," and tackled it with confidence.

Summary

This project illustrates a model of professional development that combines giving teachers materials that embody effective classroom practices providing the opportunities for teachers to use the materials in their classrooms and reflecting on and sharing their classroom experiences with colleagues. Although continued follow-up and support are needed to sustain and build on the outcomes reported, the participants clearly developed higher expectations for their students as mathematical problem solvers and a deeper understanding of the classroom practices that can lead to improved student outcomes.

References

Bruschi, Barbara, and Rosalea Courtney. *PACKETS Program Evaluation*. Princeton, N.J.: Educational Testing Service, 1997.

Collins, Paul, and Lewis J. Sinatra, eds. *Perspectives on Change in Teacher Education*. New York: New York State Teachers Corps Network, June 1976.

Corcoran, Thomas. *Transforming Professional Development for Teachers: A Guide for State Policymakers*. Washington, D.C.: National Governors' Association, 1995.

Katims, Nancy, and Richard A. Lesh. *The PACKETS Staff Development Guide*. Lexington, Mass.: D. C. Heath & Co., 1995.

Katims, Nancy, Richard A. Lesh, Bonnie Hole, Mark Hoover, and Cynthia Tocci. *PACKETS: Performance Assessment for Middle School Mathematics*. Lexington, Mass.: D. C. Heath & Co., 1995.

Lelyveld, Nita. "Teenagers Offer a Prescription for City's Schools." *Philadelphia Inquirer*, 11 May 1997.

Lesh, Richard A., Mark Hoover, and Anthony E. Kelly. "Equity, Assessment, and Thinking Mathematically: Principles for the Design of Model-Eliciting Activities." In *Developments in School Mathematics Education around the World*, vol. 3, edited by Izaak Wirszup and Robert Streit, pp. 104–29. Reston, Va.: National Council of Teachers of Mathematics, 1992.

Lesh, Richard A., and Susan J. Lamon "Assessing Authentic Mathematical Performance." In *Assessment of Authentic Performance in School Mathematics*, edited by Richard Lesh and Susan Lamon, pp. 17–62. Washington, D.C.: American Association for the Advancement of Science, 1992.

Loucks-Horsley, Susan. "Significant Advancements in Staff Development of the Past Twenty-five Years." *Journal of Staff Development* (Fall 1994): 7–8.

National Council of Teachers of Mathematics. *Curriculum and Evaluation Standards for School Mathematics*. Reston, Va.: National Council of Teachers of Mathematics, 1989.

———. *Professional Standards for Teaching Mathematics*. Reston, Va.: National Council of Teachers of Mathematics, 1991.

National Staff Development Council. *National Staff Development Council's Standards for Staff Development: Middle Level Edition*. Oxford, Ohio: National Staff Development Council, 1994.

Raizen, Susan A., and Susan Loucks-Horsley. *Formative Evaluation of the K–12 Education Programs of the Department of Energy*. Paper presented at the annual meeting of the American Educational Research Association, New Orleans, La., April 1994.

School District of Philadelphia. *Standards Curriculum Resource, Grades 5–8*. Philadelphia: Office of Curriculum Support, September 1996.

Shulman, Lee. "Teaching Alone, Learning Together: Needed Agendas for the New Reforms." In *Schooling for Tomorrow: Directing Reform to Issues that Count*, edited by T. J. Sergiovanni and J. H. Moore. Boston, Mass.: Allyn & Bacon, 1989.

Sparks, Dennis, and Stephanie Hirsh. *A New Vision for Staff Development*. Alexandria, Va.: Association for Supervision and Curriculum Development, 1997.

U.S. Department of Education, National Center for Education Statistics. *Teaching Mathematics in the Eighth Grade: An Analysis of Videos from Japan, Germany, and the United States*. Washington, D.C.: U.S. Government Printing Office, 1997.

Nancy Katims, *Educational Testing Service, Princeton, New Jersey,* and Clara F. Tolbert, *Urban Systemic Initiative, School District of Philadelphia, Philadelphia, Pennsylvania*

11

Reflections on High School Reform and Implications for Middle School

Eric W. Hart and
Jacqueline Stewart

The metaphors one chooses to describe grade levels can be revealing of current attitudes. Is middle school a bridge to high school? Or is it a continuation of the foundation building that began in elementary school? Or, as indicated by the results of the Third International Mathematics and Science Study (TIMSS), is it a holding pattern? These metaphors imply desirable characteristics for elementary and high school, but seem to give middle school an ill-defined and subordinate role. Perhaps we need to stop thinking of the school curriculum as three or four major levels, among which we struggle to make links, and instead think of it as a coordinated set of themes that are developed over all the grade levels. In this article we will describe some of the changes in content, teaching, and assessment that are common to the new reform high school programs, with examples from the Core-Plus Mathematics Project, and we will consider implications for the part that middle school mathematics education plays in the development of common themes.

Recent History of Mathematics Education Reform

This is a period of great excitement and change in mathematics education at all levels. The current reform can be viewed as an important next step in the recent history of mathematics education, as seen in the following brief summary of trends in the last fifty years.

In the 1950s the emphasis in mathematics education was on the learner and her or his social needs. Technical content and theoretical mathematics were de-emphasized in favor of practical skills needed for informed citizenship. Several events were linked to the perceived failure of this approach. Russia launched *Sputnik* and beat the United States into space, the U.S. Army found large numbers of mathematically illiterate new recruits, and in general, there was a manpower shortage for full participation in the rising technological age. During this period the educational establishment was accused of "antiintellectualism," as exemplified by a scathing attack by Arthur Bestor (1952, p. 113) in which he claimed that American mathematics education was being led by the "the specialists in knowhow rather than knowledge."

As a reaction against this approach to mathematics education, the so-called new math was born and it came to dominate the scene in the 1960s. This was a time of great activity in American mathematics education. New curriculum materials were developed, and there was a massive effort to retrain American school teachers. However, the new math came to be characterized by an emphasis on abstraction and formality.

Mathematical structure was a guiding force in much of the curriculum design at the time. Topics such as sets and functions gained prominence. Whether for reasons of content or implementation, the result of this approach was widespread public dissatisfaction. Parents did not understand the new curriculum, many teachers were unable to teach it successfully, and student performance was less than satisfactory. Despite many good features of the new math reform movement, implementation was not successful.

The 1970s ushered in a back-to-basics rebellion against the new math. This was a period in which efficient teaching and learning of basic skills was emphasized, particularly procedural skills. Despite this very focused emphasis, national tests showed that student performance in basic skills declined or stayed the same (Kenney and Silver 1997). At the same time, performance on tests of problem solving was very poor (Carpenter et al. 1981).

If one phrase could be said to characterize the mathematics education movement in the 1980s, it would be *problem solving*. The goal of problem solving connected to the trends of previous decades. To be good mathematical problem solvers, students must combine proficiency in basic skills with robust understanding of abstract mathematical concepts. The culmination of mathematics education reform in the 1980s was the development and release of the influential *Curriculum and Evaluation Standards for School Mathematics* (National Council of Teachers of Mathematics [NCTM] 1989). As an indication of beginning success for this reform movement, standardized test scores began to rise (Kenney and Silver 1997).

In the 1990s the mathematics education profession became even more proactive in the ongoing reform of American mathematics education. Most notably, two additional standards documents were developed by the National Council of Teachers of Mathematics, *Professional Standards for Teaching Mathematics* (NCTM 1991) and *Assessment Standards for School Mathematics* (NCTM 1995). These two reports, along with the original *Curriculum Standards*, fueled what is sometimes called *Standards*-based reform. It is out of this movement that the current high school reform arose.

Current High School Reform in Mathematics Education

The current reform movement has moved beyond recommendations and fragmented implementation to the creation of complete reform curricula. Recommendations from the 1980s and 1990s on how to improve the learning and teaching of school mathematics (e.g.,

NCTM 1989, 1991, 1995; Mathematical Sciences Education Board [MSEB] 1990) are now being implemeted by comprehensive new curriculum projects funded by the National Science Foundation (NSF). Some of the NSF middle school projects are discussed elsewhere in this volume; the five NSF high school curriculum projects are listed below:

- Application Reform in Secondary Education (ARISE)
- Core-Plus Mathematics Project
- Interactive Mathematics Program
- MATH Connections
- Systemic Initiative for Montana Mathematics and Science (SIMMS)

Overview of Common Themes in High School Reform

The high school programs listed above have some commonalities, both in content and approach. These commonalities provide guidance for middle school mathematics education.

Typically, reform high school programs eschew the layered approach taken in the past, where content areas were deliberately kept segregated and connections among areas were superficial or artificial. The current approach to content creates *more integration among subject areas*. However, the method of integration can vary widely. A particular program might focus on integration through thematic units. In this case, each unit is organized around a particular context, and mathematics from different strands is brought to bear on the analysis of that context. In other programs each unit might focus on a particular mathematical strand and bring in other strands as needed to solve a variety of interesting problems. Different strands might be developed equally each year, or some strands may be developed more fully, whereas others are advanced only as necessary to support contexts that invite crossover.

As an example, consider the unified content in the Core-Plus program. Four interwoven strands of mathematics are developed each year—algebra and functions, geometry and trigonometry, statistics and probability, and discrete mathematics. Each unit emphasizes a particular strand, but all units are connected by common applications; by connecting activities in every unit; by common themes of data, shape, change, chance, and representation; by common topics such as matrices, symmetry, and curve fitting; and by mathematical habits of mind, such as reasoning, visualization, and recursive thinking.

All the reform programs strive to make mathematics relevant and *build connections to the real world*. Curriculum materials are designed with the goal of setting mathematical learning in contexts that students find interesting and meaningful and in which important mathematical concepts can be effectively developed. The emphasis is shifted from rote performance of prescribed algorithms to devising, selecting, analyzing, and applying strategies to solve interesting problems. This does not mean that procedural skills are ignored but that conceptual understanding is primary. Both concepts and procedural skills are developed in the context of rich applications and engaging problem situations.

Perhaps we need to stop thinking of the school curriculum as three or four major levels, among which we struggle to make links, and instead think of it as a coordinated set of themes that are developed over all the grade levels.

Current high school mathematics education reform *emphasizes active learning*. All programs encourage a problem-solving and investigative approach. Students work in collaborative groups and individually, as they investigate, conjecture, verify, apply, evaluate, and communicate mathematical ideas. The curriculum is organized around guided student investigations that lead to construction of mathematics that makes sense to students and in turn enables them to make sense of new situations and problems.

All current reform programs *take advantage of technology*. Technology is used to make real problems accessible and to allow students to take an investigative approach. In some areas, technology makes the difference between dealing with powerful ideas and being restricted by lack of computational prowess. Appropriate use of technology permits the curriculum to highlight multiple representations (numerical, graphical, and symbolic) and focus on goals in which mathematical thinking, rather than mere computation, is central.

Assessment is an important component of the high school reform movement. Assessment practices must accommodate the changing approaches to content, teaching, and learning described above. All reform high school programs support comprehensive assessment of student learning using a variety of methods and tools.

Finally, an important goal of all the reform programs is to make *mathematics accessible to all students*.

By investigating engaging problems, making connections to the real world, using technology as a learning tool, and designing a curriculum in which mathematics makes sense, an attempt is made to be as inclusive as possible. Moreover, it is possible, and desirable, for a curriculum to be both accessible and challenging. Reform curricula are designed so that core topics are accessible to a wide range of students, while at the same time differences in student background, interest, performance, and ability are accommodated by—

- the depth and level of abstraction to which topics are pursued;
- the nature and degree of difficulty of applications;
- the rich and varied problem sets in every lesson; and
- the provision of opportunities for student choice of homework tasks and projects.

Implications for Middle School Reform

The high school reform described above dramatically changes content, pedagogy, and assessment with respect to—

- what is taught;
- how it is taught; and
- how it is assessed.

Change of this magnitude at the high school level has implications for middle school reform as well. A smooth transition between the middle grades and high school requires coordinated changes in content, teaching, and assessment. Each of these three areas is considered separately in the following sections. For each area, first the status of high school reform is summarized, and then implications for middle school are discussed.

Mathematics Content in a Reform High School Curriculum

All high school reform curricula include new content and new approaches to old content. Following the recommendations of the NCTM *Standards*, the new curricula include discrete mathematics and probability and statistics, along with algebra, geometry, and trigonometry.

Algebra

There are various perspectives on the high school subject called "algebra." These different perspectives are generally complementary and not mutually exclusive. One perspective emphasizes the idea of "function." From this point of view, traditional algebraic skills such as solving, simplifying, and evaluating are developed in the context of the unifying idea of function or relation. For example, students evaluate expressions in the context of finding the output of a function for a given input, and they solve equations in the reverse situation, that is, finding what input will result in given output. Another perspective on algebra emphasizes properties and structure such as the distributive property and the field structure of the real numbers. From a modeling perspective, algebra can be viewed in terms of representing and analyzing patterns and relations among quantitative variables. Algebra can also be characterized as "generalized arithmetic," which includes the procedural skills of algebraic manipulation. Whatever perspective or combination of perspectives is espoused by a particular high school reform program, there are general themes and topics common to all. These include function, variable, symbol sense (understanding connections between symbolic expressions and the corresponding graphs and tables), multiple-linked representations (symbolic, graphical, numerical, physical, and verbal), and symbolic reasoning (including symbolic manipulation of appropriate complexity).

Geometry and Trigonometry

With respect to geometry, all reform high school programs develop visual thinking, encourage students to construct and apply mathematical models of patterns in the visual world, and develop geometric reasoning. Although there are differences in approach, the following are some common topics and themes: describing geometric objects (shape, size, location, and motion), multiple geometric perspectives (coordinate, vector, synthetic, and transformational), symmetry, similarity and congruence, trigonometric functions, reasoning, and proof.

Statistics and Probability

There is less uniformity in the coverage of probability and statistics among the reform high school programs, but they all develop student ability to deal intelligently with data patterns, variation, and uncertainty. Themes that are present in most of the programs are the following: data analysis (graphical and numerical), simulation, variation, distribution (typically including binomial and normal distributions), and best-fitting data models (including least-squares regression). Other topics may include correlation and confidence intervals.

Discrete Mathematics

Discrete mathematics has become an important strand in the high school curriculum. In this strand, students develop the ability to model and solve problems involving enumeration, decision making in finite settings, relationships among a finite number of elements, and sequential change. Discrete mathematics topics, found to some degree in all the reform high school programs, include iteration and recursion, vertex-edge graphs, matrices, and counting (combinatorics).

Implications for Middle School Mathematics Content

Taking each of the major strands in turn and examining the topics and themes discussed above, we see that many of these ideas become accessible to middle school students. Moreover, they connect naturally to some of the traditional content of the middle school curriculum. However, adding more topics without regard to priorities, connections, and methods to teach these topics would be counteproductive. International comparisons show that typically, eighth-grade texts in the United States already contain all the topics that international texts contain, and more besides. We must proceed judiciously in considering what implications high school reform may have for changes in middle school content. With this in mind, the implications of each of the high school content strands can now be considered.

Algebra

In the case of algebra, there are at least four important points of articulation between middle school and high school: function, data, multiple-linked representations, and symbol sense. As seen in the discussion below, these four points are mutually interdependent.

Typically, reform high school programs eschew the layered approach taken in the past, where content areas were deliberately kept segregated and connections among areas were superficial or artificial.

Since *function* is a central concept of reform high school algebra, this perspective needs to be built into middle school algebra. Functions need not be studied formally in middle school, but the function perspective on algebra should be developed. The ability to model and analyze relationships between changing variables is a vital step. Students should study numerical patterns in familiar contexts. For example, since ratio and proportion are central to the middle school curriculum, it makes sense to study situations involving direct proportionality in terms of linear functions and constant rate of change. In addition, some informal work with nonlinear patterns would be helpful, so that students can see the important distinction between linear and nonlinear relationships.

The teacher assumes the roles of director, moderator, facilitator, and intellectual coach.

Another important perspective arises when we consider that algebra models not only patterns among quantitative variables determined by precise rules but also patterns given by "messy" data. This data-driven perspective is less traditional, but it also deserves attention in the middle school curriculum. Students should analyze real-world data and also perform experiments. Experiments allow students to practice measurement skills, integrate with science subjects, and produce data that may exhibit functional relationships.

Whether analyzing relationships given by precise rules or patterns exhibited by data, multiple-linked representations should be emphasized. Sometimes a pattern that is not apparent in a table of experimental data will become evident in a graph. It may be that constant rate of change is more easily seen in terms of constant increments in a table rather than by analysis of a symbolic or verbal rule. Students need to see that graphs, tables, and rules can all represent the same relationship. Being able to represent and analyze problems graphically, numerically, symbolically, and verbally and to link these representations is an essential skill that middle school students should begin developing prior to being successful high school students.

An important aspect of this idea of linked representations is *symbol sense*, the ability to make connections between a symbolic form and the corresponding table, graph, or verbal description. This is separate from, but complementary to, the skill of manipulating algebraic expressions. Students should develop familiarity and ease with symbols so that they can explain and show how the effect of a change in the symbolic form is reflected in the table, graph, or context, and vice versa.

Geometry

One way to think about the development of geometry from middle school to high school is in terms of the van Hiele theory of levels of thought in geometry. No attempt is made here to thoroughly discuss this theory, but the basic idea is that students progress in a discontinuous manner through a sequential hierarchy of levels of geometric thought, where adequate functioning at one level requires substantial mastery at lower levels. These levels, briefly, are (1) *visual*—students identify and analyze geometric objects on the basis of their appearance; (2) *descriptive/analytic*—students recognize and can characterize shapes by their properties; (3) *abstract/relational*—students can form abstract definitions, classify figures hierarchically, and understand and sometimes even provide logical arguments; (4) *formal deduction*—students can prove theorems within an axiomatic system; and (5) *rigor/metamathematical*—students can reason formally about mathematical systems (Clements and Battista 1992). Certainly middle school geometry instruction should facilitate students' experiences at the lower levels so that they can succeed at the upper levels in high school. In particular, to provide the basis for success in the reform high school geometry described above, it would be reasonable for middle schools to focus on level 2, including work with three-dimensional shapes, with some movement toward level 3 by having students carefully explain (not prove) the properties and relationships they discover.

Probability and Statistics

There are many appropriate opportunities for middle school students to examine real data graphically and numerically. Activites that take advantage of their interest in themselves, their families, and their peers can mine a rich vein of data. Learning to choose from among number-line plots, histograms, stem-and-leaf plots, and boxplots to find a representation that best illuminates a situation is an important precursor to a high school data strand. Interpreting the significance of the shape of a graph and identifying trends and patterns are skills that require experience and some sophistication, but students can begin in middle school. Some numerical data analysis is well within the ability of middle school students. They can calculate mean, median, mode, range, and quartiles to summarize their data and begin to analyze why some measures are more useful summaries than others, depending on the situation being studied.

Some concepts important to the study of probability are also accessible and appropriate at middle school. An important initial understanding is that some events are equally likely and some are not and that statements about probabilities must take this into account. Analyzing games of chance for fairness and expected outcomes is an engaging and valuable activity for middle school students. An important understanding, which takes time to develop and should be pursued in middle school, is the connection between probability and long-term relative frequency. In order to make concepts of abstract probability concrete, students should conduct probabilistic experiments. Such experiments are invaluable for informing and corroborating theoretical analysis and for developing intuition about probabilistic situations. In addition, concrete experiments in middle school can pave the way for abstract simulations in high school.

Discrete Mathematics

Discrete mathematics is an area that is sometimes perceived as appropriate only at advanced levels in high school. This is not the case. Middle school students can and should learn some discrete mathematics. Elementary treatments of vertex-edge graphs, recursion, and systematic counting would be valuable additions to the middle school curriculum. Vertex-edge graphs are powerful mathematical models used to represent and analyze situations involving relationships (edges) among a finite number of elements (vertices). Middle school students should learn how to construct and analyze vertex-edge graph models for simple situations involving nodes and connections, like networks of streets, computers, or friends.

It is also important for middle school students to begin thinking recursively—that is, thinking about how to describe the present state of a system in terms of previous states (without formal notation)—since this is a fundamental way to describe and understand processes of sequential change. Finally, middle school students should begin developing the skill of careful counting, without technical formulas, using diagrams, systematic lists, and the fundamental principle of counting.

Teaching Mathematics in a Reform High School Curriculum

So far, the mathematical content of middle school has been discussed in relation to the content in reform high school curricula. However, we must consider *how* to teach as well as *what* to teach. We need to have smooth articulation between middle school and high school in content *and* teaching.

Teaching in a reform high school curriculum is based on the notion of active student learning. This typically leads to a style of teaching that is quite different from traditional lecturing. Students tend to be actively engaged in investigating and making sense of mathematics. They are less often found sitting quietly in rows; more often they are clumped together working (noisily) in teams. The classroom environment is one of collaboration, cooperation, sense making, and communication. The teacher assumes the roles of director, moderator, facilitator, and intellectual coach.

Implications for Middle School Mathematics Teaching

The main implication for middle school mathematics *teaching* is that we should be thinking first about students' *learning*. What are our assumptions, what are desirable outcomes, and what kind of practice will support learning?

A transition period is always required when students move from middle to high school. This may require a lengthy adjustment time if the students must also acclimate to a new style of learning and teaching. When students come from middle school classrooms that involve active learning, the transition period is shortened or eliminated. Since elementary school mathematics classrooms have been moving in this direction for some time, the bridge of active learning could soon span all the grades.

Assessment in a Reform High School Mathematics Curriculum

Many guidelines for assessment have been published in the last several years, among them the NCTM *Assessment Standards for School Mathematics* (NCTM 1995). The current reform high school curricula have been influenced by these guidelines and have taken a more comprehensive approach to assessment. They acknowledge that there are many purposes for assessment, and the primary purpose is to enhance learning, not just sort students. The teacher will make instructional decisions, and the student will make judgments about what is important and about his or her own expertise, based on assessment. Thus, in keeping with expanded knowledge about learning, assessment practices in the reform high school programs tend to offer students many different opportunities to show what they know. Assessments might include optional student journals, portfolios, and extended projects.

Implications for Middle School Mathematics Assessment

The purposes of assessment are to guide instruction, promote learning, monitor student progress, and, of course, assign grades. Despite the importance of the last purpose, it should not preclude the others. Since a broad-based approach to assessment is becoming more common in high school as more reform programs are implemented, a smooth articulation with middle school requires a rich middle school assessment program as well. This could include broader assessment on quizzes and tests and a variety of other assessment methods, like student journals, presentations, writing assignments, group checklists, open-ended projects, and portfolios.

Conclusion

Mathematics education reform is in full swing at all levels. This article has described the current reform in high school mathematics education and discussed some of the implications for middle school. By working together to develop coordinated teaching, content, and assessment across all the grades, we can weave a continuum of effective student learning throughout the school curriculum.

References

Bestor, Arthur E. "Aimlessness in Education." *Scientific Monthly* 75 (August 1952).

Carpenter, Thomas P., Mary Kay Corbitt, Henry S. Kepner, Jr., Mary Montgomery Lindquist, and Robert E. Reys. *Results from the Second Mathematics Assessment of the National Assessment of Educational Progress.* Reston, Va.: National Council of Teachers of Mathematics, 1981.

Clements, Douglas H., and Michael T. Battista. "Geometry and Spatial Reasoning." In *Handbook of Research on Mathematics Teaching and Learning,* edited by Douglas A. Grouws, pp. 420–64. New York: Macmillan Publishing Co., 1992.

Kenney, Patricia Ann, and Edward A. Silver, eds. *Results from the Sixth Mathematics Assessment of the National Assessment of Educational Progress.* Reston, Va.: National Council of Teachers of Mathematics, 1997.

Mathematical Sciences Education Board. *Reshaping School Mathematics: A Philosophy and Framework for Curriculum.* Washington, D.C.: National Academy Press, 1990.

National Council of Teachers of Mathematics. *Curriculum and Evaluation Standards for School Mathematics.* Reston, Va.: National Council of Teachers of Mathematics, 1989.

———. *Professional Standards for Teaching Mathematics.* Reston, Va.: National Council of Teachers of Mathematics, 1991.

———. *Assessment Standards for School Mathematics.* Reston, Va.: National Council of Teachers of Mathematics, 1995.

Eric W. Hart, *Western Michigan University, Kalamazoo, Michigan; Maharishi University of Management, Fairfield, Iowa;* and Jacqueline Stewart, *Okemos High School, Okemos, Michigan*

PART TWO

DEVELOPING MIDDLE SCHOOL CURRICULA

12

Ports of Entry into Curricular Change

STEVEN R. WILLIAMS,
STEPHANIE Z. SMITH, JUDITH MUMME,
AND NANETTE SEAGO

In 1989, the National Council of Teachers of Mathematics (NCTM) published the *Curriculum and Evaluation Standards for School Mathematics*. The *Curriculum Standards* attempted to set a vision for what school mathematics should be for all students. The National Science Foundation (NSF) responded to this vision by providing funding for curriculum developers at the elementary, middle, and high school levels to produce curriculum materials conforming to the *Curriculum Standards*. Five such grants were awarded specifically to produce middle-grades mathematics curricula. NSF required that each of the five projects be associated with a publisher, thus insuring wide dissemination of the materials. However, a substantial period of time elapsed between publication of the *Curriculum Standards* and the widespread availability of the NSF-funded curricula. During this period, districts, schools, and teachers engaged in attempts to realize the vision of the *Standards* using any available means.

In this chapter we examine several "ports of entry" for teachers into the process of reforming their curricula. Although not strictly hierarchical, these ports of

entry entail differing levels of commitment and engagement. We describe each port of entry briefly and provide examples of how teachers have engaged in curriculum reform efforts through these ports.

Injection

The first of our ports of entry has been called an *injection model* of reform (Williams 1994). In this model, teachers inject small portions of reform into conventional curricula and classroom practices to try new pieces of curriculum or approaches to pedagogy. A common example is the introduction of a "problem of the day" or "problem of the week." These provide experience with nonroutine problems and, hence, address the problem-solving standard. In some cases, individual activities gleaned from published collections of activities, problem-solving collections, professional meetings, or in-service workshops are used as injections to replace or supplement traditional materials. Other injections include students' making journal entries, using manipulative materials, working in groups or pairs, or using calculators or computers for selected activities.

Injections of small curriculum reforms can also occur over longer periods of time or in less structured

Research reported in this paper was funded in part by a grant from the National Science Foundation (MDR-9153873). The views expressed are those of the authors and do not necessarily reflect the views of the National Science Foundation.

ways, such as a day devoted to exploring a mathematical idea suggested by a video presentation or a week devoted to a special class project. During these times the usual business of the classroom as defined by the established curriculum (usually the textbook) is put on hold, and students and teachers are freed to explore mathematics and to "try on" new materials or practices. These injections of new activities or tasks are often teacher-developed and can even be initiated as spur-of-the-moment ideas.

The injection model is characteristic of many teachers' first attempts at reform. Injections are one way to provide some experience with making connections and communicating mathematics that might otherwise be missing from the curriculum.

Examples of Curricular Injection

One example of injection comes from a project whose major goal was to study discourse in middle school mathematics classrooms (Williams 1994). The three teachers involved in the project all expressed a desire to move toward implementation of the *Standards*. In particular, all made special efforts to provide mathematical tasks that would support discourse. As they did so, it became clear that a common thread ran through their efforts.

The teachers—Ms. Rogers, Ms. Larson, and Mr. Scott—tended to depart from their usual classroom practice in bursts that varied in length but accomplished similar purposes. Ms. Larson began each day with exercises in mental mathematics. She incorporated this activity into her routine in an effort both to increase students' facility with mental computations and to make such computations meaningful. The questions she used included mental computations, definitions, and questions whose answers required straightforward deduction from definitions. In general these exercises were not related to topics being studied, and they ranged over several mathematical topics. Following her reading of the exercises, Ms. Larson and the class discussed the solutions together. During this time, Ms. Larson encouraged conjecturing, asked "why" questions, and addressed understanding of the problems more freely than she did during the regular lesson segments that followed. She was much more likely to ask, "And how did you know that?" or "Tell us how you did that," when discussing mental mathematics problems.

Ms. Larson and the other project teachers all felt an obligation to teach the established curriculum in their schools, and departures from the regular curriculum, like Ms. Larson's mental mathematics, involved some degree of risk. Although other departures from the established curriculum occurred in Ms. Larson's class-

room (e.g., during special lessons and shortened periods), her daily mental mathematics activities were one way she made changes in her teaching practice to further her goal of facilitating mathematical communication.

Although these teachers approached reform somewhat differently, each used a method that allowed him or her to experiment with new curricula and practices without uncomfortable levels of risk.

Injections also occurred in Ms. Rogers's classroom, although not as structured as Ms. Larson's (Walen 1992). More typical of Ms. Rogers's injections were further exploration and discussion of a particularly interesting problem encountered in class. These discussions could take most of the period. The problems that spawned these explorations were often ones Ms. Rogers thought would be beneficial for students to "think through," so there was an attached pedagogical goal. On other occasions, however, the problems were genuine for Ms. Rogers as well—as when the class discussed patterns in multiplying by 11, 111, and 1111. During these times Ms. Rogers encouraged conjectures, asked students to explain their thinking, and avoided premature closure of discussions. She would also point out that such activities were typical of doing "real mathematics"—the kind where the answers were not in the back of the book.

By contrast, Mr. Scott's injections were planned and lasted for days at a time. In fact, project staff characterized Mr. Scott as producing two distinct cultures within his classroom—one characterized by business as usual and one associated with trying out new curricula (Ivey 1993). Mr. Scott, a relatively new teacher, felt an obligation to cover certain basics and help all his students achieve at least a minimum level of competence. At the same time, he recognized a need to give students different kinds of experiences to stretch them beyond the basics. He did this by following a week or two of traditional instruction with periods of group work on more open-ended questions. During the latter period the classroom culture changed in ways that permitted communication, conjecturing, and justification of mathematical ideas that would not have found a place during the more traditional lessons.

Although these teachers approached reform somewhat differently, each used a method that allowed him or her to experiment with new curricula and practices without uncomfortable levels of risk. As the year progressed, these teachers also became more comfortable with the changes they made, yet the changes remained a small and distinctly separate portion of their curriculum.

Replacement Units

In contrast to what we have called injections, *replacement units* (c.f. Leonard 1989) are larger sections of curriculum, usually developed by persons other than the teacher. Like injections, they allow teachers to "try on" curriculum reform without having to develop a complete curriculum or deviate substantially from the familiar curriculum. In one sense, the development and use of replacement units grew from desires for larger injections and the perceived inadequacy of large blocks of the existing curriculum. Implicit in the use of replacement units is the notion that teachers will think more deeply about their practices, receive support and training for the use of such units, and generally take larger steps toward reform than is typical of the injection approaches. This model has been used successfully in California as part of state-supported teacher development activities.

By using replacement units, teachers experience reforms in their own classrooms and have opportunities to grapple with the difficulties that arise. Their experience with alternative curricula prompts examination, inquiry, and collaboration. Opportunities for such reflective practice and conversation deepen understanding and motivate teachers to broaden their application of the reform ideas to other parts of their curriculum. This port of entry allows teachers to be exposed to big mathematical ideas in coherent and practical chunks, "pieces small enough to seem manageable to even the most reticent" (Acquarelli and Mumme 1996, p. 482).

Ideally, replacement units focus on appropriate concepts and skills, integrate important mathematical topics, and help students make sense of mathematics. Frequently, these units also provide opportunities for teachers to explore new and different mathematics. Initial involvement with these units often requires teachers to grapple with their own understanding of mathematics, including topics not typically part of traditional curriculum, prior to thinking about planning children's experiences with the units.

Replacement units have come from a variety of sources. Some units were created to meet perceived needs for reform prior to the publication of the *Curriculum Standards*. Others were commissioned to replace existing curricula to meet the demand created by the *Standards* prior to completion of large-scale curriculum reform projects or were pulled from early versions of large-scale reform curriculum projects.

An Example of the Use of Replacement Units

Mr. Herrera, a middle-grades mathematics teacher, had been involved with improving his practice over several years and had injected "problems of the week" as well as various investigative activities into this curriculum. He then became involved with Mathematics Renaissance, a large-scale professional development network in the state of California. He attended replacement unit workshops where he spent two days as a learner experiencing a unit on mathematical growth. He was then asked to teach the unit in his classroom during the next four to six weeks. The unit's first lesson informally assessed students' knowledge of the important mathematical ideas in the unit. Mr. Herrera spent four class periods on this lesson instead of the one period recommended. He was frustrated that his students didn't understand how to "do it," so he gave them guidance in solving the preassessment problem.

Mr. Herrera spent nine weeks on the unit. During this time he continued his predetermined problems of the week, even though they were not connected to the unit. Mr. Herrera indicated that he preferred quiet in his classroom, so even though students were sitting in groups of four as suggested in the unit design, they worked independently and silently most of the time. Students regularly wrote about how they solved their problems in their journals, but individual or whole-class discussions of the mathematics were rare.

She continued to stay involved in professional growth experiences and to search for better ways to deepen her students' mathematical understandings.

At the Renaissance meeting to debrief the unit, Mr. Herrera discussed his experiences with other teachers who had taught the same unit. These discussions provided him with new tools for the next time he taught this unit. He learned a lot from hearing what other teachers did in their classrooms and from looking at their students' work. He looked forward to teaching the unit again the next year, when he would be more comfortable with it, "let go" of making sure the students mastered the material in each lesson (especially

77

the preassessment), and focus more on the progress of students' understandings.

According to Ball and Cohen, the current climate for reform leads to the perception that good, motivated teachers reject the use of a current textbook or other curricular materials in favor of creating their own materials.

Ms. Templeton attended the same unit workshop as Mr. Herrera, but she taught the replacement unit differently. She had been teaching for three years when she became involved in the Mathematics Renaissance. Ms. Templeton, like Mr. Herrera, used problems of the week, but she used them differently: she searched for and used problems that related mathematically to the ideas in the unit. In order to obtain clues to potential tough spots for the students in the unit, as well as information about the students' previous experiences, she used the preassessment in one fifty-minute period to assess students informally. That information was used throughout the unit to connect the problem contexts to students' experiences.

Ms. Templeton completed teaching the unit in five weeks. Like Mr. Herrera, Ms. Templeton had her students write daily in mathematics journals. Students were asked regularly to work collaboratively, discuss their solutions, and defend and justify the logic of their strategies. Ms. Templeton's room was noisy and active. After each lesson, she pulled the class together for a whole-class discussion of the various strategies and solutions. The important mathematical ideas in the lessons were the foci of these discussions.

Although these teachers were from different districts, they met regularly at Renaissance meetings. Ms. Templeton shared her reflections on her teaching experiences, discussed the student-work products from the unit, and indicated that she also learned from others discussing their experiences in teaching the unit. She looked forward to teaching this unit again the next year and indicated that the mathematical and pedagogical knowledge she gained would help her with the next replacement unit, which she intended to teach right away.

Later in the first year, both of these teachers taught another replacement unit, and they taught two more units each year for the next two years. Mr. Herrera's instructional program changed. Most significant, he in-corporated more student-centered activities. Yet many of the changes were superficial; it was difficult for him to change other aspects of his practice. Ms. Templeton's classroom also looked different. However, her curriculum underwent a complete transformation; she was now using new instructional materials, the core of which had come from the replacement units. She continued to stay involved in professional growth experiences and search for better ways to deepen her students' mathematical understandings.

Each of these teachers approached replacement units through a preexisting mindset that determined the degree to which each was willing to modify or abandon old behaviors. Using replacement units provided an opportunity to try new practices and beliefs about teaching and learning.

Teacher-Made or Teacher-Organized Curriculum

A third port of entry that requires a more significant initial commitment to reform is the introduction of a teacher-made or teacher-organized curriculum. Here, teachers actually abandon the old curriculum in favor of one they make themselves, either by creating materials from scratch (teacher made) or by pulling together a combination of original materials and those from other sources (teacher organized). In this case, as with injections and replacement units, the risk involved in curriculum innovation still appears manageable. Teachers control many of the choices involved with implementation; they decide what gets taught and the depth and sequence in which it is taught.

The development of teacher-made or -organized curricula seems a natural step for some teachers as they become more comfortable with reform ideas and experience success with individual injections or replacement units. Success with initial efforts naturally leads to a desire to replace more of the curriculum. In their simplest form, these curricula may look like collections of injection tasks or activities sandwiched between replacement units. Unlike injections and replacement units, however, teacher-made or -organized curricula are meant to completely replace an existing curriculum and, therefore, must attend to topic coverage and local or state curriculum frameworks. One danger is that important topics will be abandoned along with the old curriculum materials. Despite the need to cover the range of material specified by these frameworks, there is a tendency for these curricula to lack coherence, both between and within topics. Too often there is no underlying theme or philosophy that guides the assembling, sequencing, and presenting of materials. Therefore, connections between and among mathematical topics are often lacking.

Teacher-made or -organized curricula may also be supported by various pedagogical innovations, including integration of mathematics with other subjects, the use of journal entries, problems of the day, problems of the week, group activities, and so forth. These innovations typically reflect teachers' preferred approaches to pedagogical reform. At the same time, they may provide the *appearance* of curricular reform without providing a coherent set of mathematical ideas connected across topics and grade levels.

Consequently, accepting teacher-made or -organized curricula as a mark of good reform-oriented teaching may be problematic. According to Ball and Cohen (1996), the current climate for reform leads to the perception that good, motivated teachers reject the use of a current textbook or other curricular materials in favor of creating their own materials. However, teachers may, in the name of reform, reject a traditional curriculum in favor of a collection of activities with attractive surface features but with little coherence and few within- or across-topic connections.

An Example of Teacher-Made or -Organized Curricula

After trying out various replacement units, three teachers in a suburban school district convinced their district to fund the development of a full-year curriculum for the district's Math A course. (Math A was intended for students not fully prepared for the college preparatory algebra or geometry courses. See California State Department of Education [1985].) The three teachers—Ms. Jones, Ms. Hernandez, and Ms. Willow—were considered forward-looking lead mathematics teachers who had spent their summer developing curriculum materials for the course. Their first few meetings centered on gathering supplementary curriculum materials from many sources and organizing them according to content topics. It was important to these three that the content topics of the current text series be included, but they wanted the tasks to be more conceptually oriented than the procedural activities found in the text series.

The product of this work consisted of ten instructional units with the following titles: "Problem-Solving Strategies"; "Factors and Multiples"; "Spatial Visualization"; "Data and Survey Analysis"; "Graphing"; "Probability"; "Similarity"; "Mouse and Elephant"; "Growth and Decay"; and "Algebra". In addition, a collection of problem-solving materials was prepared for optional use by teachers. The unit titles indicated that the core of the new curriculum materials consisted of units from the Middle-Grades Mathematics Project,

such as "Mouse and Elephant" (Shroyer and Fitzgerald 1986), and from the Math A replacement units that had previously been developed by other teachers for the state of California, such as "Spatial Visualization" (Leonard 1989). Additional individual tasks were collected or created and folded into that core of materials.

> *When philosophies or feelings of ownership clash with a mandate to follow new guidelines, teachers may work out a compromise in which the most important elements of the old curriculum (from their viewpoint) are preserved in the new.*

The three teachers spent a significant amount of time in discussions about the structure of the units. It was agreed that a list of unit objectives was needed as a familiar organizer for other teachers. Lesson objectives were also included. A unit overview provided pacing guidelines, a description of the unit, and a list of the materials needed for the specific activities. A day-by-day teachers' planning outline of the unit followed the overview. The general lesson plan consisted of a problem of the day to be used as a warm-up, followed by a collection of problems involving a specific mathematical topic. The lessons included guidelines for structuring cooperative learning, procedures for sequencing the events of the day (including journal prompts as closure to the lessons), and masters for worksheets needed by students. Homework tasks were also included. At the end of each unit were several appendices with student pages, answer keys for the various worksheets and homework assignments, supplementary materials, and other teacher resources.

Student materials included a table of contents, which listed the problems of the day, the class and homework assignments, and the journal prompts. The table of contents also provided spaces for entering the dates that assignments were completed and the grades received. The remainder of the student materials consisted of copies of the consumable worksheets needed to complete the curriculum activities.

The district printed a set of the materials for each teacher, with each unit in a separate three-ring binder. The consumable student materials were also printed by the district for each class. Manipulatives were purchased by the district for each participating teacher; these were organized into sets in stackable containers by the three lead teachers.

Before the start of school, each participating teacher attended an in-service workshop about the use of the curriculum, where they were given the teacher materials, student materials, and manipulatives kit. Follow-up in-service training during the year consisted of sharing concerns and providing feedback from experiences using the curriculum materials. On the basis of that feedback, the materials were revised the following summer. Two additional teachers who were using the curriculum materials participated with the original three in that revision process.

The curriculum continued to be used by many teachers in the district during the next four years. The materials seemed to meet the goals of the teachers involved in organizing and revising them, and other teachers in the district were generally supportive of trying out the curriculum. The project also provided an excellent professional development opportunity for many of the teachers and a positive, enjoyable learning environment for students. However, the materials did not provide an adequate long-term solution for the district.

Adoption of a Full, *Standards*-Based Curriculum

Another port of entry comes with the adoption of a reformed curriculum typically developed by commercial publishers and university professors, with input from practicing teachers. Such a curriculum is usually developed independently of most teachers and adopted at a district or building level. Only recently have such complete reformed curricula become available, and many educators are still struggling with issues surrounding full implementation of such curricula.

Adoption of a new curriculum does not insure that teachers will feel ownership of that curriculum or that teachers will be comfortable with either the content or the pedagogy that goes with it. Teachers who agree to teach a reformed curriculum may concurrently teach pieces of the old curriculum, juxtaposing old and new. In these circumstances, teachers may see much of value in the new curriculum, but they may be either too firmly aligned with the philosophies of the old curriculum or have too much "ownership" in their past practices to be successful with the new materials. Success can be affected by the teachers' levels of comfort with the old material, their beliefs that the new curriculum does not cover given topics as well as the old, and the mindset of teachers or parents that students need the basic skills emphasized in the old curriculum in addition to the skills and understandings emphasized in the new materials. This juxtaposition of

old and new can take the form of reverse injections of traditional curricular topics, activities, and methods of teaching into the reformed curriculum. When philosophies or feelings of ownership clash with a mandate to follow new guidelines, teachers may work out a compromise in which the most important elements of the old curriculum (from their viewpoint) are preserved in the new.

Teachers who adopt a reformed curriculum can and often do come to see it as valuable, and injections of old curricula often disappear with time. This happens as teachers become philosophically aligned with the new curriculum or feel more ownership of the practices it suggests. Arriving at this point takes time and effort on the part of the teacher, along with a good deal of "trying on" reform in the ways discussed. It is also true that the metaphor of "adoption" is not perfect. Teachers never fully "adopt" a reformed curriculum but, rather, use it as a context for their teaching. In this sense, every teaching act is a *trying* of a curriculum, and every act enriches and informs the next try.

Examples of Adopting a Full, *Standards*-Based Curriculum

During the field-tests of one such reformed curriculum, it became increasingly evident that teachers' use of the new materials varied widely. The following cases taken from observations by one of the authors are examples of two extremes.

At the beginning of each week, Mr. Jensen would assign a problem of the week to his sixth-grade class, and solutions were discussed the following Friday. Also, Mr. Jensen began each day's lesson with a set of warm-up exercises, usually requiring operations with whole numbers, fractions, or decimals. Closure for this activity consisted of his checking for correct answers and demonstrating conventional procedures when students made mistakes (which was frequently). At first, these warm-up activities were completely separate from the use of the new materials. However, as the year progressed, Mr. Jensen began choosing problems and procedures that he thought fit each day's work in the new materials. These warm-up activities took ten to thirty minutes of the fifty-five–minute class period.

After the warm-up, the class corrected the homework assignment from the previous day, with Mr. Jensen focusing on correct answers and demonstrating procedures when students had errors in their work. Time for correcting the homework took five to twenty minutes, depending on how much trouble the students had with the assignment.

Mr. Jensen would then assign problems, by number, from the new curriculum materials, with little or no demonstration or discussion. Sometimes Mr. Jensen shortcut the exploration and problem solving in the materials by determining where he thought the section was headed and demonstrating a procedure that was applicable to the problems in the materials. At other times he created more sample problems to be practiced by the students in the same manner. If class time permitted, Mr. Jensen allowed students to work on the problems until the end of the period, with the unfinished problems to be done as homework. In many instances, students hurried through the problems so they would be finished and not have any homework. On the average, Mr. Jensen's students were engaged with the new curriculum materials only one to two hours per week.

In contrast, Mrs. Chester dedicated a full sixty-minute class period to the new curriculum materials every day. When she began using the new materials in class, she regularly sent home assignments from old curriculum materials as a response to parents' concerns about basic skills and the need for practice. This continued for several months, until she realized that few of the procedures the students were practicing were being used by them for problem solving in the new curriculum.

At the start of each lesson or problem sequence, Mrs. Chester was careful to prepare her students for a particular problem by discussing the problem context. During this discussion she often informally assessed her students' knowledge and provided the resources and tools she thought they needed. She then decided whether to encourage independent or collaborative exploration of particular problems.

Comprehensive, connected Standards-*based curricula include advantages with which teacher-made or -organized curricula, replacement units, and injections cannot compete.*

Mrs. Chester provided time and support for her students to engage in problem solving, present solutions, and understand and critique other students' logical arguments. In Mrs. Chester's classroom, alternative solutions were encouraged and frequently proposed, which fostered an attitude of openness to the possibility of multiple acceptable solutions to some problems. She regularly made decisions in guiding students' investigations, encouraging those who became frustrated, stimulating critical thinking, and evaluating students' logical arguments that differed from her own. Normally, Mrs. Chester's students were engaged with the new materials four to five hours per week.

As with Mr. Herrera's and Ms. Templeton's use of replacement units, Mr. Jensen and Mrs. Chester approached the adoption of a new curriculum with previously formed understandings and attitudes. These attitudes affected the degree to which the reforms intended by the authors of the curriculum were undertaken. It is clear that teachers who enter reform through this port of entry also need time to try new practices and beliefs about teaching and learning.

Issues and Summary

Although we discuss several ports of entry that differ in the level of reform undertaken, our description is not meant to suggest a developmental sequence. Teachers obviously can and do enter the process of curriculum reform at one of these levels without necessarily attending to any of the others. However, our discussion brings to light some issues common to teachers involved in curriculum reform. It is in this context that we provide the following observations.

As teachers approach changing their curricula, a major issue is controlling the risks involved. Injections and replacement units are popular because they minimize the risk of unachieved goals. If the new curriculum does not work as intended, the problem is confined to a few minutes or days. As teachers move toward changing entire curricula, the risks become greater. Acknowledging this fact is important, as is discussing the difficulties involved in asking teachers to change their practice.

It is also clear that whether change is mandated from administrative levels or initiated by teachers, time is needed for teachers to bring their beliefs and practices into alignment. Teachers who are required to teach a new curriculum may require time to align themselves philosophically with that curriculum and alter their practices in ways that support achievement of its goals. For that reason, we note that even the fourth port of entry, the adoption of a full curriculum, may require some "trying on," both of philosophies and practices. Some reverse injections of comfortable, traditional activities and practices may occur as teachers think about the beliefs that underlie the new curriculum and increase their level of comfort and expertise with new content and ways of teaching.

Still, the initial ports of entry we described are possible "boarding" points for the journey toward reform. Comprehensive, connected *Standards*-based curricula include advantages with which teacher-made or -organized curricula, replacement units, and injections cannot compete. Most important, such curricula can bring to the classroom a "big picture" of mathematics and provide the unifying themes and connections among themes that are an important part of the vision of the *Curriculum Standards*.

Our purpose in writing this chapter has been to provide glimpses into the ways teachers have approached reforming curricula in their classrooms. We agree with Ball and Cohen (1996) that curriculum developers and teachers need to work together to understand how teachers "try on" reform in the many aspects of their daily work and to understand the advantages of coherent, grounded approaches to curriculum development.

References

Acquarelli, K. B., and J. M. Mumme. "A Renaissance in Mathematics Education." *Phi Delta Kappan* 77, no. 7 (1996): 478–84.

Ball, D. L., and D. K. Cohen. "Reform by the Book: What Is—or Might Be—the Role of Curriculum Materials in Teacher Learning and Instructional Reform?" *Educational Researcher* 25, no. 9 (1996): 6–8.

California State Department of Education. *Mathematics Framework for California Public Schools Kindergarten through Grade Twelve*. Sacramento, Calif.: California State Department of Education, 1985.

Ivey, K. M. C. "World Views in the Mathematics Classroom: Students Translating Beliefs into Actions." Unpublished doctoral dissertation, Washington State University, 1994.

Leonard, J. *Spatial Visualization: A Unit Written for the State of California's Math—A Prototype Course*. Sacramento, Calif.: California State Department of Education, 1989.

National Council of Teachers of Mathematics. *Curriculum and Evaluation Standards for School Mathematics*. Reston, Va.: National Council of Teachers of Mathematics, 1989.

———. *Professional Standards for Teaching Mathematics*. Reston, Va.: National Council of Teachers of Mathematics, 1991.

———. *Assessment Standards for School Mathematics*. Reston, Va.: National Council of Teachers of Mathematics, 1995.

Shroyer, J., and W. Fitzgerald. *Mouse and Elephant: Measuring Growth*. Menlo Park, Calif.: Addison-Wesley Publishing Co., 1986.

Walen, S. B. "An Analysis of Students' Knowledge of the Mathematics Classroom." Unpublished doctoral dissertation, Washington State University, 1993.

Williams, S. R. "Temporality and Views of Change in Mathematics Teaching." Paper presented at the Research Presession of the NCTM Annual Meeting, 12 April 1994, Indianapolis, Indiana.

Steven R. Williams and Stephanie Z. Smith, *Brigham Young University, Provo Utah;*
Judith Mumme, *Mathematics Renaissance WestEd, Camarillo, California;*
and Nanette Seago, *Video Cases for Mathematics Professional Development, San Diego State University, San Diego, California*

13

Teaching and Learning in the Connected Mathematics Project

Glenda Lappan and Elizabeth Phillips

The Connected Mathematics Project (CMP) (see Lappan, Fey, Fitzgerald, Friel, and Phillips 1995) was funded by the National Science Foundation to produce a middle school curriculum that aligns with the vision of mathematical power in the National Council of Teachers of Mathematics (NCTM) *Curriculum and Evaluation Standards for School Mathematics* (1989), the *Professional Standards for Teaching Mathematics* (1991), and the *Assessment Standards for School Mathematics* (1995). To embrace the goal of mathematical power for all students envisioned in the *Standards* documents, requires attention to the tasks that we use to engage students in learning mathematics, and perhaps even more importantly, it requires attention to our teaching practices. Jerome Bruner in *The Process of Education* (1977) wrote,

> If it (new curriculum) cannot change, move, perturb, and inform teachers, it will have no effect on those they teach. It must first and foremost be a curriculum for teachers. If it has any effect on pupils, it will have it by virtue of having an effect on teachers. (p. xv)

The CMP curriculum's overarching goal is to develop student and teacher knowledge of mathematics that is rich in connections and deep in understanding and skills in the strands of number, geometry and measurement, statistics and probability, and algebra.

Having worked over a six-year period on the development of both student and teacher materials, we can summarize our mathematics goals into a statement that could be called a standard:

> *Students should be able to reason and communicate proficiently in mathematics.* This includes knowledge and skill in the use of the vocabulary, forms of representation, materials, tools, techniques, and intellectual methods of the discipline of mathematics, including the ability to define and solve problems with reason, insight, inventiveness, and technical proficiency.

This statement makes a commitment to skill, but skill is more than proficiency with computation and manipulation of symbols. Skill means that students can use the mathematics tools, resources, procedures, knowledge, and ways of thinking developed over time to make sense of new situations that they encounter. In order to provide opportunity and motivation for students to develop connected conceptual understanding and skill, we focused our development efforts on identifying "big ideas" in mathematics and organizing the curriculum around those ideas. The following section outlines the goals that we agreed on in each of the important mathematics strands from the *Standards*.

Mathematics Strands

These are the broad goals for the main strands in CMP:

Number

Students should be able to analyze situations involving relations and operations on whole numbers, integers, and rational numbers. In each number system, they should develop understanding and skill in the following dimensions of knowledge: number sense, representations, operation sense, procedural skill, and system properties. In addition, they should have an informal understanding of irrational numbers. Students should understand the multiplicative structure of numbers, including primes and composites, and be able to use these ideas to understand equivalence of fractions, ratios, and rates. Students should be able to use these concepts to reason proportionally and make comparisons.

Geometry and Measurement

Students should be able to recognize shapes and their properties, understand principles governing the construction of shapes, ascertain why shapes serve special purposes, recognize and use shapes in a variety of representations, appreciate and use important relationships (especially symmetry and similarity), and measure shapes and predict changes in one-, two-, and three-dimensional measures under size change and other transformations. They should be able to generate a rich set of examples of angles and one-, two-, and three-dimensional figures and categorize, define, and relate figures; understand what it means to measure an attribute of a figure or a phenomenon, specify a location of points or figures, and reason about the spatial aspects of situations.

Probability

Students should be able to formulate questions about situations involving chance, design and carry out simulations of gathering data to describe situations, organize and interpret data, make predictions about the long-term chances of particular outcomes, and compute the expected value of particular outcomes. They should grow in their understanding of both theoretical and experimental analyses of situations involving chance—by using lists, trees, and other informal ways of counting—to determine theoretical probabilities.

Statistics

Students should be skilled in the process of data investigation, including the use of a variety of ideas and techniques for interpreting, collecting, and analyzing quantitative data to answer questions, solve problems, and make informed decisions. They should grow in their understanding and skill in problem formulation; in data collection, representation, description, comparison, and interpretation; and in evaluation of arguments.

Algebra

Students should be able to analyze situations involving related quantitative variables by identifying variables and potentially significant patterns among the variables; representing variables and patterns among these variables using tables, graphs, symbolic expressions, and verbal descriptions; and translating information among these forms of representation. They should be adept at identifying the questions that are important or interesting in a situation for which algebraic analysis is effective in providing answers. They should develop the skill and inclination to represent information mathematically, transform that information using mathematical techniques to solve equations, and create and compare graphs and tables of functions. Students should make judgments about the accuracy and completeness of the analysis and determine if the answers are reasonable.

A Curriculum for Teachers and Students

If our primary goal is that students develop a deep, connected mathematics understanding and skill in the strands of number, geometry and measurement, statistics and probability, and algebra, then the ways in which students engage with mathematics and the instructional practices of the teacher must support this goal. We have taken a stand that curriculum and instruction are not distinct—"what to teach" and "how to teach it" are inextricably linked. The circumstances in which students learn affects what is learned. We have worked to produce a curriculum that helps teachers and those who work to support teachers to examine their expectations for students and analyze the extent to which classroom mathematics tasks and teaching practices are aligned with their goals and expectations.

The NCTM *Professional Teaching Standards* describes a set of shifts in classrooms and classroom practices that supports the learning goals of CMP. We need to shift toward classrooms as mathematics communities; toward logic and evidence as verification; toward mathematical reasoning, conjecturing, inventing, and problem solving; and toward connecting mathematics, its ideas, and its applications. And we need to shift away from mathematics classrooms where students always work as individuals; where the teacher is the sole source of authority for right answers; where students memorize procedures and apply them in a mechanistic way to find answers; and where mathematics is viewed as a body of isolated concepts and procedures.

The principles that guided us in the development of the materials for students raise issues and questions about what kind of teaching and learning is implicit in the stances we have taken and the shifts that are called for in the *Standards*.

Goals for Students

Students develop deep understanding of mathematical concepts, skills, procedures, and processes through—

- solving problems;
- observing patterns and relationships among variables in a situation;
- conjecturing, testing, discussing, verbalizing, and generalizing these patterns and relationships;
- discovering salient mathematical features of patterns and relationships and abstracting from these underlying mathematical concepts, processes, and relationships;
- developing a language for talking about problems and for representing and communicating their ideas; and
- striving to make sense of and to connect mathematics they abstract from their experiences.

Taking this stance on how students learn mathematics leads immediately to the need to examine what teaching practices will support such engagement. The development of materials was guided by the major instructional themes. These themes are tied to the content and process goals, but they point more directly to the nature of classroom discourse that supports the growth of student understanding and skill.

Instructional Themes

Teaching for Understanding

The curriculum is organized into modules around mathematical "big ideas," clusters of important, related mathematics concepts, processes, ways of thinking, skills, and problem-solving strategies, which are studied in depth with the development of conceptual understanding as the goal.

Connections

The curriculum emphasizes connections among mathematics topics and between mathematics and other school subjects.

Mathematical Investigations

Instruction emphasizes inquiry and discovery of mathematical ideas through investigation of rich problem situations.

Representations

Students grow in their ability to reason effectively with information represented in graphic, numeric, symbolic, and verbal forms and move flexibly among these representations.

Technology

The information-processing capabilities of calculators and computers have brought about fundamental changes in the way people learn mathematics and apply their knowledge to problem-solving tasks. Mathematics goals and teaching approaches have been revised to reflect these changes.

These instructional themes and the goals for student engagement indicate how the philosophy of CMP is compatible with major shifts in teaching and learning mathematics as described by the NCTM in the *Professional Teaching Standards* and in the *Curriculum and Evaluation Standards*.

The CMP curriculum's overarching goal is to develop student and teacher knowledge of mathematics that is rich in connections and deep in understanding and skills in the strands of number, geometry and measurement, statistics and probability, and algebra.

A problem-centered curriculum requires that the teacher possess a broad view of mathematics and a deep knowledge of pedagogy based on "inquiry." The curriculum materials are designed to engage teachers in a conversation about the mathematics and pedagogy needed to support a problem-centered curriculum. We have worked to engage students in worthwhile problems and provide teachers with ways to plan and carry out this problem-centered teaching in their classrooms. In the teacher's material used during planning for instruction, we point to the need for such questions as, Is this a good task for my students? What mathematical development will it support? What questions can I use to help my students engage with the task? What questions can I ask to help the students extract, explain, and generalize the embedded mathematics?

Developing a Classroom Climate

Curriculum materials, for both student and teacher, are designed to help students and teachers build a different pattern of interaction in the classroom. The materials support teachers and students in building a community of learners who are mutually supportive in their effort to make sense of the mathematics. We do this through the tasks provided, the justification that students are asked to provide regularly, the opportunities for students to talk and write about their ideas, and the help for the teacher in using alternative forms of assessment and problem-centered instructional models in the classroom. Ideas from many teachers are included in the teacher materials to help establish an environment that supports students' making sense of mathematics.

Change is hard for both teachers and students. Teachers may be frustrated in moving from a rule-based curriculum to a problem-centered one. Students may not like their past experiences with mathematics yet may resist any attempts by the teacher to change the culture of the classroom. Students may be used to a mathematics classroom where little is required of them beyond practicing the idea that was illustrated by the teacher in the first part of the lesson. CMP teachers, however, have found that perseverance works. Students, resistant in September, are fully engaged by January.

Change is hard for both teachers and students. Teachers may be frustrated in moving from a rule-based curriculum to a problem-centered one. Students may not like their past experiences with mathematics yet may resist any attempts by the teacher to change the culture of the classroom.

We are also finding that in the second year, students start the year expecting to tackle more-challenging problems and to construct arguments to justify their thinking and reasoning. They understand the demands of working in pairs, in groups, and individually. Establishing the expectation and pattern of classroom discourse is much easier. This evidence of student involvement, reasoning, flexibility and perseverance, in turn, provides the reinforcement teachers need to reflect on and refine their teaching practices.

Assessment in CMP—Part of the Environment

If interactions in pairs and small groups around big problems is the intended norm for the classroom, then assessing what sense students are making of mathematics must occur collaboratively as well as individually. Therefore, a group of teachers working with us has designed an assessment package that provides individual and pair assessments, projects, and unit tests that may have a group or a take-home portion.

Another dilemma for teachers is figuring out how to balance the different purposes of assessment—to report grades and to make instructional decisions. The teacher materials provide assessment tasks and examples of students' work and teacher commentary to help a teacher analyze students' learning in order to report grades and make instructional decisions. However, the process of changing traditions from an answer-oriented, easy-to-check test to an evidence- and explanation-oriented assessment is very difficult. Teachers who observe their students learning more with innovative materials are still hard-pressed to use rubrics and more-subjective evaluations to report students' grades to parents and school administrators. Work with teachers piloting these materials suggests that teachers need two years of experience with the curriculum before they are ready to take on the challenge of such assessment techniques.

The Teaching Model

For more than two decades, we have been experimenting with ways to help teachers think about problem-centered teaching. As we developed the student materials and the supporting teacher materials, we took into account the demands of problem-centered teaching, thereby developing an instructional model that provides a lesson-planning template. This model looks at instruction in three phases: *launching, exploring,* and *summarizing.*

During the first phase, the teacher launches a whole-class investigation by setting the context for the problem. This involves making sure the students understand the setting or situation in which the problem is posed. More important, the problem must be launched in such a way that the mathematical context and challenge are clear. The teacher needs to consider the following: What mathematical question can be asked in this situation? What are students expected to do? How are they expected to record and report their work? Will they be working individually, in pairs, or groups? What tools are available that might be helpful? This is also the time when, if necessary, the teacher introduces new ideas, clarifies definitions, reviews old concepts, and connects the problem to students' prior knowledge. Teachers need to make sure they are launching tasks in such a way that the challenge of the task is left intact and students are given a clear picture of what is expected. It is easy to tell too much and lower the challenge of the task to something fairly routine.

After the task is launched, students explore the task as the teacher circulates, asks focusing questions when a student or group is struggling, and extends questions when students have solved the problem but have not generalized the solution. The teacher takes stock of who is understanding and who needs help; who has a strategy, generalization, or interesting way of explaining the problem solution that needs to be shared in the summary; and who has a good idea that needs to be shared but perhaps does not have a complete solution.

The final phase of the instructional model is the summary. This is the most important and, perhaps, the hardest phase. Here the students and the teacher work together to explain the mathematics of the problem; generalize certain situations; abstract useful mathematical ideas, processes, and concepts; make connections; and foreshadow mathematics that is yet to be studied.

As we developed the curriculum, we believed that student writing and explaining would help students clarify their thinking and understanding. In the early drafts of the pilot materials, we had students write and explain constantly! The pilot teachers were overwhelmed with the demands of so much writing. It became clear that when students write, there should be a good mathematical reason for that writing; there should be ideas to pull together, clarify, and record for future reference. Out of our struggles evolved writing prompts, a feature that has become a real strength of the CMP materials. At the end of each collection of related problems, there is a mathematical reflection. This is a set of questions designed to help students reflect on what has been learned, why it is important, when it is useful, and how it fits with prior knowledge. The questions in the reflections point to the "big ideas" and how they fit together (abstracting and connecting); to skills (how-tos); to decisions to be made and how one makes them (when-tos); to issues about how these problems are similar to, and different from, problems encountered earlier (connecting, discriminating, and elaborating); and finally, to questions to ask in similar situations (questioning habits). These reflections are first discussed by the teacher and the class together; then students write their own answers to the questions in their journals as a part of a self-assessment. Each unit contains four to seven mathematical reflections that, read by themselves, tell a mathematical story about the unit.

Issues Faced in Developing the Curriculum

As we set out to write a complete connected curriculum for grades 6, 7, and 8, the following issues quickly surfaced:

- What are the overarching goals in each strand?
- What size of problem is feasible for the teacher and students to explore?
- What kind of sequencing or scaffolding is needed?
- How much help is needed to move from a contextual setting to a symbolic situation free of context?
- What basic skills should be developed and how?
- When is group or individual work appropriate?
- What kinds of practice or homework and reflection are needed to ensure some degree of automaticity of understanding?
- What assessment is appropriate?
- How much help with the mathematics and pedagogy does a teacher need?

There were no easy answers to these questions. Even though it took classroom trials and observations, discussions, revisions, more trials, and research and reflections to resolve such issues into a coherent curriculum, our initial analysis of overarching goals remained sound. However, our notions of what we could expect to teach in one year, in a curriculum based on bigger problems, did change. Sufficient instruction time was needed to foster deep understanding of the big ideas.

Criteria for a Mathematics Task

We have said that a good task is one that supports some or all the following:

- The problem has important, useful mathematics embedded in it.
- Students can approach the problem in multiple ways using different solution strategies.
- The problem has various solutions or allows different decisions or positions to be taken and defended.
- The problem encourages student engagement and discourse.
- The problem requires higher-level thinking and problem solving.
- The problem contributes to the conceptual development of students.

- The problem connects to other important mathematical ideas.

- The problem promotes the skillful use of mathematics.

- The problem provides opportunity to practice important skills.

- The problem creates an opportunity for the teacher to assess what his or her students are learning and where they are experiencing difficulty.

We believe that problems should not be chosen just because they are "fun" or use a manipulative that is available in the classroom. There must be the potential for students to engage in sound and significant mathematics as a part of accomplishing the task. However, the needs and interests of students must be taken into account. Therefore, a teacher is encouraged to choose an alternative setting for a problem if the students are likely to find that setting more engaging. The problem could also be presented in a more open or closed form to meet students' needs. Fundamental issues for a teacher include what the students already know and can do, what their mathematical needs are, and the level of challenge they seem ready to accept. Therefore, we encourage teachers to use their professional judgment to help students succeed.

Once we established our overarching goals for three grade levels, we worked to develop the strands into units of instruction. The struggles we faced fall into three broad categories: (1) selecting and developing a big mathematical idea; (2) problems: size, openness, sequencing, practicing, reflecting, and building understanding; and (3) basic skills and evaluation.

Examples of Tasks, Sequencing, and Skill Development

One example of an important mathematics idea includes rational numbers and proportional reasoning. Once we identified these as requisites for the middle grades, we then faced the difficult task of deciding what it meant to understand these ideas, what algorithms or processes were important, and how these would be developed.

We took the stand that the development of fractions, decimals, and percents should emphasize the equivalence of these forms of representations. The seeds of proportional reasoning began in the rational number and similarity units but moved to the forefront in the "Comparing and Scaling" unit. Rather than the traditional development of proportional reasoning as an abstract rule equating two ratios, proportional rea-

soning was cast in the broader context of finding ways to use quantitative measures to compare two situations, thus expanding students' previous experience of making comparisons only by finding differences. This view is reflected in the first problem of the "Comparing and Scaling" unit; through the context of writing ads, students informally explore strategies for making comparisons using quantitative measures.

EXAMPLE 1: WRITING ADS

An ad for Bolda Cola seeks to compare the popularity for Bolda Cola with Cola Nola. A copywriter from the advertising department has proposed four possible concluding statements:

- In taste tests, people who preferred Bolda Cola outnumbered those who preferred Cola Nola by a ratio of 3 to 2.

- In taste tests, people who preferred Bolda Cola outnumbered those who preferred Cola Nola by a ratio of 17 139 to 11 428.

- In taste tests, 5 713 more people preferred Bolda Cola to Cola Nola.

- In taste tests, 60% prefer Bolda Cola to Cola Nola.

A. Describe what you think each of the four statements means. Explain how each shows a comparison. Be sure to tell what is being compared and how it is being compared.

B. Is it possible that all four advertising claims are based on the same survey data? Explain your answer.

C. Which comparison is the most accurate way to report the survey data? Why?

D. Which comparison do you think would be the most effective advertisement for Bolda Cola?

E. Write two more statements comparing the popularity of the two colas. Explain each statement.

This problem introduces the language of ratios and then several other situations in which students explore the ideas of comparisons using ratios, differences, fractions, percents, and scaling. The familiar context of advertisement helps students make sense of proportionality, and the rest of the unit continues to deepen these understandings and techniques using a variety of settings.

The next three investigations develop deeper understandings and techniques for using percents, ratios, and rates to compare quantities. For example, in the second investigation, students work with real data from a survey about participation in sports activities. They work with the large numbers in the data either by using division to find decimals, percents, or rates or by rounding the data to numbers that can easily be changed to simple ratios. Throughout the unit, students are encouraged to think about other ways of comparing. Students quickly find that rounded, whole-number ratios are generally easier to interpret, and they often use this technique to estimate ratios and to make predictions.

Once ratios, fractions, decimals, or percents have been used to describe relationships among quantitative measures, an important next step is to make things larger or smaller while maintaining those relationships. This is the process involved in making scale models, building life-sized objects from scale models, and extrapolating from recipes proportionally. The third investigation continues the development of strategies for scaling ratios to make comparisons or find missing parts of equivalent ratios. When pizzas are to be shared, both the number of pizzas and the number of people are factors in determining how much pizza each person will get. "Pizza per person" is a kind of comparison called a *rate*. Rates are a derived quantity based on measures of two different aspects of the situation. One quantity is divided by another to produce a rate; in this example, the number of pizzas divided by the number of persons gives pizza per person. Although ratios come to the forefront in this investigation, they are informally used here and developed more fully in subsequent investigations. For example, students build rate tables as a technique for scaling in this problem:

EXAMPLE 2: USING UNIT RATES

When Madeline and Luis compared the fuel economy of their new cars, they found these rates:

- Madeline's car went 580 miles using 19 gallons of gasoline.
- Luis's car went 452 miles using 15.5 gallons of gasoline.

With this information answer the following questions.

A. For each car, find a unit rate describing the mileage. Which car got the better gas mileage? In other words, which car went more miles per gallon of gas?

B. Complete a table [like table 13.1], showing the fuel used and the miles covered by each car, on the basis of the unit rates you found in part A. We call this kind of table a *rate table*.

C. Look for the patterns in your table. For each car, write an equation for a rule you can use to predict the miles driven (*m*) from the gallons of gas used (*g*).

TABLE 13.1.
Rate table

Gallons of gas	0	1	2	3	4	5	6	7	8
Miles in Madeline's car									
Miles in Luis's car									

D. Use the rules you wrote in C to find the number of miles each car could cover if it used 9.5, 15.5, 19, 23.8, 100, 125, and 150 gallons of gasoline.

Follow-up

1. Use your data from B or D to sketch graphs of the (gallons, miles) data for each car.
2. How are the two graphs alike? How are they different?
3. What do you think makes the two graphs different?

Rates provide a powerful way to reason both formally and informally when comparing quantities. In this investigation students connect proportional reasoning and unit rates to the notion of constant growth in tables and to straight lines in graphical representations.

Once the students have a variety of techniques for reasoning about ratios and proportions, they explore a variety of applications, choosing the techniques that make sense to them. One such problem is estimating the size of a population when the entire population is not known (for example, the size of a deer population in a region). In another set of problems, population densities are explored. For example, in the next problem, students compute the densities of North and South Dakota and then "equalize" the densities by moving people from one state to the other.

EXAMPLE 3: COMPARING THE DAKOTAS

South Dakota and North Dakota rank 45th and 47th in population of all the states in the United States. South Dakota has 721 000 people in 75 896 square miles of land, and North Dakota has 638 000 people in 68 994 square miles of land.

A. Which state, North Dakota or South Dakota, has the greater population density?

B. How many citizens of one state would have to move to the other state to make the population densities in the two states equal? Explain how you arrived at your answer.

Follow-up

Find the population density of your state. How does it compare to the population densities of North and South Dakota?

Students' Reasoning

Students use a variety of techniques to solve this problem. Two strategies follow:

- *Belinda's Group*: "Since South Dakota has the greater population density, we moved 5 000 people to North Dakota to see what it did to the densities. After that move, we had these numbers:

South Dakota: $\frac{716\,000}{75\,896} = 9.43$ people per square mile

89

North Dakota: $\dfrac{643\,000}{68\,994}$ = 9.32 people per square mile

"We were moving in the right direction, so we moved 5 000 more people.

South Dakota: $\dfrac{711\,000}{75\,896}$ = 9.37 people per square mile

North Dakota: $\dfrac{648\,000}{68\,994}$ = 9.39 people per square mile

"That was too many, so we tried 9 000 in all.

South Dakota: $\dfrac{712\,000}{75\,896}$ = 9.38 people per square mile

North Dakota: $\dfrac{647\,000}{68\,994}$ = 9.38 people per square mile

"About 9 000 people must move from South Dakota to North Dakota."

- *Armin's Group*: "First we put together all the land area and all the people and computed the overall density.

$$\dfrac{721\,000 + 638\,000}{75\,896 + 68\,994}$$

$$= \dfrac{1\,359\,000}{144\,890} = 9.38 \text{ people per square mile}$$

"Then we thought about how to spread out the people so that each state would have this overall density. If we multiply the area of North Dakota by this rate, we get

$$68\,994 \times 9.38 = 647\,164 \text{ people}$$

"This means that about $647\,164 - 638\,000 = 9\,164$ people need to move from South Dakota to North Dakota."

The unit culminates in a larger, more open-ended problem in which the students organize a national youth conference. This is a "fair division," or apportionment, problem. Students consider questions about population characteristics that may be relevant in making decisions about who will be invited to an environmental conference to represent their geographic areas. They use data from the U.S. 1992 Census Bureau of Statistics to apportion the 1000 delegates on the basis of population size of geographical regions, metropolitan or rural areas, ethnic groups, and sex. In addition, an appropriate amount of land for camping at the convention site must be divided proportionally for each region. In this last problem, students are working with both numeric and geometric settings.

Through their work in this and other units, students learn important questions to ask themselves about any situation that can be represented and modeled mathematically, such as:

When you have two or more quantitative measures related to different situations, how can they be compared? When can a comparison be made by subtraction? When can rates be used? When is a ratio a good tool for comparison? How can a ratio be scaled up or down?

Facing the Issues

Developing a problem-centered curriculum posed an interesting dilemma: "How big should a problem be so that a teacher can conduct a class based on inquiry, guide the students to make conjectures, provide sound reasoning, and refine strategies?" Bigger and more open problems allow for many patterns and conjectures to be generated by the students. Which conjectures to follow up on and how becomes a challenge for both the teacher and the students. We struggled to select and sequence problems in a way that allows both the students and the teachers a chance to make sense of the mathematics.

The discussion of "Comparing and Scaling" gives a quick glimpse at how a big mathematical idea, proportional reasoning, was developed through a series of investigations. The first investigation starts out with an informal, rather open look at making comparisons. The second example given above, in using rate tables, shows a more closed and structured problem designed to develop in more depth one particular way to make a comparison. The decision on the size of a problem was based on classroom experience, on how much time should be spent in discovering a technique (in this instance a rate table), on the subtlety of the mathematical idea, and on whether we were trying for some closure on an important concept, strategy, or skill.

Introducing a mathematical idea through a contextual problem is important because the problem embodies the concept. Thus the context helps carry the meaning of the idea for the student and serves as a vehicle to quickly retrieve the understanding when needed. We found that when we moved to symbolic situations without a context, students were able to go back to the context to help them make sense of the symbols. Each investigation ends with a set of problems called Applications, Connections, and Extensions (ACE), which provides homework practice with applications and "naked" symbols. Through our extensive pilots and field-testing (each unit went through a three-year development and testing cycle), we found the appropriate mix of skills and applications. Finally, the mathematical reflections at the end of each investigation and the assessment package described earlier provide an opportunity for the teacher and the students to assess their understanding throughout the unit.

Student Achievement

At the end of the development pilot phase, a comparative study of sixth-, seventh-, and eighth-grade CMP classes and non-CMP control classes (Hoover, Zawojewski, and Ridgeway 1997) was conducted. Premeasures and postmeasures on the Iowa Test of Basic Skills (ITBS) and a *Standards*-based problem-solving test developed by the Balanced Assessment group were collected and analyzed. The CMP students significantly outperformed the non-CMP students on the *Standards*-based test. The CMP students held their own on the Iowa Test of Basic Skills in the sixth and seventh grade, and they scored significantly better than the non-CMP students by the eighth grade. An additional comparative study of proportional reasoning in grades 7 and 8 (Ben-Chaim, Fey, Fitzgerald, Benedetto, and Miller 1997) was conducted. CMP students again scored significantly better than the non-CMP students. The graphs in figures 13.1 to 13.3 show the scores of students on the ITBS, the Balanced Assessment Test, and the proportional reasoning tasks.

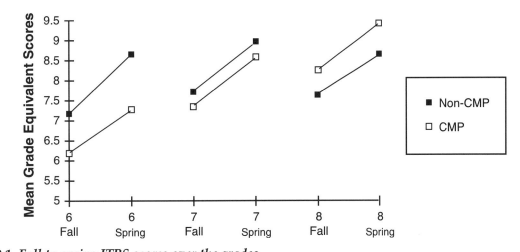

Fig. 13.1. *Fall to spring ITBS scores over the grades*

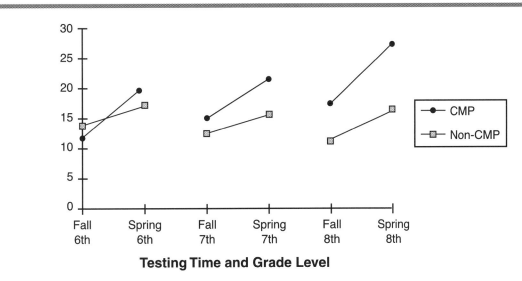

Fig. 13.2. *Balanced assessment achievement scores*

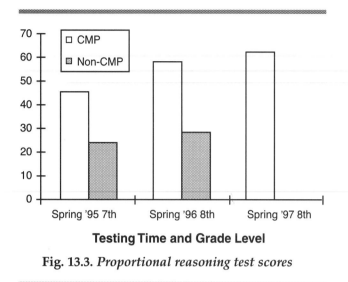

Testing Time and Grade Level

Fig. 13.3. *Proportional reasoning test scores*

From our experience, it takes three years for a teacher to become comfortable with the curriculum. Since the materials do not look like the traditional rule-bound mathematics textbook, it is difficult for teachers and parents to thumb through them. We are finding that in assessing a curriculum like CMP, careful attention must be paid to helping teachers, parents, and community leaders see the mathematics potential of the curriculum. They need to recognize the skills and understanding, flexibility, and retention of mathematical ideas and skills that can be reached by their students through engagement with important mathematics embedded in interesting contexts (real world, whimsy, and mathematics). To reach its full potential, such a curriculum must be supported by pedagogical practices that focus on making sense of mathematics.

We also included the test results for the grade 8 students in CMP classes in 1997 on the proportional reasoning tasks. We retested in the classrooms of the same eighth-grade teachers a year later to see if the results from 1996 held. Collectively, the results from these studies suggest that we may have achieved the right balance between understanding and skill. Additional studies that move beyond the pilot schools are needed to confirm these results and specifically assess students' knowledge in algebra, probability, geometry, number sense, and data.

Summary

The power of a problem-centered curriculum is not developed in one or two units, but it is the continual building and connecting of one unit to the next that produces the kind of results described. During our work with pilot teachers and our present work on professional development, we have found that teachers need help with both the mathematics and the pedagogical skills needed to implement the curriculum.

References

Ben-Chaim, David, James T. Fey, William M. Fitzgerald, C. Benedetto, and Jane Miller. *Development of Proportional Reasoning in a Problem-Based Middle School Curriculum.* Chicago: Paper presented at the annual meeting of the American Education Research Association, 1997.

Bruner, Jerome. *The Process of Education.* Cambridge, Mass.: Harvard University Press, 1977.

Hoover, Mark N., Judy S. Zawojewski, and James Ridgeway. *Analysis of Sixth-, Seventh-, and Eighth-Grade Student Performance for the Connected Mathematics Project.* Chicago: Paper presented at the annual meeting of the American Education Research Association, 1997.

Lappan, Glenda, James T. Fey, William M. Fitzgerald, Susan N. Friel, and Elizabeth D. Phillips. *The Connected Mathematics Project.* Palo Alto, Calif.: Dale Seymour Publications, 1995.

National Council of Teachers of Mathematics. *Curriculum and Evaluation Standards for School Mathematics.* Reston, Va.: National Council of Teachers of Mathematics, 1989.

———. *Professional Standards for Teaching Mathematics.* Reston, Va.: National Council of Teachers of Mathematics, 1991.

———. *Assessment Standards for School Mathematics.* Reston, Va.: National Council of Teachers of Mathematics, 1995.

Glenda Lappan and Elizabeth Phillips, *Michigan State University, East Lansing, Michigan*

14

Middle Grades Math Thematics: The STEM Project—a Look at Developing a Middle School Mathematics Curriculum

RICK BILLSTEIN

In *Everybody Counts: A Report to the Nation on the Future of Mathematics Education* by the Mathematical Sciences Education Board (MSEB 1989), the following observation is made: "As technology has mathematized the workplace and mathematics has permeated society, a complacent America has tolerated underachievement as the norm for mathematics education. We have inherited a mathematics curriculum conforming to the past, blind to the future and bound by the tradition of minimal expectations" (p. 1). Further, "As children become socialized by school and society, they begin to view mathematics as a rigid system of externally dictated rules governed by standards of accuracy, speed, and memory. Their view of mathematics shifts from enthusiasm to apprehension, from confidence to fear" (p. 44). No part of the grades K–12 mathematics curriculum exemplifies the view of "bound to minimal expectations" more than that found in grades 6 to 8. As discussed in *Reshaping School Mathematics: A Philosophy and Framework for Curriculum* (MSEB 1990), the restructuring of mathematics education requires more than simply replacing parts. MSEB states, "What is required is a complete redesign of the content of school mathematics and the way it is taught" (p. 1).

In 1991, in response to a call from the National Science Foundation (NSF), the University of Montana submitted a proposal to redesign a middle school mathematics curriculum based on the *Curriculum and Evaluation Standards for School Mathematics* (National Council of Teachers of Mathematics [NCTM] 1989). Five years later the the resultant Six through Eight Mathematics (STEM) project's student and teacher materials were being prepiloted and field-tested by more than 250 teachers of more than 35 000 students in twenty-four states. The field-test schools were chosen by an outside evaluator to assess the effectiveness of the STEM materials in a variety of schools and classroom settings throughout the country. The states ranged from Washington, Montana, and California in the West to Illinois, Missouri, and Indiana in the Midwest and Connecticut, Massachusetts, and Florida in the East. The information provided by the evaluator, teachers, and students involved in the prepilot and field tests was used to revise and edit the materials. The commercial version was published in 1998 by McDougal Littell under the name *Middle Grades Math Thematics: The STEM Project* (Billstein and Williamson 1999).

The STEM curriculum—whose writers chose a dream catcher as the project symbol (figure 14.1)—strives to help all students develop mathematical power by emphasizing positive approaches to learning mathematics while filtering out undesirable practices. This article will focus on the project's philosophy and goals

93

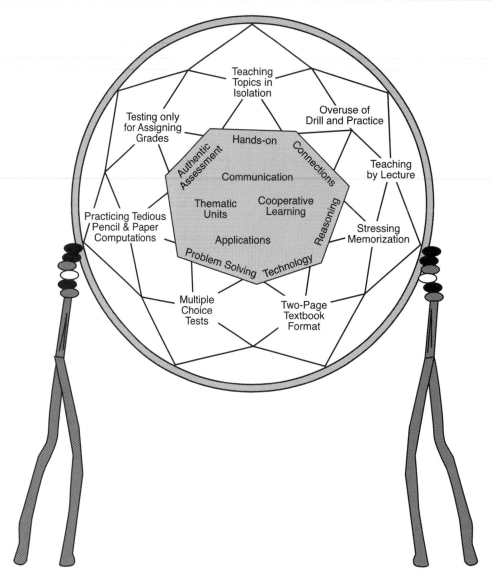

Fig. 14.1. *The dream catcher.* *Native Americans hung dream catchers in their tepees or lodges and on babies' cradle boards. According to legend, the air is filled with both good and bad dreams. Good dreams pass through the web of the dream catcher to the sleeping person; the bad dreams are trapped in the web, where they perish in the light of the dawn. STEM's hope is that the new curriculum along with changes in teaching practices will make the good dreams come true and bad dreams disappear.*

and how the curriculum changed over a five-year period.

STEM Writing Team

To ensure that the project incorporated multiple views of mathematics education, a writing team was formed consisting of a research mathematician, mathematics education faculty, school mathematics specialists, ad-

ministrators, technology specialists, and, most important, high school and middle school classroom teachers. Classroom teachers on the writing team provided input on what would interest middle school students and methods to implement activities in a classroom. The high school and middle school teachers were chosen from Presidential Award winners and national, innovative, teaching-award winners on the basis of written materials submitted for review. More than thirty people served as writers, from Arizona, Florida, Maryland, Vermont, New York, North Carolina, Oklahoma, California, Montana, Pennsylvania, Missouri, and Massachusetts. As with any project, it took a while to channel thinking in the same direction and at the same level. It wasn't long before everyone realized that different writers with diverse strengths could contribute to the curriculum development in a variety of ways; as a team they produced exciting materials.

Mathematical Content

The mathematical content of the STEM curriculum was driven by the conviction that students who have learned the basic number structure in a *Standards*-based grades K–5 curriculum are ready for new, interactive, meaningful, and interesting mathematics. The mathematical content considered important for middle school was organized around two components: *content strands* and *unifying concepts*.

Content Strands

Content strands are needed to delineate the mathematical concepts to be presented each year and ensure that the curriculum is broad and balanced at each of the three years. The strands—number, measurement, geometry, statistics, probability, algebra, and discrete mathematics—provide the framework on which the curriculum is built and identify the procedural knowledge—computational skills, facts, definitions, concepts—that students need to acquire. Material from each strand is taught every year to ensure sufficient depth of understanding.

Unifying Concepts

During STEM's development four unifying concepts were identified as relevant to almost every strand:

- Proportional reasoning
- Multiple representations
- Patterns and generalizations
- Modeling

These unifying concepts are important in middle school mathematics because they act as catalysts for all mathematics at this level and serve to prepare students for the transition to high school mathematics. By using the unifying concepts, middle school students develop depth of understanding and learn to make connections among mathematical ideas and between mathematics and the real world.

Instructional Approach

The STEM vision is that the middle school years—a time for investigating new, meaningful mathematics, not just a period of review—should be a time when students practice mathematics in a variety of settings. To achieve this goal, the typical textbook design—one lesson per day completed in a single period—was abandoned and the emphasis on computational skills was reduced.

STEM's initial vision also included the recognition that a middle school mathematics curriculum must consider the personal characteristics of middle school students. Extensive intellectual, social, and physical changes occur at this age level. Because middle school students are physically active, their environment needs to include activities in which they work with manipulatives, build things, and gather data. Because they are curious, a problem-solving approach based on interesting problems and real-world applications appeals to them.

As students work through the modules, they seldom ask, "When are we ever going to use this?"

Many of the questions students investigate through STEM are designed to appeal to the vivid, expansive (and sometimes very strange) imaginations of middle-grades students. For example, in the "Wonders of the World" module, there are questions such as, How many students would it take lying head-to-toe to cover the length of the Great Wall of China? What benchmark might be used when estimating the length of the world's largest cockroach? What would it cost to deliver the Great Pyramid by mail? Through questions like these, students see that mathematics can be imaginative. Other questions or projects show the practical applications of mathematics; for example, in the "Search and Rescue" module, students design search techniques for finding a person lost in the mountains by using geometry, probability, and algebra as well as computation and number sense.

Middle school students are social beings who need interaction with, and approval from, their peers. To accomplish this, cooperative learning is incorporated into STEM's learning activities. "Cooperative learning has been shown to help students learn course material faster and retain it longer and to develop critical reasoning power more rapidly than working alone" (Carnegie Council on Adolescent Development 1989, p. 50). However, cooperative learning is not the only educational style used; others, including lecture, class discussion, and independent work, are sometimes more appropriate.

Additionally, a variety of application-based and problem-solving instructional approaches have evolved through the STEM project. When appropriate, the approaches—

- require students to communicate ideas orally and in writing;
- integrate mathematics topics;
- use cooperative groups as structures for learning;
- incorporate hands-on activities;
- utilize existing technology;
- involve the teacher as listener, questioner, prober, and facilitator; and
- measure with an assessment package that views learning as its prime goal.

Modular Organization

The STEM curriculum is organized around thematic modules. Each module is integrated in terms of the mathematics covered with cross-curriculum connections to other subjects such as science, language arts, and social studies. The modules have titles such as "Patterns and Design," "Health and Wellness," "Creating Things," "Wonders of the World," "At the Mall," and "Our Environment." The mathematics listed earlier as content strands are integrated around the themes of the modules. Assessment is embedded in the instructional materials, and open-ended questions and writing activities are important components of each module.

Each module is broken down into sections intended to last two to three days each. Each section begins with a "grabber"—a reading, game, or activity—called Setting the Stage, which provides a strong lead-in to the mathematics content and its connection to the theme. An example of Setting the Stage from the sixth-grade materials providing a tie to language arts is shown in figure 14.2.

The mathematics content of each section is taught in instructional units called Explorations. Each section also includes Practice and Applications, Reflecting on the Section, Spiral Review, Key Concepts, and Extra Skill Practice. Many investigations include Extensions that provide challenges for those students who are ready for them. An Extended Exploration (called an E^2

by the students) is included in each module. E^2's are typically open-ended or open-response problems that students work on outside of class. Students are usually given one to two weeks to work on these problems and polish their solutions, which are assessed using a generalized assessment rubric. A sixth-grade student from Chicago commented on the E^2's as follows:

> Problem solving is fun and hard at the same time because some problems are hard, but then you figure out one portion of the problem and it starts to get easier and easier until you are done. I think this class is fun because I like playing the games working on the E^2's, and playing Olympiad.

Another student from the same class reported,

> Problem solving has always been my worst thing in math. I've never liked problem solving at all. I guess it could be good sometimes. Sometimes the math just charges to my brain right away.

An example of an Extended Exploration from the seventh-grade "Search and Rescue" module is given in figure 14.3.

Initially the prepilot materials for grade 6 consisted of thirteen modules. Because no teacher could cover the thirteen modules in a year's time, the number of modules was reduced to nine in the field-test version and shortened to eight in the commercial version. It was also found that six weeks was too long for a particular theme to hold the students' interest, so the length of time required for each module was shortened to approximately four weeks.

Field-test teachers indicated that timelines were not being met because teachers were producing drill and practice pages and spending extra time trying to achieve mastery the first time students were exposed to a topic. By integrating the mathematical content, each topic is now presented in many settings and covered at different levels in different modules. Teachers were not used to this approach because traditional textbooks broke down mathematical topics by chapter, and individual topics were never revisited; hence, it was difficult for teachers to postpone teaching to mastery the first time a topic was introduced. When teachers became more comfortable using a thematic, integrated approach, the pace of progress through modules improved. However, the field-test teachers' responses confirmed that more skill practice was needed; therefore, additional practice was included in the final version.

Another reason for the slow progress through the modules was that teachers and students were not used to so much reading and writing in a mathematics class. Students were asked to explain their solutions and tell

Section ④ Mean, Median, Mode

IN THIS SECTION

EXPLORATION 1
◆ Finding Mean, Median, and Mode

EXPLORATION 2
◆ Appropriate Averages

Animal Averages

Setting the Stage ▸▸▸▸▸▸▸▸▸▸▸▸▸▸▸▸▸▸▸▸▸▸▸▸▸

In *The Phantom Tollbooth*, by Norton Juster, Milo is surprised to see what seems to be half of a child.

> "Pardon me for staring," said Milo, after he had been staring for some time, "but I've never seen half a child before."
>
> "It's .58 to be precise," replied the child from the left side of his mouth (which happened to be the only side of his mouth).
>
> "I beg your pardon?" said Milo.
>
> "It's .58," he repeated; "it's a little bit *more* than a half."
>
> "Have you always been that way?" asked Milo impatiently, for he felt that that was a needlessly fine distinction.
>
> "My goodness, no," the child assured him. "A few years ago I was just .42 and, believe me, that was terribly inconvenient."
>
> "What is the rest of your family like?" said Milo, this time a bit more sympathetically.
>
> "Oh, we're just the average family," he said thoughtfully; "mother, father, and 2.58 children—and, as I explained, I'm the .58."

Think About It

1   **a.** What do you think the word *average* means?

   b. How do you think the average 2.58 was found?

2   Do you think the average number of children for families in your class is 2.58? Why or why not?

Fig. 14.2. *From* Math Thematics, Book 1, *by Rick Billstein and Jim Williamson. Copyright © 1999 by McDougal Littell Inc. All rights reserved. Reprinted by permission.*

A PHONE CHAIN

The Situation

When a search and rescue team is needed, all members of the search and rescue team must be notified as quickly as possible. This is often accomplished through a phone chain. In a phone chain, the first person calls two people. Each of those people call two more people. Each of those people call two more people and so on, until everyone in the search and rescue team is notified of the emergency.

The Problem

Estimate the least amount of time it would take using a phone chain like the one described above to notify all the members in a 55-person search and rescue team.

Something to Think About

◆ How might a table or drawing help you solve this problem?

◆ Could you modify the procedure to shorten the total amount of time involved? If so, how?

◆ What are some assumptions you might need to make about phone calls?

Present Your Results

Describe what you did to solve the problem. Explain why you solved it this way. Show any drawings, diagrams, charts, or tables that you used to solve the problem. Why do you think your solution is accurate?

Fig. 14.3. *From* Math Thematics, Book 2, *by Rick Billstein and Jim Williamson. Copyright © 1999 by McDougal Littell Inc. All rights reserved. Reprinted by permission.*

why procedures work. A teacher from Massachusetts reported, "The teachers in the other subject matter areas can always identify the STEM students in their class because they are the ones that add 'because' to every question that you ask them." Teachers reported that not only mathematics scores were increasing but so were the reading and writing ability of the students.

Traditional textbooks typically develop chapters with separate mathematical topics. STEM materials portray a very different view of mathematics, and students recognize the difference. A sixth-grade student from North Carolina stated,

> Before I was taught STEM by my teacher this year, I thought the only thing math was were problems in a book. Boy was I wrong! Thank you STEM for opening my eyes to the world of math!

As students work through the modules, they seldom ask, "When are we ever gonna have to use this?" The applications are obvious and integral to the mathematical development of the lesson. Many of the sections can be taught in conjunction with other subjects, and there are many cross-curricular connections. Students become involved in building materials such as zoetropes (motion wheels) or whirligigs (a popular toy in colonial America). When building a whirligig, students must use a single piece of cardboard and apply their understanding of fractions to plan the layout so they have enough material to cut out the pieces necessary for the construction. Within this context measurement conversions also become meaningful. It is through building some of these items that students learn the importance of using and reading measuring devices accurately.

Multiculturalism also takes on a new look in STEM materials. Simply reading about a people or cultures often fails to interest students. The STEM project tries to take the multicultural connection a step farther. For example, in the Setting the Stage for the investigation Over and Under, students read about the Pomo Indians and the magnificent baskets and mats they weave. As they continue the section, students develop their mathematical abilities by weaving mats using one-inch paper strips. In this way, they gain a deeper appreciation of the skills of the Pomo Indians, who wove intricate patterns with reeds less than one-sixteenth of an inch wide.

Format

Parents, teachers, students, and administrators all influenced the evolution of the curriculum into its final format. In many cases, parents and outside reviewers who examined the materials recognized and appreciated the thematic nature of the modules but had a hard time "seeing" the mathematics. As revised, the mathematical content is more evident and Key Concepts and Examples have been added; as a result, parents and teachers feel more comfortable. This was a change in the project format and made the materials appear more traditional than originally intended. Parents are a very important factor in the education of middle school students, and we learned throughout the field-testing that it is important to consider their needs when developing the materials. The luxury of developing and field-testing over five years using actual classrooms allowed time to refine the materials on the basis of teacher, student, and parent feedback to make the final product more acceptable.

The Role of Technology

Mental mathematics and estimation along with paper-and-pencil work are stressed throughout the STEM curriculum, but early in the project its designers realized that if students were to engage in real-world mathematics and problem solving, they should not be hampered by the size or complexity of the numbers often involved. For this reason, graphing calculators and computer activities are included for classrooms and students who have access to them. An example of a student page from the grade 7 "Health and Wellness" module using spreadsheets is shown in figure 14.4.

Assessment

There are three major purposes for student assessment:

- To inform students of the mathematical outcomes they are expected to achieve
- To inform teachers of the instruction that must be provided to assist students in achieving the desired outcomes
- To document the progress of students in meeting the outcomes

STEM developed its assessment package with the enhancement of learning as its primary goal. The project believes that documenting student achievement should be an integral part of the instructional process rather than an add-on. Open-ended problems are included, and students are involved in activities that require interaction, communication, and decision making in nonroutine situations. Alternative approaches are encouraged and discussed. The assessment package

You can use spreadsheet software to answer Question 23 on page 477. You can set up the spreadsheet to find the differences between resting heart rates and active heart rates, as well as the percents of increase.

Step 1 Set up your spreadsheet with the same headings as the table on Labsheet 2A. Enter the class data about heart rates.

File	Edit	Format	Calculate	Options	View

RESTING AND ACTIVE HEART RATES

| B4 | ✕ | √ | 120 |

	A	B	C	D
1	Resting Heart Rate	Active Heart Rate	Difference (Active – Resting)	Percent of Increase
2	50	90		
3	70	140		
4	80	120		

Step 2 In cell C2 (the box in column C and row 2) enter a formula that will calculate the difference between resting and active heart rates. Every formula must begin with an equals sign.

The formula takes the number in cell B2 and subtracts the number in cell A2.

File	Edit	Format	Calculate	Options	View

RESTING AND ACTIVE HEART RATES

| C2 | ✕ | √ | = B2 – A2 |

	A	B	C	D
1	Resting Heart Rate	Active Heart Rate	Difference (Active – Resting)	Percent of Increase
2	50	90	40	
3	70	140		
4	80	120		

The result appears in cell C2.

Step 3 In cell D2, enter the formula "= C2/A2*100" to find the percent of increase.

Step 4 Use the *fill down* command in columns C and D to apply the formulas to the data in the remaining rows.

Calculate
Move…
Fill Right
Fill Down
Sort…
Insert Cells…
Delete Cells…
Calculate Now
Auto Calc

File	Edit	Format	Calculate	Options	View

RESTING AND ACTIVE HEART RATES

| D2 | ✕ | √ | = C2 / A2 * 100 |

	A	B	C	D
1	Resting Heart Rate	Active Heart Rate	Difference (Active – Resting)	Percent of Increase
2	50	90	40	80
3	70	140	70	100
4	80	120	40	50

Fig. 14.4. *From* Math Thematics, Book 2, *by Rick Billstein and Jim Williamson. Copyright © 1999 by McDougal Littell Inc. All rights reserved. Reprinted by permission.*

includes real-world applications and permits full use of technology.

Embedded Assessment

In the prepilot of the sixth-grade materials, the structure of the materials did not provide sufficient guidance for teachers on how and when to interact with students. A basic premise of the project is that as students work through the materials, they will construct their own meaning for mathematical concepts. As might be expected in such a process, students occasionally develop incomplete or incorrect conceptualizations. If these misconceptions are not noticed by the teacher, they are compounded, and extra time and effort are required to correct them. To remedy this situation, an icon was placed in the margin telling the students to stop at this point and proceed only when the teacher has checked their understanding of the topic. This feature has evolved into Checkpoints that are simple tests for understanding, Discussion Questions that groups discuss among themselves and with the teacher, and Try This as a Class exercises intended to be used by teachers to lead class discussions to bring closure to concepts. The information that is to be checked at a Checkpoint is listed on the student page. The Checkpoint also gives students and parents an indication of what learning should be occurring. Examples of a Checkpoint, a Discussion Question, and a Try This as a Class exercise are given in figure 14.5.

Multidimensional Assessment

One of the unique features of the project—and a reason for more change in student performance than any other—is the Assessment Criteria. The criteria are used to evaluate open-ended or open-response problems that students may have been working on for a week or more. There are two forms of criteria, one for student *self-assessment* and the other for *teacher assessment* (see figure 14.6, pages 103 and 104). Student self-assessment has not been a part of the traditional curriculum, and yet, it is a very important part of student learning. Students' learning is enhanced if they become involved in the assessment process.

The Assessment Criteria allows the teacher to recognize a student's strengths and helps the student focus on areas where growth is needed. Through these tools, students learn exactly what is important in good problem solving and communication and evaluate their own progress in these areas. Students will respond if they know what is expected, and the criteria make that clear. These tools, used in all three years of the project, are introduced in the first module in grade 6 and re-

viewed in the first module of each subsequent grade level. The assessment criteria are not an add-on to the curriculum but are an integral part of the materials.

The STEM vision is that the middle school years—a time for investigating new, meaningful experiences, not just a period of review—should be a time when students practice mathematics in a variety of settings.

In the prepilot version of the materials, the criteria were user-*un*friendly and hard to interpret. If this very important component of the project were to produce the intended results, it had to be revised and made easier to use. The rubrics have undergone more than ten revisions before reaching the forms they are in now.

Cheryl Wilson, a former middle school mathematics teacher turned principal, reports on her experience with the Assessment Criteria:

> This year I have used drafts of this tool in my classroom and was amazed at how quickly students improved in their ability to solve complex problems and to write up their problem-solving solutions. This is a tool whose time has come. Assessment has been the focus of several recent professional journals, conferences, and discussions. It is exciting to see a curriculum project develop a quality assessment instrument to accompany the curriculum materials.

Teacher Training

To prepare teachers to use the STEM curriculum, they were brought to the University of Montana for a two-week workshop. During the workshop, teachers were exposed to the project's philosophy and the changing role of the teacher in the mathematics classroom. The workshop included sessions on reform mathematics, cooperative learning, assessment, and various kinds of technology. The teachers worked through most of the modules and built many of the hands-on materials their students would make. It was necessary to spend time on mathematical content with which some teachers did not feel comfortable. Changing assessment techniques to measure what is valued instead of what is easy to measure was difficult and time-consuming for teachers. Most teachers wanted more time to learn and understand the assessment process and to become proficient at using the Assessment

12 Solve the proportion in the Example on page 348 to find the Audience Approval rating for Movie A. Round your answer to the nearest whole percent. How does the answer compare with your estimate in Question 11?

13 ✔ **CHECKPOINT** Set up and solve a proportion to write each ratio as a percent.

    a. $\frac{27}{90}$ **b.** 35 to 105   **c.** $\frac{18}{63}$

✔ **QUESTION 13**

…checks that you can set up and solve a proportion to find a percent.

14 a. Set up and solve a proportion to find the Audience Approval rating for Movie B to the nearest whole percent.

    b. Which movie received a higher Audience Approval rating, Movie A or Movie B?

    c. Is $\frac{19}{30} = \frac{15}{24}$? Explain why rounding to the nearest whole percent may be misleading.

15 Discussion Sometimes rounding to the nearest whole percent may not give the best answer.

    a. Find the Audience Approval rating for Movie B to the nearest tenth of a percent.

    b. Does your answer in part (a) change your answer to Question 14(b)? Explain.

Audience Approval rating for Movie A rounded to the nearest tenth of a percent

$$\frac{x}{100} = \frac{19}{30}$$

$$30x = 1900$$

$$x = \frac{1900}{30}$$

$$\begin{array}{r} 63.\overline{3} \leftarrow \text{about} \\ 30\overline{)1900.0} \quad 63.3\% \\ \underline{180} \\ 100 \\ \underline{90} \\ 100 \end{array}$$

Write each ratio as a percent. Round to the nearest tenth.

16 $\frac{8}{35}$ and $\frac{22}{97}$ **17** $\frac{14}{29}$ and $\frac{15}{35}$ **18** $\frac{7}{35}$ and $\frac{8}{49}$

19 Try This as a Class Use your class's star ratings from page 344.

    a. Set up and solve a proportion to find the Audience Approval rating for each movie or television program. Round each answer to the nearest tenth of a percent.

    b. Which movie or program had a higher Audience Approval rating?

    c. Find a fraction that has a percent equivalent within 0.5% of each class Audience Approval rating.

HOMEWORK EXERCISES ▶ See Exs. 8–14 on pp. 353–354.

Name _____ Problem _____

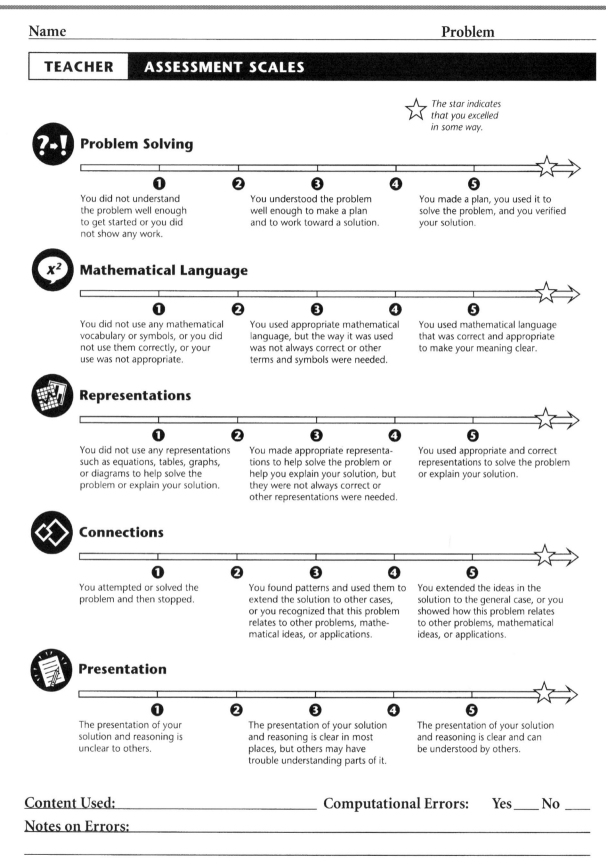

TEACHER   ASSESSMENT SCALES

The star indicates that you excelled in some way.

Problem Solving

❶ You did not understand the problem well enough to get started or you did not show any work.

❷ **❸** You understood the problem well enough to make a plan and to work toward a solution.

❹ **❺** You made a plan, you used it to solve the problem, and you verified your solution.

Mathematical Language

❶ You did not use any mathematical vocabulary or symbols, or you did not use them correctly, or your use was not appropriate.

❷ **❸** You used appropriate mathematical language, but the way it was used was not always correct or other terms and symbols were needed.

❹ **❺** You used mathematical language that was correct and appropriate to make your meaning clear.

Representations

❶ You did not use any representations such as equations, tables, graphs, or diagrams to help solve the problem or explain your solution.

❷ **❸** You made appropriate representations to help solve the problem or help you explain your solution, but they were not always correct or other representations were needed.

❹ **❺** You used appropriate and correct representations to solve the problem or explain your solution.

Connections

❶ You attempted or solved the problem and then stopped.

❷ **❸** You found patterns and used them to extend the solution to other cases, or you recognized that this problem relates to other problems, mathematical ideas, or applications.

❹ **❺** You extended the ideas in the solution to the general case, or you showed how this problem relates to other problems, mathematical ideas, or applications.

Presentation

❶ The presentation of your solution and reasoning is unclear to others.

❷ **❸** The presentation of your solution and reasoning is clear in most places, but others may have trouble understanding parts of it.

❹ **❺** The presentation of your solution and reasoning is clear and can be understood by others.

Content Used: _____   Computational Errors: Yes ____ No ____

Notes on Errors: _____

Fig. 14.6. *From* Professional Development Handbook for Math Thematics, Book 2, *by Rick Billstein and Jim Williamson. Copyright © 1999 by McDougal Littel Inc. All rights reserved. Reprinted by permission.*

STUDENT   SELF-ASSESSMENT SCALES

If your score is in the shaded area, explain why on the back of this sheet and stop.

The star indicates that you excelled in some way.

Problem Solving

1 I did not understand the problem well enough to get started or I did not show any work.

3 I understood the problem well enough to make a plan and to work toward a solution.

5 I made a plan, I used it to solve the problem, and I verified my solution.

Mathematical Language

1 I did not use any mathematical vocabulary or symbols, or I did not use them correctly, or my use was not appropriate.

3 I used appropriate mathematical language, but the way it was used was not always correct or other terms and symbols were needed.

5 I used mathematical language that was correct and appropriate to make my meaning clear.

Representations

1 I did not use any representations such as equations, tables, graphs, or diagrams to help solve the problem or explain my solution.

3 I made appropriate representations to help solve the problem or help me explain my solution, but they were not always correct or other representations were needed.

5 I used appropriate and correct representations to solve the problem or explain my solution.

Connections

1 I attempted or solved the problem and then stopped.

3 I found patterns and used them to extend the solution to other cases, or I recognized that this problem relates to other problems, mathematical ideas, or applications.

5 I extended the ideas in the solution to the general case, or I showed how this problem relates to other problems, mathematical ideas, or applications.

Presentation

1 The presentation of my solution and reasoning is unclear to others.

3 The presentation of my solution and reasoning is clear in most places, but others may have trouble understanding parts of it.

5 The presentation of my solution and reasoning is clear and can be understood by others.

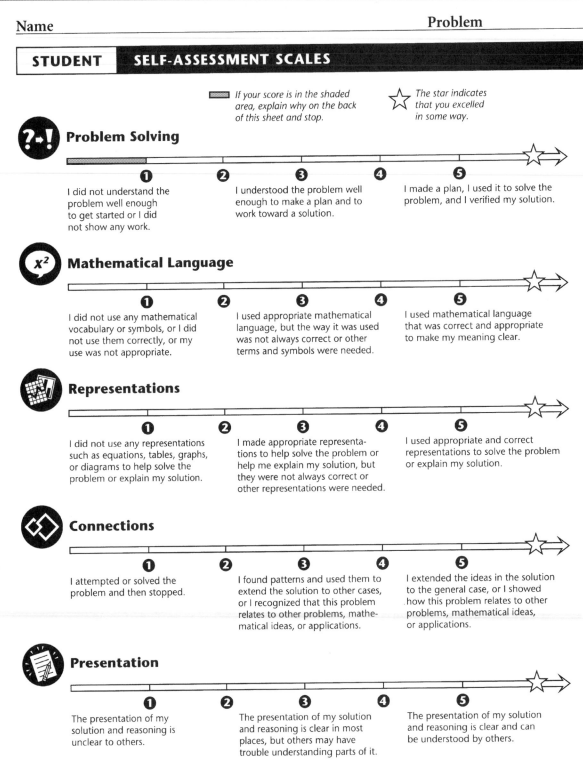

Fig. 14.6. (*continued*)

Criteria. The workshops showed that change can take place, but teachers need training to implement the new curricula.

Outside Evaluator Findings

Research Communications Limited (RCL) acted as the outside evaluator for the project. RCL used various methods, instruments, and analyses to assess whether specific objectives were being achieved through the use of the modules and to provide feedback on the strengths and weaknesses of the materials to writers and publishers. RCL measured teacher reaction to the materials, classroom implementation of the materials, student attitudes, and student learning outcomes. Student learning outcomes were measured by designing a seventh-grade criterion referenced test (CRT). The test was designed to measure forty-two learning outcomes. Each learning outcome was related to one of twelve NCTM Standards (Standard 4 was not included). Table 14.1 summarizes the average scores for each tested standard. The scores are compared across three groups of students. Eighth-grade students were not included in this comparison because a control group was not used in the eighth-grade evaluation. The following groups of students are compared in the table:

- *Control Group Students.* ($N = 176$) These students were taught seventh-grade mathematics with a curriculum other than STEM.

- *STEM Grade 7 Students.* ($N = 386$) These students were taught seventh-grade mathematics with STEM but had been taught with a different curriculum for sixth grade.

- *STEM Grades 6 and 7 Students.* ($N = 201$) These students were taught both sixth- and seventh-grade mathematics with the STEM curriculum.

The scores that represent significant differences are boldfaced. It is important to note that the CRT was designed as a tool for the continuing development of the curriculum and should not be considered as a summative evaluation of whether or not the curriculum was successful.

The Next Steps

This paper has been a discussion of the evolution of one particular reform curriculum project over a five-year period. The materials are now ready for classroom use. This article has discussed—

- thematic modules;
- authentic assessment;
- cooperative learning;
- hands-on activities;
- open-ended problems;
- use of technology;
- connections; and
- interdisciplinary work.

TABLE 14.1.
Scores on the Criterion Referenced Test (CRT)

NCTM Standard		Control	STEM 7	STEM 6 & 7
Standard 1*	Mathematics & Problem Solving	**30**	**45**	43
Standard 2	Mathematics & Communication	25	34	36
Standard 3*	Mathematics & Reasoning	**28**	**44**	**47**
Standard 5	Number & Number Relationships	38	39	46
Standard 6*	Number Systems & Number Theory	**35**	**54**	50
Standard 7	Computation & Estimation	19	28	32
Standard 8*	Patterns & Functions	**23**	**40**	**46**
Standard 9	Algebra	33	45	44
Standard 10	Statistics	32	41	43
Standard 11	Probability	29	41	44
Standard 12	Geometry	35	42	42
Standard 13	Measurement	18	24	28

Scale: 0 to 100
Significant differences ($p \leq 0.05$) are indicated by * and boldface.

Middle school teachers and administrators need to begin thinking about the next steps when examining new curricula. Some old-fashioned Montana advice seems appropriate here: "If the horse you are riding dies, get off of it." This is what we must do with the traditional middle school mathematics curriculum. It has not worked, and we should not continue to use it just because it is what we have always done. It takes time to gentle a horse before it can be ridden, and it takes time for a horse to grow to adult size and be able to carry a rider. Middle Grades Math Thematics (formerly STEM) is now ready to carry riders.

References

Billstein, Rick, and Jim Williamson. *Middle Grades Math Thematics: The STEM Project.* Evanston, Ill.: McDougal Littell, 1999.

Carnegie Council on Adolescent Development. *Turning Points: Preparing American Youth for the Twenty-first Century.* New York: 1989.

Educational Testing Service. *The Mathematics Report Card: Are We Measuring Up?* Washington, D.C.: National Library of Education Office of Educational Research and Improvement, U.S. Department of Education, 1988.

Mathematical Sciences Education Board, National Research Council. *Everybody Counts: A Report to the Nation on the Future of Mathematics Education.* Washington, D.C.: National Academy Press, 1989.

———. *Reshaping School Mathematics: A Philosophy and Framework for Curriculum.* Washington, D.C.: National Academy Press, 1990.

National Council of Teachers of Mathematics. *Curriculum and Evaluation Standards for School Mathematics.* Reston, Va.: National Council of Teachers of Mathematics, 1989.

Rick Billstein, *University of Montana, Missoula, Montana*

15

Designing Middle School Mathematics Materials Using Problems Created to Help Students Progress from Informal to Formal Mathematical Reasoning

THOMAS A. ROMBERG

Two essential elements in the reform of school mathematics have been (1) creating new curricular materials that emphasize having students understand mathematical ideas so they can solve nonroutine problems, and (2) using those materials in classrooms. Accomplishing these two goals has not been easy. This chapter illustrates how one group approached the task of designing new curriculum materials for middle school mathematics and describes some of the consequences of those efforts.

One of the goals for students is that by the end of grade 8 they be able to use algebraic representations (both graphical and symbolic) to model a variety of problem situations. A nonroutine problem students might be expected to solve is shown in figure 15.1, as an example of an intended endpoint of the middle school mathematics curriculum. To investigate this problem, a grade 8 student might write algebraic equations to represent both the area and perimeter of rectangles, graph those equations, consider the constraints given in the problem, and use those ideas to answer the questions raised. A possible student solution to this problem is also shown in the figure.

The primary engineering task faced in this curriculum project involved creating a sequence of learning activities across all of the domains in middle school mathematics (such as algebra, number, geometry, meas-

urement, statistics, and probability), with each activity being justifiable in terms of the intended endpoints of the learning experiences. This sequencing of student activities required making fundamental design decisions about how learning would proceed. Although the intended endpoints of the learning sequence included understanding formal mathematics in the domains mentioned above, to achieve those goals the instructional sequence was designed to begin with informal models and strategies for solving contextualized problems as a foundation for understanding the formal models and representations. In the domain of algebra, for example, this implied creating a set of activities that would provide opportunities for students to progress from informal notions about variation, formulas, and graphs toward using formal algebraic concepts, reasoning, and representations to model and solve nonroutine problems with understanding. Paul Cobb (1994), in his analysis of the approach to instruction used in this problem, stated,

> This implies that students' initially informal mathematical activity should constitute a basis from which they can abstract and construct increasingly sophisticated mathematical conceptions. At the same time, the starting point situations should continue to function as paradigm cases that involve rich imagery and thus anchor students' increasingly abstract mathematical activity. (Pp. 23–24)

Here are two constraints for all rectangles with two sides along the axes:

I. The area is at least 900 square meters, and it is at most 1,200 square meters.

II. The horizontal side is at least 20 meters and it is at most 60 meters.

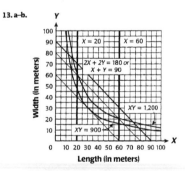

13. a. Graph the feasible region for these constraints.

 b. Graph the line for the upper-right vertices for all rectangles with perimeters of 180 meters.

 c. Use the rolling line strategy to find the rectangle that satisfies constraints **I** and **II** and minimizes the perimeter.

 d. Do the same thing to find the rectangle with the maximum perimeter.

13. a–b.

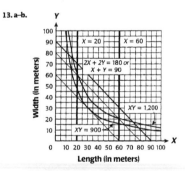

 c. See the graph above. The point in the feasible region that is closest to the origin that can be found with the rolling line is the point (30, 30). So the minimum perimeter forms a rectangle with dimensions of 30 m by 30 m. The perimeter is 120 meters.

 d. See the graph above. There are two points in the feasible region that are farthest away from the origin and that can be found with the rolling line: (20, 60) and (60, 20). So the maximum perimeter forms a rectangle with dimensions of 20 m by 60 m. The perimeter is 160 meters.

Fig. 15.1. *An algebra problem from Get the Most Out of It (Used with permission of Encyclopaedia Britannica.)*

Cobb went on to argue:

> Instructional sequences should involve activities in which students create and elaborate symbolic models of their informal mathematical activity. This modeling activity might involve developing informal notations or using conventional mathematical notations. (P. 24)

The point of this instructional approach is that with appropriate guidance from teachers, a student's informal models can evolve into models for increasingly abstract mathematical reasoning (Gravemeijer 1991).

With this design task in mind, a brief overview of the project is presented. Next, examples from the algebra strand are given to illustrate the progression of problems in a given context, designed so that students have the opportunity to progress from informal to formal reasoning in algebra. Following that, evidence about the quality of the program and its effectiveness is presented. Finally, issues related to the implementation of these materials in classrooms are discussed on the basis of research conducted during the developmental process.

Overview of the Development of Mathematics in Context

An "Achieved" Curriculum for Middle School Mathematics project was funded in 1991 by the National Science Foundation to develop a comprehensive mathematics curriculum for the middle grades 5–8. The materials, entitled Mathematics in Context (MiC) (National Center for Research in Mathematical Sciences Education and Freudenthal Institute 1997), were designed to reflect the content, teaching, and assessment standards for school mathematics proposed by the National Council of Teachers of Mathematics (NCTM) (1989, 1991, 1995). Collaborating on this project were research and development teams from the National Center for Research in Mathematical Sciences Education (NCRSME) at the University of Wisconsin—Madison and the Freudenthal Institute (FI) at the University of Utrecht (Netherlands), a group of field-test teachers in the United States, and artistic, editorial, and production teams at Encyclopaedia Britannica Educational Corporation. MiC consists of forty curriculum units (ten at each grade level, 5–8) and a teacher's guide for each unit that includes assessment materials. MiC also includes two supplementary packets: News in Numbers, which provides extra opportunities for students to develop estimation skills in contexts similar to those in the curriculum units, and Number Tools, consisting of additional problems designed to help students maintain basic skills. (A complete listing of MiC program references and individual units appears in the appendix to this article.)

The development of the MiC materials took more than six years and involved the following steps. First, an international advisory committee of mathematics educators, mathematicians, scientists, curriculum supervisors, principals, and teachers was formed to ensure that MiC conformed to the goals and philosophy of both the *Curriculum and Evaluation Standards for School Mathematics* (NCTM 1989) and the *Professional Standards for Teaching Mathematics* (NCTM 1991). Initially, this committee prepared a blueprint document to guide the development of the materials. Second, Freudenthal Institute staff prepared initial drafts of individual curriculum units based on the blueprint. Researchers at the University of Wisconsin—Madison then modified these units and developed them further to create a curriculum appropriate for U.S. students and teachers. Third, pilot versions of the individual units were tested in middle school classrooms in Wisconsin, where both students and teachers provided feedback and suggestions for revisions. Fourth, the units were then revised and field-tested at additional schools in other states and Puerto Rico. The field tests included trials of the entire year's curriculum at each grade level. Data collected during the field tests were used to again revise the units and prepare detailed guides for teachers for the final step, the commercial publication of the materials. The final product, Mathematics in Context, is a complete mathematics program, with the resources and support materials necessary for successful implementation: student booklets, teacher's guides, and assessment materials.

If reform curricula are to be widely used, data are needed on student mathematical performance as a consequence of the use of these curricula in classrooms.

The mathematics content included in the program is organized in two ways: first by grade level and second by mathematics strand. The notion of strands is based on a metaphor for mathematics expressed by William Thurston (1990): "Mathematics isn't a palm tree, with a single long straight trunk covered with scratchy formulas. It's a banyan tree, with many interconnected trunks and branches—a banyan tree that has grown to the size of a forest, inviting us to climb and explore" (p. 8). Roots of the curriculum are grounded in quantita-

tive and spatial situations, and its trunks are number, algebra, geometry, and statistics and probability.

Over the course of this four-year curriculum, middle school students explore and connect the mathematical domains that are the trunks, which MiC calls strands. These include—

- number (whole numbers, common fractions, ratios, decimal fractions, percents, and integers);
- algebra (creation of expressions, tables, graphs, and formulas from patterns and functions);
- geometry (measurement, spatial visualization, synthetic geometry, coordinate and transformational geometry); and
- statistics and probability (data visualization, chance, distribution and variability, and quantification of expectations).

Although each unit in MiC emphasizes specific topics within a particular mathematical strand, most units involve ideas from several strands and emphasize the interconnectedness of those ideas.

The instructional design and sequencing of the MiC units involved two related assumptions. First, students come to understand mathematics from their experiences solving problems. This involves making sense of a situation by seeing and extracting the mathematics embedded within it. This also involves learning to represent quantitative and spatial relationships in a broad range of situations; to express those relations using the terms, signs, and symbols of mathematics; to use procedures with those signs and symbols following understood rules to carry out numerical and symbolic calculations; and to make predictions and interpret results based on the use of those procedures. Students need to understand the rationale for the use of the mathematical terms, signs, symbols, and rules.

The second assumption was that the sequence of contextual activities should help students gradually develop methods for modeling and symbolizing problem situations. Thus, all activities are related to end goals and seen as helping students in their transition from informal to formal symbolization. This implies that instruction should not start with presenting students the formal terms, signs, symbols, and rules and then expect them to use these formal ideas to solve problems. Instead, the activities should lead students to the need for the formal symbolization of mathematics. Students should gradually develop more formal ways of representing complex problems.

MiC is designed to support teaching as envisioned in the *Professional Teaching Standards*. Each unit includes tasks and questions to engage students in mathematical thinking and discourse. Students are expected to explore mathematical relationships, develop strategies for solving problems, use appropriate problem-solving tools, work cooperatively, and value one another's strategies. They are encouraged to explain their thinking as well as their solutions. Teachers are expected to help students develop common understanding and usage of the terms, signs, symbols, and rules of mathematics in order to assist students in articulating their thinking. Other activities have been designed so that students can extend their ideas to new problem situations.

MiC Approach to Algebra

Examples from the MiC algebra strand are provided in this section to illustrate how MiC supports students' progression from informal to formal reasoning in algebra through representing and analyzing realistic situations and solving problems related to those situations. Fourteen algebra units were developed for grades 5–8.

The diagram in figure 15.2 shows the grade level for which each unit was intended, with the interconnections and the sequencing of the units shown by directed arrows.

In this strand, students initially approach problems and acquire algebraic concepts and skills in an informal way. Words, pictures, and diagrams invented by students are used to describe mathematical situations, organize their own knowledge and work, and solve problems. In later units, students gradually begin to use symbols to describe situations, organize their mathematical work, or express their strategies. At this level, students devise their own symbols or learn some nonconventional notation. A mixture of words and symbols is used to represent problem situations and explain their work. In later MiC units, students learn and use standard, conventional algebraic notation for writing expressions and equations, for manipulating algebraic expressions and solving equations, and for graphing equations. Although students are actually

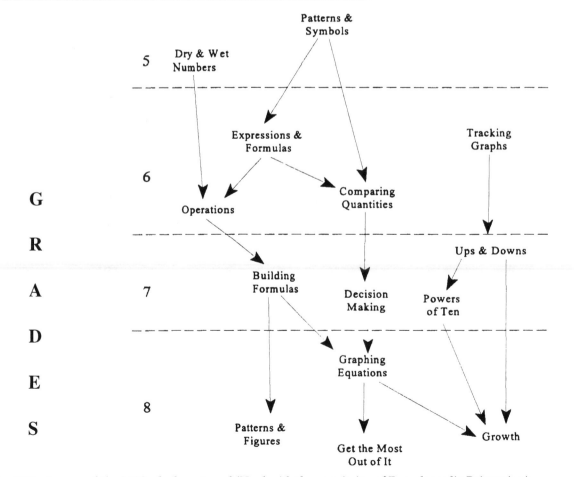

Fig. 15.2. *A map of the MiC algebra strand* (*Used with the permission of Encyclopaedia Britannica.*)

doing algebra less formally in the earlier grades, they are not forced to generalize their knowledge to a more formal level nor to operate at a more formal level before they have had sufficient experience with the underlying concepts.

Three themes run throughout the MiC algebra strand: (*a*) the study of change, (*b*) consideration of constraints, and (*c*) the study of patterns. Similar to themes in a symphony, sometimes one theme is stronger than others; sometimes they are evident simultaneously. Overall, the themes set the tone and determine the shape of the algebra strand.

In the grade 5 unit, Dry and Wet Numbers, students study *change* in water levels as the basis for developing notation and ways of computing with positive and negative numbers. In the grade 6 unit, Tracking Graphs, students produce their first graphs by analyzing phenomena that change over time (e.g., temperature). In the grade 7 unit, Ups and Downs, students graph and describe different kinds of change (e.g., linear, exponential, periodic); this is also central to one of the culminating grade 8 units, Growth. The study of change is important elsewhere as students build knowledge of concepts, such as slope, or move to formal notation and procedures for developing formulas or solving equations.

Considering *constraints* first becomes prominent in the grade 7 unit, Decision Making, as students solve a realistic problem about building housing on a reclaimed landfill. In the grade 8 unit, Graphing Equations, students develop the understanding and skills needed to graph linear inequalities and learn to use these graphs to define restricted regions on the coordinate system. Considering constraints is again prominent in the grade 8 unit, Get the Most out of It, when students tackle a complicated problem in which they use all their graphing skills and accumulated knowledge of linear programming.

In the grade 5 unit, Patterns and Symbols, students begin using symbols to represent *patterns* they see in such things as the growth rings of a tree or blocks used to make a border along a garden. Recognizing and describing patterns is important as students write algebraic formulas in the grade 6 unit, Expressions and Formulas, and in the grade 7 unit, Building Formulas. The grade 8 unit, Patterns and Figures, centers on the study of patterns as students analyze sequences and write formulas for finding terms in the sequence. Students encounter several classic topics in mathematics that deal with patterns (e.g., Pascal's triangle). Patterns also play an important part as students write formulas and equations, work on graphing, describe various kinds of change, and make connections between equations and graphs.

The following four related units illustrate the kinds of problem situations students are expected to investigate and the way these situations have been orchestrated in the MiC algebra strand.

Patterns and Symbols

Patterns and Symbols is a unit designed for grade 5. It introduces students gradually to the use of symbols as an efficient way to represent real situations. For example, in one lesson students are given information about how the red and black growth rings develop on a snake (see figure 15.3). They describe this growth pattern symbolically, and they systematically record the number of red and black rings for a snake's first five growth cycles. They then predict the number of red and black rings a snake would have after a certain number of growth cycles or determine the age of a snake with a given number of red and black rings.

Throughout the unit, students observe patterns in realistic situations and use symbols to describe them. In doing so, they are introduced to concepts of equivalence and opposites (or inverse relationships).

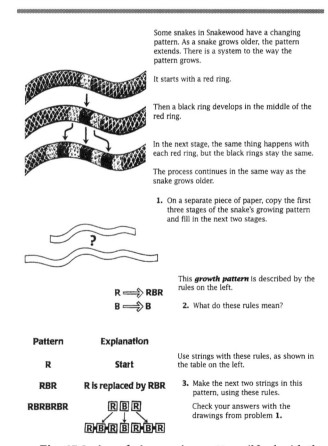

Some snakes in Snakewood have a changing pattern. As a snake grows older, the pattern extends. There is a system to the way the pattern grows.

It starts with a red ring.

Then a black ring develops in the middle of the red ring.

In the next stage, the same thing happens with each red ring, but the black rings stay the same.

The process continues in the same way as the snake grows older.

1. On a separate piece of paper, copy the first three stages of the snake's growing pattern and fill in the next two stages.

This **growth pattern** is described by the rules on the left.

R ⟹ RBR
B ⟹ B

2. What do these rules mean?

Pattern	Explanation
R	Start
RBR	R is replaced by RBR
RBRBRBR	

Use strings with these rules, as shown in the table on the left.

3. Make the next two strings in this pattern, using these rules.

Check your answers with the drawings from problem 1.

Fig. 15.3. *A snake's growing pattern (Used with the permission of Encyclopaedia Britannica.)*

They also begin to find symbolic ways to represent a certain number of repetitions of a pattern and, later in the unit, begin to substitute numbers for symbols to determine how many blocks, placed in a given pattern, are needed to make a wall of a given length.

Expressions and Formulas

Many problems in Expressions and Formulas are posed in the context of buying and selling. Among other things, students make change; determine grocery bills when buying produce, meat, or cheese by the pound; and figure out a plumber's bill. In order to keep track of the complicated sequences of calculations necessary to do these problems, students are introduced to several new tools. First, they use "arrow strings." For example, given a story about someone earning and spending various amounts of money, students might use the arrow language in figure 15.4 to help them figure out how much money is left.

As problems and calculations become more complicated (e.g., buying three kinds of produce, all at a different price per pound), students adapt their "arrow language" to include multiplication and division and they add another calculation tool, tables. When dealing with problems requiring multiplication or division and addition or subtraction, students learn about the order of operations and use another new tool, arithmetic trees, to help them organize and keep track of their work. Finally, students begin to generalize their calculations for specific problems to represent broader mathematical relationships. For example, for a problem about buying tomatoes, grapes, and green beans for different prices per pound, students might form a generalization such as the following:

amount of tomatoes × 1.50 + amount of grapes × 1.70 + amount of green beans × 0.90 = total cost

or an arithmetic tree such as the one shown in figure 15.5.

Building Formulas

In the unit Building Formulas, students use formulas to solve a variety of realistic problems. These problem sit-uations involve designing and mathematically describing patterns for tile walkways or for a metal framework used in building construction, converting temperatures from Fahrenheit to Celsius, figuring heart rate as related to age and exercise, and designing staircases to meet various building code requirements for rise (height of a step) and tread (depth of step).

Students informally encounter the distributive property as they describe brick patterns for a garden border. They then formalize both the concept and the notation, recognizing and using equivalences such as $4(2S + 5L) = 8S + 20L$, where S and L represent bricks either standing or lying on their sides. Students also encounter the need to square and "unsquare" numbers and use a variation of their familiar arrow language to express this (see figure 15.6). They then learn formal notation and use calculators to find square roots more exactly. In figure 15.6 students are given the area (154 000 m²) covered by a giant fungus discovered in northern Michigan in 1992. They imagine the fungus is in the shape of a square and are asked to find, to the nearest whole number, the length of the side of this fungus square and to explain how they found it.

Patterns and Figures

In the unit Patterns and Figures, students start by studying sequences that are arithmetic progressions. This means any number in the sequence (any *term*) can be found by adding or subtracting a certain number from the previous number in the sequence. This is a *recursive* rule, and students describe it in words and algebraic formulas (see figure 15.7).

They also describe, in words and formulas, how to find any term in the sequence without knowing the previous term (see figure 15.8). This is a *direct* rule, or formula. Students apply and practice this in the context of real situations (e.g., the arrangement of seats in a Greek amphitheater and the flight patterns of migrating birds).

Students learn they can combine sequences by addition and subtraction. Among other things, they determine and describe the relationship among the vertices, edges, and faces of pyramids; relate this to their

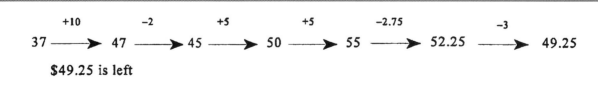

Fig. 15.4. *An example of arrow language (Used with the permission of Encyclopaedia Britannica.)*

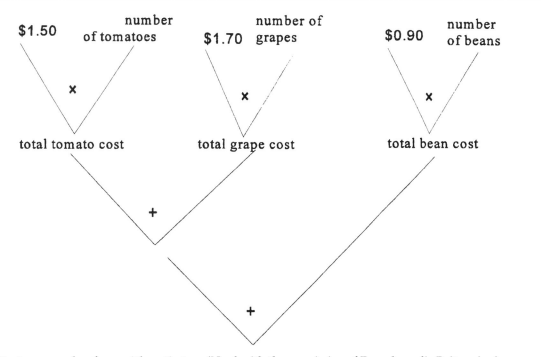

Fig. 15.5. *An example of an arithmetic tree* (*Used with the permission of Encyclopaedia Britannica.*)

work with the vertices, edges, and faces of prisms in the grade 7 geometry unit, Packages and Polygons; and recognize Euler's formula. Finally, through studying sequences that involve squaring numbers, students are introduced to Pascal's triangle.

In Patterns and Figures, students also encounter other important mathematical topics such as binary coding, tessellations, and triangular numbers. This unit broadens their mathematical experience and makes connections between algebra and geometry.

As a consequence of studying the problems in this sequence of units, students have the opportunity to reason, reflect on, and use the terms, symbols, and rules of algebra to solve problems.

Evidence about the Quality and Effectiveness of the Materials

When the MiC materials were being developed, considerable information was gathered about the quality and effectiveness of the materials (cf. Romberg and Pedro 1997; Romberg 1997b). During both pilot and field tests of the materials, information was gathered from teachers, students, administrators, and parents through surveys, teacher logs, unit tests, and classroom observations. Most of the data were used to revise and improve the activities and the teacher's guides that ac-

company the units. The evidence about the program is briefly summarized here.

Review of Content

Simon Hellerstein, former chair of the department of mathematics at the University of Wisconsin—Madison, commented on the MiC units in the algebra strand:

> Incorporating pre-algebraic ideas and skills into the middle school math curriculum, culminating in the 8th grade with some basic formal algebra, is a splendid undertaking. The end goals of the algebra strand as listed in teacher guide are commendable. In those schools where the goals are actually achieved, students will have been well served and better prepared to tackle high school algebra. . . .
>
> Where the students are encouraged to find their own strategies or to write a description of their reasoning, the role of the teacher, while important for the rest of the material, becomes critical. . . . Encouraging independent thinking is ideal, reinforcing sloppy independent thinking is poor. Controlling the latter while not at the same time also squelching the former is a challenge that too few teachers may be able to handle. (S. Hellerstein, personal communication, 30 March 1995)

Other reviewers have made similar comments about the quality of the mathematics in each strand and the

The numbers that result from squaring a whole number are called *square numbers*, or *perfect squares*.

5. Find at least five different square numbers. Share your list with a classmate. Each of you can try to guess what numbers the other person squared.

There are several ways to indicate the square of a number:

3^2, 3 ↑ 2, 3 times itself, and 3 ∧ 2 all mean 3 × 3. Three squared is nine.

When using arrow language you can write:

$$14 \xrightarrow{\ ^\wedge 2\ } 196$$

Or, using words, you can write:

$$\begin{matrix} \text{length of} \\ \text{side} \end{matrix} \xrightarrow{\ ^\wedge 2\ } \begin{matrix} \text{area of} \\ \text{square} \end{matrix}$$

Recall that the *Armillaria bulbosa* fungus was found covering an area of 154,000 square meters.

Suppose that the fungus is in the shape of a square. To find the length of one side of the square, translate the problem to:

$$? \xrightarrow{\ ^\wedge 2\ } 154{,}000$$

The squaring has to be undone. In other words, you have to "unsquare" 154,000.

6. Estimate what number is the result of unsquaring 154,000. How can you check your estimation?

For some numbers, unsquaring is easy.

7. Write some numbers that are easy to unsquare. Then unsquare them.

Fig. 15.6. *Squaring and unsquaring numbers (Used with the permission of Encyclopaedia Britannica.)*

instructional approach. Each, however, cautioned the developers about the difficulties they could see in implementing the program in many schools.

Information Collected from Teachers

On every unit taught, all teachers were surveyed about the forms of assessment they used during the unit, the amount of time allowed for the assessment activities, and the results (for specifics, see Romberg [1997b]). For example, one teacher of the field-test version of Expressions and Formulas said, "I was very pleased with the [students'] understanding of the math-ematics in this unit. Students understood the concepts and were able to apply them on the assessment [activity]."

Teachers were also asked to provide examples of students' work representing low, medium, and high performances and a list of scores for the end-of-unit assessment activity, with students identified by gender and grade level. Some general comments for the field-test version of Expressions and Formulas were negative:

"Formulas were generally hard for students."

"This unit needed teacher direction."

Here is a different strip made with the repeating pattern red–white–blue–red–white–blue.

Any list of numbers that goes on forever is called a *sequence.*

How can you figure out the color for 253,679?

Fig. 15.7. *An example of a recursive pattern (Used with the permission of Encyclopaedia Britannica.)*

Look at the following sequence of W-patterns.

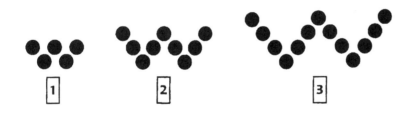

12. a. Copy and complete this chart for the W-patterns.

Number of Dots	5	—	—	—	—	—
Pattern Number	1	2	3	4	5	6

b. Write a step-by-step formula for the number of dots in the W-pattern sequence.

c. How many dots are in pattern number 16?

d. Find a direct formula to describe the number of dots in any W-pattern. Then use your formula to find the number of dots in pattern number 25.

Fig. 15.8. *An example of developing a direct rule (Used with the permission of Encyclopaedia Britannica.)*

"There were no parts my students could accomplish in small groups."

Some were positive:

"Students as a whole were quite successful as exhibited by their discussions, journals, and assessments."

"Content was presented in such a way that it was meaningful and related to a variety of situations in everyday life."

"Arrow language was very useful, especially in helping students reverse the order when looking for a factor rather than final product or answer."

Teachers also were asked whether students had understood the mathematics in the previous unit. Some comments were positive:

"Most students did well on all but the section about the Forest Fire Fighting, especially problems 3 and 4 where they had to think."

"Students were able to apply the concepts on the assessment."

"I noticed several using trees to solve other math problems after we completed the unit."

"When given a Continental Math League test, many students used reverse arrow strings to figure out answers!"

Some were negative:

"Students were confused and anxious but demonstrated effort to understand. Towards the end they 'clicked.'"

"Students struggled with every part of this unit except the arrow language."

"Occasionally the students would not understand how a problem was worded and we would have to discuss it as a group."

One significant outcome for teachers in these studies was a changed view of their students' capabilities. In fact, all the teachers were surprised by the work their students were able to do. As one field-test teacher commented, "What we're finding in some of our work, too, is that the kids get things that we thought might be hard for them" (Romberg and Shafer 1995, p. 8). Romberg and Shafer (1995) also commented that "most teachers were amazed that students could communicate and were excited about talking and doing math. They were able to make connections to the world around them and to other areas of study in school" (p. 16).

The impact of having students "do mathematics"

in this manner had two consequences. First, as Burrill (quoted in de Lange et al. [1993]) found, "Students who had been labeled as 'poor in math' found they could succeed," and second, "some who considered themselves 'good in math' decided 'this isn't math'" (p. 160). Similar results were found during the field tests, when teachers administered open assessment tasks as a part of the suggested end-of-unit tests:

One teacher even discovered something new about the students' understanding by means of the test: "Some of my quieter students displayed a greater understanding than I had given them credit for." This same teacher went on to make the following comment about the assessment for the unit: "I feel it offers more than most objective sorts of tests. It allows students to explain their thinking—a very valuable piece of information." (van den Heuvel-Panhuizen 1995, p. 71)

Performance-Test Data

If reform curricula are to be widely used, data are needed on student mathematical performance as a consequence of the use of these curricula in classrooms. Such data were not collected systematically by the project staff during the development of MiC because they needed to be related to the final, commercially published version of the curriculum used continuously with students over a four-year period. In 1996 the National Science Foundation funded a four-year study— "A Longitudinal/Cross-Sectional Study of the Impact of Mathematics in Context on Student Mathematical Performance"—to determine the impact of the final version of the MiC curriculum on the mathematical knowledge and understanding, attitude, and performance of middle school students when used continuously over a four-year period.

. . . even if the teachers themselves were familiar with the mathematics, they were often unsure how to proceed because they had never taught that mathematics to students.

Nonsystematic performance data were gathered during the development of the MiC units. Assessment tasks were included with every unit. However, teachers often adapted the tasks or used only some of them to judge students' progress. Students often found the material challenging and different from their past mathematical experiences. Nevertheless, the evidence on each unit showed that most students learned the intended content. Furthermore, school districts that used the MiC materials often shared the districts' standardized-test data with the developers. Overall, they reported improved test scores for the students using MiC compared to scores for similar students in prior years (Romberg and Pedro 1997).

In summary, the evidence shows that Mathematics in Context is a quality product and, if appropriately implemented in middle school classrooms, can be an effective means of teaching students to understand and use mathematics to solve nonroutine problems.

Implementation Issues

From the beginning, we were confident a middle school curriculum that met the expectations of the NCTM *Standards* could be created; yet we anticipated implementation would be challenging. However, from research carried out during the pilot and field-testing of the materials, it is now clear that wide-scale implementation of such a program presents several challenges. As Sarason (1971) argued, "[A]ny attempt to introduce a change into the school involves [challenging] some existing regularity, behavioral or programmatic" (p. 3). As MiC units were being taught in classrooms in the pilot and field tests, the traditional school culture and the common instructional routines for mathematics classes were being challenged. The following examples come from a series of ongoing case studies and the formative information gathered during field trials of the materials (Romberg 1997a). To summarize the findings, four topics were chosen: instructional sequence, coverage, unfamiliar content, and authority.

Instructional Sequence

In Weller's (1991) study of traditional mathematics classrooms, he found a common daily pattern of instruction in both classes: "It was evident that a repeating pattern of instruction occurred which consisted of three distinctive segments: a review, presentation, and study/assistance period. This 'rhythm of instruction' was not unplanned or coincidental" (p. 128). NCTM's *Professional Teaching Standards* (1991) called for a different pattern of instruction. The MiC materials were designed to support the shift to posing worthwhile problems, solving those problems, and discussing solution strategies and mathematical thinking as central features of instructional routine. In fact, MiC field-test teachers found that teaching a Mathematics in Context unit constituted a departure from the the traditional daily pattern.

Coverage

The recent report from the Third International Mathematics and Science Study (TIMSS), *A Splintered Vision: An Investigation of U.S. Science and Mathematics Education* (Schmidt et al. 1996), showed that U.S. textbooks cover more topics, repeat topics more often, and spend less time on any one topic than textbooks in other countries. Further, many teachers see their primary job as covering the topics in their textbooks.

As the materials were being pilot- and field-tested, teachers using MiC often voiced concern over whether to teach traditional topics. The danger, of course, is two-fold: the tendency, first, to augment reform instruction with traditional practices and, second, to modify and change activities so that they resembled past lessons. For example, B. Clarke (1995) found that "there was also a tendency on the part of one of the teachers, having taught the lesson once, to vary the presentation in subsequent lessons, with increasing levels of structure, as a response to feelings of personal discomfort" (p. 159).

Unfamiliar Content

B. Clarke (1995) found that "tasks within the unit and students' attempts at these led to the introduction of a variety of mathematical content areas some of which were unfamiliar to the teachers" (p. 157). When this occurred, teachers were unsure how to proceed. Further, even if the teachers themselves were familiar with the mathematics, they were often unsure how to proceed because they had never taught that mathematics to students. The latter is important because it focuses on the teacher's understanding of the learning process of their students. D. Clarke (1993) found that teachers floundered when "they lacked knowledge of most students' learning of the content of the unit and the means by which such knowledge could be obtained" (p. 222). This lack of familiarity with the specific mathematics in a unit and the potential connections to other content was often reflected in the assessment tasks teachers created. For example, van den Heuvel-Panhuizen (1995) found that "the teacher-made problems made clear that [they] had a preference for computational problems and problems which are firmly connected with the contexts and the tasks that are used in that teaching" (p. 70). Similar comments related to assessments were made by many of the field-test teachers when interviewed by the staff as a part of the review process (Romberg and Shafer 1995).

Authority

Weller (1991) found that in traditional classrooms, "the expert knowledge of the teacher was deliberately

117

subjugated to that of the textbook authors. As a result of that process, the teacher was able to camouflage his or her role as authoritarian, thus eliminating student challenges of authority" (p. 133). In the field-testing of Mathematics in Context, student booklets contained tasks for students to read and make sense of under the guidance of the teacher. This approach to instructional authority changed the work environment for both teachers and students. For example, when reflecting on the work of the two teachers in her study, B. Clarke (1995) commented that "the teachers encouraged conjecturing and inventing as students solved problems. This led to critical incidents for the teachers as they tried to understand the students' methods of solution on the spur of the moment. Insightful student responses led to more critical incidents than any other type" (p. 156). In particular, she found that for these teachers, "the reality of changing authority is difficult. There were a number of times when the students were able to provide the clarification of a difficulty. This was powerful, though potentially threatening to the authority of the teacher" (pp. 157–58). In fact, in most classes teachers occasionally had to admit they did not know how to approach a problem and thus had to work on the tasks with the students as equals.

In summary, information from these studies makes it clear that this approach to mathematics teaching "represents, on the whole, a substantial departure from teachers' prior experience, established beliefs, and present practice. Indeed, they hold out an image of conditions of learning for children that their teachers have themselves rarely experienced" (Little 1993, p. 130). Such departures from traditional practices were evident in every classroom in these studies.

As Chevellard (1988) pointed out, currently there is a gap between what is taught and what is learned. He argued that this gap is created when we treat a pupil only as a "student" (someone who studies) and not as a "learner" (someone who learns). The MiC approach was developed to close this gap. The transition from working with students to working with learners is difficult for teachers, but it can be done and it is very rewarding.

Concluding Comments

This chapter has summarized the story of the development of Mathematics in Context and provided a glimpse of the possibilities it provides for furthering the reform of middle school mathematics.

Our experience suggests that it is possible to create a set of activities to be taught over a four-year span that provides students an opportunity to progress from informal notions in a mathematical domain (for exam-

ple, algebra) toward using formal reasoning and representations to model and solve nonroutine problems. Thus, the goal of conveying mathematics that makes "sense" to students and that can be used by students to make sense of their worlds has been achieved.

References

Chevellard, Yves. "The Student-Learner Gap." In *Proceedings of the Third International Conference on the Theory of Mathematics Education,* edited by Alfred Vermandel, pp. 1–6. Antwerp, Belgium: Universitaire Instelling Antwerpen, 1988.

Clarke, Barbara. "Expecting the Unexpected: Critical Incidents in the Mathematics Classroom." Ph.D. diss., University of Wisconsin—Madison, 1995.

Clarke, Douglas. "Influences on the Changing Role of the Mathematics Teacher." Ph.D. diss., University of Wisconsin—Madison, 1993.

Cobb, Paul. "Theories of Mathematical Learning and Constructivism: A Personal View." Paper presented at the Symposium on Trends and Perspectives in Mathematics Education, Institute for Mathematics, University of Klagenfurt, Austria, September 1994.

de Lange, Jan, Gail Burrill, Thomas Romberg, and Martin van Reeuwijk. *Learning and Testing Mathematics in Context—the Case: Data Visualization.* Scotts Valley, Calif.: Wings for Learning, 1993.

Freudenthal, Hans. "Mathematics Starting and Staying in Reality." In *Proceedings of the USCMP Conference on Mathematics Education on Development in School Mathematics Education around the World,* edited by Izaak Wirszup and Robert Street, pp. 279–95. Reston, Va.: National Council of Teachers of Mathematics, 1987.

Gravemeijer, Koeno. *Developing Realistic Mathematics Education.* Utrecht: CD β Press, 1991.

Hellerstein, Simon. Comments on the MiC algebra units, personal communication, 30 March 1995.

Little, Joyce. "Teachers' Professional Development in a Climate of Educational Reform." *Educational Evaluation and Policy Analysis* 15, no. 2 (1995): 129–51.

National Center for Research in Mathematical Sciences Education and Freudenthal Institute, eds. *Mathematics in Context.* Chicago: Encyclopaedia Britannica, 1997.

National Council of Teachers of Mathematics. *Assessment Standards for School Mathematics.* Reston, Va.: National Council of Teachers of Mathematics, 1995.

———. *Curriculum and Evaluation Standards for School Mathematics.* Reston, Va.: National Council of Teachers of Mathematics, 1989.

———. *Professional Standards for Teaching Mathematics.* Reston, Va.: National Council of Teachers of Mathematics, 1991.

Romberg, Thomas A. "Mathematics in Context: Impact on Teachers." In *Mathematics Teachers in Transition,* edited by Elizabeth Fennema and Barbara S. Nelson, pp. 357–80. Mahwah, N.J.: Lawrence Erlbaum Associates, 1997a.

———. "The Development of an 'Achieved' Curriculum for Middle School Mathematics." Unpublished report to the National Science Foundation, National Center for Research in Mathematical Sciences Education, University of Wisconsin—Madison, 1997b.

Romberg, Thomas A., and Joan Pedro. "Developing Mathematics in Context: A Research Process." Unpublished report to the National Science Foundation, National Center for Research in Mathematical Sciences Education, University of Wisconsin—Madison, 1997.

Romberg, Thomas, and Mary Shafer. "Results of Assessment." Unpublished manuscript, National Center for Research in Mathematical Sciences Education, University of Wisconsin—Madison, 1995.

Sarason, Seymour B. *The Culture of the School and the Problem of Change.* Boston: Allyn & Bacon, 1971.

Schmidt, William, Curtis McKnight, and Senta Raisen. *A Splintered Vision: An Investigation of U.S. Science and Mathematics Education.* Boston: Kluwer, 1996.

Thurston, William P. Letters from the editors. *Quantum* 1, no. 1 (1990): 8.

van den Heuvel-Panhuizen, Marja. "Developing Assessment Problems on Percentage." Paper presented at the annual meeting of the American Educational Research Association, San Francisco, Calif., April 1995.

Weller, Mark. "Marketing the Curriculum: Core versus Non-Core Subjects in one Junior High School." Ph.D. diss., University of Wisconsin—Madison, 1991.

Appendix

National Center for Research in Mathematical Sciences Education and Freudenthal Institute, eds. *Mathematics in Context.* Chicago: Encyclopaedia Britannica, 1997.

The following MiC units are referred to in this chapter:

Building Formulas. Monica Wijers, Anton Roodhardt, Martin van Reeuwijk, Gail Burrill, Beth Cole, and Margaret A. Pligge.

Decision Making. Anton Roodhardt, James A. Middleton, Gail Burrill, and Aaron N. Simon.

Dry and Wet Numbers. Leen Streefland, Anton Roodhardt, Beth R. Cole, and Laura J. Brinker.

Expressions and Formulas. Koeno Gravemeijer, Anton Roodhardt, Monica Wijers, Beth R. Cole, and Gail Burrill.

Get the Most out of It. Anton Roodhardt, Martin Kindt, Margaret A. Pligge, and Anton Simon.

Graphing Equations. Martin Kindt, Monica Wijers, Mary S. Spence, Laura J. Brinker, Margaret A. Pligge, Aaron N. Simon, and Jack Burrill.

Growth. Anton Roodhardt, Jack Burrill, Mary S. Spence, and Peter Christiansen.

News in Numbers. Marja van den Heuvel-Panhuizen, Mary C. Shafer, Sherian Foster, and Aaron N. Simon.

Number Tools. Jack Burrill and Beth R. Cole.

Operations. Mieke Abels, Monica Wijers, Gail Burrill, Aaron N. Simon, and Beth R. Cole.

Packages and Polygons. Martin Kindt, Mary S. Spence, Laura J. Brinker, and Gail Burrill.

Patterns and Figures. Martin Kindt, Anton Roodhardt, Aaron N. Simon, Mary S. Spence, and Margaret A. Pligge.

Patterns and Symbols. Anton Roodhardt, Martin Kindt, Gail Burrill, and Mary S. Spence.

Tracking Graphs. Jan A. de Jong, Nanda Querelle, Margaret R. Meyer, and Aaron N. Simon.

Ups and Downs. Mieke Abels, Jan A. de Jong, Margaret Meyer, Julia A. Shew, Gail Burrill, and Aaron N. Simon.

Thomas A. Romberg, *University of Wisconsin—Madison, Madison, Wisconsin*

16

What Should a Middle School Mathematics Classroom Look Like? Watching the "Seeing and Thinking Mathematically" Curriculum in Action

Glenn M. Kleiman, Dan Tobin,
and Shelley Isaacson

The Seeing and Thinking Mathematically project (STM) began with Education Development Center, Inc.'s proposal to the National Science Foundation (NSF):

> To be human is to seek to understand. Mathematics, along with science, has made possible dramatic advances in our understanding of the physical universe. To be human is to explore. Throughout history, mathematics has been essential for exploration, from navigating by the stars to travel into space. To be human is to participate in a society. Societies require mathematics to keep records, allocate resources, and make decisions. To be human is to build, and mathematics is essential for the design and construction of everything from tents to temples to skyscrapers. To be human is to look to the future. Mathematics enables us to analyze what has been, predict what might be, and evaluate our options. To be human is to play, and mathematics is part of our games

and our sports. To be human is to think, to create, and to communicate. Mathematics provides a vehicle for thinking, a medium for creating, and a language for communicating. Indeed, to be human is to develop mathematics. Mathematics has been developed in every culture for the purposes of counting, locating, measuring, designing, playing, and explaining. Without mathematics, as without language, the nature of humanity and human society would be fundamentally different.

In 1991, NSF awarded the Education Development Center (EDC) a five-year grant to develop the STM middle school curriculum based on this humanistic view of mathematics and on the National Council of Teachers of Mathematics (NCTM) *Curriculum and Evaluation Standards* (1989). True to the interdisciplinary approach to mathematics in the proposal, we set out to form an eclectic project team and a diverse group of partners. Mathematicians, classroom teachers, curriculum and software developers comprised the core STM team. We worked closely with EDC colleagues specializing in mathematics curricula, professional development, and research, and we formed key partnerships with international curriculum experts who helped broaden our perspectives and pushed our thinking (several units were developed in partnership with the Shell Centre for Mathematical Education at the Uni-

The Seeing and Thinking Mathematically project is based at Education Development Center, Inc. ([EDC] Newton, Mass.) and funded by the National Science Foundation (grant no. 9054677). The opinions expressed in this article and the curriculum are those of the authors and not necessarily those of the National Science Foundation. The authors would like to thank the major contributors to the curriculum design and the ideas expressed in this paper: Amy Brodesky, Rebecca Brown, Dan Brutlag, Hugh Burkhardt, Al Cuoco, Paul Goldenberg, Kristen Herbert, Susan Janssen, Charles Lovitt, and Sandra Ward, along with the many other colleagues, teachers, and students.

versity of Nottingham, England, and EdMath Curriculum Services in Victoria, Australia).

Perhaps our most important partnerships, however, were with middle school teachers and school districts. Although our vision of mathematics was broad and sweeping, our approach to building a curriculum began and ended in classrooms: we wanted to find out what worked and what didn't work in real classrooms. We knew from our previous experience that designing an elegant mathematics activity on paper was relatively easy; the real challenge was making that activity work, achieving intended goals in a wide variety of classrooms. For that reason, we spent the first two summers of the project running intensive institutes with fifty middle school teachers. The sessions were designed to gather information on the characteristics of middle school students; teaching conditions; advantages and disadvantages of current mathematics textbooks; areas of difficulty in mathematics for many middle school students; and common students' misconceptions of mathematics. Teachers shared mathematics activities they thought exemplary and helped develop some preliminary investigations for future units.

Collaborative Research: What's Happening in the Classroom?

We carried that collaborative approach throughout the life of the project—particularly throughout the four years we spent field-testing units. Field-test teachers worked closely with STM research staff, who spent hours observing them in their classrooms, interviewing them, and reading their journals and students' work. Following the field test, the STM researchers worked closely with the curriculum developers to revise the units on the basis of extensive classroom data. The research process consisted of two phases: the first was conducted by EDC curriculum developers and involved the summer institutes with middle school teachers and early formative testing in which project staff tried out activities with groups of students. These research activities helped to define the design principles used throughout the curriculum. The second phase was conducted by an EDC research team and Inverness Research Associates and consisted of extensive field testing by teachers in their classrooms and reviews of the unit drafts by mathematics educators, mathematicians, and middle school teachers.

The research team carefully selected field-test sites to insure that there would be a diversity of teachers, students, and school settings. In Massachusetts, middle school teachers in nine school districts and more than twenty schools field-tested STM units. In California,

more than 1000 teachers used STM units, primarily in conjunction with two NSF-funded teacher development projects: the Middle Grades Mathematics Renaissance project, and the Math Matters project. Inverness Research Associates in California conducted research on how nine middle school teachers used the units in their classrooms. The Inverness researchers observed classrooms, interviewed teachers, and analyzed student work. In addition, Inverness and EDC conducted telephone interviews with a large number of teachers who were using STM materials.

Although our vision of mathematics was broad and sweeping, our approach to building a curriculum began and ended in classrooms: we wanted to find out what worked and what didn't work in real classrooms.

All this research was guided by a topical framework developed and continually revised throughout the course of the project. The framework consisted of dozens of questions regarding everything from the appropriateness of the mathematics for the intended grade level to the clarity and tone of the writing in the teachers' guide. Underlying all these issues was one central question that framed the ongoing discussions between STM researchers and curriculum developers: "If the unit works as we intended, what should we see happening in the classroom?"

Of course, the answer to that question depends to some degree on which classroom you are observing. Every classroom differs in the teacher's approach, students' backgrounds, the physical environment, materials available, explicit and implicit rules, school context, and ways students interact with each other and with the teacher. Therefore, activities that result from a given set of curriculum materials will vary greatly across classrooms. The materials do not control what happens but simply play one role in a complex interaction of teachers, students, and materials. We designed the STM materials with this interaction in mind, aiming to develop materials sufficiently flexible and robust to be used successfully in many different classrooms. However, there were certain benchmarks or traits we expected to see in *every* classroom using these materials. In this article, we will describe ten of these traits, which together would be a measure of the success of our materials (fig. 16.1). Some examples of how research findings assisted the design of materials will also be provided.

121

1. Students demonstrate meaningful understandings of mathematical concepts.

2. Students' work and class discussions involve three components of mathematical understanding.

3. As they progress through the curriculum, students move from using their own approaches to more precise and powerful mathematical language and techniques.

4. Students share discoveries, discuss, and write about mathematics, and engage in collaborative projects.

5. Students engage in creative mathematical work.

6. Students use computers to enhance their learning.

7. Students connect mathematics to other subjects and to their lives outside the classroom.

8. Teachers learn as well as teach.

9. Teachers adapt the curriculum to best meet the needs of their students.

10. All students are successful mathematics learners.

Fig. 16.1. *Ten benchmarks of classroom success*

The Ten Benchmarks of Classroom Success

1. *Students demonstrate meaningful understandings of mathematical concepts.*

In our project discussions, phrases such as "meaningful understanding" triggered lively and productive exchanges. What constitutes meaningful understandings of particular mathematical concepts? How would we—and the teacher—know whether or not a student has gained them?

We could not answer these questions without considering their opposites: Where do we see examples of a *lack* of meaningful understandings? We began to look for evidence of student misconceptions and to probe student thinking so we could identify where materials or instruction may have failed. For example, one of the observers was visiting in a sixth-grade classroom where, using a traditional curriculum, the topic of the day was "multiplying an integer by a fraction." The teacher began by demonstrating the standard two-step procedure: divide by the denominator and then multiply by the numerator. After working a few problems on the chalkboard, the teacher assigned a set of word problems in the student text.

The following problem was presented:

John took 24 pictures and 2/3 of his pictures were of his cat. How many pictures did John take of his cat?

Edward had written the answer "8" for this problem, so he was asked how he solved it. He reread the problem, wrote 24 ÷ 3 on his worksheet, found the quo-

tient, 8; and then repeated that John would have eight pictures of his cat.

To help Edward see that he was leaving out the second part of the two-step procedure, the observer gave him a revised problem in which 1/3 of John's 24 pictures were of his cat. Edward repeated exactly what he had done before and again gave the answer of 8. The observer asked, "Could 1/3 of a number and 2/3 of the same number both be the same?" Edward carefully examined the work on his paper and responded, "I guess so; they are both 8." The observer probed Edward's understanding of fractions, found that he could not show 1/3 or 1/4 of a simple shape, did not know whether 1/3 or 1/4 was larger, and did not understand that 2/4 equals 1/2. He could not represent, compare, or sequence fractions. And yet, had he remembered the second step of the procedure, he would have been able to solve all the assigned problems correctly, and his lack of understanding would have gone unnoticed.

Within the STM materials, we provide opportunities for students to work with important concepts in a variety of forms and contexts—to explore fractions, for example, through using shapes, pictures, measures, and numbers involving creating scale drawings, finding "best buys," comparing rates of change, and designing probability games. We ask students to describe how they arrive at their solutions, to compare different approaches, and to find alternative means of checking their answers. We also ask students to—

- generalize their approaches to related problems and to pose their own problems;

- represent mathematical ideas in different ways and show how the different representations are related; and

- describe connections of new ideas to what they have learned.

All these elements of the curriculum are designed to help students gain meaningful understandings of the mathematics, to provide teachers (and researchers) with opportunities to see how students' understandings are developing, and to reveal students' misconceptions and gaps in understanding so that teachers can address them.

For example, consider the Crossing the River problem from a grade 6 STM unit called Patterns in Numbers and Shapes:

A group of 8 adults and 2 children needs to cross a river. They have a small boat that can hold either 1 adult and 1 child, or 2 children. How many one-way trips are required to get everyone across the river?

Many students approach this problem by modeling the situation with materials such as blocks, whereas others draw various types of diagrams. They find that four trips are required to get one adult across the river and return the boat to the original side (see figure 16.2). After all eight adults are moved across the river, one additional trip is necessary to get the last child across. So the answer is $4 \times 8 + 1 = 33$ trips. Students then generalize their solution process for different numbers of adults. Students who have meaningful understandings will be able to extract the pattern and develop a method of solution for any number of adults, including numbers too large to act out or diagram step-by-step. They can also describe how they solved the problems and explain why their approach makes sense—to say, for example, why there is a 4, an 8, and a 1 in their solution to the first problem, and why only the 8 changes as the number of adults in the problem situation varies.

This student articulated the generalized rule in symbols and explained how it relates to the original situation.

The rule is that it always takes 4 one way trips to get 1 adult across. So what you would do is multiply the number of adults by four and add 1 to your answer. You'd add the 1 because the children need to get back with the adults. For 100 adult you would do 100 times 4 & +1. Example: $100 \times 4 = 400 + 1 = 401 =$ answer

$$(A \times 4) + 1 = T$$

Another student drew the generalized rule and explained how it relates to the original situation.

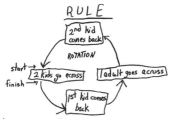

The rotation begins at the start arrow. It occurs once for every adult. When all of the adults are across, the 2 kids go across for the final time.

For 100 adults and 2 children it would take 401 trips.

Fig. 16.2.

The information given and the question asked are then changed in a second problem:

> It takes 13 trips to get all the adults and the 2 children across the river. How many adults were there?

Students with meaningful understandings will use their solution for the first type of problem to help them solve the second. Students can explore variations of the problem with different numbers of students or even different size boats.

2. *Students' work and class discussions involve three components of mathematics understanding.*

In our field tests, we looked for evidence of mathematical understanding in three different areas: concepts and skills, central ideas, and mathematical processes. In the STM curriculum, as in any mathematics curriculum, there is a large set of specific concepts and skills for students to learn. We group these specifics into four general strands: (1) number and operations; (2) algebra and functions; (3) probability and statistics; and (4) geometry and measurement. Within each strand, we include the concepts and skills appropriate for grades 6–8 as described in the NCTM *Standards* and in a variety of state and local curriculum frameworks. Defining these concepts and skills and dealing with the issues of balance between depth and breadth of content were a major challenge for the project.

We also defined a set of "mathematical themes" or "central ideas" that permeate the curriculum and help connect the specific concepts and strands. These include proportional reasoning, multiple representations, patterns, and functional relationships. Consider, for example, the theme of proportional reasoning. In geometry and measurement, we introduce the concept of similarity and procedures for making scale drawings; in number and operations, the concept of ratio and procedures for solving problems involving proportions; in statistics and probability, the concepts of theoretical and experimental probabilities, and the procedures for representing and comparing them; and in algebra and functions, the concept of a linear function and the procedures for solving unknowns in linear equations. In STM classrooms, we hope to see students not just working with each of these concepts and applying each of these procedures appropriately, but also reflecting upon and discussing how they all relate to the general idea of proportionality.

The third component of the essential content consists of mathematical processes. We hope to see students engaged in doing, at appropriate levels, the same kinds of things that mathematicians do. These include making and testing conjectures; using physical and pictorial models; searching for patterns and generalizations; posing problems; testing ideas against new cases; conducting mathematical experiments; using mathematical tools such as calculators and measuring devices; visualizing relationships; seeking precision in communication; developing proofs; and systematizing ideas. We believe that students should learn mathematics by doing mathematics, and doing mathematics involves all of these processes.

3. *As they progress through the curriculum, students move from using their own approaches to more precise and powerful mathematial language and techniques.*

Students must construct their own understandings by building on what they already know, gradually revising and extending their knowledge, and learning to use more precise and powerful mathematics techniques. These are the ways in which meaningful understanding can be developed; otherwise, we risk students acquiring mathematical formalism devoid of meaning.

For example, in the grade 8 unit Mathematics of Motion, one of the early tasks asks students to describe in writing and with a picture or diagram how they get from home to school. Students then analyze their work to see which dimensions of the trip, such as distance, speed, time, direction, are included in their representations.

Early in the unit, students work in pairs to measure each other's paces in walking and other movements. They then find their own ways to estimate or calculate to solve problems based on those measurements, such as "how long would it take you to walk a mile at the speed you walked across the room?"

As students progress through the unit, they learn to use the mathematical relationships to calculate distance, speed, or time when the other two are known; to use distance/time and speed/time graphs to represent motions; and to compare the information about a journey that can best be provided by text, maps, and graphs.

4. *Students share discoveries, discuss and write about mathematics, and engage in collaborative projects.*

Mathematics should not be a lonely or isolating enterprise. In STM classrooms, we seek mathematics learning that involves interactions with classmates, teachers, and families. Many activities throughout the curriculum are designed to foster this goal.

For example, in the grade 6 unit Designing Spaces, students engage in several design tasks. Early in the unit, they design a model house using cubes or blocks. Later in the unit they design a house using a set of two-dimensional geometric shapes. During the unit, students learn various ways to represent three-dimensional shapes in two dimensions, such as orthogonal drawings, isometric drawings, and perspective draw-

ings, and they learn the geometric terms for describing shapes and shape properties. They use these representation techniques and language in creating plans for their buildings. The test of their plans is to have classmates try to reconstruct the original building from the plans; that is, the building plans provide an opportunity for students to communicate to a real audience (their classmates) for a real purpose (to enable them to reconstruct their designs) and obtain feedback about how successful they were (by seeing whether their classmates' reconstructions match their original structures). Figure 16.3 shows some examples of students' structures and plans.

5. *Students engage in creative mathematical work.*

In English class, students write their own essays; in social studies, they offer their own interpretations of current and historical events; in science, they collect their own data and conduct their own experiments. But in traditional mathematics class, as students learn facts and procedures and apply them to given problems, all too often they see mathematics as devoid of creativity and personal involvement.

In the STM curriculum, we provide activities in which students engage creatively in real mathematical tasks. For example, the grade 6 unit The Language of Numbers begins with students constructing a "mystery device"—something like a circular abacus with four sets of four beads and three sets of three beads (see figure 16.4). Students are asked to create a system for showing all the numbers from 0 to 120 on their mystery device. They then explain their systems to others, compare systems, and consider certain properties of their systems, such as the largest number that can be shown, whether every number up to the largest can be shown, and whether there are multiple ways to show some numbers. Students' work creating and describing systems for representing numbers forms a basis for later exploring the properties of the base ten place value system.

There are many other examples wherein students create physical models, drawings, games, and stories; collect and analyze data in their own projects; and develop their own strategies for solving problems. In classrooms we hoped to see students eager to show and explain their own work—to find many examples of student work that elicited responses like "We never would have thought of that!" One such example, of a student's concentric circle system for representing numbers on the mystery device, is shown in figure 16.5.

6. *Students use computers to enhance their learning.*

While computers are not required for most STM units (the exception is a grade 7 unit, Getting Down to Business, in which spreadsheets are introduced), computer software and Internet access can enhance and extend students' learning. Students can conduct mathe-

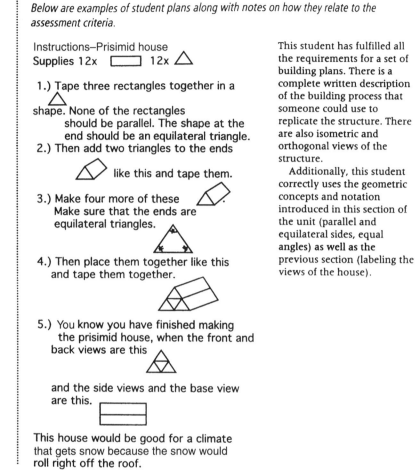

From the Classroom

Below are examples of student plans along with notes on how they relate to the assessment criteria.

Instructions–Prisimid house

Supplies 12x ▭ 12x △

1.) Tape three rectangles together in a △ shape. None of the rectangles should be parallel. The shape at the end should be an equilateral triangle.

2.) Then add two triangles to the ends ◁ like this and tape them.

3.) Make four more of these ◁. Make sure that the ends are equilateral triangles.

4.) Then place them together like this and tape them together.

5.) You know you have finished making the prisimid house, when the front and back views are this

and the side views and the base view are this.

This house would be good for a climate that gets snow because the snow would roll right off the roof.

This student has fulfilled all the requirements for a set of building plans. There is a complete written description of the building process that someone could use to replicate the structure. There are also isometric and orthogonal views of the structure.

Additionally, this student correctly uses the geometric concepts and notation introduced in this section of the unit (parallel and equilateral sides, equal angles) as well as the previous section (labeling the views of the house).

Fig. 16.3. *From* Designing Spaces *(Used with the permission of Education Development Center, Inc.)*

matics experiments and investigations that would be impossible without them. For example, in the Chance Encounters unit for grade 7, physical experiments with spinners, number cubes, and coins are an essential part of the unit. Each physical experiment takes time and effort, and when studying probability, a number of trials is often needed. As students develop their ideas about probability, they are unlikely to conduct many experiments in which they collect hundreds of trials. A simulation program was developed to enhance this unit. This program enables students to quickly simulate the types of experiments, vary key parameters (e.g., the number and size of the "slices" on a circular spinner), and collect hundreds or even thousands of trials. It also can represent the results as counts, percentages, circle graphs, and bar graphs, to enable students to explore the relationships among these repre-

sentations. As the class combines results, they investigate patterns and learn concepts such as variability, theoretical versus experimental probability, and the law of large numbers.

The World Wide Web can be used to enhance those units that involve gathering and sharing data, such as What Does the Data Say?, Buyer Beware, and What Comes Next? Other software—such as geometry construction programs, computer-aided design tools, simulations, spreadsheets—provide valuable enhancements for many of the units.

7. Students connect mathematics to other subjects and to their lives outside the classroom.

Throughout the STM curriculum, we have intertwined "thematic challenges" with mathematical investigations to provide motivation. Some examples are shown in table 16.1.

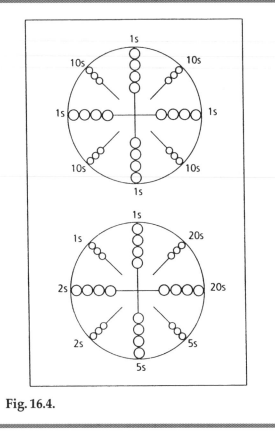

Fig. 16.4.

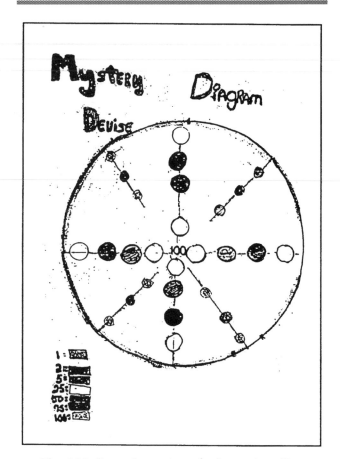

Fig. 16.5. *Jasper's mystery device system.* *From* The Language of Numbers *(Used with the permission of Education Development Center, Inc.)*

Throughout our design and testing of the curriculum, we sought contexts and challenges that are "real" for middle school students—that engage their interests and stimulate their thinking. We often asked whether an idea was a "context or a pretext." Since the distinction depends not upon the developers' view but on the responses of the students, this question could only be resolved by field tests of activities. We abandoned a number of thematic contexts when field tests revealed them to be uninteresting or artificial to students, or in the worst cases, when the contexts interfered with students' understanding of the mathematics. For example, in testing the Getting Down to Business unit, many realistic business terms or scenarios clouded students' understanding of the functional relationships involved. In that case, we simplified the contexts; for other units, we decided to forego a thematic context altogether.

8. *Teachers learn as well as teach.*

The STM curriculum differs in many ways from a traditional middle school mathematics curriculum. For most teachers, there is new content, including more about functions and algebra and probability and statistics. There are new types of classroom activities involving kinesthetics, design, writing, and modeling. The curriculum encourages discussions and interactions

different from those traditionally found in many classrooms.

Our vision of mathematics education shares a great deal with the vision of the writing process approach (see, for example, Graves 1983 and Hansen 1987). A key to both is the development of a community of learners within the classroom, in which everyone is involved in both teaching and learning. The teacher is the key to making this vision a reality. Our role as curriculum developers is to provide guidance and support for the teachers.

The design of the STM materials contains many elements to support teachers in meeting the challenges of the new curriculum. These include—

- mathematics background sections in each unit, to provide an overview of key mathematical ideas;
- suggestions developed during field-testing of the units (e.g., common misconceptions or areas of difficulty, and how the teacher might address them);

TABLE 16.1.
Sample thematic challenges and mathematical investigations

Thematic challenges	Mathematical investigations
Determine which brands of cereal should be purchased for a school breakfast.	Determine cost per serving and other "per" quantities.
Design a house in which you would like to live to fit a given plot of land, and to be built within certain cost constraints.	Building 3-D shapes with 2-D nets; measuring surface areas of 3-D shapes; and calculating cost-per-unit.
Determine whether a game of chance is fair for all the participants.	Find all possible outcomes with tree diagrams and outcome grids.
Identify patterns in the number words of a language that make it easier to learn to count in that language.	Explore number patterns and the use of addition and multiplication in number composition.
Analyze changes in the population of a town to plan whether new schools will be needed in the future.	Explore the differential results of linear, geometric, and exponential growth.
Create a life-size object at the scale it would be in the land of giants that Gulliver visited.	Determine the effects of rescaling on linear, area, and volume measurements.

- notes to teachers explaining the rationale for certain lessons;
- teacher reflection essays, providing more detailed accounts of classroom activities, with student and teacher responses; and
- samples of students' work and suggested assessment criteria to help teachers evaluate students' work.

We also sought connections with professional development projects. We encouraged such projects to provide opportunities for teachers to use one or two of the units as "replacement" or "transition" units in a supportive environment in which teachers have opportunities to discuss the experience with their colleagues and with mentors. Support for teachers and the opportunities for teachers to be learners must be provided if any reform-based curriculum project is to flourish.

9. Teachers adapt the curriculum to best meet the needs of their students.

As we defined our curriculum goals at the beginning of the project, we were faced with certain dilemmas. A major goal was to enable middle school students to achieve the NCTM *Standards* for that level, but we could not assume that they entered middle school having achieved the elementary standards. Students could come from a traditional elementary curriculum or a "reform" curriculum. STM should prepare students well for most high school curricula but many are undergoing revision, so we could not make strong assumptions about the curriculum students would have after STM.

Further, as stated in the introduction to this article, we knew that every classroom and every school faces a unique set of conditions. To meet this range of needs

and conditions, a high degree of flexibility was built into STM at all levels (curriculum, grade, unit, and lesson). The curriculum consists of twenty-one units, with seven assigned to each grade in the "standard" plan. These units can be reconfigured in many ways. For example, some districts may replace certain units with locally developed ones that connect well with the community and cover the same content. Other districts may use some of the units in grade 5 and move others units down a year from the standard sequence, in order to prepare students for a more formal algebra course in grade 8.

Within each unit, we provide a standard schedule and notes about some alternative paths. Many of the From the Classroom Notes within lessons include suggestions for adapting the lesson to the students. At both the unit and lesson level, the adaptations consider such things as students' prior mathematical backgrounds, their work on prior lessons, their reading and writing abilities, and the time and resources available.

10. All students are successful mathematics learners.

Edward, the fifth-grader who did not understand fractions, said something that indicated much more than his lack of knowledge of fractions: "I'm not very good at this math stuff." He seemed to know his mathematics facts—he was quick to say that $24 \div 8$ equaled 3—but he still believed that he could not succeed at it.

By the time they reach middle school, most students believe that some people are good in mathematics and some are not and classify themselves in one category or the other. Students bring different strengths and need different support in learning mathematics, and some students will need extra work to be ready to begin middle school mathematics. But all students are

127

capable of understanding the mathematics contained within the STM curriculum.

The most rewarding feedback from STM field testing are the many cases of students who had been identified as weak in mathematics—by their teachers, their families, their peers, and themselves—but who find they have mathematical insights and abilities that did not come to light when their mathematics consisted primarily of computation.

Many students have strong visualization skills—a type of skill very important to mathematicians—but have had few chances to apply and develop these skills in traditional mathematics classes. These "poor mathematics students" may find themselves very able to visualize and represent shapes in units such as Designing Spaces and others in the STM curriculum.

Other students show real mathematical insights when the context is motivating. For example, in the grade 7 unit Chance Encounters, students explore probability and statistics in a variety of game contexts, investigating, for example, whether games of chance played with spinners and certain rules are fair or unfair. At the end of this unit, students collect data about the likelihood of events in a real situation, and then design their own simulation. Poor mathematics students have surprised many teachers and parents with their level of motivation and the quality of their work in these tasks.

We hope that, as we visit STM classrooms, we never hear children describe themselves as "not very good at this math stuff" but that we hear phrases like "I think I can figure this out," "Let me show you how I did it," "Let's try this . . . ," and "I'm still working on . . ." —phrases that convey confidence, persistence, and engagement in middle school mathematics class.

References

Graves, Donald. *Writing: Teachers and Children at Work.* Portsmouth, N.H.: Heinemann, 1983.

Hansen, Jane. *When Writers Read.* Portsmouth, N.H.: Heinemann, 1987.

National Council of Teachers of Mathematics. *Curriculum and Evaluation Standards for School Mathematics.* Reston, Va.: National Council of Teachers of Mathematics, 1989.

Glenn M. Kleiman, Dan Tobin, and Shelley Isaacson, *Education Development Center, Newton, Massachusetts*

17

Engaging Middle Schoolers in and through Real-World Mathematics

SHELLEY V. GOLDMAN, JENNIFER
KNUDSEN, AND MICHELLE LATVALA

Success or failure in school mathematics has the power to qualify or exclude students from future school or employment opportunities. Without successful completion of high school mathematics—algebra and beyond—students are unprepared for entrance to college, technical education, or, in many instances, work.

When the Middle-school Mathematics through Applications Project (MMAP) began in 1992, mathematics learning in schools was in a crisis: over 90 percent of the students who began the high school mathematics sequence were not finishing; girls' achievement in mathematics was dropping during the middle school years; inner-city youth were failing in school; and patterns of alienation were firmly reflected in high drop-out rates. All of these indicators pointed to a need for change in mathematics teaching and learning. The problem was not that mathematics was too hard for most to learn; instead, children were failing because of our reliance on traditional mathematics instruction in a radically changing world. The National Council of Teachers of Mathematics (NCTM) *Curriculum and Evaluation Standards for School Mathematics* (1989) had established reform at the policy level, and now the classrooms needed resources to begin to implement reform. Teachers who were seeking new approaches to mathematics content needed a variety of new resources and materials to use with students.

Grants from the National Science Foundation (NSF) allowed MMAP to develop and study the use of materials that experimented with an applied approach to middle school mathematics. However, it would not be enough simply to create new classroom materials. We would need to understand more about mathematics practices outside of schools, challenge standard conceptions of how mathematical content is learned and incorporated in classrooms, and better understand and address issues affecting teachers' work. This meant attention to curriculum, teaching, learning, assessment, and technology—none could be left out of the mix.

The challenge to MMAP was to take guidance from research on learning, the concerns of middle school students, and conjectures about pedagogy and content in order to create curriculum materials that would work within national constraints for standards and accountability. MMAP made several commitments to materials development and research, including—

The Middle-school Mathematics through Applications Project was funded by NSF grant numbers MDR-9154005, ESI-9154119, and ESI-9452771. Opinions presented in this article are those of its authors and not the NSF.

129

- defining and testing the feasibility of an applications-based approach to learning mathematics by creating and field-testing a series of application units and assessments for middle school mathematics classrooms;

- learning more about the ways that technologies might be integrated into the mathematics classroom through a research and development process;

- bringing to the curriculum design process a collaborative community of education researchers, teachers and teacher educators, curriculum developers, mathematics-using professionals, and students;

- working with teachers to learn about the issues they face as they make changes in their perspectives and practices (see Greeno et al. 1997); and

- conducting research to improve on materials design and generate new understandings of mathematics teaching and learning.

In meeting these commitments, MMAP developed a comprehensive set of middle school mathematics materials. At its center are projects that engage students in real-world problem solving and require them to learn and use mathematics. Our hypothesis was that real-world problem contexts would engage students who were alienated from mathematics as a school subject as well as provide grounding for all students' mathematical reasoning and argumentation. Our research and development confirm what teachers, students, researchers, and policymakers thought—that new approaches to mathematics learning were necessary for raising the level of student engagement and learning. We have constructed our version of mathematics through applications to address equity issues, engage students in continued growth of mathematical ideas, skills, and practices, and relate to what matters in their lives.

In this paper, we outline the MMAP curriculum and discuss its features as a comprehensive set of middle school materials that engage students in learning mathematics through real-world applications. In section I, we describe the MMAP application units and comprehensive plan and how they support mathematical growth during the middle school years. In section II, we invite you into a classroom where we describe an application project in action, the Antarctica project, that brings to life some of the important curriculum features that support middle school mathematics learning. In section III, we outline and elaborate on the features of the curriculum that are introduced by the Antarctica vignette. In section IV, we conclude with a short summary and highlight some research and assessment results.

I: Curriculum Components and Mathematics Coverage

Curriculum Components

MMAP is a series of technology-integrated, project-based units that fit together into a comprehensive middle school mathematics plan. The curriculum consists of modules that can be arranged to meet the course needs and standards of students, teachers, schools, and districts. MMAP has three types of modules—application units, extensions, and investigations—from which teachers and curriculum decision makers can choose to construct a complete and balanced *Standards*-based middle school curriculum.

Application units require six to eight weeks of classroom time and the use of specially created MMAP design software. The application units plunge students into an extended role-play as "employees" involved in real-world problems such as creating codes, designing floor plans, making maps, or building biological models. Accompanying software applications provide easy-to-use tools for exploring the real-world context and require the use of mathematics to solve the problem. Mathematical concepts and skills are integrated within the project work and are progressively developed throughout the unit. Each unit introduces at least two new mathematical concepts along with several minor mathematical themes and provides opportunities to practice skills.

Nine applications units are included in the comprehensive curriculum. An introductory unit guides students into design and group work in the context of event planning, supported by the use of an appropriate spreadsheet. The eight central units have been developed around each of four real-world work themes: architecture, population biology, cryptology, and cartography. Each theme forms the basis for two units, one targeting lower middle school (grades 6 and 7) and the other targeting upper middle school (grades 7 and 8).

Extensions are two- to three-week units that build directly on the mathematical insights and skills students develop within the major application units. These materials introduce students to the standard mathematical notations associated with concepts such as proportion, help students develop specific skills such as manipulating algebraic expressions, and deepen their conceptual understanding of central mathematical ideas such as function. At least one extension is designed to lead or follow each application unit, for a

130

total of thirteen extensions in the comprehensive curriculum.

Investigations are one- to two-week explorations that introduce mathematical concepts either from a pure mathematics point of view or within fanciful contexts. In these miniunits, students learn geometric vocabulary in the context of quilting or methods of proof while exploring relationships between even and odd integers. Mathematics concepts, common notations, and vocabulary are emphasized, along with mathematical practices such as making conjectures, coming up with counterexamples, and writing proofs. Eleven investigations complete the comprehensive curriculum.

These three different types of modules are designed to be used flexibly, within parameters. Although most extensions follow a specific application unit, investigations can be inserted anywhere, depending on teachers' and students' needs and local curriculum requirements. We provide teachers with a provisional plan that sequences application units, extensions, and investigations. This plan provides students with mathematics learning trajectories that link prior learning and new experiences to concepts, skills, and conventions.

Primary Content Foci

Proportional reasoning becomes a primary focus during middle school as students make the transition from additive to multiplicative reasoning about relationships between quantities. By the end of grade 8, students need to be able to use multiplication, ratios, and proportions to express relationships between quantities and make predictions.

Proportional reasoning is addressed through a range of MMAP materials for sixth through eighth grade. In units based on architectural problems, students grapple with scale (the ratio that defines proportionality between the real world and the paper or computer screen world). Then, in an extension, they map their experiences in the units onto standard proportional notation, developing and verifying rules for manipulating the proportion equation. In contrast, in two population biology units, ratios represented by decimals and percents explain the growth rates of populations over time. Students compare and manipulate growth ratios with historical data. In a third, more mathematically sophisticated approach to proportionality students examine proportional covariation in an extension, developing an analysis of covariation from examples found in applications units.

Through three years of the comprehensive curriculum, students use proportions, ratios, fractions, and percents to express the relationships between quantities and find missing quantities. Students learn to recognize and describe proportional covariation. They use and develop their proportional reasoning skills in a variety of mathematics and nonmathematics contexts.

Algebra and functions become a second curricular focus as middle schoolers develop their abilities to track changes in two variables and describe the change of one in terms of the other. In doing so, they need to use a variety of representations of functions, from tables to algebraic formulas. By the time students leave middle school, they should be comfortable with standard algebraic notation, have a rich understanding of variable, and be able to use functions to solve problems.

The areas of algebra and functions are addressed not only from different real-world contexts but from different mathematical vantage points. Architectural units provide opportunities to conceptualize variables in two ways: students represent and manipulate variables with the software, and they build tables comparing two variables (such as level of outside insulation and building cost). In population biology units, students learn to represent their knowledge of the world through algebraic functions and track the results of those functions over a period of time.

Facility with algebraic notation and words used for variables is developed through using the software and unit activities. In units based on cryptology, students develop facility with algebraic notation and investigate functions. Functions are first used to build codes; then learning about function properties enhances students' ability to break codes. A standard algebraic notation for functions (for example, $y = x^2 + 3$) is used in the software.

Extensions for each of the application units move students from informal, implicit use of functions to understanding and flexibly using the standard symbolic notations associated with functions. In a variety of extensions, students build on their familiarity with geometric patterns to make simple function tables and graphs; compare multiplicative and additive linear functions; examine covariation in a variety of real-world settings; and write equations to represent patterns and situations.

After three years of the comprehensive, applications-based curriculum, students will have experienced designing investigations of covariation, used functions to represent real-world phenomena, and explored the mathematical properties of functions. They will be able to use standard algebraic notation and verbal description of functions, tables, and graphs to solve problems.

In addition to these two foci, the MMAP curriculum addresses all the NCTM Standards for middle school.

The mathematical processes of problem solving, communication, reasoning, and making connections are central to each application unit. Probability and geometry are addressed in a series of investigations; number theory is used in an application dealing with codes on the Internet; opportunities for computation and estimation arise in many units.

II: At Work in the MMAP Classroom

The scenario that follows illuminates features of the MMAP curriculum in use in the classroom. This scenario is a composite of data gathered over five years in a number of Bay Area classrooms.

The Antarctica Project

As you enter the classroom, you see thirty seventh graders and their teacher, working in small groups at tables and at five computers set around the periphery of the room. Their project involves designing a research station in Antarctica. Students at the computers are making laboratory floors plans using ArchiTech, a software environment in which they can do architectural design work using concepts of proportionality and function. As they lay out sections of walls, windows, and doors, one group is busy discussing the percentage of the building that will be needed as space for laboratories and research equipment. A second group constructs a circular building but must approximate a circle by means of the straight-line segments allowed by the software. Part of the group turns to centimeter graph paper to sketch out an approximation of a circle with line segments; two students check a research station constraint list generated to determine the largest possible diameter for their near-round station.

At the tables, the teacher has asked a group that has finished its preliminary design to estimate how much garbage the laboratory will generate in two years. After a lively discussion of how much garbage each of their own families sets on the curb each week, the students settle on some estimates. For starters, they estimate that a can of garbage a week takes up 0.75 m³ of space; then they find out how much space would be needed for storing two years' garbage.

The groups spend the last ten minutes of the class period in peer reviews of their designs, checking that all the constraints have been met: fitting their design within a 17 m by 30 m building site, setting a scale for their design, and having proportional (and realistically scaled) walls, doors, and furnishings.

Each group is then ready for the next part of the project: an analysis of the most economical grade of insulation (R value) to install in their Antarctic station,

taking into consideration building and heating costs over the expected twenty-year life span of the building. This phase begins when the teacher distributes a memo from the client requesting the analysis (figure 17.1) and leads a discussion about insulation. She asks all the groups to use the software to experiment with the insulation values and conjecture how these affect the building and heating costs.

Over the next few class periods, students are guided through a systematic investigation of insulation values. They examine and interpret two graphs that show, for a specific building size, the relationship between roof insulation and building cost and between roof insulation and heating cost (see figure 17.2). Next, students investigate the insulation extremes for their own building designs, predict what the costs for a medium insulation will be, and verify their predictions. They write a formula, in words or symbols, for combining building costs and twenty years of heating costs. Finally, through building a table in ArchiTech and calculating the total costs by paper and pencil, students look systematically at what happens to the heating, building, and total costs as the value of the roof insulation varies from low to high. After graphing that relationship, they make a choice of insulation for their station.

As a culminating activity, each group presents its research station design and the special analyses conducted. Each group's presentation is made to local community members, who inquire about the details of each design and analysis and make commentary about the likely success of the students' designs.

Throughout this five-week project, these students use and further develop their sense of proportional reasoning as they make and refine scale drawings of their design. Students learn new skills and acquire conceptual understanding by writing a formula relating two variables to a third and by examining patterns in the changes of these variables, two at a time, to solve the realistic insulation problem.

After the Antarctica project is complete, the entire class will spend two weeks with extension activities that guide them through explorations of direct and inverse variation. Thus, students' new understanding of functions is refined, elaborated, and connected to standard mathematical conventions and language.

III: MMAP Applications—Features and Issues

The Antarctica project provides a scenario of a class using a specific application unit. (See also figure 17.3, teacher pages accompanying the Antarctica project.) General features of the curriculum can now be addressed.

MEMO 3

To: **ANTARCHITECTS**
From: Booker Vega, Principal Designer
Re: Analyzing and Revising

You're now "AAT" a very important phase in the design process. **The Frozen Scientific Group** needs a design that can not only be built at a reasonable cost but won't break the budget on heating costs.

1   FIND THE BEST R VALUE

Now that you've met the design needs of your Requirements List, it's time to consider the energy efficiency of this design. Find the R value that will give *the lowest total building and heating costs for 20 years.*

2   CONSIDER THE COSTS

Review your design. Investigate and then make any other changes you can to lower costs or improve your design. Look at other **ANTARCHITECTS'** designs. You can learn a lot from others' work.

Fig. 17.1. *Antarctica project memo*

What do we mean by an application? Students in the Antarctica scenario are working within an application—an extended real-life problem with several solutions. MMAP application units reverse the usual relationship in the mathematics curriculum between applications and mathematical content. Most traditional mathematics curricula approach applications by identifying a mathematical concept to be learned and then building a series of activities that illustrate that particular concept. In contrast, we start with a compelling, real-world problem to be solved and then find relevant mathematics that occur naturally within the problem-solving process. As evidenced in the Antarctica vignette, the curriculum materials place students in the role of designers who need to create solutions for real-world problems.

Why did we choose the contexts we did? Many of the application topics and software environments were inspired by observations of mathematics—using professionals at work. MMAP chose specific real-world contexts because of their connections to work-world problem solving and global issues, both of which proved interesting to young teenagers. We discovered that students are intrigued by work-world–related problems, possible vocations, and work tools relevant to their futures. As students act as workers who are designing solutions to problems, teachers find that such questions as "Why do we have to learn this?" and "When will we ever use this?" are rarely asked. As the vignette implies, the Antarctica project proved very appealing to students. The isolation and harsh winter conditions made Antarctica a strange and curious context

133

MAKING THE BEST OF IT

MEMO 3 asks you to find the best insulation for your station. This activity will help you figure out strategies for doing that. Record your answers in your logbook.

1. These two graphs are based on data collected from ArchiTech for a 310 square meter design: For each graph write a paragraph that tells what they say. Then write a sentence or two that compares the two graphs.

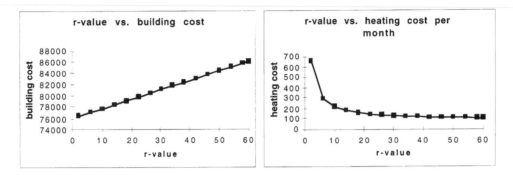

For steps 2–4, use your own design. Don't change the shape or size; only use the sliders.

2. Test out the heating and building costs for R 2 and R 60 for your design. Write down what you get.

3. Predict what the heating and building costs will be if you set the insulation value at 31 R. Now test your prediction, and explain what you find out.

4. MEMO 3 asks you to figure out "the R value that will give *the lowest total building and heating costs for 20 years.*"

Explain, in words, symbols or pictures, how to calculate the total cost for heating and building for twenty years.

5. Make a table that shows the effect of increasing the R value of one kind of insulation on the total cost for heating and building. Make sure you don't change anything else during this part of the activity.

6. Describe at least two patterns that you see in your table. Use this table to help you choose the most effective insulation value for *that kind of insulation* for your design. Explain how you made your choice.

Fig. 17.2. *Student page for activity*

for almost all students, but they eagerly took on the responsibility for making an Antarctic stay comfortable for others.

How does the curriculum support student work? Bringing these rich applications to the classroom means devising materials that guide students through this process, since students and teachers are not used to working on such a long-range problem with so many

parts. The problems in the units are broken into a series of steps approximating what adult workers do, but simplified for use in the classroom. A series of memos, similar from unit to unit, break student work into manageable segments with specific tasks to be accomplished. An introductory memo welcomes students to their new job, previews the project, and demarcates the stages they will follow. Succeeding memos direct research on the application topic, the design work, the mathematical analyses, and the final report.

How do we ensure ongoing opportunities for learning and using significant mathematics? Specially designed mathematics activities are embedded in each application unit. Teacher notes and student handouts direct students' project investigations in particular ways, highlight and name the mathematics students are using, and support students' learning of new mathematics in the context of the application problem. For example, in the Antarctica project, a mathematics activity handout guided students' investigation of the most economical insulation value for their home. The handout asked students to examine and interpret existing graphs and make predictions, then develop their own set of graphs and tables to determine the best insulation values for their designs. In this way, students learned how to investigate covariation, an important aspect of functions for middle schoolers. Other mathematics activities throughout the Antarctica project help students understand metric measurement and support an exploration of the relationship between area and perimeter.

As students work through an application unit, they use and learn several different mathematics topics, since it is difficult to design a solution to a real-world problem by using only one kind of mathematics at a time. Instead of being a liability, this is an opportunity to help students learn and use mathematics in more integrated ways. Whereas traditionally students learn one topic at a time, rarely having the opportunity to integrate their learning, application units integrate several topics together in solving a problem. Students find it easy and natural to work with more than one kind of mathematics when real-world problem solving demands it.

With this potential for learning several topics in one unit, ongoing choices need to be made. To some extent, students and teachers choose how deeply to delve into specific content. For example, the Antarctica project contains materials for helping students explore the relationship between area and perimeter by building a series of rectangular storage sheds. The teacher can introduce these materials if this topic is one her students need to explore. Or, on the basis of diagnostic assessment work, she can eliminate those materials altogether and concentrate on the mathematics of the insulation optimization problem.

What are the mathematical benefits of design work? All the application units use a design environment to engage students in mathematical work and provide opportunities for constructing mathematical understanding. The design work starts in each application unit when students have a set of constraints to meet. Math-

ematical discourse and analysis occur around the negotiation of these constraints. Design work requires multiple representations, so that design teams frequently have to negotiate moving from one representation to another. Such fluidity requires a variety of tools, and design teams seek out the computer, calculators, and rulers to help them with their designs (Berg and Goldman 1996). Throughout the design work, multiple solutions to mathematical problems are generated. All of these characteristics of design environments create learning opportunities in which the mathematics is contextualized, functional, and meaningful for the students involved.

How does the software support learning the mathematics? The computer tools allow students to build, display, and interpret models, tables, data, and representations. The software handles excessive and complicated calculations while still leaving room for grade-appropriate pencil-and-paper calculations. The tools become a focal point for mathematical conversation; thus, software encourages group participation rather than single-user activity. In keeping with adult work practices, students use the computer software only when it is useful during a project and to accomplish design and mathematics work.

Although MMAP designed the computer tools for the application units based on what professionals were using, we needed to add or subtract features from real adult tools. For example, in the vignette students used computer software to investigate a variety of levels of insulation and associated costs of a building design. Real computer-aided design (CAD) systems do not contain tools for this, but we found the insulation value investigation to be a relevant and useful way to get students to work on an optimization problem and learn about functions. We included "sliders" in the software that enable students to control inside and outside insulation, as well as inside and outside temperature, and easily track these changes in tables.

The vignette showed an ideal arrangement of five to eight computers in the classroom throughout the unit. However, teachers with only one computer in their classroom have managed to complete application units by rotating groups through the computer station. Teachers can also complete the unit by taking the class to the computer lab every few days.

How do we support assessment throughout project work? The term *assessment* is used to describe a variety of activities that help teachers and students engage in, capture, reflect on, and demonstrate mathematical growth. Within the vignette, the teacher used several different forms of assessment that were seamlessly embedded in the curriculum: a peer review, a mathematics activity handout, and a final presentation. In an applied

Help with R Value

Intent: Help students understand the difference between the effect of changing R values on heating cost and building cost.

Students' Product: Notebook entries based on student handout.

Math Concepts and Skills: interpreting graphs, comparing changes in related variables, making predictions, describing patterns, using multiple representations to describe the relationship between two related variables.

Time Frame: 1-2 class sessions

Materials:

- Student Handout: MAKING THE BEST OF IT
- ARCHITECH software

What to Do:

• Give students the handout, MAKING THE BEST OF IT. After they have had some time to compare the graphs in #1, take some time to discuss their comparisons.

• Give students time to complete the activity. When students get to #5, make sure that they understand what it means to change only one variable at a time. This means that they must choose one type of insulation to analyze and leave the other ones alone. You may want to tell students to choose either roof or wall insulation. These insulations have the greatest effect on the heating cost of the building. Another option is to have your students take some time to figure out which insulation has the greatest effect on heating cost.

Teaching Strategies:

This activity will help students in doing Memo 3, which sets up an optimization problem. Students should also use the handout, ARCHITECH INFORMATION.

After students complete #1, you could ask students to tell the "story" of the second graph. One story: "When the R value of the roof is low, the heat cost is high. As you add just a little bit of R, you get big payoffs on heat savings right away. You continue to save on the heating cost, but you save less and less as the R value gets closer and closer to 60."

Possible Solutions:

1. The first graph shows that the relationship between R value of the roof and building cost is linear: the building cost goes up at a constant rate as the R value of

Fig. 17.3. *Teacher page for activity*

the roof insulation increases. This makes sense, since every unit of R costs the same amount. The second graph shows that the relationship between R value of the roof and heating cost is definitely not linear! The heating cost declines very fast as the R value of the roof insulation goes up. See the extension **Direct and Inverse Variation** for a more in-depth look at the difference between these types of variations from a pure mathematical point of view.

3. You can't just get the heating cost at R 31 by averaging the costs at R 2 and R 60, although that does work for the linear function of R value vs. heating cost. This is another hint about how the heating cost and building cost are changing. You could ask students to use the graphs from activity 1 to show why this is so.

4. Example answers:

Example 1.
total cost = heating cost x 240 + building cost (240 is number of months in 20 years)

Example 2.
You take the heating cost for one month and you multiply it by 12 to make it a year, then by 20 for 20 years, then you add that on to the building cost.

Example 3.
24,000 <———building cost   month heat cost———> 123 x 12 = 1476 x 20 =
29,520 <———20 years heating cost
53,520 <———total cost

Help students see connections between the different ways they answer this question. Tying example 1, a very algebraic representation, to example 3, an algorithmic representation using specific values, can help students understand algebraic representations.

5. Tables can be made on paper or on a spreadsheet. Help students use what they did in #4 to set up a formula in the spreadsheet for "20 year total."

Fig. 17.3. *(continued)*

curriculum of this kind, assessment is especially important for focusing students on mathematics in their projects and helping students build from informal experience to more formal mathematics.

The assessment system provides opportunities for students to show their mathematical progress. (An assessment activity example is shown in figure 17.4.) Much complex activity is occurring, and there are many chances for any growth to be measured. Teachers can combine different types of assessments in order to generate the information they need to help students recognize their mathematical growth, demonstrate growth to

parents and administrators, and calculate performance scores.

How does the curriculum support students of all abilities? In the vignette, one group of students was working on an advanced problem they had discovered themselves. All of our application units have a "low floor and high ceiling"—meaning students can enter at various achievement levels, make progress, and advance to more sophisticated or challenging levels, if appropriate. While some students are developing benchmarks for measuring and estimating in meters, others in the class are estimating in cubic meters. The

A SHORT DESIGN PROBLEM

Scary Harry, the mega rock star, needs a new tour bus to carry him around the country on his Mock Rock Tour. You are responsible for designing the interior of this bus. Harry needs a place to sleep, a place to hang out with the band and practice, and a bathroom with a Jacuzzi tub. The band sleeps in another bus, but they all practice together on Harry's bus.

Part 1: Below is a diagram of the empty bus your bus company makes.

(a) Make a rough sketch of how you would divide the space between the three rooms (bedroom, practice room, bathroom).

■ = .5 meter

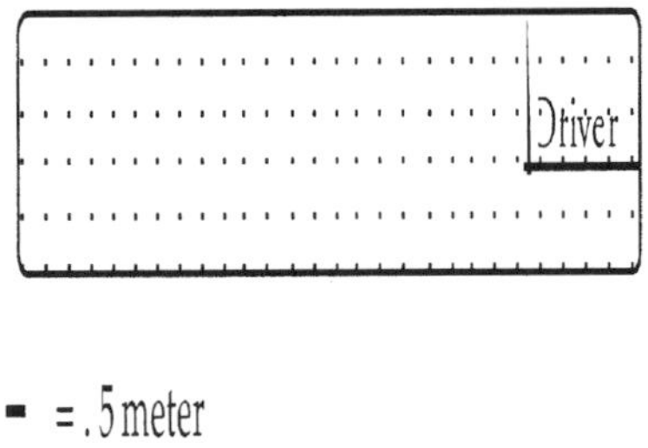

(b) On the basis of your sketch, what do you estimate to be the size of each room?

ROOM	SIZE (in square meters)
Bedroom	
Practice Room	
Bathroom	

Part 2: How did you decide how big to make each space?

Fig. 17.4. *Assessment activity example*

mathematics activities are developed so teachers can match opportunities for mathematics learning to the students' needs. Teachers make the decisions about the particular, available directions and tailor any project to the learning needs of individual students, groups, or classes. Similarly, teachers are able to use extensions and investigations to target and assess individual topic areas.

How do we ensure these units are do-able in today's class-rooms? Although the application units push the boundaries of what has been thought possible in middle school classrooms, they provide an innovative way to use computers while remaining sensitive to access issues in many schools. They furnish curricular reasons for mathematics teachers to get assigned time in computer labs, to cobble together a small group of computers for about a month's time, or to lobby for dismantling the computer lab.

Do a Short Design Problem (Posttest)

Intent:

Student Product:

Math Concepts and Skills:

Time Frame: 1 class period

Materials:
• Student Handout: **A SHORT DESIGN PROBLEM**

What to Do:
•

Teaching Strategies:
We recommend that you grade the post-test based on how well each student employs the particular math learned in the unit to solve the test problem. Use the following suggestions as guidance.

Part 1:

(a)

(b)

Part 2:

Part 3:

Part 4:

(a)

(b)

Fig. 17.4. *(continued)*

IV: Conclusions

The Middle-school Mathematics through Applications Project sought an alternative approach to middle school mathematics. We chose to engage students in mathematics problems, practices, and tools inspired by real-world contexts. The materials integrate real-world applications and middle school mathematics. We constructed the application problems to provide reasons for students' engagement in a wide variety of mathematical practices. Extensive field testing has shown these materials to be usable in today's classrooms, while introducing new ideas, practices, and technologies into middle school mathematics.

We are currently completing development of the final application unit and the last few extensions and investigations. The materials have been extensively field-tested in classrooms in California, Michigan, and

Oregon and have proved extremely engaging to middle school students. At this point, close to 300 teachers have used the units as supplementary materials and over 60 000 students in California and five other states have learned mathematics through an application unit.

Teachers who have used the materials were almost uniformly positive about the experience, believing that the materials encouraged *Standards*-based teaching and increased their students' ability to think, act, and communicate mathematically (Sukenik 1994). Several veteran teachers reported they were finally teaching the way they had always imagined they would and feeling invigorated in their work with students.

Teachers found the introduction of computers into their classrooms somewhat stressful because the technology introduced new management issues, such as troubleshooting problems or dividing students between mathematical activities and computer-design tasks. Even so, most teachers thought computers worth the effort on the basis of the positive response they got from students. Most teachers could gather together a group of computers to use for a month or six weeks at a time or arrange to use the school computer lab. Only a few of thirty teachers were unable to equip their classrooms with a set of computers year-round.

Data on students indicate positive trends. In field-test schools, more students are being placed into algebra. For instance, one teacher found higher numbers of students passing the district's eighth-grade algebra readiness test. All of the students are completing algebra successfully. In past years there was a significant (almost 50 percent) failure rate. Other teachers reported increased numbers of eighth-grade students recommended for placement in ninth-grade algebra.

MMAP materials propose a comprehensive version of a mathematical application, challenge coven-

tional assumptions about the sequence of mathematics learning, integrate the use of computers, and rely heavily on performance-based assessments. The materials have a flexible component organization that enables teachers to use them cumulatively as they both gain comfort with applications in mathematics and gain access to computers. The research and evaluation results available confirm that teachers and students working with these materials reap exponential learning rewards both in middle-grades mathematics and beyond.

References

Berg, R., and S. Goldman. "Learning through Design: Why Design Activities Involve Middle Schoolers in Learning Mathematics." Paper presented at the American Educational Research Association Meeting, New York, April, 1996.

Greeno, James G., Ray McDermott, Karen Cole, Randi A. Engle, Shelley Goldman, Jennifer Knudsen, Beatrice Lauman, and Charlotte Linde. *Research, Reform and Aims in Education: Modes of Action in Search of Each Other*. Working Paper No. 115. Middle-school Mathematics through Application Project. Menlo Park, Calif.: Institute for Research on Learning, 1997.

National Council of Teachers of Mathematics. *Curriculum and Evaluation Standards for School Mathematics*. Reston, Va.: National Council of Teachers of Mathematics, 1989.

———. *Professional Standards for Teaching Mathematics*. Reston, Va.: National Council of Teachers of Mathematics, 1991.

———. *Assessment Standards for School Mathematics*. Reston, Va.: National Council of Teachers of Mathematics, 1995.

Sukenik, Michal. "Evaluation of the Middle-school Mathematics through Application Project (MMAP)." Tel Aviv, Israel: Center of Educational Technology, April, 1994.

Shelley V. Goldman, Jennifer Knudsen, and Michelle Latvala,
Institute for Research on Learning, Menlo Park, California

18

Classroom-Based Curriculum Development: A Case History

LINDA COOPER FOREMAN

As my views of mathematics, learning, and teaching have transformed over time, so has my view of curriculum. Early in my teaching, when my district asked me to develop curricula, I collected activities that would help students remember mathematical procedures and facts, activities that lead students through a logical sequence of steps to solve a complex problem or show why an idea works. If an activity disguised drill and practice in a "fun" mathematics game or puzzle, used manipulatives, or required students to work with partners, it was innovative.

My criteria for identifying and creating worthwhile mathematical activities are very different today:

- Is the emphasis of the curriculum on how students think rather than on getting students to think a certain way?

- Will students' mathematical thinking become public?

- Is the emphasis on understanding concepts and inventing procedures?

- Are a variety of strategies and approaches likely to emerge?

- Are students likely to formulate conceptions and questions that set the stage for thinking about more complex ideas?

- Are there opportunities for students to view in a new light, question, or contradict their prior mathematical conceptions?

- Are the ideas and actions developmentally appropriate, accessible, and challenging for all students?

- Are meaningful extensions and "what if" investigations possible?

- Do manipulatives and models provide a context for seeing meaning and relationships, and will the models remain mathematically faithful as ideas become more complex?

- Will the activity promote meaningful "math-talk"—debate, questions, conjectures, student-invented procedures, and generalizations?

- Are students likely to make connections to other mathematical topics they have studied and to ideas outside of school?

- Is there commentary that helps the teacher anticipate ways that students may respond and the possible mathematical implications of such responses?

Implicit in these questions are the notions that knowing and doing mathematics involve more than knowing procedures and facts, and understanding a mathematical idea is not something that can be scripted or timed. An important moment in my shift to this view of mathematics happened in 1984, when one of my former professors, Eugene Maier, invited me to participate in Math and the Mind's Eye, a project supported by the National Science Foundation (NSF Grant Numbers MDR 8470371 and MDR 8954770) and the Math Learning Center, a nonprofit organization with over twenty years of experience supporting the improvement of the learning and teaching of mathematics. The purpose of the project was to make mathematics accessible and understandable to middle school students by creating teaching methods and materials based on visual thinking.

Dr. Maier described visual thinking as "thinking that draws upon the processes of perceiving, imaging, and portraying. Perceiving is becoming informed through the senses, through sight, hearing, touch, taste, smell, and also through kinesthesia, the sensation of body movement and position. Imaging is experiencing a sense perception in our mind or body that, at the moment, is not a physical reality. Portraying is depicting a perception by a sketch, diagram, model or some other representation" (Maier 1985, p. 3). A major premise of visual thinking is that carefully designed sensory experiences enable students to develop meaningful mental and kinesthetic images of mathematical concepts and processes. These images help students understand, retain, and recall this information. Listening to others talk about their thought processes and mental images fascinates students and prompts new ideas. As students explore mathematics in this manner, ideas make sense, math anxiety diminishes, and confidence grows.

The following personal journal entry describes an episode that occurred early in the Math and the Mind's Eye project and led me to rethink my teaching practice:

MARCH, 1985

Last Tuesday in my general math class I presented the following as the first four tile arrangements in a sequence of arrangements formed according to a pattern:

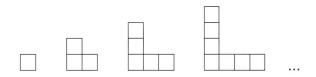

I asked the students to describe their ideas about what the 20th arrangement in the pattern looks like and how many tiles it contains. While the students agreed there are 39 tiles in the 20th arrangement, their ways of looking at it varied. For example:

"There is one tile in the corner with 19 tiles going up and 19 tiles going right."

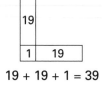

$$19 + 19 + 1 = 39$$

"There are two rows of 20, but the corner has been counted twice so subtract one."

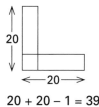

$$20 + 20 - 1 = 39$$

"There is a row of 20 tiles across the bottom with a column of 19 tiles on the left."

$$20 + 19 = 39$$

Several students noted that the number of tiles would always be odd, and that the numbers of tiles in the first 20 arrangements were the first 20 odd numbers.

Casey (repeating general math for the 2nd year) came to the overhead and showed how he could "see" each arrangement as a square whose side length was determined by the number of the arrangement, and removed from the upper right corner of this square was a smaller square whose side length was one less than the arrangement number. Casey said that "what was left" was always an odd number of tiles.

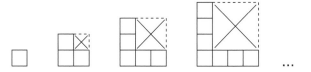

Casey used his diagram to show what he meant and to clarify questions that other students raised. Although he didn't have the language to say so directly, he went on to prove visually—and elegantly—why the difference between n-squared and $(n-1)$ squared is the nth odd number. The class buzzed for the rest of the period and for two days afterward, as they discussed odd numbers and square numbers, generalized about the nth odd number and nth square number, investigated the difference between squares that aren't consecutive, and invented a pattern for the even numbers. In all, the mathematical dialogue was incredibly rich. Students had developed intuitions about the concept of a variable, used inductive reasoning, made and tested conjectures, generalized, discovered a model for square numbers, computed mentally, explored the concepts of oddness and evenness, and were excited by the many "right" ways to view a problem.

Ironically, the textbook lesson for Thursday in my algebra class *stated* the following, with no illustrations: "The difference between the nth and $(n - 1)$st square numbers is the nth odd number, as shown here: $n^2 - (n - 1)^2 = n^2 - (n^2 - 2n + 1) = n^2 - n^2 + 2n - 1 = 2n - 1$." So, before asking the algebra students to open their texts, I wrote $n^2 - (n - 1)^2$ on the overhead and asked the students to describe their ideas about the meaning of the expression. Several read the symbols aloud and others expanded and simplified the expression to obtain $2n - 1$. When asked to discuss their ideas about the meanings of the terms "square number" and "odd number," students responded that square numbers were the numbers 1, 4, 9, 16 . . . and that each square number was the product of some integer times itself. Odd numbers were simply 1, 3, 5, 7, 9 . . .

Next, I posed the visual pattern the general math class had explored. None viewed it as Casey had. I told them that a student in another class had seen each arrangement as the difference of two squares. I asked groups to investigate that idea. They quickly "saw" Casey's thinking and a meaningful discussion and generalization of the difference of consecutive squares followed, including algebraic representations of this and other relationships they could "see." Finally, I asked them to read the text lesson. Some were irritated that the author hadn't included models so they could see what the symbols represented. Others said they felt proud that, based on the models, they had invented an algebraic statement very close to the author's.

Two thoughts strike me after using this activity with both groups of students. First, it is unfair to set limits on what students can do by not providing them with opportunities to try. Second, students at all levels deserve to experience mathematics in a way that brings meaning to symbols and rules. The fact that some students are better at memorizing or mimicking procedures should not preclude them from experiences that enhance understanding. This episode makes me think that teaching isn't something I "do to" students; it's more about providing opportunities for them to discover their mathematical selves by seeing meaning in mathematics.

Shortly after this occurred, I attended a National Council of Teachers of Mathematics (NCTM) annual meeting and heard a presentation about the changing mathematics curriculum and the difficulties teachers face in changing their practice to align with a reformed curriculum. The presenter said that, to change, a teacher must first develop a sense of guilt about the status quo—a feeling that the status quo is wrong. Without guilt, one tends to remain frozen by old practices; with guilt comes a readiness for change. This helped me realize that my first year's experiences in the Math and the Mind's Eye project, particularly the episode involving Casey, had caused me to feel guilt. Thus, I had begun a conscious process of reconstructing my views of mathematics, teaching, learning, and curriculum (Foreman 1987). However, a dilemma soon emerged—my teaching was in transformation, but curriculum materials to support a reform-based practice were limited.

AUGUST, 1986

In my classes now I strive to:

- listen more and talk less
- emphasize understanding rather than remembering
- encourage students to explain, discuss, debate, wrestle with, question, and make sense of ideas
- have students write and talk about their thinking and reasoning
- ask "what do you think?" instead of saying what I think
- ask questions that show genuine interest in students' thinking rather than questions that lead them to a certain way of thinking
- honor students' right and ability to solve challenging problems

Few curriculum materials exist today that view students as mathematical sense-makers or do more than disguise drill and practice. In theory, once we teachers explore activities that give us a feel for what it means to use conceptual models to promote mathematical understanding, and once we have experienced activities that promote invention, we will be able to bring these ideas to whatever mathematical topic we teach and whatever materials we use. In practice, this is a challenge.

This issue came up recently when I led a workshop about the ideas I have learned in the Math and the Mind's Eye project. Teachers were excited by the simplicity and power of the "leveling off" model for the concept of average. All agreed that it seems natural to think of numbers as columns of cubes, and to think of averaging those numbers as the process of leveling the columns. Besides helping us understand the meaning of average, this model prompted insights and strategies for thinking about ideas ranging from mental calculation to finding the average value of a function. Everyone laughed to think that, after years of teaching averaging, not one of us had ever seen or thought of this model. For many, it is a new notion to think of the *concept* of average as something other than the "add and divide" *procedure*. The thought of creating activities that are based on conceptual models can be overwhelming; just sorting activities that use manipulatives to foster conceptual understanding from activities that use manipulatives to disguise drill and practice is a challenge for those of us still sorting out the difference between concepts and procedures.

By the summer of 1987, the Math Learning Center had offered numerous workshops based on the methods and materials from the Math and the Mind's Eye project. Teachers wanted to implement the ideas they experienced in a workshop but felt limited by their mathematical upbringing. They asked for more materials that would support them as they transformed their teaching. Hence, Professor Al Bennett and I agreed to create a guide for organizing and implementing Math and the Mind's Eye activities and other available activities that reflected a similar spirit and philosophy. We had no idea this would become a twelve-year project!

Being in the classroom kept me focused on the curriculum: to support mathematics teachers as educators—*those who educe, or draw out, each student's inner mathematician.*

In 1988 we completed the guide for implementing Math and the Mind's Eye. Next, in response to teacher requests for more classroom materials philosophically aligned with constructivist views of learning and with an expanded view of classroom assessment, we wrote and published *Visual Mathematics* (Bennett and Foreman 1990). Interest in workshops based on these materials spread (in 1993 alone, there were more than 140 nationwide week-long workshops about *Visual Mathematics*). National Science Foundation funding in 1995 led to the 1998 publication of *Math Alive!* (Foreman and Bennett 1998), a comprehensive grades 5–8 curriculum that replaces *Visual Mathematics* and reflects our current thinking.

I no longer view mathematics as a collection of isolated procedures and facts. Similarly, I no longer view curriculum development as assembling a collection of student activities, connected only by chance. I now view curriculum development as creating a cohesive mathematical story line that develops depth and breadth as the teacher and students bring the story to life.

An effective curriculum enables teachers to imagine how their classrooms might look and feel, offering examples of what might come up, not what should come up. It offers teachers the opportunity to examine and question mathematical ideas, to consider mathe-

matical concepts from their own and others' perspectives. Thus, curriculum and professional development are intertwined; the materials provide private in-service opportunities, engaging the teacher in meaningful thought about mathematics and providing options and possibilities for engaging students in the same. *Math Alive!* is structured according to this view of curricula (see figure 18.1).

Determining the specific mathematics content for each grade level of Math Alive! was a challenge. We first considered the mathematical "big picture." We developed activities and models that promoted connections to ideas explored previously and laid conceptual groundwork for more complex ideas. In particular, we focused on mathematical models that would remain faithful over time—for example, we included explorations involving the area model for multiplication that progress naturally across the grades to include products of whole numbers, fractions, decimals, and binomial expressions (see figure 18.2).

Perhaps the greatest challenge in determining content was avoiding assumptions about what students can and cannot do and thus not setting artificial limits on student achievement—a precondition most limiting to youngsters. Working with fifth graders taught me not to make assumptions regarding appropriate questions and engaging content. Sense making comes naturally to children when explorations emphasize concrete representations of concepts and opportunities arise to reason about, puzzle over, and debate situations involving those representations.

Manipulatives and meaningful mathematical models enable understanding and make many topics typically taught in high school accessible to middle school students. For example, teachers from field-test classrooms for Math Alive! report that, with *meaningful models* on which students can base their thinking, sixth graders do far more than enhance their understanding of number systems and increase their facility with computing whole numbers, fractions, decimals, and percentages. Such models enable students to build understanding of the concept of a variable, solve linear equations and some quadratics, establish the Pythagorean theorem, and create sound statistical, probabilistic, and geometric arguments.

By building on models and concepts examined in fifth and sixth grade, seventh-grade students invent formulas and algorithms, explore and generalize about arithmetic sequences, graph and solve linear and quadratic equations (with and without the graphing calculator), conduct and analyze statistical experiments, devise geometric constructions, create "Pythagorean proofs," carry out simulations, and grasp complex probability concepts.

144

Visual Reasoning
Focus Teacher Activity (cont.)

ACTIONS

4 Select one of your student's methods from Action 2 or 3. Ask the class to imagine the 50th (and/or 100th, 75th, etc.) figure usin... ...dent's method and to determine the numb... ...cuss. Repeat as appro...

5 (Optional) Pose ...tions for groups to ... sequence. Ask for ... methods.

a) How many tile ... spaces" (i.e., tile ...

b) Which figure ...

c) Two consecuti... other) have a to...

Lesson **5**   Visual Reasoning
Focus Teacher Activity (cont.)

ACTIONS

COMMENTS

2 (continued.)

"The 1st figure has 5 tile; for each subsequent figure, you add 2 tile (1 on each side); so the 10th figure has 5 plus 9 groups of 2 tile, or 5 + 9 × 2 = 5 + 18 = 23 tile."

...nd 1 in the middle of
...side and 1 in the
...side and 1 in the
...side and 1 in the
...1 tile."

...l tile missing tile; the
...sing tile; and the 3rd
... So the 10th is a 3 by
...ence, it has 3 × 11 −10

...scribing their think-
... the 10th figure and
...f tile it contains. It is
...out this lesson that
...lving visual pattern-
...d that students show
... Eyes to Mathematics,
...tivities.)

...to see how many
...eard others share in
...the 20th figure. This
...the value of sharing

Visual Reasoning   Lesson **5**

◉ Focus Teacher Activity

OVERVIEW & PURPOSE
Students use visual reasoning to predict the size and shape of the 4th, 5th, 10th, and other figures in sequences of arrangements of tile. They examine these visual patterns from many points of view and have the opportunity to extend their own and their classmates' ways of thinking about the patterns. This is the first of many Visual Mathematics patterning activities that lay important groundwork for the study of algebra.

MATERIALS
✔ Tile, 30 per student.
✔ Tile for use at the overhead.
✔ Focus Master A (optional), 1 transparency or 1 copy per group.

ACTIONS

1 Arrange the students in groups and give tile to each student. Form the 3 tile figures shown below on the overhead.

Tell the students the above figures are the first 3 figures in a sequence that is based on a pattern that you have in mind. Ask them to use their tile to form what they think are most likely to be the 4th and 5th figures in your sequence, based on what they observe about the first 3 figures. Have volunteers build their 4th and 5th figures at the overhead and describe how they decided their shape and size.

2 Ask the students to each imagine in their mind's eye what they believe the 10th figure in the sequence would look like, without building the intervening figures. Have volunteers build or sketch their 10th figure at the overhead and describe how they decided its shape and the number of tile it contains.

COMMENTS

1 Encourage students to think and work privately before sharing, thus allowing several ways of thinking about the pattern to emerge. The 4th and 5th figures most commonly formed by students are shown here:

Asking students to guess what pattern you have in mind, allows you to acknowledge all ideas but focus on a specific pattern. You may want to extend an interesting alternate pattern suggested by a student.

2 Some students may find imagining larger figures difficult at first. However, this usually becomes easier after listening to others explain their reasoning. Thus, it is important to elicit a variety of approaches.

Here are some possible descriptions of the 10th figure, based on the pattern suggested in Comment 1:

"The 1st figure has 3 tile on top and 1 tile on each side; the 2nd has 3 on top and 2 on each side; the 3rd has 3 on top and 3 on each side. So the 10th has 3 tile on top and 10 on each side, or 10 + 10 + 3 = 23 tile."

(Continued next page.)

Math Alive!, Course I / **53**

Fig. 18.1. Sample activity from Math Alive! Course I (Used with the permission of the Math Learning Center.)

In the eighth grade, students' work in algebra, geometry, probability, and statistics takes on a more symbolic, traditional look. At first glance, one might question the appropriateness of such symbolic work in middle school—until one listens closely to the thinking behind the students' work. For example, in eighth grade much of the students' work with Algebra Piece models (manipulatives produced at the Math Learning Center and included throughout the Math Alive! curriculum) goes on in their minds or in quick sketches, and

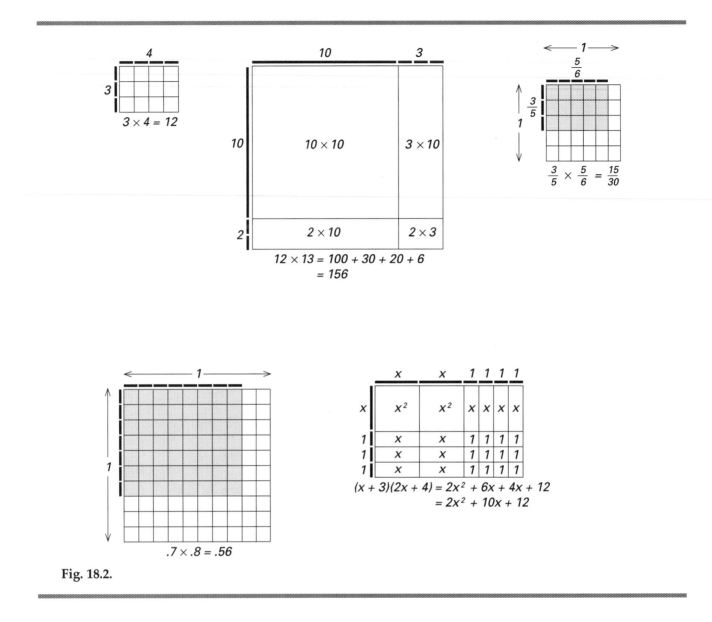

Fig. 18.2.

students use algebraic symbols to represent and communicate their images and actions. Students regularly build sophisticated inductive and deductive arguments that are based on relationships they "see" in images — "I wonder . . . I notice . . . I conjecture . . . I can prove that . . . What if . . ." are part of their everyday dialogue.

To inform my writing and keep moving forward with development of the Math Alive! curriculum, I taught the same group of students for four years. Although working in the classroom slowed the curriculum-writing process, it kept me grounded in the realities of daily classroom life, led to surprising adaptations, and prompted curriculum ideas that I might never have considered at each grade level. I gained first-hand knowledge about the thinking an action

might elicit, the mathematical implications of such thinking, and possible responses. Being in the classroom kept me focused on the real purpose of the curriculum: to support mathematics teachers as *educators*— those who educe, or draw out, each student's inner mathematician.

Spending extended time with the same group of students provided evidence of the potential for developing mathematical power in students immersed over time in reform. This experience, combined with extensive conversations with other teachers struggling to reform their practice, also heightened my sensitivity to the tensions created by implementing a different curriculum and instructional style. Such tensions include the following:

- Adopting an investigative spirit about teaching—a willingness to explore with the students—implies not always having answers.

- Honoring the constructivist view of learning implies letting students' mathematical thinking determine the direction of an activity; this also means not always knowing the direction or amount of time a lesson will take.

- Engaging students in group work, hands-on activities, discussions, and debate implies a noisy, active classroom.

- Subscribing to the belief that within every student exists an accessible and capable mathematician implies allowing students to struggle with ideas and resolve their own questions.

- Breaking away from traditional habits, such as comforting puzzled students by showing them methods and solutions and asking questions that lead the student to a certain way of thinking, means students, parents, and colleagues accustomed to a traditional approach may resist and suggest a teacher's job is to give answers.

- Moving on to another topic, knowing that students still have questions and misconceptions, implies abandoning a mastery-based, behaviorist approach.

- Viewing assessment as an ongoing process of seeking insights about the development of a student's mathematical thinking means more than testing and giving grades.

For a reform curriculum to be effective, there must be options and support for dealing with such issues. A teachers' resource book, *Starting Points for Implementing Math Alive!*, provides philosophical background about the curriculum, options for addressing issues that may arise in the classroom, and an extensive collection of assessment possibilities (figure 18.3). In addition to the discussion in *Starting Points*, suggestions for working with parents, assessing student thinking, organizing and pacing instruction, and other classroom-related issues are embedded throughout the Math Alive! lessons.

To support students in the shift to an NCTM *Standards*-based approach and help their families understand the approach, the students from my classroom are editing, under the guidance of Luise Wilkinson, a series of home reference books titled *What's the Big Idea?* in which different "big ideas" in mathematics are discussed and illustrated (Wilkinson and Foreman forthcoming). The sequence of topics parallels the sequence of lessons in Math Alive!, and actual discus-

sions from classrooms are presented as dialogues. The "characters" in *What's the Big Idea?* model typical mathematical discourse and thinking. Parents can glimpse classroom activity and get support for helping their children with homework. Teachers see how their classrooms might look—students collaborating to solve problems, using manipulatives and models to reveal meaning, sharing their thinking and questioning ideas. At the end of each chapter are problems and activities for students to investigate with family members.

Many studies support the need to involve parents in the mathematical development of their children, and there is evidence across the United States that parents can be effective in either facilitating or blocking reform. To promote parental support for mathematics reform, Lou Saponas, a parent volunteer and graduate student in mathematics education, has created a set of materials and workshops called *Math Roundtables* (Saponas and Foreman forthcoming) that outlines activities illustrative of the Math Alive! curriculum to help parents, teachers, administrators, and others prepare to lead "math nights." The goals of "math nights" are—

- to help parents support their children's creative thinking, mathematical understanding, and confidence;

- to expose parents to the benefits of reform;

- to enable parents to promote change in their children's school; and

- to encourage home environments supportive of a reformed view of middle school mathematics.

Although effective curriculum materials provide built-in opportunities for teachers to grow in their thinking about mathematics and pedagogy, even more dramatic growth occurs when groups of teachers engage in in-service experiences that enrich their mathematics backgrounds, address the challenges of implementing a *Standards*-based curriculum, and promote the development of collegial support networks. To provide such experiences, there is a nationwide network of teacher-leaders who use Math Alive! in their classrooms and lead workshops for teachers.

Why use an approach that requires such hard work and may create discomfort in parents and teachers? My answer is that it offers students access to their potential. Over the past four years, I witnessed students changing from a heterogeneous group with a wide range of mathematical achievement to a group of powerful thinkers with an average score in the 92nd percentile on *Standards*-based statewide tests.

A larger-scale documentation of student achievement comes from the QUASAR Project (Quantitative

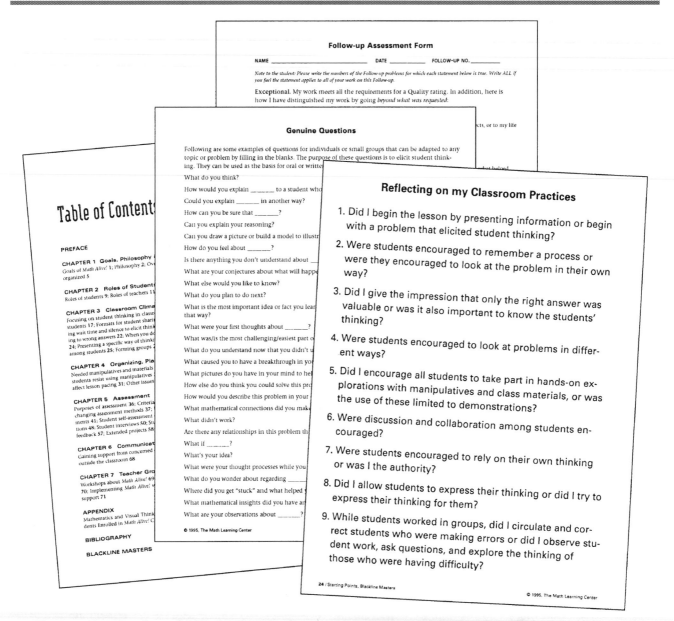

Fig. 18.3. *Excerpts from the Math Alive! teachers' resource book,* **Starting Points for Implementing Math Alive!** *(Used with the permission of the Math Learning Center.)*

Understanding: Amplifying Student Achievement and Reasoning), conducted from 1990 to 1995 by the Learning Research and Development Center at the University of Pittsburgh. The QUASAR researchers studied the development and implementation of enhanced mathematics-instruction programs for students in middle schools in economically disadvantaged communities. One focus of this study was the implementation of the Visual Mathematics materials (the precursor to, and foundation for, the Math Alive! curriculum) in

grades 6 through 8 at Portsmouth Middle School in Portland, Oregon. Portsmouth is an inner-city school with a high percentage of economically disadvantaged students. The only curriculum materials used at Portsmouth during this five-year study were Visual Mathematics and preliminary Math Alive! materials.

Throughout the study, students were assessed regularly using the QCAI, a set of open-ended tasks designed by QUASAR researchers to measure student proficiency with complex mathematical ideas and thinking. Portsmouth students showed substantial and steady gains throughout the project in "the kind of complex thinking and reasoning skills and mathematical knowledge deemed essential by the mathematics education community" (George and Smith 1995). Caucasian students' average scores increased 36 percentage points between the sixth and eighth grades, and African American students' average scores increased 40 percentage points over the same time. The outcomes at Portsmouth Middle School exceeded those at the five other sites in the study, all of which used *Standards*-based materials but not the Visual Mathematics curriculum.

Further documentation comes from the results of standardized tests given each spring to all district eighth graders to determine their high school mathematics placement. The number of Portsmouth students who qualified for high school algebra or geometry increased steadily from 8 percent in 1991 (no eighth graders had studied Visual Mathematics that year or previously) to 41 percent in 1994. In 1995, more than 60 percent qualified. Further, beginning in the fall of 1992, in spite of the fact that students entered ninth-grade instructional environments that were substantially different from those in Portsmouth classrooms, the researchers found that Portsmouth students "enrolled in nonremedial mathematics classes in high school in much greater numbers and increased numbers of students have experienced success in these courses" (George and Smith 1995).

Another positive outcome at Portsmouth relates to computation, an area of concern to many who are considering adopting a reform curriculum:

> Students have continued to grow in computational proficiency over the course of the project, even though this is not the focus of the curriculum and no special preparation for standardized testing occurred. This suggests that by focusing on the development of understanding of concepts, rather than on procedures, students are able to apply meaning to more algorithmic situations and hence also to develop proficiency in basic skills. (George and Smith 1995)

Teachers from schools using the Math Alive! curriculum confirm this result. When the curriculum is implemented consistently for several years, students have opportunities to construct deep and lasting mathematical understandings that positively affect their ability to reason, solve problems, and compute.

As demonstrated by the Portsmouth data, a curriculum such as Math Alive! that embraces the spirit and content of the NCTM *Standards* can have a dramatic effect on students' achievement, even in the most challenging settings. My own classroom experiences, to-

gether with reports such as the Third International Mathematics and Science Study (National Center for Education Statistics 1997), provide further evidence to refute the common myths reinforced by traditional mathematics curricula: there is only one right way to solve a mathematics problem; the teacher's role is to give answers; manipulatives and models are used only in the primary grades or for remediation; mathematics is arithmetic; some people can't do mathematics; sharing ideas and working together on mathematics problems is cheating.

Yet, even with such compelling evidence, changing the way mathematics is taught prompts uncertainties, as illustrated by this more recent journal entry:

FEBRUARY, 1998

An important moment happened yesterday. At the end of a class period filled with conjectures and debate about a locus problem, Morgan wrote in her journal, "In our class we are mathematicians. We do the work of mathematicians instead of imitating their results."

In spite of all that I have learned about good teaching, old beliefs still affect my practice. There are times I still struggle with letting students struggle, with letting wrong ideas just sit for a while, with holding back my ideas so students can find theirs, with knowing when to step in with a clue and when to step back, and with finding the "right" question to draw out their thinking rather than to impose mine. So, a moment like Morgan's is important for me in my search for signs that my practice is changing.

My learning about mathematics, learning, teaching, and curriculum development is a journey. Where I am now is reflected in the Math Alive! curriculum, informed by thousands of experiences, people, and ideas. But most of all, where I am now is an outcome of the incredible lessons I have learned by watching young mathematicians at work.

What I wonder about most these days is: What are the questions we haven't thought to ask these young mathematicians? What are the questions we haven't given them opportunity to ask? Perhaps answers will come in the next stage of my journey. For now, I hope that Math Alive! will provide other teachers opportunity to accelerate their journey and provide young mathematicians unimpeded progress in theirs.

References

Bennett, Albert B., Jr., and Linda Cooper Foreman. *Visual Mathematics*. Vols. 1 & 2. Salem, Oreg.: The Math Learning Center, 1990.

Foreman, Linda. "On Guilt and General Math." *The Oregon Mathematics Teacher* (September 1987): 26–27.

Foreman, Linda Cooper, and Albert B. Bennett, Jr. *Math Alive!* Salem, Oreg.: The Math Learning Center, 1998.

George, Elizabeth, and Margaret Smith. QUASAR Progress

Report, Fall 1995, Portsmouth Middle School, Portland School District. Pittsburgh, Pa.: University of Pittsburgh, Unpublished manuscript.

Maier, Eugene. "Mathematics and Visual Thinking." *Washington Mathematics* (Spring, 1985), pp. 1–3.

National Center for Education Statistics. *Third International Mathematics and Science Study—Eighth Grade.* Washington, D.C.: U.S. Government Printing Office, 1997.

National Council of Teachers of Mathematics. *Assessment Standards for Teaching Mathematics.* Reston, Va.: National Council of Teachers of Mathematics, 1995.

———. *Curriculum and Evaluation Standards for School Mathematics.* Reston, Va.: National Council of Teachers of Mathematics, 1989.

———. *Professional Standards for Teaching Mathematics.* Reston, Va.: National Council of Teachers of Mathematics, 1991.

Saponas, Louise, and Linda Cooper Foreman. *Math Roundtables.* Salem, Oreg.: The Math Learning Center, forthcoming.

Wilkinson, Luise, and Linda Cooper Foreman. *What's the Big Idea?* Salem, Oreg.: The Math Learning Center, forthcoming.

Linda Cooper Foreman, *The Math Learning Center, Portland State University, Portland, Oregon*

PART THREE

IMPLEMENTING CHANGE IN THE CLASSROOM

19

Standards-Based Middle School Mathematics Curricula: What Do Students Think?

ROBERT E. REYS, BARBARA J. REYS,
DAVID E. BARNES, JOHN K. BEEM,
RICHARD T. LAPAN, AND IRA J. PAPICK

Lawyers never knowingly ask a witness a question that will provide an unexpected answer or an answer they don't want to hear. This may be common practice in courtrooms; however, in schools teachers often ask students questions that produce a range of surprising answers. This was our experience in examining responses from students about new *Standards*-based middle school mathematics curriculum materials being used in their classrooms. Examining students' responses helped us learn about the mathematical experiences they liked and disliked, and it reminded us of the challenges associated with constructing and implementing new mathematics curricula in a manner that satisfies all constituents.

Background

During the 1995–1996 school year, middle school teachers and students in fifteen school districts in a midwestern state investigated four emerging *Standards*-based middle school mathematics curricula—Six through Eight Mathematics (STEM) (now Middle Grades Math

Thematics), Connected Mathematics Project (CMP), Mathematics in Context (MiC), and Seeing and Thinking Mathematically (STM) (see appendix to this article). Each curriculum is unique, although all illuminate a vision of mathematics learning that—

- focuses on applications or problem-based learning in environments that interest and motivate students to investigate;

- launches and connects significant mathematical concepts, building a strong base for various high school mathematics options;

- provides opportunities for significant interactions among students and teachers using a variety of communication methods (writing, explaining, presenting, defending, etc.);

- provides a rich source of materials for teachers at various professional development entry levels to learn from and use; and

- incorporates various forms of assessment to gauge student understanding and inform instruction.

The teachers were participants in a National Science Foundation (NSF) project that used collaborative curriculum investigation as a vehicle for professional development (Reys et al. 1997). They represented a

Research reported herein was supported by a grant from the National Science Foundation (#ESI 9453932). The findings and opinions expressed are those of the authors and do not necessarily reflect either the position or policy of the NSF.

153

range in academic preparation and experience, but all shared a strong desire to implement significant change in the mathematics programs of their middle schools. During the school year, they field-tested units from each of the four curriculum projects and met once every four to six weeks to interact with colleagues about the curricula and instructional techniques they were using.

"What I liked best was the problems— the way they all hooked together and how one question led to another. The worst is probably that they asked you to explain and write about your answer to questions . . . you really can't explain."

Throughout the school year, students were experiencing "pieces" (one or two units) from each project rather than the complete program. Every six weeks, teachers interrupted their traditional curriculum with a unit from one of the *Standards*-based curriculum projects. These units were selected by the teachers and in most cases matched mathematical content that was being omitted from the traditional program. As the year progressed, many teachers devoted more time to these units than their textbooks (Reys and Reys 1997).

Near the end of the school year, we asked project teachers to invite their students to write the project directors a letter describing their thoughts about the "new" mathematics curriculum materials. Their answers revealed a range of thinking, including conceptual strength, weakness, misunderstanding, insight, prejudice, and brilliance. Responses were not received from students in every teacher's classroom, nor did every student within a class write a letter. However, over 300 letters—ranging in length from one or two sentences to several pages—were received.

In general, student responses focused on specific activities, games, lessons, units, or projects within a unit. However, students also reflected on global issues that transcended the curricula and seem to have broad relevance for all involved with curriculum development, teaching, and helping children learn mathematics. Our purpose here is neither to report the students' endorsement nor condemnation of their experiences but rather to offer a sampling of the multiple perspectives these middle school students had as they reflected on their experiences with *Standards*-based mathematics curricula. Their exact expressions (warts and all, in-cluding misspellings and grammatical errors) provide a level of authenticity that would be forever lost in any editing of their comments. We have organized the student comments around some common themes frequently voiced in the letters:

- Is this mathematics?
- Doing mathematics is better than hearing about it!
- Solving problems is hard / challenging.
- The "old" mathematics was more comfortable.
- Working in groups is good / hard / awful.

Is This Mathematics?

Everyone has a personal definition of what mathematics is as well as what it means to learn mathematics. These meanings are formed by an accumulation of experiences and encounters, usually within school. By the time students reach middle school, they have studied mathematics for hundreds of hours and established what mathematics means to them. If their experiences have consisted of reading and reviewing two pages from textbooks, learning a variety of new vocabulary and computational procedures, or regularly doing a series of practice exercises, then the students' view of learning mathematics is closely associated with these experiences.

When students think of mathematics as computation, they are likely to associate mathematical learning only in this context. Conversely, they may think, if they are not computing, they are not doing mathematics. Each of these notions was expressed in the following responses:

"In the other math you just bacialey learn adding, subtracting, multiplying, and dividing. In new math you have word problems." —6th grader

"It wasn't really like math." —7th grader

"Math ain't suposed to be stories. Its numbers." —8th grader

Students recognized that the new materials were different, not only in appearance but substance.

"I liked this material, because it had things related to life. I hate our regular book because we never do anything interesting." —7th grader

"They give you more knowledge than the math books & they're alot of fun." —7th grader

"I think you learn more than you would with math books." —7th grader

One characteristic of the new middle school curricula is their emphasis on mathematics in the real world.

The establishment of contexts for real-world exploration required more reading than in traditional texts. This placed a heavier responsibility on students to read and to tell or write about their solutions.

> "I didn't really like the books because it was a lot of reading." —7th grader

> "There was a lot of writing! . . . more of an english class than math. We write way too much compared to usually just writing down #'s." —8th grader

> "What I liked best was the problems—the way they all hooked together and how one question led to another. The worst is probably that they asked you to explain and write about your answer to questions [that] you really can't explain." —6th grader

The students' expectations, based on previous experiences in mathematics classes, were quite different from their experiences with the new material. Time is needed to help students view communication, specifically reading and writing, as integral parts of mathematics learning.

Doing Mathematics Is Better than Hearing about It!

Research documents the value of students being actively engaged in learning mathematics. Mathematics is not a spectator sport but one that requires a sustained commitment of time and energy. A central tenet of *Standards*-based middle school curricula is the necessity of active involvement in learning mathematics (NCTM 1989, 1991); this involvement includes measuring, using manipulatives, gathering data, and building models. The added attention given to using hands-on activities was noticed by many of the middle grade students.

> "I liked this because of the physical activies we did. We got to move around instead of sitting in our seats working and listening to the teacher the whole time." —6th grader

> "It makes learning easier because you get to actually do it."—7th grader

> "You get to get involved. I like hands-on units better, you learn by doing." —8th grader

> "I liked doing these experiences because you can find out by yourself and learn without the teachers help." —8th grader

> "I liked it because it got you more involved in the activity, therefore it was easier to understand." —8th grader

> "I liked it because it was a change of what you normally do in a math class. The thing that I liked the best was when I actually got to do the experiment because I think I learn better." —7th grader

Support for activities and projects that involved the students was strong and almost unanimous. The activities increased student interest in learning and made the mathematics more meaningful, contributing to greater understanding.

Solving Problems Is Hard/Challenging

Problem solving—a standard that cuts across all grades and is an integral part of learning—is the heart of mathematics. Yet, problem solving represents different things to different people, and student responses often reflected their preconceived ideas and experiences concerning problem solving. One of the expectations middle school students seem to have established is that solving problems should neither be hard nor require much time. Nearly all students stated directly or suggested that the problems encountered in the new curricula were significantly more challenging than problems they had experienced previously.

> "I did not like these experiences because they are too hard thinking problems and I don't think they should be so hard. I found them too hard because I had to think about them. They were very interesting but they were not fun." —6th grader

> "I found the books to be complicated, maybe for hard thinkers and for me my mind starts to wander when I concentrate on one problem too long." —7th grader

> "Solving problems is very complicated. It seems to me that there are simpler ways of doing math." —8th grader

We view these remarks as an indictment of traditional mathematics that, under the guise of problem solving, have conditioned students to expect relatively quick and easy solutions to mathematical tasks.

The NSF middle school curriculum projects have taken a significant step toward implementing more challenging, yet appropriate, problem solving in which students find a solution to a situation wherein no ready-made solution exists. Thus, problem solving, in its reformed nature, creates some tension and uneasiness as students struggle to arrive at a solution. Although some students were critical of the challenging

155

problem-solving experiences they encountered, other students appreciated the challenge.

> "I liked the new material. It is interesting. They made it more fun and interesting. I liked the different scenarios and problems the best."
> —7th grader

> "I found them hard because you really had to pay attention and you definetly had to think! It was not that easy to do. It was interesting because I found out things I never knew in lower grades. It was fun!" —7th grader

> "I liked it because it really streached my brain."
> —7th grader

> "I found that the questions in the books were challenging. And I liked it because I think thats what teachers should do, challenge younger minds to the extream and I think that can be good. I would like to do this next year because it was like a challenge, and I feal much better when my mind has had a challenge because its like exersizing. I am going into 8th grade next year."

> "Yes, some of it I did find hard . . . but you would get into it and you wouldn't want to stop."
> —7th grader

The "Old" Mathematics Was More Comfortable

Change is difficult for all of us. Each teacher and principal participating in this project personally experienced challenges and frustrations associated with implementing the new instructional strategies and curricula. They had to be flexible and adapt to the philosophy of the programs, learn about the content of units they chose to teach, often study them carefully to become familiar with the mathematics, learn to incorporate new forms of assessment, and sometimes even reconfigure their classroom and school schedule. The project focused on the participating teachers and how change affected them; however, the letters told a different story and provided a vivid reminder that students are also concerned about change in their classes. Some students were excited about the changes and the opportunities to learn new and interesting ideas.

> "Its fun to learn new stuff, especaly when you learn stuff your parents dont know how to do the stuff." —7th grader

> "I never liked math until we got out of those old, boring books and got into these units."
> —7th grader

> "I liked it because it was a change of what you normally do in a math class. The thing that I

liked the best was when I actually got to do the experiment because I think I learn better."
—8th grader

> "It is way better then having the teacher bore you by telling how to do it then telling you what page it is, but the new math material is more hands on and learn more about math not just #ers."
> —8th grader

> "The old way of teaching was just fine. I had no problem with it. I wish that you would use more traditional ways of teaching." —7th grader

Working in Groups Is Good/Hard/Awful

One philosophical component of reformed middle school mathematics curricula is the value placed on group work in facilitating mathematics learning. Group activity may take different forms, from reaching a consensus on what the problem is to collecting data to making sure everyone in the group contributes to, or at least understands, a solution. These experiences lead to making presentations that explain different approaches and solutions. The *Standards* advocates collaboration in mathematics classrooms as an approach to learning and teaching that will promote greater success for all students. The message from students was quite mixed on the value of this approach.

> "If you didn't understand something then some one in the group did." —6th grader

> "What I like the best is groups we got to help each other figure things out." —6th grader

> "I really need a tutor to help me with math because I never did like math. I think it works out with me in a group because they actually explain things to me so that I understand!"
> —7th grader

> "Yes, I liked these activities, because you got to work in groups and when you got a wrong answer it wasn't just you getting it wrong but the whole group." —7th grader

> "It was fun and easier working in groups when you have more heads thinking together."
> —8th grader

Strong responses arguing against mandatory group work were also voiced. Some students were concerned about who they worked with; others felt that too much time was wasted in their groups.

> "The thing I like the least is working in groups, because I think its easier to work by myself."
> —6th grader

"I think it is harder to work with friends because you want to talk so much. It is also hard to concentrate working with someone you don't like."
—7th grader

"The groups slowed me down. I like to learn new things but I don't want to wait until everyone in our group learns it before we get to go on."
—8th grader

Perhaps the most adamant of these responses was from a seventh-grade student:

"You are trying to lift up the bottom 35% of students at the expene of the top 5–10%. You're doing this by forcing us into group work with low students and putting us into slave labor by helping them."

This note is from a bright and articulate student who sees herself as being held back by the extensive involvement in group work. It could be ignored; yet, it seems important to reflect on what this student is saying about how she wants to learn. It also provides a vivid reminder that individual learning styles and preferences exist. Designing classroom instructional approaches that accommodate *all* students is truly a challenge.

Conclusion

Our discussion has focused on student reactions to the new curriculum materials. Certainly, we recognize and acknowledge the critical role teachers play in the successful implementation of any materials. In fact, in many student letters, it was not possible to differentiate between impressions about materials and the teacher's role in using materials. For example, one seventh-grade student summed up her evaluation of the new materials in this way:

"I think everything was great because Mrs. _____ made the mathematics fun and interesting."

We learned from reading and reflecting on the students' responses about specific aspects of the new curriculum materials they liked and disliked. We were also reminded how difficult it is to create materials that appeal to everyone. Perhaps most important, we learned these middle-grades students are developing attitudes and beliefs about mathematics and are willing to share their thinking. These students are the real con-

sumers of emerging reform mathematics programs. They are the recipients of both the process and product of mathematics being espoused in the *Standards*-based curricula. Their thoughts and impressions provide a valuable perspective on curriculum change that must not be lost in our continuing effort to reform mathematics.

References

National Council of Teachers of Mathematics. *Curriculum and Evaluation Standards for School Mathematics*. Reston, Va.: National Council of Teachers of Mathematics, 1989.

———. *Professional Teaching Standards for School Mathematics*. Reston, Va.: National Council of Teachers of Mathematics, 1991.

Reys, Barbara J., and Robert E. Reys. "Standards-Based Mathematics Curriculum Reform: Impediments and Supportive Structures." *NCSM Journal of Mathematics Education Leadership* 1 (July 1997): 3–8.

Reys, Barbara J., Robert E. Reys, David Barnes, John K. Beem, and Ira Papick. "Collaborative Curriculum Investigation as a Vehicle for Teacher Enhancement and Mathematics Curriculum Reform." *School Science and Mathematics* 97 (May 1997): 253–59.

Appendix

The following four middle school curricula were explored in the M[3] Project:

Connected Mathematics, developed at Michigan State University (Glenda Lappan, Project Director). Publisher: Dale Seymour Publications

Mathematics in Context: A Connected Curriculum for Grades 5–8, developed at the University of Wisconsin (Tom Romberg, Project Director). Publisher: Encyclopaedia Britannica

Seeing and Thinking Mathematically (MathScape): Connections in a New Middle School, developed at the Educational Development Center. Publisher: Creative Publications

Six through Eight Mathematics (Middle Grades Math Thematics), developed at the University of Montana (Rick Billstein, Project Director). Publisher: Houghton Mifflin

Information about these curricula, including staff development opportunities, publisher information, sample lessons, scope and sequence, implementation stories, and related literature, can be obtained on the Show-Me Center Web site: www.showmecenter.missouri.edu

Robert E. Reys, Barbara J. Reys, David E. Barnes, John K. Beem, Richard T. Lapan, and Ira J. Papick, *University of Missouri, Columbia, Missouri*

20

The Power of Discourse

CONNIE LAUGHLIN AND
JOHN C. MOYER

A growing number of school districts have decided to require all students to enroll in an algebra course, usually at grades 8 or 9. Equity arguments are often the impetus for these mandated algebra decisions. In 1987, the U.S. Department of Education (Mathematical Sciences Education Board 1988) found that, other than demographic factors, the strongest predictor of earnings nine years after graduation from high school was the number of mathematics courses taken. Yet, many students, particularly students in poor communities, are not given an opportunity to study algebra.

Mandates alone, however, only force access to algebra; they do not ensure success. Failure rates of inner-city, ninth-grade students who *voluntarily* enroll in algebra have traditionally hovered around 50 percent. Further, assessments of those who do pass imply they are not able to apply basic algebraic concepts in problem-solving situations, and they do not understand many of the structures underlying algebra. As a result, many urban districts are struggling as they attempt to implement algebra-for-all mandates. Districts and teachers struggle to answer fundamental questions:

- What is algebra?
- How can teachers know when students know algebra?
- How can teachers nurture the development of algebraic thinking across grade levels?
- What is a proper balance between understanding and skills?
- What principles can teachers use to inform teaching decisions as they attempt to implement the NCTM (National Council of Teachers of Mathematics) *Curriculum and Evaluation Standards* (1989) and the *Professional Standards for Teaching Mathematics* (1991)?

Clearly, there is a serious need to reform the algebra curriculum in the nation's schools. Reform, however, cannot occur solely within the ninth-grade classroom. Edward Silver (1997, p. 3) suggested that we take—

> . . . seriously the recommendations of the *Standards* regarding the development of algebraic proficiency throughout the school curriculum, beginning with experience with patterns and the development of informal understanding of variable in grades K–4, moving to a deeper understanding of, and greater facility with, variables and equations and different representations for functional relationships in grades 5–8 . . .

The authors gratefully acknowledge the participation of Rosann Hollinger, a mathematics teacher at Fritsche Middle School, Milwaukee, Wis., and her eighth-grade students in the preparation of this article.

This article describes how Ms. Conroy, a middle school mathematics teacher in a large urban school district, is able to help her eighth-grade students gain a deeper understanding of variables and different representations for functional relationships. The students in her classes are more than 50 percent minority, heterogeneously grouped, and of low socioeconomic status, with 75 percent of them qualifying for free or reduced-cost lunch.

I See a Pattern

Ms. Conroy planned to spend the evening assessing her students' written work from the day's mathematics activity, I See a Pattern, which she adapted from an activity in *Math and the Mind's Eye* (Arcidiacono and Maier 1993). All three of her prealgebra classes had been engaged in the forty-five–minute activity and had worked well in their groups. Discussions among the students had been lively and productive. At the end of the period, Ms. Conroy asked students to individually describe what their groups had found; she was curious about how well her students had written up their findings.

The students' written work confirmed the conclusions she had drawn while observing her classes. Each group, as a whole, had arrived at a solution to the activity. However, close to one-third (twenty-six out of ninety-one students), when working individually, could not discuss the pattern their groups had seen in the blocks and the table. (Figure 20.1 is representative of some of these students' work on these papers.) From

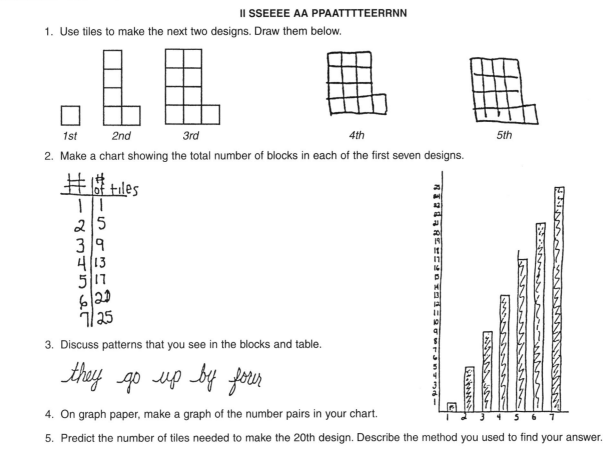

II SSEEEE AA PPAATTTTEERRNN

1. Use tiles to make the next two designs. Draw them below.

   1st 2nd 3rd 4th 5th

2. Make a chart showing the total number of blocks in each of the first seven designs.

# of tiles
1	1
2	5
3	9
4	13
5	17
6	21
7	25

3. Discuss patterns that you see in the blocks and table.

   they go up by four

4. On graph paper, make a graph of the number pairs in your chart.

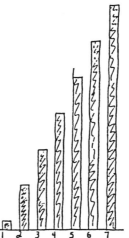

5. Predict the number of tiles needed to make the 20th design. Describe the method you used to find your answer.

   just add 4 ~~1~~ until you get up ~~3~~ to 20
   77

Fig. 20.1.

these results, Ms. Conroy knew that she would have to spend more time in a class discussion about I See a Pattern. Many questions passed quickly through her head:

- What would be the best format for this discussion?
- How much more time should she spend on this problem?
- How could she orchestrate the discourse to nurture deep reasoning about variables and functional relationships?
- What could she do to engage every student in the discourse?

The key to Ms. Conroy's success is a teaching–learning cycle that relies heavily on classroom discourse and incorporates an assessment loop (see figure 20.2) that she adapted from the *Assessment Standards for School Mathematics* (NCTM 1995). The activity above demonstrates how Ms. Conroy *interprets* the evidence she has *gathered* from her students so she can *use* the results to devise a *plan* for the subsequent lesson.

The *Professional Standards for Teaching Mathematics* (NCTM 1991) emphasizes the importance of meaningful, high-quality discourse in the classroom. Ms. Conroy works very hard to make her classroom a place where everyone participates in meaningful discourse, carefully orchestrated to achieve predetermined learning goals. She takes her own role in the discourse very seriously and expects her students to take their roles seriously, too. Ms. Conroy has previously discussed her expectations with her students. For her own part,

she is guided by five tips for improving classroom discourse:

- Never say anything that a student can say.
- The option of not participating does not exist.
- Everything that a student says is valued, even if it is incorrect.
- Do not repeat student answers.
- Answer the question "Is this right?" with another question, not yes or no.

Discourse on I See a Pattern

Ms. Conroy decided to spend a whole day helping her classes understand how to write the patterns in I See a Pattern using algebraic representations. As she pondered what the best format for class discussion would be, she recalled Standard 2 of the *Professional Standards* (NCTM 1991, p. 36), which states:

> A key aspect of the teacher's role in orchestrating classroom discourse is to monitor and organize student participation. . . . Teachers must judge when students should work and talk in small groups and when the whole group is the most useful context.

She began the second day of I See a Pattern with a whole-group discussion focusing on the table (below) that nearly everyone in class had made correctly, despite the fact that they did not have a deep understanding of the functional relationship. She planned to break the class into groups of four as soon as the students became engaged in the problem. By using both small- and large-group discussion, she hoped the discourse would lead the students to a deeper understanding of variables and functional relationships.

Design #	# of Tiles
1	1
2	5
3	9
4	13
5	17
6	21

For the whole-group discussion, she placed the table on the overhead, and the students quickly began discussing patterns they had seen the day before.

MARCUS: They go up by four.

Ms. Conroy knew that this imprecise language should be clarified.

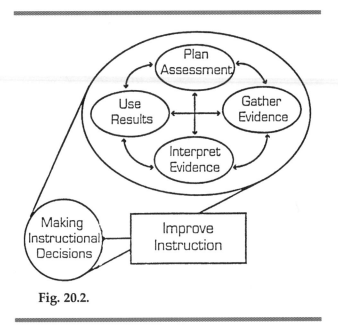

Fig. 20.2.

MS. CONROY: You know that we have been emphasizing precise mathematical language. What goes up by four?

MARCUS: The number of tiles goes up by four.

MS. CONROY: What about the design number?

ANITA: That's easy—the design numbers just go up by one.

MS. CONROY: How do these patterns help you predict the number of tiles needed to make the twentieth design?

ANITA: That's easy, too. Just add 4 until you get up to 20.

Because one of the discourse goals Ms. Conroy adopted from the *Professional Teaching Standards* (NCTM 1991) was to provoke students' reasoning about mathematics, she seized this opportunity to do so.

MS. CONROY: OK, everyone. In your group, discuss what Anita just told us. Will her method help you predict the number of tiles needed to make the twentieth design?

Students began their discussions in groups of four. Ms. Conroy walked around with a notebook, listening intently to what the groups of students were saying. In her class, the students were expected to communicate about mathematics. They were used to paying attention to one another's ideas and reasoning together. They also accepted responsibility for helping each other. Here is the dialogue that occurred in one group:

JUANITA: Well, I understood what Anita said, and I think she is right.

TONY: What did she say?

JUANITA: See, you weren't listening! She said to just add 4 until you get to 20.

TONY: OK, I think that is what I did, too, until my answer was 77.

NICKY: I can add 4 five times and get to 20 . . . 4, 8, 12, 16, 20. But that is not what Anita meant. So maybe we can say what she was doing in another way.

JUANITA: Well, when the first design was built, there was one tile. To get the second design, you add 4 to the number of tiles in the first one, and then there are five tiles. To get the third design, add 4 to the number of tiles in the second design to get nine tiles. So, see, that's where the "Add 4" comes from.

MICHAEL: You have to add 4 twenty times, and then you know the number of tiles in the twentieth design.

NICKY: Well, I sort of get it. But if I add 4 twenty times, well $20 \times 4 = 80$, but our answer is 77. . . .

TONY: OK, we didn't add 4 twenty times, only add 4 nineteen times. See (pointing to the chart up to the sixth row), you add 4 five times to get to the sixth design, and we started with 1 for the first design. I think I see a new pattern.

Discussions similar to this one occurred around the room. The nature of this discourse is important. As noted in Standard 3 of the *Professional Standards* (NCTM 1991, p. 45):

> Whether working in small or large groups, students should speak to one another, aiming to convince or to question their peers. Above all, the discourse should be focused on making sense of mathematical ideas, on using mathematical ideas sensibly in setting up and solving problems.

The follow-up whole-group discussion was spirited, and many groups began to offer various algebraic generalizations either discovered during the class discussions or written the day before. Standard 2 of the *Professional Teaching Standards* (NCTM 1991, p. 36) says: "For the discourse to promote students' learning, teachers must orchestrate it carefully." Since the ability to make algebraic generalizations was the weakness in her students' oral and written work the day before, Ms. Conroy capitalized on the points raised and presented a new challenge to the whole class. She wrote some formulas on the overhead that she had observed the students generate while in small groups.

$$4x - 3 \qquad (x + (x + 1))2 - 1 \qquad (n - 1)4 + 1 \qquad x + 4$$

She hoped these expressions would challenge the students to think.

MS. CONROY: I want you to determine which of these formulas will work to predict the number of tiles for *any* design. You may have discussed one or more of these rules in your group. How do you think that someone came up with each of these rules? I will give you some time in your groups to discuss this, and then we will share what we have learned in a large-group discussion. Everyone in every group should be prepared to contribute to this discussion.

Groups attacked this new challenge with confidence. Some of the generalizations were harder to analyze than others. The large-group discussion revealed that many of the students understood which formulas were correct and, more important, possible ways to start making generalizations.

MS. CONROY: Let's start with $4x - 3$. Does this work? How could you get this formula?

CORY: Yes, it works. I tried it with several rows in the chart [see figure 20.3], and it always gives you the correct number of tiles for a design. But I am still having a hard time knowing how to get that in the first place.

MS. CONROY: Who wants to explain how you get this formula?

CHRIS: Well. I didn't see it yesterday, but I started to see it today. Look at the pictures, not the chart. (Chris comes up to the overhead.) After the first design, there are always some towers of four tiles. In the third design, there are two towers of 4. This one tile hanging off the end could be another tower, but it is missing three tiles. See . . . on the fifth design, there are four towers of 4 and one that is missing three. You multiply by 4 because there are four tiles in every tower and then you subtract 3 because of the three that are missing.

MS. CONROY: Cory, can you retell us what Chris just explained?

CORY: Sort of. Can I draw another design? OK, on the sixth design, there are really six towers of four tiles, but one is missing three. . . . Yes, I see now. But I still think this is hard.

MS. CONROY: Yes, it can be, Cory. But you worked hard and you got it. Now we have to explain the next one: $(x + (x + 1))2 - 1$. Who can do that?

LORENA: I think that one came from our group. I'll start, but you guys help me if I get stuck. We did not look at the tiles. We were just using the chart. Can I come up to the overhead? . . . OK. Look at these numbers:

2	5
3	9
4	13

We were just looking for number patterns. The first one I noticed was $2 \cdot 3 - 1$ gave me 5. But

Clockwise from lower left: Sarah Wierzbinski, Katie Rothe, Danielle Washington, Rosann Hollinger (teacher), Lucy Rodriguez (at board), Jessie Jones, and Jim Lopeman

that did not work for the next pair. See $3 \cdot 4 - 1 = 11$, but we wanted the answer to be 9.

BILL: We just kept looking and then I saw that $(2 + 3) \cdot 2 - 1 = 9$. And this pattern does work all the way down the chart. See

3	9
4	13
5	17

$(3 + 4) \cdot 2 - 1 = 13 \ldots (4 + 5) \cdot 2 - 1 = 17$

LORENA: Yes. So then we said that the first number is x and the second number is $(x + 1)$ and our formula is $(x + (x + 1))2 - 1$.

MS. CONROY: Did you check that it worked for any other numbers not on this chart?

ANNA: Well, it worked for four pairs of numbers, so we thought that it must be OK!

MS. CONROY: Would everyone please verify that this formula really works for any number?

GEORGE: Our chart from yesterday went down to ten designs, and our answer on the chart for 10 is 37

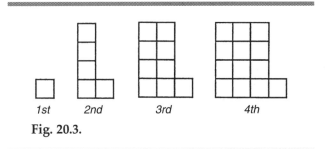

1st   2nd   3rd   4th

Fig. 20.3.

tiles. But when I use Bill's rule, I get 41. Something is wrong.

SARAH: It doesn't seem to work for 8 either. My answer is 29 and this rule gives an answer of 33.

MS. CONROY: OK, Lorena's and Bill's group. What is happening here? It sure sounded good a few moments ago.

BILL: I don't see why our rule is wrong. It always gives a number on the chart.

SANDY: Wait. I think I see it. You *are* right. It always gives a number on the chart, but the answer you get is one below the one you really want. Look back at $(3 + 4) \cdot 2 - 1 = 13$. You started with 3, so $x = 3$. The answer for design #3 is 9, but you get 13, which is really the answer for 4. So you are off by 1.

GEORGE: Not really 1. The answer is off by 4.

SANDY: I meant the design number is off by 1.

MS. CONROY: I think this class discussion has highlighted a very important point for us to remember. When you are using a variable it is important to know what the variable represents. In this case x represented a design number and the answer from the formula should give you the number of tiles in that design. So Lorena's group will need to revise their formula. Who can tell us what the revised formula should be?

Similar discussions occurred for $(n - 1)4 + 1$ and $x + 4$. Each time, Ms. Conroy solicited many students' reactions, instead of stopping after a correct answer or showing them the right answer. Each time, her tone of voice and her questions showed the students that she valued their thinking more than the answer they gave.

The whole-group discussion continued for fifteen more minutes. The analysis of other students' reasoning about patterns was fruitful. The students understood how two answers could look very different and, yet, represent the pattern. Some of the generalizations were more easily explained by using the chart. Others came directly from using the tiles. For some (e.g., $x + 4$), the students needed to know the previous number of tiles. They realized this was a drawback, especially if asked to find the answer for larger numbers. They also gained a clearer understanding of the importance of identifying specifically what a variable represents and how it can unify both columns of a table.

Near the end of the period, Ms. Conroy placed on the overhead the completed assignment of a student from a different class (see figure 20.4). She led the class in a brief discussion of the qualities that made that student's solution an example of good written communi-

cation. The students then discussed what could make the paper even better; in particular, a lively discussion centered on whether the points on the graph should be connected. The class concluded that the line connecting the points highlighted the linearity of the relationship between the design number and the bricks. However, the line should not have been drawn because the design numbers were whole numbers and the ordered pairs were discrete.

. . . many students, particularly students in poor communities, are not given an opportunity to study algebra.

Both good oral and written communication skills must be modeled for students. The majority of this lesson focused on discourse and sense making of the various mathematical formulas, but these students are often asked to communicate their reasoning in writing. By showing all the students a well-written response to the previous day's activity, Ms. Conroy gave them a model to use the next time they might have a similar problem.

Conclusion

Ms. Conroy's goals in promoting discourse in her classroom were shaped by her knowledge of the *Professional Standards*. They are (1) to provoke students' reasoning about mathematics; (2) to actively listen to her students' discourse so she can orchestrate the discourse in ways that will promote students' learning; and (3) to monitor and organize the discourse so that all students participate in some way. The instructional decisions that Ms. Conroy made were guided by these three goals. The implementation of her decisions produced fruitful discussions in small groups and in whole-class sharing. The analysis of the first day's work revealed weaknesses in student thinking clarified in the subsequent discussion. If she had not spent this time in class discussion, she would have wasted a valuable learning opportunity. The students, led by a master teacher who made good decisions about discourse and content, moved farther along the road to understanding various representations of algebra.

References

Arcidiacono, Michael J., and Eugene Maier. "Picturing Algebra." In *Math and the Mind's Eye*. Salem, Oreg.: The Math Learning Center, 1993.

II SSEEEE AA PPAATTTTEERRNN

1. Use tiles to make the next two designs. Draw them below.

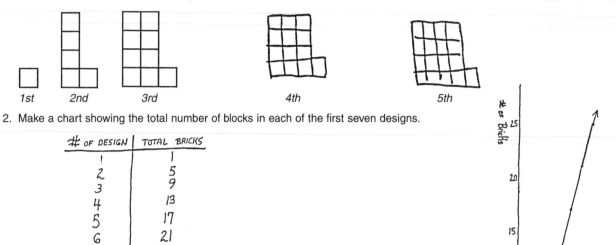

1st   2nd   3rd   4th   5th

2. Make a chart showing the total number of blocks in each of the first seven designs.

# OF DESIGN	TOTAL BRICKS
1	1
2	5
3	9
4	13
5	17
6	21
7	25

3. Discuss patterns that you see in the blocks and table.

TOTAL # OF BRICKS GOES UP BY FOUR. FOR EACH ˅DIAGRAM ~~THE # Complete~~ ~~Add~~ THE # OF COMPLETE ROWS IS ONE LESS THAN THE DESIGN #. Total # of bricks is always an odd number. The # design goes up by 1. The total # of bricks added on each time is always a multiple on 3. Graph is linear. Formula can't ~~be~~ ~~*****~~ because graph is linear. have an exponent

4. On graph paper, make a graph of the number pairs in your chart.

5. Predict the number of tiles needed to make the 20th design. Describe the method you used to find your answer.

77. Used formula 4x-3.

So,
4·20-3=
80-3=
=77

Fig. 20.4.

Mathematical Sciences Education Board. Report of a Symposium: *Mathematics Education: Wellspring of U.S. Industrial Strength.* Irvine, Calif.: December 15–16, 1988: 6.

National Council of Teachers of Mathematics. *Assessment Standards for School Mathematics.* Reston, Va.: National Council of Teachers of Mathematics, 1995.

———. *Curriculum and Evaluation Standards for School Mathematics.* Reston, Va.: National Council of Teachers of Mathematics, 1989.

———. *Professional Standards for Teaching Mathematics.* Reston, Va.: National Council of Teachers of Mathematics, 1991.

Silver, Edward A. "Algebra for All—a Real-World Problem for the Mathematics Community to Solve." *NCTM Xchange* 1(2) (1997): 1–4.

Connie Laughlin, *Steffen Middle School, Mequon, Wisconsin,* and John C. Moyer, *Marquette University, Milwaukee, Wisconsin*

21

Mathematics the Write Way

ANN M. ENYART AND
LAURA R. VAN ZOEST

"What good is writing in a math class? We work with numbers, not words."

"Maybe writing does have a place in math class, but where do I start?"

Writing can enhance mathematics instruction and provide opportunities for students to deepen their mathematical understanding. Writing in mathematics class can provide benefits for both teachers and students and improve the overall classroom environment. In the following, we share ideas for using writing in the mathematics classroom, examples of students' writing from Ann's middle school classes, and suggestions for getting started.

Benefits to Students

Writing to Increase Reasoning Skills

More than ever before, employment opportunities require mathematical thinking. Teachers have an obligation to help their students become more than efficient calculators. As one student commented, "Knowing the math but not being able to explain it is kind of like having a car and not being able to drive it." When students write about their solutions to problems, they are required to interpret the meaning of their answers.

One technique to help students reason through in-formation is to have them write a letter to a student (real or fictional) who has been absent from class. The theme of the letter could be to explain a specific concept, review an extended lesson or unit, or tell the student what he or she had missed on a certain day and how to make it up. We have found that students really enjoy this activity and are willing to ask questions if they can't explain things clearly. An extension is to have students exchange papers to see if they can understand what the others have written.

Writing also provides opportunities for students to use higher-order thinking. One example from Ann's seventh-grade mathematics class is the "jump experiment." Students in three classes used a calculator-based laboratory (CBL) to collect data on the height of their individual jumps. This activity involved a flashlight aimed at a light sensor; each time a student jumped and landed, the CBL program calculated the amount of time the sensor sensed light and converted this air-time into jump height. The students used these data to find basic statistics for each class, as shown in table 21.1 and figure 21.1. After creating several graphs and charts, the students were asked to interpret the data in a whole-class discussion.

The interpretation of the data turned out to be far more challenging for the students than either calculating the statistics or creating the graphs and charts.

TABLE 21.1.

Hour	1st	4th	7th
Mean	12.6	13.3	14.6
Minimum	5.5	1.3	1.3
First quartile	9.2	8.2	9.6
Median	12.1	10.9	11.5
Third quartile	14.9	12.7	16.0
Maximum	22.8	48.2	50.7
Number of jumpers	21	21	21

After the class discussion, the students were asked to respond individually to the following questions in a report format:

- The mean of each class is very close. How could this happen?
- "Your class is the best group of jumpers." Support this statement with evidence.
- Using all of the evidence, which class is the best group of jumpers?

The following are representative selections of student responses to the third question:

> "I think that [7th hour] had the best group of jumpers. As I looked through my information the thing we did that really caught my eye was the box-and-whiskers plot. The box-and-whiskers plot showed me that there were more higher jumpers in that class than lower ones. This struck me because all of the other classes were opposite with more lower jumpers than higher jumpers. [7th hour]'s higher numbers were also more

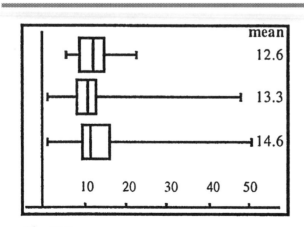

Fig. 21.1.

spread out than any others. . . . Another reason I believe they are the highest jumpers is because they jumped the highest on average (14.6)."

> "I think that [first hour] has the best group, because if you look at the chart. They have a close range of jumps. They also have one of the highest Q3's [3rd Quartile]. They also have the highest minimum. They also have a higher Q1 than [fourth hour]."

The individually written reports required *each* student to make sense of the discussion and come to her or his own conclusions about the data. Putting their thoughts in writing encouraged the students to synthesize multiple representations of the data. After the reports were written, the class discussion was richer and student involvement increased. Errors in analysis, such as the student's conclusion that a closer range of jumps means higher jumpers, were exposed by classmates who focused on the data rather than the individual whose conclusion was incorrect.

Writing to Encourage Self-Reflection

Reflective writing encourages students to *think about* their thought processes and become self-regulators of their learning, an important skill of successful problem solvers (Schoenfeld 1992). Reading reflective writing also provides the teacher with greater insight into the students' thought processes and levels of understanding. Requiring students to comment specifically on the *sense* of their answer encourages them to develop the practice of questioning whether their answers are reasonable.

Learning logs provide an opportunity for students to generate a record of their learning and practice self-reflection. One practical approach to compiling a "log" is to have students do their homework on the right-hand page of a notebook and write comments about their thinking and questions on the corresponding left-hand page (the reverse for left-handed students). These comments can help students when they study and also become a record of their growth over time. The students' questions provide an opportunity for the teacher to respond to them on a one-on-one basis by jotting a quick note or suggestion. If a particular question is shared by a number of students, the teacher will be cued to address it during the next class session.

Another easy way to encourage self-reflection and provide useful feedback to the teacher is the "exit pass" —an index card or other small piece of paper on which students write one thing they learned during class and one question they still have. These "exit passes" must be turned in before they leave the class. The passes are quick to read, and yet, they force students to reflect on the day's lesson while it is still fresh in their minds. In particular, this technique motivates students to write without adding any additional grading to the mounting "to do" pile of most middle school teachers.

Writing to Deepen Student Understanding

Writing can become an integral part of mathematics instruction through the opportunities it provides students to deepen their understanding of mathematical concepts. One example of this occurred when one teacher's class was working with percentages using the vehicle of sales taxes and tips. Students were given the sales tax or tip percent and asked to find the sales tax or tip amount, given the original cost, or to find the original cost, given the sales tax or tip amount; one side of the question requires multiplication and the other division. When the students were given a set of questions, the teacher heard them say, "Now, do you divide or multiply here?" and observed them trying both operations and choosing the more reasonable result.

Although this approach produced the correct answer, the students did not understand why their chosen operation worked. To improve their understanding, they were asked to explain their reasoning in writing; this required them to think about what they were doing and analyze why an operation worked in a given situation. Writing helped clarify and deepen their understanding of the process.

Benefits to the Teacher

Writing to Assess Student Understanding

Along with deepening students' understanding, writing provides teachers with valuable feedback: the teacher can discover if students really understand, regardless of the correctness of their answer. When an answer is correct, the students' written explanations help a teacher distinguish whether the students really understand a concept or simply mimic a demonstrated process. Conversely, having the students explain their thinking about a problem can help the teacher see whether errors involve miscalculations or misunderstandings. For example, on one question a student was one number "off" on the median and the teacher initially assumed that he had just written it down incorrectly. On reading the student's explanation of his work, however, she found that the student did not understand the importance of putting the numbers in order before picking the middle number.

Writing can also be beneficial in assessing student understanding during a class session. For example,

when students communicate that the teacher doesn't make sense, it is not always clear what is confusing and who, exactly, is confused. A few vocal students may be speaking for the whole class. Are only a few students confused or the majority of the class? Having students quickly jot down what they do and don't understand gives each student an equal voice and helps the teacher prepare for the next class meeting.

Writing helped clarify and deepen their understanding of the process.

Other times, writing can verify or disprove a *teacher's* sense of the students' understanding. For example, a teacher spent considerable time discussing units, square units, cubic units, and the importance of having the same units for each dimension before finding the perimeter, area, or volume of a shape. The students had worked on converting fractions to decimals specifically so they would not make common mistakes such as changing 1 1/4 to 1.14 instead of 1.25. She then gave them a routine exercise:

> Carlton Michael Strutherford III found the volume of his class's chameleon cage. Unfortunately, he was not paying attention to his wise and beautiful math teacher and made some errors. Please point out Carlton's mistakes and explain what he did wrong.
>
> length = 1′6″   w = 9″   h = 10 1/2″
>
> $1.6 \times 9 \times 10.12 = 145.73$ volume = 145.73 square feet

When the teacher read her students' work, she found that the exercise had been far from routine. In fact, she was shocked at how many students defended Carlton's work despite his volume of *145.73 square feet* for the class's very ordinary chameleon cage. The following responses are representative of her students' lack of understanding:

> "I don't think that Carlton did anything wrong. He was supposed to multiply and he did."
>
> "The only mistake he made was he forgot to change all of his units to inches or to feet before he multiplied to find the volume. The volume would be either in feet or inches."
>
> "The volume should be in cubic feet. Volume has 3 dimensions so it should be in cubic units."

If not asked to write, the students' misconceptions would have gone undetected. This experience provided insight into how firmly rooted misconceptions can be and pointed out the need for more intense experiences that would help students confront their misconceptions.

Writing to Assess Student Perceptions

Writing can identify students' feelings and attitudes toward mathematics class and help the teacher monitor the effects of classroom activities on them. In some cases, students can become partners in professional development. For example, one student's comment— "When we ask questions you should get to the point and not go and on about unnecessary stuff we know"— prompted one teacher to think hard about her approach to answering student questions. Although she was answering the questions the students had *asked*, she wasn't specifically answering the questions they had. This led to a concentrated effort on her part to understand what the students already knew before responding to their questions.

At the end of the year, it is helpful to have students respond to this prompt: "What I liked most this year was . . ." This allows the student to choose an activity, approach, or theme that had particular meaning for them. Asking the students to respond to "What I would change from this year is . . ." also provides insight that can be used in planning future classes. Examples of practical suggestions that students have provided in the past include:

> "Writing down the agenda on the board and keeping it there for absent students would really help them to catch up."

> "Slow down. When you talk to [*sic*] fast I can't understand what you're talking about."

Building Student-Teacher Relationships

Writing to Understand Students

Knowing who the students are and what they know can help teachers design courses to better meet student needs. Mathematical autobiographies are an interesting way to find out students' past mathematical experiences and current attitudes toward mathematics. For example, at the beginning of the year students can create a bar graph to show their feelings about mathematics at different grade levels; this can be combined with a mathematics autobiography: "Tell me about your mathematical journey." Later, reading these autobiographies again—after having time to connect names with faces—can be particularly helpful. By that time, the teacher has seen examples of the students' behav-

iors and abilities in class and can connect their past experiences to their current actions.

Middle school students will often reveal deeply personal experiences and feelings that help their teachers understand them. For example, the following are responses to the prompt "Dear Mrs. Enyart, I think you should know . . .":

> "My foot just fell asleep. I have 2 dogs & 2 guinea pigs. I did have 3 but one died. I have a brother that has AIDS. I have a brother that is getting married. My mom yells at me alot [*sic*]."

> "I think you need to no [*sic*] that my parents are divorced and my mom's last name is [last name] so you can't mess up saying her last name."

> "What I think you need to know is that I like your class very much and it is starting to inspire me for being an engineer or architect. Math is one of my favorite subjects. I also want to tell you that when I'm older I'm going to be rich, because I need enough money to pay my working maid. I'm going to hire a maid because I HATE cleaning. I'm going to also have a big beautiful house in Connetecut [*sic*] and work in New York City."

Although this information is not related directly to mathematics, it can help teachers understand why a student is or is not "connecting" with mathematics.

Personal needs are revealed naturally when students are given the opportunity to write.

Josh was a very quiet, polite, and well-mannered student who appeared so well adjusted that his teacher did not feel he required much attention. He did seem to need some help mathematically (at times he seemed to "give up" on problems) but not emotionally or behaviorally. As part of a unit on percents, Josh's class was required to write a story that involved percentages in the context of burns and their severity. The students were asked to describe a burn situation and perform calculations to indicate the nature and type of burn. The following is an excerpt from Josh's story: "There was a kid who was cookin [*sic*] eggs and moping [*sic*] the floor. He smellet [*sic*] something burning so he went to check his eggs and he sliped [*sic*] and his hand hit the bottom of the pan . . ."

Josh's teacher shared the excerpt with a teacher aide in her classroom and found out that much of the story was real. Josh had four younger brothers and sisters and, as a seventh grader, did a large share of the work around the house. In fact, he was responsible for much of the care of his siblings. This information helped the teacher understand some of Josh's behavior in mathematics class. When Josh gave up on doing his work, she encouraged him in ways appropriate to his situation.

Writing to Increase Communication

Journals can be an exciting way to develop ongoing communication between the teacher and individual students. The most effective journal entries grow out of specific classroom experiences or events in the students' worlds and do not have short correct or incorrect answers. Some examples of journal prompts that have worked well are these:

> Today we used graphing calculators in math class. What did you learn about linear equations that you didn't know before?

> Yesterday we elected a new president. What math was involved in displaying the election results?

> What was the most important thing you learned in class today? Explain.

> If you were teaching this class, how would you figure out how well students understood fractions?

> Last weekend's ice storm caused severe tree damage. What does surface area and the fact that the trees hadn't yet lost their leaves have to do with the damage?

Prompts allow students a positive outlet for thinking, ideas, emotions that they might otherwise express in negative behavior. Middle school students are not the most tactful writers, therefore thick skin is often needed when reading their journals. It is important to provide students the freedom and confidentiality to share negative feelings about the class, their fellow classmates, and their teacher. Although this can be uncomfortable, knowing how students feel allows teachers to see more clearly how their actions affect students.

Once students realize that teachers read and care about what they write, the content and writing naturally improves over time. It is very important that the teacher respond to what each student has written. Even if the response is "Yes, I see what you mean" or the sketch of a "smile face," the student will know that the teacher cares about what was written. Middle school students are often excited when journals are returned, turning quickly to see what the teacher wrote. It is important that any comments made be upbeat and encouraging as well as empathetic and thought-provoking.

Journals, however, can be well intended but easily set aside because of impractical implementation. Determining what is practical for an individual teacher requires experimenting with the frequency of collection and with different formats, such as notebooks, single pages, or folders. If using journals in a number of classes, stagger the collection dates. Do not expect to collect and read a hundred journals the week grades are due.

Getting Started

As you begin to incorporate writing in your mathematics class, here are some closing suggestions. Start with small steps that don't radically change the nature of your class; this can ease you into writing in mathematics class and convince you of its effectiveness. For example, if you are in the habit of giving multiple-choice or short-answer tests, try adding one or two questions that require that students explain their thinking or describe their problem-solving strategy. You can also use "exit passes" and individual prompts as easy ways to try out writing in your mathematics classes.

Clearly communicating expectations to students in advance can alleviate some of the discomfort they may feel when asked to write in mathematics class for the first time. Reassuring students that the focus is not on writing skills encourages them to participate. Starting small and keeping things simple will ease any discomfort that writing in mathematics class might cause you or your students. Remember also that English teachers in your building will be your allies as you join them in helping students become literate.

Like all things, writing in mathematics class should be done in moderation. We have presented a wide range of ideas, but it would be unrealistic to think that any one teacher can incorporate all of them into classes at all times. A small number of carefully selected writing tasks can provide significant feedback without placing a burden on either the students or the teacher. Setting reasonable objectives for incorporating writing into classrooms will ensure that writing becomes an enjoyable and natural part of teaching. Modify these ideas as needed so that they will fit into your curriculum and be practical for *you* to implement.

Reference

Schoenfeld, Alan H. "Learning to Think Mathematically: Problem Solving, Metacognition, and Sense Making in Mathematics." In *Handbook of Research on Mathematics Teaching and Learning,* edited by Douglas A. Grouws, pp. 334–70. New York: Macmillan; and Reston, Va.: National Council of Teachers of Mathematics, 1992.

Ann M. Enyart, *Hastings Middle School, Hastings, Michigan,* and Laura R. Van Zoest, *Western Michigan University, Kalamazoo, Michigan*

22

Mathematics by E-Mail

EVELYN M. SILVIA

Access to electronic mail (e-mail) offers many interesting sources of information on mathematics and numerous opportunities for exchanges of mathematical ideas among people who would have no contact otherwise. This article offers highlights of my recent experience assisting a middle-grades student with a science project on a topic in mathematics. With a few exceptions, all contacts were by electronic mail. The few exceptions were the initial contacts, the sending of ideas for consideration, copies of references, and a copy of the completed project.

This process illustrates a way to create links between middle-grades students and mathematicians and mathematics educators. Completion of such projects offers students a more realistic picture of what it means to do mathematics. The better the students' understanding of the many-faceted nature of mathematics—particularly beyond computation—the more likely they are to make connections and meaningful applications.

Electronic mail facilitated the whole process by allowing more efficient exchanges of information than afforded by regular post. There were several times when my being able to respond quickly averted costly misdirection of energy. E-mail offers the capacity for almost instantaneous feedback. With e-mail, if a point raised by the student is easy to answer, the answer or guidance is returned quickly; if the point raised requires a more significant response, the student can be told an approximate time when response will be forthcoming. This greatly minimizes unnecessary frustration and increases likelihood of the student's persistence on long-term projects. Because a particular project might take longer than the student had ever experienced, the near-immediate response afforded by e-mail can be important to the level of success achieved.

Some Background

In September of 1995, I was pleasantly surprised to receive (by regular post) a short inquiry from an eighth grader requesting my assistance with the design of a mathematics research project. (The student was one of many attendees at a Center for Talented Youth awards ceremony at which I spoke in May of 1995. This particular ceremony was for the purpose of distributing awards to Northern California youths who had achieved the distinction of having scored in the 700–800 range on the SAT-M or SAT-V before the age of thirteen. After the program, I talked with him briefly and gave him several mathematics problems on which to work; at the time, I offered to send him additional problems on request.) The student's letter stated he had "an upcoming science project in which he was considering using a mathematics-related subject" as his research. I responded with a willingness to assist and included my e-mail address. In addition, I requested more information and asked the student to reply to the following questions:

Are you thinking of something that starts with an idea from science and then uses mathematics, or can the whole focus be something from mathematics?

Has your teacher given you some basic rules to follow in terms of format, length, when due, etc.?

There are several ways to research a project in mathematics. The three that come to mind right away are (*a*) start with a problem in mathematics and see how much of it can be solved or what ideas can be obtained from working on it, (*b*) do a thorough study of some area of mathematics or of a famous mathematician including explaining some of the mathematics that has been done in connection with that area or person, or (*c*) study the mathematics that is related to some career in mathematics. Is one of these what you had in mind?

The student responded by e-mail. The research project, assigned for the student's eighth-grade sciences class, could focus on mathematics; the format of the project needed to offer a problem or research title with a hypothesis followed by the application of methods, procedures, or mathematical proofs of results obtained in pursuit of the hypothesis; the result of the study needed to be reported with both a poster display and a written report; and the project was due in January, which allowed for about three months of work. Of the three ways suggested, the student preferred "the idea of starting with a problem in mathematics, trying to solve it, and obtaining results from it." I acknowledged receipt of the response by e-mail and indicated that possible problems would be forthcoming.

Armed with the needed information, I forwarded three ideas for consideration. One of them was a Faux Billiards Investigation, described below: the other two consisted of excerpts from books (see Pappas 1992; Perl 1978; Sobel 1975) that would lend themselves to generating appropriate problems. The three ideas were sent by regular post because the excerpts from books would have been difficult for the student to find if only the references had been sent, and the Faux Billiards Investigation had figures and graphics available in software to which the student was unlikely to have access. The enclosures were accompanied by a letter offering to send more problems if the ideas sent did not pique the student's interest. The following advice was given:

It is most important that you find a question that will interest you! Since you are going to be spending a fair amount of time working on your problem, you want it to be something that you will look forward to working on and that looks like fun.

The Faux Billiards Investigation Prompt

A normal billiards table looks like a pool table with fewer holes; a billiards table has holes only in the corners (i.e., no side pockets). For "Faux Billiards" we form rectangular tables using graph paper and assume that there are holes or exit pockets only in the upper right (R), upper left (L), lower left (l), and lower right (r) corners. We trace out paths for the ball according to the rules given below and then record the corner of exit (C) for the ball.

FAUX BILLIARDS PROBLEM

Find $C(m, n)$ = the exit corner for an "*m* by *n*" faux billiards table where *m* is the number of rows (height) and *n* is the number of columns (width) and travel of the billiard ball is according to the following:

Rules for Travel

1. The ball always starts from the lower left hand corner.
2. The path is determined by going along the possible diagonals given by the grid of the graph paper (no retracing or backtracking);
3. The ball exits when and only when you reach one of the other three corners of the faux billiards table.

Examples

(*a*) Use the "4 by 6" faux billiards table in fig. 22.1 to show that $C(4, 6) = L$.

(*b*) Find $C(3, 2)$.

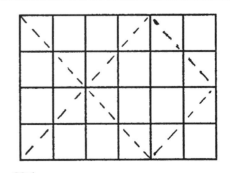

Fig. 22.1.

We want to be able to predict (conjecture, know) the corner of exit for any faux billiards table without actually having to trace out the path. To get some ideas for how $C(m, n)$ might be predictable, we first collect some information (data).

Fill out the following chart for $C(m, n)$, using the notation r = lower right corner, l = lower left corner, R = upper right corner, and L = upper left corner. In the table, the width (number of columns) for the table is given across the top row, and the height (number of rows) is given in the first column. We have filled in $C(4, 6)$ and $C(3, 2)$ to help you get started.

A completed chart (see figure 22.2) is the first step toward the search for hypotheses or results. Remember that the goal is to come up with general statements concerning the outcomes $C(m, n)$ based on properties of m, n, or relationships involving m and n. The chart is *only an aid* toward a scientific process.

1. Did you notice any patterns?

2. Are there any general statements you can make that would hold for all the values that you obtained in your chart? These observations are descriptions of properties of the chart only.

3. Is there anything that you observed for the chart that you believe is true in general? You can state such claims as conjectures. Something holding for your chart does not necessarily mean that it would be true in general. You may observe something that is true only for five cases, twelve cases, etc. Until you can prove any of them, claims based on your observations can be labeled as conjectures only.

C	1	2	3	4	5	6	7	8	9	10
1										
2										
3		r								
4						L				
5										
6										
7										
8										
9										
10										
11										
12										

Fig. 22.2.

Highlights of Interactions

The following are excerpts from some of the e-mail exchanges that occurred as the project progressed; they offer a good picture of how the student's thinking changed as the investigation proceeded. It was exciting to see how the student's thinking matured. When things started to come together for the student, I became very appreciative of access by e-mail. The first few exchanges of e-mail were to encourage work in a productive direction and to make sure that the student's initial collection of data was correct.

December 5, from me:

I look forward to learning about your progress towards making some conjectures. When you get a chance, e-mail what you got for rows 2, 4, 8, and 10 of your $C(m, n)$ table. This will give me a quick cross-check.

December 9, from student:

width (n)		1	2	3	4	5	6	7	8	9	10
	2	L	R	L	r	L	R	L	r	L	R
	4	L	L	L	R	L	L	L	r	L	L
length (m)	6	L	R	L	r	L	R	L	r	L	R
	8	L	L	L	L	L	L	L	R	L	L
	10	L	R	L	r	L	R	L	r	L	R

After finishing the chart, I noticed some sort of pattern.

The student went on to offer some statements for $C(m, n)$ outcomes with various conditions on m and n. The list was improved upon with the following e-mail communication.

December 11, from student:

After I wrote you last time, I spent more time studying the chart. These are some of the observations I have:

1) $C(m, n) = R$ when both m and n are odd
2) $C(m, n) = r$ when m is odd and n is even
3) $C(m, n) = R$ when $m = n$, m and n could be even or odd
4) $C(m, n) = L$ when m is even and n is odd
5) $C(m, n) = R$ when both m and n are odd
6) $C(8, n) = L$ except when $n = 8$ then $C(8, 8) = R$ as in 3) above
7) I noticed that rows with $m = 2, 6, 10$ have the same repeating pattern
8) I noticed $m = 8$ seems to break some of the pattern.

I am working on some similarity from #1 and #8 above so that I could set up some kind of pattern or formula relating m, n and $C(m, n)$.

Also, my teacher likes what I am working on.

Because the student was still only describing the chart, my response sought to encourage movement to the next phase, which involved conjectures in general and some thinking about proofs. Some subtle hints were offered with the following excerpt from a December 12th e-mail, from me. (The comments after ">"s are the parts of the student's remarks to which my responses were directed.)

You should be able to come up with a simple proof that $C(m, m) = R$ for any natural number m. Does an argument pop into your mind? Let me know.

> These are some of the observations I have:

>1) $C(m, n) = R$ when both m and n are odd
>2) $C(m, n) = r$ when m is odd and n is even

This fits the chart. Now, can we look at a few pictures (on graph paper) to come up with a counting argument that will actually justify the observation, when m is greater than 12 and n is greater than 10?

>3) $C(m, n) = R$ when $m = n$, m and n could be even or odd
>4) $C(m, n) = L$ when m is even and n is odd
>5) $C(m, n) = R$ when both m and n are odd
>6) $C(8, n) = L$ except when $n = 8$ then $C(8, 8) = R$ as in #3 above
>7) I noticed that rows with $m = 2, 6, 10$ have the same repeating pattern
>8) I noticed $m = 8$ seems to break some of the pattern.

It might be nice to try to find a different way of grouping that will fit all the time. Notice that 2, 4, and 8 are powers of 2. Think about that for a while. . . .

I am very impressed with your progress thus far. You are doing a great job of formulating hypotheses, based on your data. It seems like a good idea to keep on the track of classifying by nature of m and then the corresponding n's.

By the way, do you know anything about similar shapes?

The next e-mail from the student shows the first movement toward proof and toward some self-designed work that sought to make things clearer. I was delighted to see the subtle and important shift indicated with the following January 3rd e-mail, from the student:

I was able to think more about the "hints" that you sent me in a previous letter. You wrote that $C(m, m) = R$ for any natural number m.

The proof for this is: Because it is a square, the diagonal leads right to the upper right corner, without rebounding off of any of the walls of the table.

Another thing that I did was to make three separate charts on graph paper. One chart for L, one for R, and one for r. I used n as the x-axis, and m as the y-axis. Then

I plotted a point for each corner, at its location on the chart. After doing this, I noticed a line of symmetry for each chart. For the L chart, the line was horizontal at the 8. For the r chart, the line was vertical at the 8. For the R chart, the line was diagonal.

Also in your letter, you mentioned 2, 4, and 8 are powers of 2. I thought about this and could not think of anything, so I looked at the chart that you had originally sent to me to complete. I noticed something in the vertical columns of 2, 4, and 8. In column 2, there is an L every 4th box down. In column 4, there is an L every 8th box down. Based on this observation, I am guessing that for the 8th column, there is an L every 16th box down. . . .

For my project, I have to know who or what to credit for each thing that I do . . ., so that I will be able to write it down in my bibliography.

My e-mail response on January 7th offered information concerning references (see Grant 1971; Hamel 1977; Jacobs 1970). In addition, ideas for looking at a few specific cases, a suggestion to look at the paths traced out to find $C(2, 3)$, $C(4, 6)$, and $C(8, 12)$, and a copy of the promised reference (Hamel 1977) were sent by regular post.

What was exciting about the next communication is that it shows the student is interpreting and moving beyond information that he is receiving. In the following excerpt from January 15th e-mail, the student makes an important leap.

> After more carefully observing the data that I have, along with the information that you sent me in your last letter, I think that I now have a better understanding of what you meant on how to organize my conjectures.
>
> In your letter, you described 3 cases that will cover all of the natural numbers: (1) m is odd, (2) $m = 2^k$ for some natural number k, and (3) $m = 2^k \exists j$ where j is an odd natural number. After I finished, though, I found that I only needed cases 1 and 3 to cover all of the natural numbers. Case 1 covered all the odd #'s and case 3 took care of all the even #'s.
>
> This is what I came up with: When m is odd, $C(m, n)$ = R when n is odd; $C(m, n)$ = r when n is even; $C(m, n)$ = $C(m, n)$ for all $m = 2^k \exists q$ when q is any odd #, k is any natural #.

The student went on to request some suggestions for how things could be organized for the reporting stage of his project. With the following excerpt from a January 17th e-mail, I offered the student some guidelines for fine-tuning what was going to be reported.

> You are conjecturing that the RrRrRrRr . . . pattern continues beyond the chart. The m bigger than 12 and n bigger than 10 case is a conjecture until you can come up with some kind of a proof. If you can't prove it, then it stays a conjecture (or open problem).
>
> In addition to the results that you can claim for $m =$

1, 2, . . ., 12 and $n = 1, 2, . . .,$ 10, you have proved that $C(m, m)$ = R. The argument that you mentioned about the 45 degree angle is fine.

> The three pictures that I asked you to compare suggested another conjecture: If $mq = np$, then $C(m, n) = C(p, q)$. This stays a conjecture until you can expand upon your similar rectangles idea to show that the "paths are similar."
>
> In summary, your outline has several parts: Definition of the Problem—Describe $C(m, n)$; Data Collection (this gives you a set of known outcomes and a set of conjectures.); Some Theorems (this consists of $C(m, m)$ = R, the known outcomes for $m = 1, 2, . . ., 12$ and $n = 1, 2, . . .,$ 10, and whatever can be proved for other values or situations.); and Some Open-Ended Problems (this will consist of your conjectures that don't get proved by the time you need to finish your project) . . . .
>
> You have been doing a wonderful job on this. I am really impressed with how far you have taken things and how nicely things have been shaping up.

In response to an e-mail in which the student offered a statement that did not correctly reflect some of the conclusions that he had drawn, I sent the following e-mail on January 18th:

> About your
> > $C(m, n) = C(m, n)$ for all $m = 2^k \exists q$
> > when q is any odd #, k is any natural #:
>
> This is correct but doesn't say what I think you meant to say. I think that you are wanting to say that $C(m, n) = C(p, n)$ where $m = 2^k$ and $p = 2^k \exists q$ when q is any odd number, k is any natural number.
>
> This statement gives the formula form for your observation that you only needed two cases: m odd and $m = 2^k \exists$(an odd).
>
> There is something more that you have conjectured that is also not shown in this formula. From an earlier e-mail, you described the proposed outcomes. Your conjecture for this can be written neatly in the form:
>
> $$C(2^k, n) = \begin{cases} R, \text{ if } n = 2^k \\ r, \text{ if } n = 2^{(k+1)} \\ L, \text{ otherwise} \end{cases}$$
>
> The two things above take care of your conjecture for m even.

Finally, on January 21st, the student sent the following e-mail:

> Thank you for all the info. you sent me. Since my science teacher moved the due date for the report to middle February, I have more than enough time to finish it. I am working on proving $C(m, n) = C(p, q)$ when $mq = np$. I am [still] trying to expand the idea of similar rectangles to "similar paths." Overall, I am just right in finishing the report. I will send you a copy when I finish it.

Postscript

The student successfully completed the project on time. It included a heuristic argument in support of the claim that $C(m, n) = C(p, q)$ when $mq = np$.

It has been over a year since the student completed his project. In preparation of this article, it seemed timely to ask him to address some of the questions that have been asked of me. Consequently, I sent him an e-mail in which I asked him to address the following questions concerning his work on the project:

What do you think that you got out of the experience of having completed the project?

How and what did you like about the interactions that we worked out via e-mail?

What things didn't you like about using e-mail the way that we used it while you were working on your project?

In response, I received the following:

1. I found the project to be very interesting. Most math that is taught in school is almost all textbook problems. Completing the project taught me about math, but from a different approach. This helped me to better realize the practicalities and real world approaches to math.

2 & 3. I found the e-mail communication to be quite beneficial, with very little setbacks. What I liked about it was the efficiency. With regular mail, information generally has to be sent in larger blocks of information, making clarification difficult and time consuming. With e-mail, if I ever had any questions, I could just send them out one at a time, and quickly get back responses, plus the information is all laid out on the screen, in case I ever needed to refer back to it. I really don't have any complaints about working things out via e-mail, except that sometimes it was time consuming to send out things like charts, which have to be placed in rows and columns.

Some Conclusions

My involvement in this project was rewarding. The student's progress was impressive, and I had a real sense of having had impact on the direction of his investigation. As noted by the student, completion of the project provided a valuable opportunity for a more realistic view of what it means to do mathematics. This had been one of my hopes. In addition, it was important to have an expectation of proofs or heuristic arguments for at least some of the conjectures; otherwise, students are misled into believing that a few examples are sufficient to justify a claim. The responsibility to prove statements is a distinguishing feature of mathematics. I was pleasantly surprised with the progress that the student made with this aspect of the project and the pace at which progress was made. The extent to which the e-mail exchanges felt like personal contacts was also a surprise. In fact, I was amazed when I experienced the awareness of "the light going on" for the student in much the same way it happens when a student I am working with individually seems suddenly to get the point.

E-mail has opened up wonderful opportunities for rich exchanges between students and mathematicians at all levels.

There were several times in the process when the accessibility to e-mail was what made the timing ideal. Prior to e-mail, the logistics of such exchanges were unwieldy enough to limit the number of mathematicians who would undertake such challenges. E-mail has opened up wonderful opportunities for rich exchanges between students and mathematicians at all levels. Mathematicians interested in initiating such collaborations can do this by offering a selection of problems on their personal Web pages and responding to questions directed from curious students. In addition to responding to inquiries, it is encouraging to forward an analogous or deeper problem. Problems should be clearly stated and offered with several illustrative examples. Investigations that relate or compare properties of numbers lend themselves nicely to proofs that make use of techniques and computational skills that are being taught in middle grades.

Although I did not have any contact with the student's science teacher, her approval of our project was communicated to me on numerous occasions. For this instance, the selection and set-up of an appropriate science project had been part of the teacher's assignment. She gave the student permission to do the science project on something in mathematics on the condition that his study meet the criteria established. For the project discussed in this article, the student contacted me directly. I then offered to send him mathematics challenges by mail. For a more general situation, it would be a good idea for interested middle-grades teachers to make the initial inquiries to mathematicians and mathematics educators to ascertain their openness to supporting such activities. By having an established cadre who will respond positively when contacted by a student and a short list of accessible projects with specific contact people, the initial stages of setting up such projects will go more smoothly.

Directories for professional societies are good sources of names and e-mail addresses. These include the Mathematical Association of America (MAA), the American Mathematical Society (AMS), the Association for Women in Mathematics (AWM), and the National Council of Teachers of Mathematics (NCTM). There are also professional societies of statisticians and engineers that would be good sources.

References

Grant, Nicholas. "Mathematics on a Pool Table." *Mathematics Teacher* 64 (1971): 255–57.

Hamel, Thomas R., and Ernest Woodward. "Developing Mathematics on the Pool Table." *Mathematics Teacher* 70 (1977): 154–63.

Jacobs, Harold. *Mathematics—a Human Endeavor*. San Francisco: W. H. Freeman & Co., 1970.

Pappas, Theoni. *The Joy of Mathematics*, pp. 28–29. San Carlos, Calif.: World Wide Publishing/Tetra, 1992.

Perl, Teri. *Math Equals*, pp. 13–26. San Francisco: Addison-Wesley Publishing Co., 1978.

Sobel, Max A. and Evan M. Maletsky. *Teaching Mathematics: A Sourcebook of Aids, Activities, and Strategies*, pp. 134–42. Princeton, N.J.: Prentice-Hall, 1975.

Evelyn M. Silvia, *University of California at Davis, Davis, California*

23

Infusing Shape and Dimension into the Mathematics Curriculum

DeAnn Huinker, Connie Laughlin,
and Joseph Georgeson

We live in a three-dimensional world surrounded by shapes, yet much of what we do in mathematics classrooms occurs in the two-dimensional world of paper, chalkboard, overhead projection, or computer screen, and usually involves symbols. We have forgotten how mathematics began—by studying the shape, dimension, and pattern of our world. The consequence has been a mathematics curriculum devoid of context and dominated by arithmetic. It is time to rethink and revitalize middle school mathematics so students are able to experience mathematics as an integrated whole involving numeric and visual connections.

The important mathematical strands of shape and dimension were brought to the attention of mathematics educators by Lynn A. Steen's landmark book, *On the Shoulders of Giants: New Approaches to Numeracy*, which stimulated dialogue and creative approaches to mathematics curricula for the new century. The chapters by Marjorie Senechal (1990) on "shape" and Thomas F. Banchoff (1990) on "dimension" provided the framework for a group of middle school teachers to bring a new "eye" to their teaching of mathematics. This group of twenty middle school teachers participated in a year-long project that focused on infusing shape and dimension into their mathematics curriculum.

Shape is the study of visual patterns. Senechal (1990) stated that the goal of studying shape is "to dis-cover similarities and differences among objects, to analyze the components of form, and to recognize shapes in different representations" (p. 140). It involves the examination of how shapes can change and, yet, in some way stay the same, the creation of images, and the reconstruction of shapes from their images.

Dimension is the study of numeric patterns within shapes—where number and geometry intermix (Banchoff 1990). It includes examining how properties such as area, perimeter, and volume change from one dimension to another, including fractal dimensions.

The study of shape and dimension overlaps the traditional geometry curriculum and broadens it to include fractals, networks, and topology. However, shape and dimension are not topics that should be absorbed into the study of geometry as a brief module or seen as something extraneous to the curriculum. As Senechal noted, "Shape is a vital, growing, and fascinating theme in mathematics with deep ties to classical geometry but goes far beyond it in content, meaning, and method. Properly developed, the study of shape can form a central component of mathematics education, a component that draws on and contributes to not only mathematics but also the sciences and the arts" (Senechal 1990, p. 140).

The infusion of shape and dimension into the curriculum provides opportunities to examine many mathematical ideas in new ways. What often appear to be mundane topics, such as making factor trees and finding prime factorizations, can be transformed into rich mathematical investigations that are highly engaging for students. A study of factor lattices is one example of an investigation that connects shape and dimension with number theory and allows students to construct their own understanding of factors and the shape of numbers (Rachlin, Mattsumoto, and Wada 1988; Woodrow Wilson National Fellowship Foundation 1995).

Factor Lattices: An Example of Infusion

All numbers have a shape, although not all are unique shapes. All numbers have a dimension. These notions form the basis for an investigation of factor lattices. A teacher commented, "This is the richest example of connecting number theory to a geometric model that I know of." One of her students commented, "This is the best math we've done all year." Factor lattices provide students with a method to represent small and large numbers that illustrates many number properties visually and makes numbers more interesting to them. Students are able to further their understanding of factors, factor pairs, prime numbers, prime factors, square numbers, square roots, exponents, divisibility rules, points, line segments, and rectangular prisms.

A factor lattice visually demonstrates the relationship between a natural number and its factors; it displays both the shape of a number and its dimension. The factor lattices for the numbers from 1 through 12 are shown in figure 23.1. The students were shown these lattices one at a time and asked to find patterns and think about why a number has a particular shape. The students quickly realized that the lattices displayed the factors for each number.

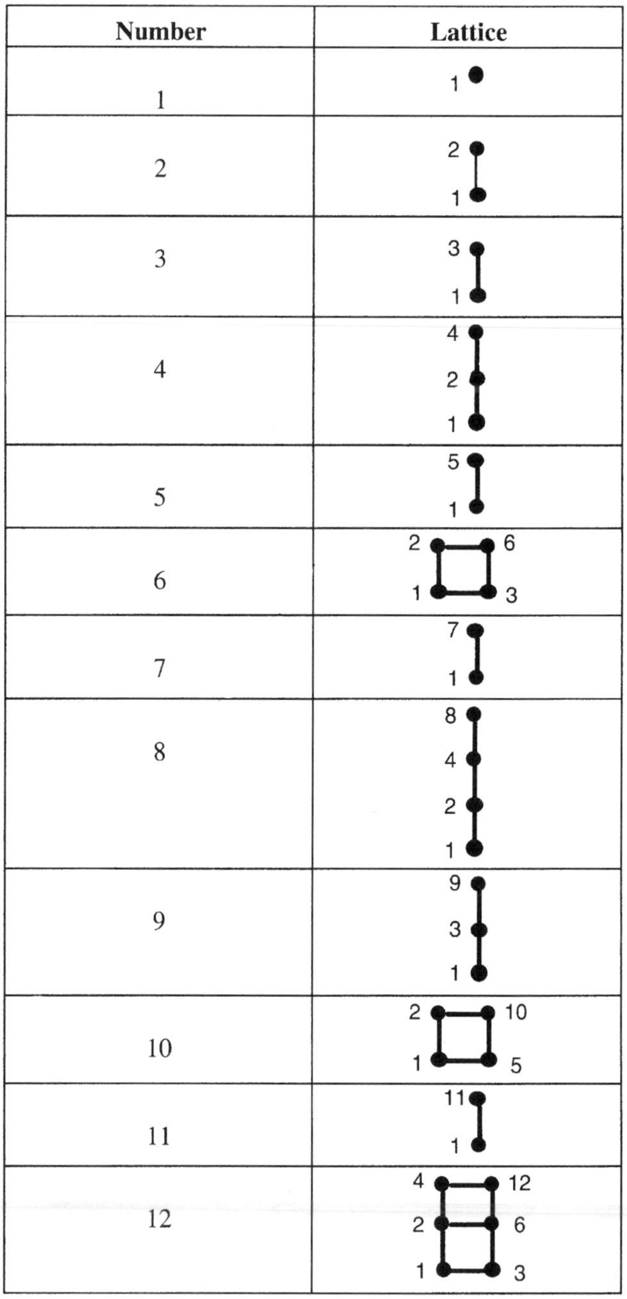

The students worked in small groups to discuss and write down any observations they could make about the first twelve factor lattices. At first, generalizations came slowly, but soon the room buzzed as students began to discover the secrets of the lattices. A first draft of the rules for factor lattices emerged. The student-generated list with some annotation is shown in figure 23.2. This initial list was incomplete, but the teacher did not try to correct any misconceptions. She knew it would make more sense to the students if they revised the rules on their own in the following days.

For homework that night, the students listed the factor pairs, made a factor tree, wrote the prime factorization using exponents, and drew a factor lattice for each of the numbers 14 through 29. The next day the students displayed the lattices on the board and justi-

Number	Lattice
1	
2	
3	
4	
5	
6	
7	
8	
9	
10	
11	
12	

Fig. 23.1. *Factor lattices for 1 through 12*

fied their shapes with the rules that the class had generated. The students discovered that the shapes of all prime numbers are one-dimensional and consist of a single line segment. The shapes of the composite numbers raised many questions. Does 3 have to be connected to 1? Doesn't 16 have to be a rectangle? Does the factor 2 always have to be placed on that specific dot above 1? Can the factor 6 be connected to 1? The stu-

1. The number 1 is in every factor lattice and is always at the bottom. (Note: The number 1 does not have to be at the bottom, but in the examples shown, that is where it was placed.)

2. The number of the factor lattice is always at the top or in the upper right-hand corner of the lattice. (Note: This is not always the case, it depends upon the placement of the number 1.)

3. The number of factors tells you the number of dots.

4. Prime numbers have only one line.

5. Numbers that are not prime are either lines or boxes. (Note: They have not yet considered three-dimensional numbers.)

6. On the factor lattices that are squares, if you multiply the diagonals, you get the same answer. (Note: Students need to be careful as to which corners this rule applies.)

7. When numbers go up a line, they are all multiples of the first number.

8. The factor 2 is always placed above the number 1. (Note: This is not always the case. Because 2 is a prime number, it needs to be attached to the number 1, but not necessarily above it.)

9. Numbers that make squares have two prime factors. (Note: Students referred to all two-dimensional lattices as squares rather than rectangles.)

10. The prime factors need to be connected to 1.

Fig. 23.2. *First draft of student-generated factor lattice rules*

dents arrived at a common understanding that composite numbers might be either line segments or rectangles. They also solidified their understanding of the relative position of the prime factors within each lattice.

It was time to move on to three-dimensional numbers. Working in groups, students were told to draw a factor lattice for 30. The students began by listing the factor pairs and circling the prime factors. Suddenly, they realized they had three prime factors. They knew they were to connect all the prime factors to 1 on the lattice, but that would mean drawing three line segments from that point. This is exactly what several groups did, but then they didn't know where to proceed from there. (See Matthew's work in figure 23.3.) Through class discourse, the students generalized that one-dimensional numbers have one prime factor and two-dimensional numbers have two prime factors; thus, numbers with three prime factors must be three-dimensional. Excitement spread as students realized they were moving into the third dimension, space, and they had to draw a cube to illustrate the number 30. Inevitably, one student asked, "Can we have fourth-dimension numbers?" They were assured they could and that the topic would be explored in a few days.

The focus in the next lesson was to connect the pieces of knowledge that students had about factors. The teacher posed the question, "If you know all the factors of a number, what does that tell you about the lattice?" Most of the students realized that this tells you the number of dots on the lattice. The other key question posed was, "How does the prime factorization of a number help you draw a factor lattice?" The following discussion occurred for the number 40:

JOSH: The prime factorization is $2 \times 2 \times 2 \times 5 = 40$.

TEACHER: How would we write it using exponents?

SARAH: 2 to the third power times 5: $2^3 \times 5 = 40$.

TEACHER: How does this help you know how to draw the lattice?

PAULA: You know it's going to be a rectangle because there are two prime factors, 2 and 5.

TEACHER: So this tells us the lattice will be two-dimensional because of the two prime factors. What else do we know based on the prime factorization?

AIMEE: You know it's going to be a rectangle and not just a square because you have three 2's.

TEACHER: How does having three 2's tell us that?

AIMEE: Because we're going to have more than just four factors.

TEACHER: Can we tell how big the rectangle is going to be?

BRETT: We know there are eight factors, so the rectangle will have eight points.

TAMARA: But you can't tell how many factors just from the prime factorization. All we know is that we have three 2's and a 5.

TEACHER: What about those three 2's? Does that tell us anything about either of the dimensions? Draw the factor lattice and think about what all those 2's tell us as you do it.

Some students were still unsure of where to place the factors. The relationship between the number of each distinct prime and the size of the lattice was still not apparent for many students. The teacher prompted them to write arrow rules along each dimension, as shown in the student work in figure 23.4, to highlight when you move across you multiply by 2 and when you move up you multiply by 5. Some students noticed when you went up once, there was only one 5, and when you went across three times, there were three 2's. The students were starting to see the relationship between the prime factorization and the shape of the lattice.

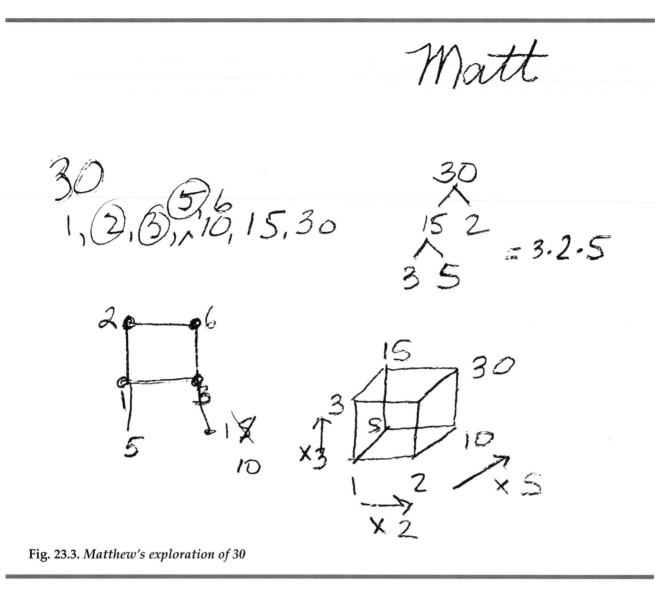

Fig. 23.3. *Matthew's exploration of 30*

The homework assigned after this lesson was to find a one-dimensional, a two-dimensional, and a three-dimensional number between 50 and 100 and write a paragraph describing how each number was determined. Everyone in the classroom put at least one of their lattices on the board and shared the strategies they used to find these numbers. This sharing allowed the teacher to gain an understanding of the various strategies used by the students and to assess each student's understanding of factor and what it means to have one, two, or three dimensions in a number.

Jonathan explained, "I started with 5, and I multiplied 5 × 5—that was 25; but that wasn't big enough. So I multiplied by 5 and got 125, but that was too big. So I went back to 25 and multiplied by a smaller number. I used 3 and got 75." Most students used this building-up approach to generate their numbers because it al-

lowed them to control the number of prime factors. Other students just picked a number, for example 88, and found its factors and determined its shape. This latter approach was more time-consuming, because there are not many three-dimensional numbers between 50 and 100.

The rest of the class period involved putting blank factor lattices on the overhead and asking students what number could be represented by each shape. The teacher observed the use of larger numbers seemed to help her students feel more confident about their generalizations. Once the students realized that a specific lattice represented a number with exactly two prime factors, they became very creative in using larger prime factors. For example, 143 and 899 both have the same shape because each has only two prime factors, 11 × 13 = 143 and 29 × 31 = 899.

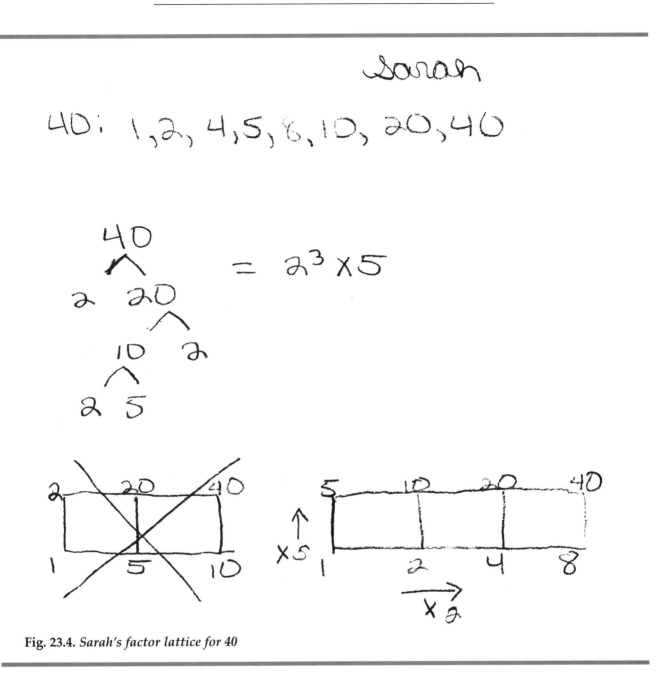

Fig. 23.4. *Sarah's factor lattice for 40*

During the final lesson, the students built models of the factor lattices out of toothpicks and marshmallows. Each group of four students was assigned a one-dimensional number, two two-dimensional numbers, and a three-dimensional number. Before they were allowed to get their building supplies, each student had to find the prime factorization, list all the factors, and make a sketch of each factor lattice. The physical building of the models helped students solidify their understanding of the lattices, especially for the three-dimensional numbers.

As a follow-up activity, students could challenge themselves to build larger, three-dimensional numbers of their own choosing or begin to explore four-dimensional numbers, called hypercubes. The following day, Kristin brought in a three-dimensional factor lattice representing 3 000 000 built out of toothpicks and marshmallows. Amelia took up the challenge of modeling a four-dimensional number and built a factor lattice out of toothpicks and marshmallows for 210. Because she was so fascinated by the hypercube, the teacher helped her draw a model of her hypercube using the computer program, The Geometer's Sketchpad (Key Curriculum Press 1991). The students found it hard to

and bring new content into the mathematics curriculum.

In the study of factor lattices, students learned several big ideas and developed important mathematical skills. They became accustomed to looking for patterns and making generalizations about numbers. They became aware of why 1 is not prime and why it is such a special number in our number system. They improved spatial visualization in the third dimension, both visualizing it and drawing it. They gained entry to the fourth dimension. Students' natural curiosity about numbers was also heightened, and large numbers became more accessible to them.

Most of the middle school teachers in the project on infusing shape and dimension used the factor lattice investigation with their students. An additional benefit noted by many teachers was that their students were no longer confusing factors and multiples, a common occurrence previously, because of the power of the visual images. The experiences with the factor lattices provided a strong visual reference that the teachers and students referred to throughout the year. A sixth-grade teacher commented:

> It was really interesting to discover that working with the factor lattices would carry over into teaching sixth graders about equivalent fractions. We had completed the factor lattice activity several months ago. As I began my lesson on equivalent fractions, the students themselves did an "Ah-ha! This is like factor lattices!" It was really cool to see their eyes light up and make a connection between the two.

believe that, four days before, they barely understood factor lattices, and now not only could they build any one-dimensional, two-dimensional, and three-dimensional numbers, but their knowledge now extended to the fourth dimension. The teacher found it hard to believe that her students were so excited about studying factors and that their understanding was so strong.

Rich Mathematical Connections

Infusing shape and dimension gives teachers another way to present mathematical ideas and provides students with opportunities to engage in imaginative, exploratory, and problem-based learning. Shape and dimension can be used to make connections among mathematical topics, bring new life to traditional ideas,

Activities promoting pattern-based thinking, like factor lattices, can assist students in making similar generalizations about the shape of other numbers and

TABLE **23.1.**
Shape and dimension examples

Investigation	Mathematical connections
Paper Folding (Franco and Schimizu-Yost 1991)	Visual problem solving, two-dimensional shapes, bisecting, perpendicular, diagonals, symmetry, edges, faces, Euler's rules, networks, area, fractions, listening skills, following oral directions
Perimeter Search (Brummett and Charles 1989)	Triangular area, perimeter, relationship of area and perimeter, constant area and varying perimeters, concepts of even and odd numbers, generalizations regarding adding odd and even numbers
Pascal's Triangle (Peitgen, Jürgens, and Saupe 1992)	Shaded visual patterns, number patterns, exponents, fractals, noninteger dimensions, probability
Golden Rectangle	Visual perception, Fibonacci sequence, area, perimeter, fractions, ratios
Pentominoes (Cowan 1987)	Visual problem solving, making an organized list of visual patterns, three-dimensional open cubes, tessellations, networks

their relationships, as well as develop initial notions of important number concepts such as odd, even, and prime. Additional examples of investigations used by these middle school teachers to infuse shape and dimension into their curriculum are listed in table 23.1.

The topics of shape and dimension are vital for the future success of students in a world dominated by computer-generated images that model minute aspects of atoms and expansive regions of space. The future will demand individuals who can use imaginative and creative approaches to solve problems. Activities like the one described, which combine spatial and numerical components, establish important mathematical and real-life connections.

References

Banchoff, Thomas F. "Dimension." In *On the Shoulders of Giants: New Approaches to Numeracy*, edited by Lynn A. Steen, pp. 11–59. Washington, D.C.: National Academy Press, 1990.

Brummett, Micalelia. R., and Linda H. Charles. *Connections: Linking Manipulatives to Mathematics Grade 5*. Sunnyvale, Calif.: Creative Publications, 1989.

Cowan, Richard A. "Pentominoes for Fun and Learning." In *Geometry for Grades K–6*, edited by Jane M. Hill, pp. 138–40. Reston, Va.: National Council of Teachers of Mathematics, 1987.

Franco, Betsy, and Jeanne Schimizu-Yost. *Using Tomoko Fuse's Unit Origami in the Classroom*. Berkeley, Calif.: Key Curriculum Press, 1991.

Fuse, Tomoko. *Unit Origami: Multidimensional Transformations*. New York: Japan Publications, 1990.

National Council of Teachers of Mathematics. *Curriculum and Evaluation Standards for School Mathematics*. Reston, Va.: National Council of Teachers of Mathematics, 1989.

Rachlin, Sidney L., Annette N. Mattsumoto, and Li Ann T. Wada. *Algebra I: A Process Approach*. (Draft). Honolulu: University of Hawaii: Curriculum Research and Development Group, 1988.

Senechal, Marjorie. "Shape." In *On the Shoulders of Giants: New Approaches to Numeracy*, edited by Lynn A. Steen, pp. 139–81. Washington, D.C.: National Academy Press, 1990.

The Geometer's Sketchpad. Berkeley, Calif.: Key Curriculum Press, 1991. Software

Woodrow Wilson National Fellowship Foundation. *Teacher Outreach (TORCH) Program: Shape and Dimension Summer Institute Handbook*. Princeton, N.J.: Woodrow Wilson National Fellowship Foundation, 1995.

DeAnn Huinker, *University of Wisconsin—Milwaukee, Milwaukee, Wisconsin;*
Connie Laughlin, *Steffen Middle School, Mequon, Wisconsin;* and Joseph Georgeson,
Glen Hills Middle School, Glendale, Wisconsin

24

The Pentomino Project: Moving Students from Manipulatives to Reasoning and Thinking about Mathematical Ideas

SUSAN MERCER AND
MARJORIE A. HENNINGSEN

[M]athematics is far more interesting when one gets to think about it. . . . By replacing memory tasks with creative interactions, we allow students to enjoy mathematics classes so that they want to take more of them. (Alper et al. 1995).

Since the 1950s, pentominoes and other polyominoes have most commonly been used for recreational mathematics and in the elementary school classroom as puzzles or games (Wah and Picciotto 1994; Onslow 1990). One of the most popular electronic puzzle games, Tetris and its variations, involves pentominoes. Polyominoes have long provided mathematicians with fodder for challenging problems in combinatorial geometry. Exploration with pentominoes in the elementary grades, however, has most often involved finding how many different pentominoes can be made with five tiles and then trying to fit them like puzzle pieces into some specified area; this type of activity is also suggested for use with all grade levels in the Family Math materials, in which pentominoes are referred to as "pentasquares" (Stenmark, Thompson, and Cossey 1986, pp. 188–89).

In more recent years, activities involving pentominoes, or polyominoes more generally, have been recommended for use in the middle grades (Geddes 1992) to explore measurement concepts and patterns and also in algebra to introduce algebraic concepts involving perimeter, area, volume, patterns and functional relationships, and optimization problems (Wah and Picciotto 1994).

In the unit described in this article, pentominoes are used as a device for exploring the mathematical concepts of measurement in one, two, and three dimensions (Geddes 1994). Pentominoes, as the primary representation, provide a unifying theme for the unit. Rather than calling the unit the "perimeter, area, and volume project" we refer to it as the Pentomino Project. In order to fully understand the design of the unit, a brief explanation of the context will be provided.

Spurgeon Intermediate School is located in Southern California and enrolls 1300 students. The school serves a large Spanish-speaking population, grades 6

The authors gratefully acknowledge the invaluable suggestions and support of Rick Doty, Teresa Garcia, and Glenn Crosswhite, who are teachers at Spurgeon Intermediate School; Charlotte Griswold of Valley High School in Santa Ana, Calif., for suggesting the Pentomino Project; Dennis Estrada of Creative Publications; and the support of our classroom efforts by the QUASAR Project directed by Edward A. Silver at the University of Pittsburgh's Learning Research and Development Center. Preparation of this article was partially supported by a grant from the Ford Foundation (Grant no. 890-0572) for the QUASAR Project. Any opinions expressed herein are those of the authors and do not necessarily reflect the views of the Ford Foundation.

through 8. Our demographics currently show that 99 percent of our students represent ethnic and racial minorities; 96 percent speak a language other than English at home; 75 percent are designated Limited English Proficient (LEP); and 75 percent fall below the federal poverty level. In addition, a large percentage of our students score below the 25th percentile in overall mathematics and reading on the Comprehensive Tests of Basic Skills (CTBS). Class sizes range between thirty and forty-two. Thus, ours is a challenging environment in which to provide students with a meaningful mathematics curriculum.

The primary goal of the Spurgeon teachers has been to develop and maintain a rigorous and cohesive mathematics curriculum across all three grade levels. Our instructional program is aimed at providing *all* students with opportunities to learn a broad range of mathematics content, engage in high-level thinking and reasoning, and acquire deep and meaningful understanding of significant mathematical ideas. Because of our large LEP population, the program also has an overarching emphasis on the development of English language skills in the context of learning mathematics. The seventh-grade Pentomino Project described in this article provides an example of the type of mathematics classroom instruction and learning environment our site has been trying to enact.

The Pentomino Project

Before working on the Pentomino Project, the students had limited knowledge of perimeter, area, and volume and often confused these concepts. During the Pentomino Project, students explored the measurement of two- and three-dimensional shapes. They informally investigated the growth of perimeter, area, and volume of similar shapes, and by doing so they were better able to discriminate between these concepts, commonly a problem for middle school students. It is important to note that the development of these concepts takes time. Marzano et al. state that "concept formation can be a long, detailed process—one that teachers cannot expect to occur incidentally" (1988, p. 36). As students learned the difference between perimeter, area, and volume, they informally developed algorithms to determine area without counting squares and volume without counting cubes. The manipulatives used allowed immediate feedback when calculating the area and volume and provided a means for students to test their hypotheses. During the project, students worked in groups to discuss and share ideas about possible "shortcuts" to calculate the perimeter, area, and volume of similar shapes. Within our mathe-

matics curriculum, this unit provides the experiences needed to develop a more in-depth understanding of perimeter, area, and volume. It is important for students to learn not only to perform algorithms and recall facts but also to know when and why they are doing them (Silver and Stein 1996).

> "I really enjoyed doing this project with a group, if I could change something about this project I wouldn't change nothing."

Throughout the unit an emphasis is given to the development of mathematical vocabulary. At the beginning of the unit, many of the students did not know the meaning of mathematical terms such as *doubling, inches, length, height, side, edge, square, cube, two- and three-dimensional,* in English or in their primary language. These words may be familiar terms for English-speaking students, but the development of the meaning needs to be included within the context of the unit to address the needs of our large population of LEP and Special Education students. As the unit progressed, other mathematical terms such as *perimeter, area, volume, similar, congruent, base, square inches,* and *cubic inches* were added to the list. As stated by Marzano et al., "[V]ocabulary knowledge is one of the cornerstones of learning . . . the relationship between words and concepts suggest that we must link teaching concepts to teaching vocabulary" (1988, p. 35).

Part 1: What Is a Pentomino?

As students began the Pentomino Project, they were asked if anyone could describe a pentomino. No one could. I explained that a pentomino is a two-dimensional shape created by linking five congruent squares so that each square shares at least one adjacent side with another square. I gave students two examples and asked them to find all twelve pentominoes using one-inch tiles. Following, I asked students to cut out the pentominoes using one-inch graph paper.

Next, I asked students to sort the pentominoes into two sets. One set contained the pentominoes that fold into an open box, the second set contained the pentominoes that do not. Figure 24.1 shows the two sets of pentominoes.

This introduction allowed every student to clearly understand that five congruent squares are needed to form a pentomino. In addition, every student was able

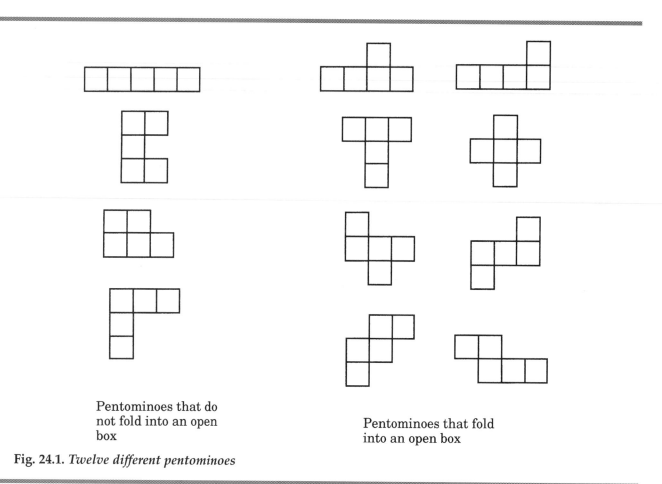

Pentominoes that do
not fold into an open
box

Pentominoes that fold
into an open box

Fig. 24.1. *Twelve different pentominoes*

to complete the sorting activity and therefore developed a positive predisposition for the rest of the project.

Part 2: Making Similar Pentominoes

First, students had to select one of the pentominoes that folded into an open box. Second, using one-inch tiles, students had to make five 2 × 2 squares. Finally, using these 2 × 2 squares, students had to make the same-shaped pentomino. This is an essential aspect of the project because, in order to continue, students must be able to visualize the pentomino and comprehend the concept of doubling the sides of each square that forms the pentomino and what effect this growth in the unit size might have on the area and perimeter of the pentominoes. Students can then develop strategies that aid them in making pentominoes using 3 × 3, 4 × 4, and 5 × 5 inch squares.

Part 3: Calculating Perimeter, Area, and Volume

Using one-inch graph paper, students created five different, yet similar pentominoes using 1 × 1, 2 × 2, 3 ×

3, 4 × 4, and 5 × 5 squares respectively. Figure 24.2 shows five similar pentominoes created using squares of different sizes. These squares are examples of a set of pentominoes students created. All of these would form an open box.

Next, students had to find the perimeter and area of the pentominoes and the volume of the open box formed by folding the pentominoes. In order to keep track of their answers, students completed a summary table (see table 24.1) that included the length of the unit square used to generate the pentominoes, the perimeter and area of each pentomino, and the volume of the open box.

The use of manipulatives allowed all students to calculate the area using tiles and the volume using cubes. As the project progressed, I encouraged students to look for more efficient ways to determine the area, perimeter, and volume; this triggered their interest and enthusiasm. Students discussed "shortcuts" within their groups. They were also required to record their thinking and findings.

Throughout the project, I walked around the classroom asking questions that made students think and

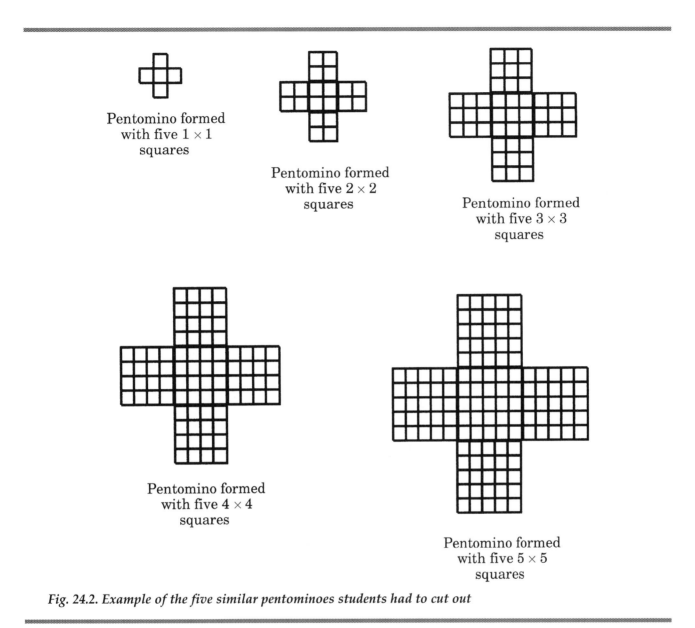

Pentomino formed
with five 1 × 1
squares

Pentomino formed
with five 2 × 2
squares

Pentomino formed
with five 3 × 3
squares

Pentomino formed
with five 4 × 4
squares

Pentomino formed
with five 5 × 5
squares

Fig. 24.2. Example of the five similar pentominoes students had to cut out

TABLE 24.1.
Sample summary table used by students to detect patterns

Length of the unit square in inches	Perimeter of the pentomino in inches	Area of the pentomino in in²	Volume of the open box in in³
1	12 × 1 = 12	1 × 5 = 1 × 1 × 5 = 5	1 × 1 = 1 × 1 × 1 = 1
2	12 × 2 = 24	4 × 5 = 2 × 2 × 5 = 20	4 × 2 = 2 × 2 × 2 = 8
3	12 × 3 = 36	9 × 5 = 3 × 3 × 5 = 45	9 × 3 = 3 × 3 × 3 = 27
4	12 × 4 = 48	16 × 5 = 4 × 4 × 5 = 80	16 × 4 = 4 × 4 × 4 = 64
5	12 × 5 = 60	25 × 5 = 5 × 5 × 5 = 125	25 × 5 = 5 × 5 × 5 = 125
. . .			
L	12 × L	$L × L × 5$	base × L = $L × L × L$

plicated, students started looking for "shortcuts," procedures that allowed them to find the answer without using the cubes. As they found patterns and developed algorithms, students tested their "theories" using the cubes and explained them to the rest of their group. At the end of the project, most groups were finding the volume by calculating the base, then multiplying by the number of "layers going up." A student explained how she calculated the volume of the open box formed by folding the pentomino created with 3×3 squares: "In my mind, I picture the box so there are nine cubes in the bottom and three layers, so I multiplied 9 times 3 for my answer. So my answer is 27 cubic inches. Another way to write my answer is 27 in³."

In one group, a Vietnamese student told the four LEP Spanish-speaking students in his group that he knew how to calculate the volume without cubes. However, the Hispanic students were not convinced of his procedure, so they checked their answers using the one-inch cubes. The Vietnamese student knew an algorithm and could recall it but not explain why he used it. Using cubes allowed him to understand the algorithm. By the end of the unit, he could explain what he was doing in terms of the visual representation: "I multiply length times width to get the bottom (base), then I multiply by the height, which is the number of layers going up." After checking four of the five open boxes, all the students in the group were convinced and started using the algorithm.

One group told me they found that the area and volume of the pentomino formed by squares with an edge length of five inches was the same, 125. I looked at their numbers and asked, "Are you sure?" They looked puzzled and started talking among themselves. After a while, they said that it was possible and explained to me that they had five big squares with an area of 25 in² each; therefore, the area was 125 in² and the volume was 25 cubes for the base times five "layers going up," and that also was 125. They added that in both cases they had five squares with 25 squares or cubes each. Students were able to present a valid and convincing mathematical argument for their theory and felt proud about it. Questioning what students are doing, even when the answer is correct, forces them to explain the mathematics not only to me but to each other.

Part 4: Looking for Patterns

Without actually cutting the pentominoes out, students had to calculate the perimeter and area of pentominoes formed with squares of unit sizes 6, 7, and 10, along with the volume of the open box formed by folding the pentominoes. In order to facilitate this, we had a class discussion in which each group explained to the rest of

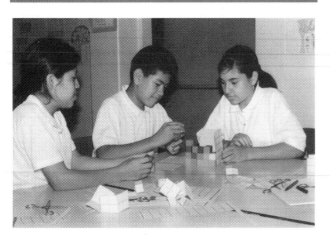

Left to right: Oralia Perez, Jorge Gamboa, Ana Gonzalez

Elizabeth Frias and José Hernandez

make connections. "Are you sure?" "Is there an easier way?" "How could you calculate the volume without the cubes?" "How can you prove that the answer is correct?" challenged most students. These questions helped students move beyond the level of recording and evaluate and analyze what they had done and why. Having students make their analysis explicit allowed me to accurately determine students' understanding.

It was interesting to observe how students moved from using manipulatives to the abstract ideas in order to calculate the volume. To find the volume of the open boxes formed by folding the pentominoes constructed with 2×2 and 3×3 squares, students filled them with one-inch cubes. However, as the task of "filling" the open boxes with cubes became harder and more com-the class how they had calculated the perimeter, area, and volume. Students described patterns and "short-cuts" they had found; these results were recorded on the board. Using the table and the patterns, students explained how they would calculate the perimeter, area, and volume for larger pentominoes.

"This project must of been an interesting and a fun way for my son to learn about geometry."

The discussion of the problem allowed students to describe patterns and move toward generalizations. In addition, it allowed every group to hear different approaches. This communication among the students was stimulating and productive. For example, in one class a group explained they calculated the area by counting the one-inch squares of one square in the pentomino and then multiplied by 5; another group added they did the same but calculated the area of one square by multiplying length times width. To this, a different group added they just multiplied the length times itself because the length and width were the same. As the students explained what they had done, I recorded results on the board as a reference. Keeping a record of the discussion is essential. Students can look back and reflect on what was discussed. Keeping such a record also helps groups find mistakes without the teacher having to point them out.

Part 5: Student Presentations

Students were asked to make a poster to display the five similar pentominoes. They had to provide a written explanation describing how they determined each measurement along with a summary table, including the length of the square that forms the pentomino, the perimeter of the pentomino, the area of the pentomino, and the volume of the open box formed by folding the pentomino, and the various algorithms they found as a group. Having students do this addresses one of the major recommendations of the *Curriculum and Evaluation Standards* (National Council of Teachers of Mathematics [NCTM] 1989)—that students become better communicators of their thinking about mathematics. This is important because "communication is the vehicle by which teachers and students can appreciate mathematics as the process of problem solving and reasoning. But communication is also very important in and of itself, since students must learn to describe phe-

nomena through various written, oral, and visual forms" (NCTM 1991, p. 96). Figure 24.3 provides two examples of the pentomino created with 5×5 squares as presented by students on their posters. The explanations and descriptions are similar to what each of these groups presented for the other four pentominoes they created.

As seen in Example 2 of figure 24.3, students calculated the perimeter by multiplying the length of the unit square times 12. Students applied the pattern they "discovered" while completing their summary tables; in other words, the perimeter of a pentomino is formed by twelve sides of the unit square, and therefore, to calculate the perimeter of a pentomino, students multiplied the length of the unit square times 12. To calculate the area of the pentomino students determined the area of the unit square and then multiplied by 5 because pentominoes have five congruent squares. To calculate the volume, students found the number of cubes that "fit" in the base of the open box and then multiplied by the number of "layers going up."

Part 6: Assessment and Reflection

For this project, each student received two grades. One was a group grade based on the completeness, creativity, and depth of the group poster. The second grade was an individual grade. As homework, each student prepared a report that included (1) the pentominoes formed with one- and two-unit squares; (2) a definition of perimeter, area, and volume and a written explanation on how to determine each; (3) a table with the length of each square, the perimeter and area of the pentominoes, and the volume of the open top box formed by each pentomino; and (4) a written explanation of the procedures used to find the perimeter and area of the pentominoes formed with units of 6, 7, and 10 and the volume of the open boxes formed by these pentominoes. The students' report together with the students' class participation determined their individual project grade. By preparing a report, every student had the opportunity to show what he or she had learned.

Before ending the project, I asked students to reflect on what they had learned, what they liked regarding the project, and what they felt could be improved. The following quotes reflect some of the students' impressions and learning:

> "I learned how to do the area, perimeter and volume in a shortcut because before this project I did the area, perimeter and volume the long way but now I know a faster and quicker way."

> "I learned to calculate the volume by timing [*sic*] the length, width and layers going up together.

Example 1:

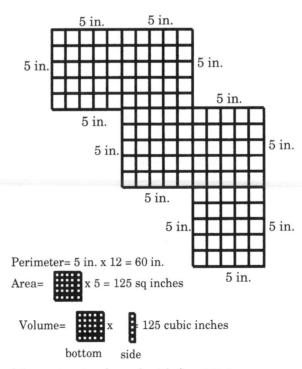

Perimeter= 5 in. x 12 = 60 in.

    because the length of each
    square is 5 inches and you
    can count 12 sides around
    the pentomino

Area= 25 x 5 = 125 sq inches

    Why times 5 ? because there are 5
    full squares, and 25 because in one
    of the 5 squares there is 25 in each
    one.

Volume= 25 + 25 + 25 + 25 + 25 = 25 x 5 = 125 cubic inches

    because in the bottom we can fit 25
    cubes and we put another layer, and
    another until we fill the box.

Example 2:

Perimeter= 5 in. x 12 = 60 in.

Area= [grid] x 5 = 125 sq inches

Volume= [grid] x [column] 125 cubic inches

bottom   side

Fig. 24.3. *Two examples of the pentomino formed with five 5 × 5 squares as presented by students in their posters*

First when you time [*sic*] the length and width that will give you the base. Then when you time [*sic*] it by the layers going up, you will get the volume."

"I really enjoyed doing this project with a group, if I could change something about this project I wouldn't change nothing."

"I learned that for area you write a small 2 on top. (inches^2), which stands for 2 dimensional. I also learned to put a 3 on top of my answer (inches^3) for volume which stands for 3 dimensional."

The importance of having students reflect on their work cannot be overemphasized. Self-reflection gives students an opportunity to think about what they have gained from the project, to see how their work might connect to other topics or to their real-world activities, and to feel ownership of the work they have done. It also provides the teacher with important feedback that can be used to plan subsequent units and revise the unit for future students.

Finally, in order for students to present their projects and explain what they learned, I requested that students take their individual projects home and share them with their parents. In a letter to the parents, I encouraged them to ask questions and invited them to write a short evaluation. Even though students were apprehensive about this homework assignment, parents' responses and reflections were positive and encouraging for the students. The following are examples of parents' comments:

"This project must of been an interesting and a fun way for my son to learn about geometry."

"What I found by talking with my son is that he enjoyed the Pentomino project and at the same time he learned that math can also be fun too, which is great."

"I thought this was an interesting project. I learned something myself in reviewing this."

"Yo pienso que este project que mi hija ha terminado parece un poco complicado para mi. Pero mi hija me a explicado lo que es un pentomino y perimetro y como calcularlo . . . he revisado el projecto y me dado cuenta que ha contestado todas las preguntas y estoy de acuerdo con mi hija que ha hecho un buen projecto y que se ha esforzado en hacerlo. Y estoy orgullosa de ella. [I think that the project my daughter has finished is a bit complicated for me. But my daughter has explained what a pentomino is, what perimeter is and how to calculate it . . . I have reviewed her project and she has done a good

project and has put a great effort in doing it. I am so proud of her.]"

Conclusion

The experiences of the Pentomino Project allowed students to explore and develop a greater understanding of the concepts of perimeter, area, and volume. This project helped create a classroom environment where problem solving, concept development, and the construction of learner-generated solutions and algorithms are more important than merely memorizing procedures to get the right answers (Brooks and Brooks 1993). The Pentomino Project is also in alignment with the NCTM *Standards*, which describe the importance of middle school students developing and constructing their own procedures for finding measures of one-, two-, and three-dimensional figures and communicating their mathematics knowledge (NCTM 1989).

Providing the experiences described in this paper is not a simple task and involves hard work on the part of the teacher. Using a unit like this requires planning, preparation, and organization of activities in such a way that the project goes beyond just "playing" with manipulatives and having fun. The teacher has to plan and deliver rich activities that will lead students to reason, think, and discover as well as allow learners to move from working with physical objects to working with mathematical ideas. The teacher is responsible for keeping students engaged, managing the supplies and manipulatives, and keeping the noise at a reasonable level, all within the constraints of a class period. The teacher must also determine the appropriate amount of time for students to investigate and discuss among themselves and continuously assess the progress made by each student or group of students. Furthermore, the teacher needs to listen attentively to explanations of the students' thought processes and respond in ways that will challenge students' thinking.

What makes all this hard work worthwhile? Recent research has shown that giving students the opportunity to grapple with cognitively complex mathematical tasks is beneficial with respect to student learning outcomes, even when students are not completely successful at solving the tasks during the lesson (Stein and Lane 1996). From the perspective of a classroom teacher, the payoff is evident in a variety of places: watching students become more articulate about their thinking, reading students' mathematics reports and reflections, seeing the finished product, listening to students excited about what they have learned about mathematics, and most important, seeing students transfer their understanding to new situations and problems. When students say "this is just like the Pentomino Project" or "it is easy, we can solve it using what we learned with the pentominoes," the teacher knows that students are building on their previous experiences in new situations and going beyond the memorization of facts.

Engaging students with units like the Pentomino Project challenges teachers to create classroom environments in which they and their students are encouraged to think, reflect, and explore. Teachers learn about students' thinking processes, and this provides insight into how students best learn and what motivates them. Learning and discovering together with the students is a challenging and gratifying experience.

References

Alper, Lynne, Dan Fendel, Sherry Fraser, and Diane Resek. "Is This a Mathematics Class?" *Mathematics Teacher* 88 (November 1995): 632–38.

Brooks, Jacqueline G., and Martin Brooks. *In Search of Understanding: The Case for Constructivist Classrooms.* Alexandria, Va.: Association for Supervision and Curriculum Development, 1993.

Marzano, Robert J., Ronald S. Brandt, Carolyn S. Hughes, Beau F. Jones, Barbara Z. Presseisen, Stuart C. Rankin, and Charles Suhor. *Dimensions of Thinking: A Framework for Curriculum and Instruction.* Alexandria, Va.: Association for Supervision and Curriculum Development, 1988.

National Council of Teachers of Mathematics. *Curriculum and Evaluation Standards for School Mathematics.* Reston, Va.: National Council of Teachers of Mathematics, 1989.

———. *Professional Standards for Teaching Mathematics.* Reston, Va.: National Council of Teachers of Mathematics, 1991.

Geddes, Dorothy, with Juliana Bove and others. *Geometry in the Middle Grades. Curriculum and Evaluation Standards for School Mathematics* Addenda Series, Grades 5–8. Reston, Va.: National Council of Teachers of Mathematics, 1992.

Geddes, Dorothy, with Robert Berkman and others. *Measurement in the Middle Grades. Curriculum and Evaluation Standards for School Mathematics* Addenda Series, Grades 5–8. Reston, Va.: National Council of Teachers of Mathematics, 1994.

Onslow, Barry. "Pentominoes Revisited." *Arithmetic Teacher* 37 (May 1990): 5–9.

Silver, Edward A., and Mary Kay Stein. "The QUASAR Project: The 'Revolution of the Possible' in Mathematics Instructional Reform in Urban Middle Schools." *Urban Education* 30 (January 1996): 476–521.

Stein, Mary Kay, and Suzanne Lane. "Instructional Tasks and the Development of Student Capacity to Think and Reason: An Analysis of the Relationship between Teaching and Learning in a Reform Mathematics Project." *Educational Research and Evaluation* 2 (1996): 50–80.

Stenmark, Jean K., Virginia Thompson, and Ruth Cossey. *Family Math.* Berkeley, Calif.: Lawrence Hall of Science, University of California at Berkeley, 1986.

Wah, Anita, and Henry Picciotto. *Algebra: Themes, Concepts, Tools.* Mountain View, Calif.: Creative Publications, 1994.

Susan Mercer, *Spurgeon Intermediate School, Santa Ana, California,* and Marjorie A. Henningsen, *Learning Research and Development Center, University of Pittsburgh, Pittsburgh, Pennsylvania*

25

Technology-Based Geometric Explorations for the Middle Grades

MARY C. ENDERSON AND
AZITA MANOUCHEHRI

Consider the following exploration:

Complete the conjectures below by writing *always, sometimes,* or *never* in the blanks provided. After completing the statements, return to each response and justify it by using the following criteria:

- If you wrote "always," provide three examples.
- If you wrote "sometimes," provide two examples (one true and one false).
- If you wrote "never," provide a counterexample.

In each case, label the sketch(es) with appropriate measurements.

- Quadrilaterals _____ have at least two lines of symmetry.
- The diagonals of a trapezoid divide the trapezoid into four triangles, _____ having the same area.
- The diagonals of a rectangle _____ bisect each other.
- The angle bisectors of a convex quadrilateral _____ meet at a point.
- The perpendicular bisectors of the sides of a parallelogram _____ meet at a point.

We shared the statements above with nearly 200 middle school teachers and asked them to decide if they were worthwhile geometry tasks for middle-level students. In addition, we asked them to discuss how their students would react to such questions and to identify potential problems associated with using these problems with middle school students. Nearly all teachers agreed that the problems were worthwhile and quite significant for the middle grades. They believed that the problems addressed goals of the National Council of Teachers of Mathematics (NCTM) *Curriculum and Evaluation Standards* (1989) for middle school curricula in that they promoted reasoning, communication, and problem solving. However, the teachers also expressed concern that their middle school students would not be able to successfully complete such problems. Some major sources of difficulty teachers identified were (1) Student conclusions based on an examination of specific cases of quadrilaterals. For instance, they would explore the relationship only for squares and, if it was valid, then they would assume the statement was true for all cases. (2) False conclusions about the relationships under investigation due to students' inaccurate drawing and measurement techniques. (3) Students' lack of knowledge about how to construct perpendicular line segments or angle bisectors of various quadrilaterals.

The problems identified by teachers are certainly valid. Too often, students' mathematical explorations are restricted by the limitations of static paper-and-pencil environments. Frequently, students generalize about certain mathematical relationships after examining an inadequate number of cases. Although these constraints are serious, they can be confronted through the use of appropriate computer software. By using geometry software that facilitates explorations, students can consider numerous cases in a short period of time and thus be more involved in an interactive learning environment.

In what follows, we share some tasks useful in teaching geometry at the middle levels through informal exploratory activities supported by interactive computer software. Implementation of such software has the potential to enhance students' growth in mathematical thinking, develop students' geometric intuition, and improve students' construction of logical arguments.

Appropriate Software for Exploring Geometry

Two pieces of interactive geometry software appropriate for middle levels are Geometer's Sketchpad (GSP) (Jackiw 1995) and CABRI Geometry (Laborde 1990). These software programs are similar and provide students with an environment that allows them to construct points, lines, line segments, rays, or circles by "clicking" special tool icons. Measurements of various segments, angles, arc lengths, perimeters, and areas can be found quickly and easily with "a point and click" for different comparisons and calculations. Students discover that constructed geometric relations will be preserved regardless of any adjustment or change to the figure or situation. The visual medium provided by these software programs, along with the ability to dynamically transform figures and examine a large number of cases, allows for experimentation on the part of learners.

Exploring Quadrilaterals

Let us revisit the quadrilateral tasks posed in the opening of this paper. The concept of a quadrilateral as being a four-sided figure is presented early in the elementary grades. Later, in middle grades, students are introduced to different types of quadrilaterals and the measurable aspects associated with them. Measuring the sides and angles, calculating the sum of the angles, and finding area and perimeter are considered typical of middle-grades geometry curricula. These topics are organized in a way that gives students only a vague notion of the behavior of each feature within different classes of quadrilaterals and with respect to one another. Investigations of these topics often include only preconstructed figures with given measurements. Students are asked to work with formulas to determine specific aspects of the figures; at other times they are requested to physically measure lengths of sides or angles of quadrilaterals. A great deal of time, some accompanied by

frustration, is spent trying to determine how to properly read and use rulers and protractors. As a consequence, very little time remains for investigation of concepts involving attributes and class-relationships among different types of quadrilaterals. Although we do not underestimate the importance of teaching students how to properly use measurement, construction tools, and procedures, research has failed to show that such exercises are effective in developing inductive or deductive reasoning (Grunbaum 1981; Osserman 1981; Fey 1984) or geometric intuition.

Consider the study of quadrilaterals within the GSP or CABRI software environments. Students could be asked to draw four points on a worksheet by selecting the drawing tool and constructing a quadrilateral by connecting those points (see figure 25.1). They could find the angle measures in quadrilateral *ABCD* by selecting the appropriate vertices and then calculate the sum of all angles (see figure 25.2).

By moving any of the four vertices, they can generate various figures representative of quadrilaterals. Students may look for similarities and differences in the numerical and visual data generated as the result of continuous transformations. At this point, students could make conjectures about the angle sum in convex quadrilaterals (figure 25.3).

Working within this environment also provides students with an opportunity to explore exterior angles of a quadrilateral and analyze their relationship to interior angles. Students could determine if there is a relationship between the sum of exterior angles of quadrilaterals and the interior angles (see figures 25.4 and 25.5). Students could examine such relationships for concave quadrilaterals and explain why differences

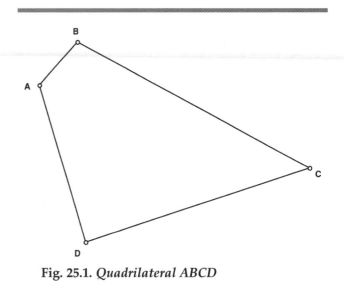

Fig. 25.1. *Quadrilateral ABCD*

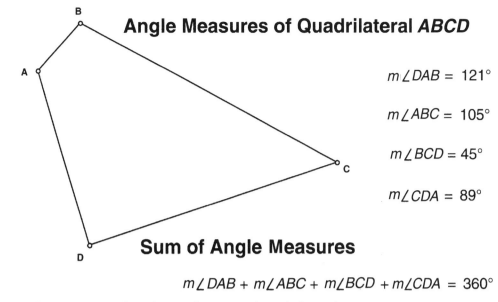

Angle Measures of Quadrilateral *ABCD*

$m\angle DAB = 121°$

$m\angle ABC = 105°$

$m\angle BCD = 45°$

$m\angle CDA = 89°$

Sum of Angle Measures

$m\angle DAB + m\angle ABC + m\angle BCD + m\angle CDA = 360°$

Fig. 25.2. *Angle measures and angle sum for original quadrilateral ABCD*

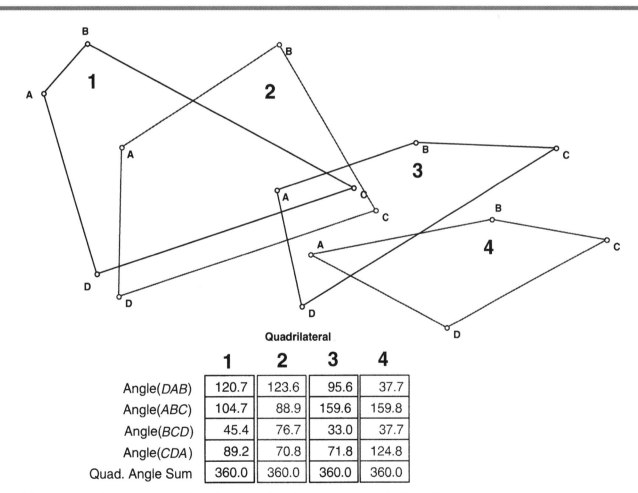

	Quadrilateral			
	1	**2**	**3**	**4**
Angle(*DAB*)	120.7	123.6	95.6	37.7
Angle(*ABC*)	104.7	88.9	159.6	159.8
Angle(*BCD*)	45.4	76.7	33.0	37.7
Angle(*CDA*)	89.2	70.8	71.8	124.8
Quad. Angle Sum	360.0	360.0	360.0	360.0

Fig. 25.3. *Angle measures and angle sum of various convex quadrilaterals*

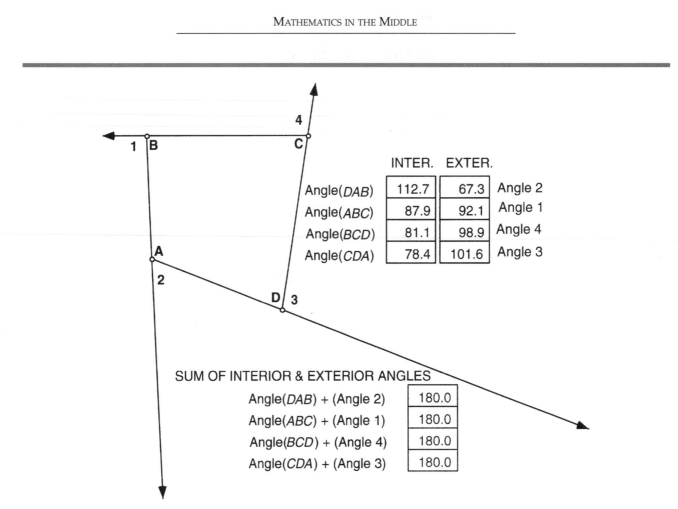

Fig. 25.4. *Interior-exterior angle relationship for a convex quadrilateral*

between the two types of quadrilaterals exist. Explorations in a static environment often do not provide students with enough insight to recognize the existence of exterior angles of polygons or to determine their measures with respect to interior angles.

As students continue investigating quadrilaterals and the properties associated with them, the teacher may redirect attention from the angles of quadrilaterals to the lengths of the sides. Students may be asked to find the measure of the lengths of the sides of various quadrilaterals and make observations about possible relationships. In other instances, the teacher may want to provide students with specific criteria to satisfy, related to sides and angles, in trying to determine what types of quadrilaterals would exist (see figure 25.6). Some interesting questions to explore at this time could include these:

- What type of quadrilateral has three equal sides?
- What type of quadrilateral has two equal sides?
- If two angles of the quadrilateral are equal, what class of shapes can be constructed?

- If all four angles are equal, what shapes can be constructed?
- Is it possible to create two distinct quadrilaterals that have the same angle measures?
- Is it possible to create two distinct quadrilaterals that have the same side length measurements but do not have the same shape?
- Given the measurement of four lengths, could we construct a quadrilateral with them? Is this quadrilateral unique?
- Can you determine a special quadrilateral (e.g., square, rectangle, rhombus, etc.) given the lengths of three sides?
- How many quadrilaterals can you construct given a certain length as the perimeter? Which has the largest area? Which has the smallest area?
- How many quadrilaterals can you construct given a specific area measurement? Which would have the largest perimeter? Which would have the smallest perimeter?

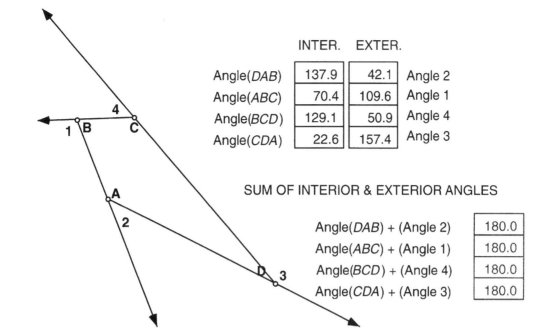

	INTER.	EXTER.	
Angle(*DAB*)	137.9	42.1	Angle 2
Angle(*ABC*)	70.4	109.6	Angle 1
Angle(*BCD*)	129.1	50.9	Angle 4
Angle(*CDA*)	22.6	157.4	Angle 3

SUM OF INTERIOR & EXTERIOR ANGLES

Angle(*DAB*) + (Angle 2)	180.0
Angle(*ABC*) + (Angle 1)	180.0
Angle(*BCD*) + (Angle 4)	180.0
Angle(*CDA*) + (Angle 3)	180.0

Fig. 25.5. *Interior-exterior angle relationship for a second convex quadrilateral*

GIVEN: Segments *AB* and *CB* are congruent and angle *DAB* is a right angle. What type(s) of special quadrilateral(s) can be created with these conditions (e.g., rectangle, square, trapezoid, rhombus)?

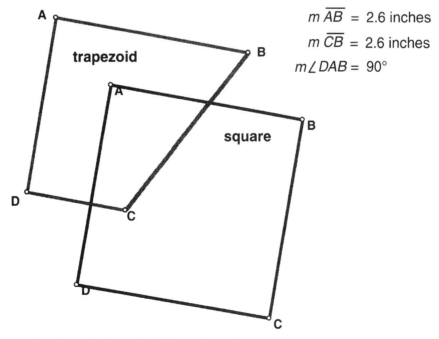

$m \overline{AB}$ = 2.6 inches
$m \overline{CB}$ = 2.6 inches
$m \angle DAB$ = 90°

Fig. 25.6. *Two examples of quadrilateral side length exploration*

Students could concentrate on generating specific quadrilaterals, for instance, squares or rhombi. By examining different components of each type, students might formulate definitions for these special quadrilaterals, defining them not only in terms of their sides and angles but also in terms of their angle bisectors and diagonals, then investigating whether quadrilaterals can adequately be defined in terms of their diagonals or angle bisectors.

. . . geometry curriculum for the middle grades should focus on building students' geometric intuition by using a variety of useful tools for experimentation and exploration.

These investigations are qualitatively different from the traditional paper-and-pencil study of geometry included in middle school mathematics curricula. These activities guide students to a deeper understanding of the attributes of geometric figures and theorems concerning the essential aspects of Euclidean geometry. Investigations of this nature have traditionally been inaccessible to the middle school population because the standard Euclidean constructions have not yet been developed.

Every teacher of geometry has at one time or another experienced some level of frustration at being unable to explain certain concepts or engage students in certain explorations because of poor reproductions of figures. Precision, accuracy, and visualization are often lost when teachers and students try to reproduce figures on chalkboards, overheads, and paper. Moreover, there is always a certain amount of error inherent in the measurement process within a paper-and-pencil environment. Lack of access and availability of adequate tools have often prevented students and teachers from exploring problems aimed at fostering the conjecturing spirit echoed throughout the *Standards*. Technology serves as a valuable vehicle to assist students and teachers in facing these obstacles. The interactive software programs provide students with immediate feedback on their actions; such technologies greatly facilitate the process of experimentation, formulating definitions and theorems, and testing them. Although students are not expected to be able to prove the conjectures and the generalizations they make, the visual nature of these investigations influences the de-

velopment of their mathematical reasoning. Moreover, these investigations provide students with opportunities to make sense of and to build "if-then" arguments that are the backbone of deductive proofs in future mathematics classes.

Such investigations can connect to other geometrical concepts. The quadrilateral exploration has the potential to engage students in a study of transformational geometry, which is often ignored even at the senior high school level. Again, using a quadrilateral environment, students could be asked to explore tasks related to lines of symmetry and reflections, rotations, and dilations, such as the following:

- Is it possible for a quadrilateral to have only one line of symmetry? Is it possible for a quadrilateral to have more than one line of symmetry?

- How many distinct quadrilaterals have only one angle of rotation, which results in the image being identical (same position) to the preimage?

- Given a square, is it possible to copy it, rotate its image, and combine both to result in a hexagon? Octagon? What if you begin with a different quadrilateral?

- Does a relationship exist between your original quadrilateral and its dilated image. State any generalizations that you observe.

Students can easily use the transformation option of each software program to draw and identify a line of symmetry or a center of rotation anywhere on the workspace and explore any of these questions.

Too often, students' mathematical explorations are restricted by the limitations of static paper-and-pencil environments.

Each of the previously presented tasks could be done with other types of polygons. Because of the ease in generating a large number of models and the ability to manipulate them continuously in a short period of time, relationships can be extended from one class of figures to another. We strongly recommend posing questions that encourage students to explore similar polygon patterns or relationships in other convex polygons. Questions such as "What is the sum of the interior and exterior angles of a pentagon? Hexagon?" naturally emerge as a result of engaging in an investi-

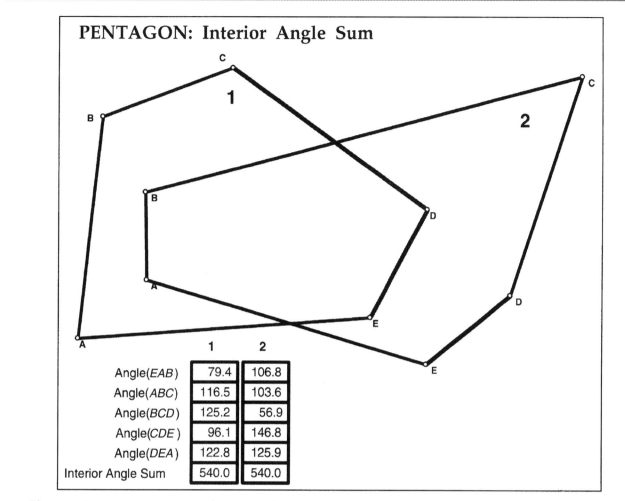

Fig. 25.7. *Pentagon interior angle sum exploration*

gation of quadrilaterals. These situations can easily be constructed and explored by students (see figures 25.7 and 25.8). Moreover, these investigations would allow the students to make generalizations about polygons of *n* sides as they try to identify patterns among different classes of polygons.

Concluding Remarks

The mission of traditional geometry instruction in the middle grades has exposed students to definitions, formulas, and basic drawing and measurement exercises. These goals are experiencing a major transformation as a consequence of the NCTM's movement to improve students' mathematical thinking, reasoning, and communication of mathematical ideas. The *Standards*

(NCTM 1989) recommend that the study of geometry in the middle grades provide students with opportunities to explore and analyze various geometric figures, make conjectures and generalizations about their relationships, and use plausible reasoning in justifying their findings. Geometry activities at the middle levels should concentrate on refining concepts that have been introduced in earlier grades by carefully examining the attributes of plane figures, while allowing a deeper understanding of the class structures and relationships. In order to achieve such goals, geometry curricula for the middle grades should focus on building students' geometric intuition by using a variety of useful tools for experimentation and exploration. Use of appropriate computer software is one means of providing students with a valuable interactive learning environment. It allows them to explore a wide range of mathematical

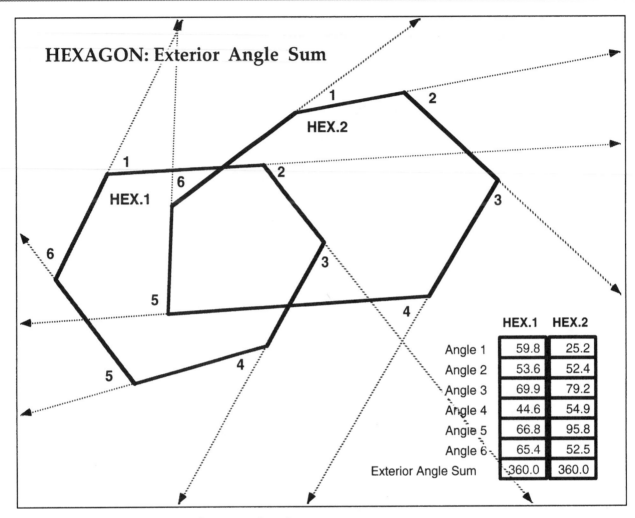

Fig. 25.8. *Hexagon exterior angle sum exploration*

problems and to visualize and experience important connections among various concepts that promote worthwhile learning.

References

Fey, James T., ed. *Computing and Mathematics: The Impact on Secondary School Curricula.* Report of a conference sponsored by the National Science Foundation. Reston, Va.: National Council of Teachers of Mathematics, 1984.

Grunbaum, Branko. "Shouldn't We Teach Geometry?" *Two-Year College Mathematics Journal* 12 (1981): 232–38.

Jackiw, Nicholas. The Geometer's Sketchpad. Berkeley, Calif.: Key Curriculum Press, 1995.

Laborde, J. M. CABRI Geometry. Grenoble, France: Université de Grenoble, 1990.

National Council of Teachers of Mathematics. *Curriculum and Evaluation Standards for School Mathematics.* Reston, Va.: National Council of Teachers of Mathematics, 1989.

Osserman, Robert. "Structure vs. Substance: The Fall and Rise of Geometry." *Two-Year College Mathematics Journal* 12 (1981): 239–46.

Mary C. Enderson, *Indiana University of Pennsylvania, Indiana, Pennsylvania,* and Azita Manouchehri, *Maryville University of Saint Louis, Saint Louis, Missouri*

26

Building Foundations for Conceptual Understanding of Arithmetic Average in the Middle-Grades Classroom

JINFA CAI

In a sixth-grade classroom the teacher, Ms. Garth, started her lesson: "Today we will discuss the concept of *average*. What might we see, hear, or say about averaging?" Within a few minutes, her students listed more than twenty examples, such as average income, average allowance, and grade point average. This discussion gave Ms. Garth a preliminary idea of her students' concept of average and helped her students realize the usefulness of the concept in real life. Then she asked her students to solve the following problem:

> For their club's food drive, Jason has 12 cans of food, Deon has 5 cans, Tonya has 4 cans, and Essie has 3 cans. When Deandre came in with his cans, the average number of cans for Jason, Deon, Tonya, Essie and Deandre became 7. How many cans did Deandre have so that the average for the five people was 7?

Ms. Garth told the students to work in pairs and walked around the room to assess their progress. After fifteen minutes she led the students in a whole-group discussion of the problem. As usual, many students raised their hands, eager to share their solutions with the class. Ms. Garth pointed to Roberta.

MS. GARTH: Roberta, what do you get there?

ROBERTA: Six.

MS. GARTH: Six. Six what?

ROBERTA: Six cans of food for Deandre.

MS. GARTH: Could you please explain to us how you found the answer 6?

ROBERTA: Because 12 plus 5, plus 4, plus 3, plus 7 equals to 31, and 31 divided by 5 is 6 something. So the answer should be 6.

Many students solved the problem the same way Roberta did. Ms. Garth was puzzled: "These students seem to know the algorithm for calculating an average (adding something up and dividing), but they used it in a wrong way here. I should correct their misunderstandings, but how?" The bell was ringing. Class was over. Ms. Garth dismissed the students and resolved to figure out a way to help her students develop a correct understanding of the concept of average.

Why Is a Conceptual Understanding of Average Important?

During the time Ms. Garth was teaching the unit on average, she was working collaboratively with a university professor on a mathematics education reform project. Coincidentally, they were planning ways to make

This article is based on work supported by a grant from the Ford Foundation, grant number 890-0572, for the QUASAR Project. Any opinions expressed herein are those of the author and do not necessarily represent the views of the Ford Foundation.

arithmetic mean understandable to students. They realized that, in the age of information and technology, it is important for students to develop an understanding of the concepts and processes used in data analysis and decision making (National Council of Teachers of Mathematics [NCTM] 1989). Arithmetic average is an important and basic concept. Thus, it is vital for a teacher to teach the concept with understanding.

Arithmetic average can be defined as the sum of the values divided by the number of values summed. The algorithm for calculating an average is straightforward, but Ms. Garth's students experienced difficulties using the algorithm flexibly to solve problems. Ms. Garth knows teaching the concept of average is more than teaching the algorithm. In fact, the arithmetic average is also a statistic used to describe and make sense of a data set. It is a tool, used in conjunction with the standard deviation, for summarizing a data set and comparing data sets. Therefore, conceptual understanding of average includes both an understanding of the computational algorithm and the statistical aspects of the concept (Cai 1998).

This article describes how Ms. Garth used manipulative materials and an open-ended problem-solving approach to build her students' conceptual understandings of arithmetic average.

How Can a Leveling Model Build Conceptual Understanding?

Over the course of several meetings, the university professor and Ms. Garth discussed a variety of instructional materials and techniques for developing the concept. Through discussions with the professor and reflections on her own approaches to teaching the activities, Ms. Garth expanded her mathematical knowledge and developed her insights into students' difficulties understanding the concept. She learned the computational and statistical nature of arithmetic average and also became aware of the properties of the concept. For example, she realized the sum of the deviations from the average is zero. She understood the importance of building on her students' existing knowledge and making connections among various representations (NCTM 1989). With this awareness she developed an instructional strategy to build a foundation for her students.

She decided to begin by introducing a leveling model that emphasized the concept of average as an evening-off process. Her lessons involved the evening-off or "leveling" of columns of tiles, recognizing that the height of the evened-off columns is the average of the original columns. The class then discussed relationships between the heights of the original columns and the evened-off columns.

Ms. Garth started her next lesson by asking her students the following question:

> Tasha has 5 candies and Billy has 13 candies. They are going to share equally. How many will each have? You need to find not only the answer, but also you must explain how you found your answer.

She asked the students to work in pairs and gave each pair a bag of tiles.

Students determined various ways to share the candies fairly. One group said: "If you add 5 and 13, then divide by 2. The answer is 9." Another group said: "It's like you have 18 tiles. You make the 18 tiles into two equal piles. You will get the answer." The third group said: "Billy has 13, but Tasha only gets 5. Billy gives one to Tasha, then Billy gets 12 and Tasha gets 6. Billy gives another to Tasha, then Billy gets 11 and Tasha gets 7. You keep going, and finally each of them gets 9; that is the answer."

Ms. Garth discussed each solution the students presented and indicated their commonalties. She then focused on the process used in the third solution. She used the tiles to model the process and indicated that equal sharing can be reached using "leveling" (see figure 26.1).

In her later lessons Ms. Garth helped her students establish a mental image by emphasizing the leveling model. She also used the leveling model to build knowledge about the properties of average. The number of tiles moved from the higher columns was always equal to the number of tiles moved onto the lower columns (i.e., the sum of the deviations from the average is zero). If the height of one of the columns was changed, the height of the evened-off columns would be changed accordingly (i.e., the average is influenced by values other than the average).

Ms. Garth also designed new problems to illustrate various aspects of the concept of average, such as situations when the average is not a whole number, when one of the numbers being averaged is zero, and when one of the numbers is unknown but the average is known.

What Does Average Mean?

The average value is a representative of the values that were averaged. Therefore, in many cases, average is used to describe a data set or compare two data sets. In order to deepen her students' understanding of this feature of the concept of average, Ms. Garth described how meteorologists determine the monthly average temperature. She introduced temperature data from January

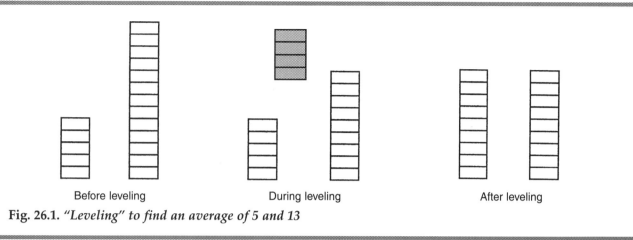

Fig. 26.1. *"Leveling" to find an average of 5 and 13*

and February for the class to use for comparisons and asked her students to write the answers to three questions:

1. What does the meteorologist mean when she or he makes the statement, "The average temperature for the month of January is 35 degrees"?

2. What steps do you think the meteorologist took to get the average temperature?

3. So far this month, Delaware's temperatures have been quite high (45 degrees on Monday, 41 degrees on Saturday). How will our high January temperatures affect the average?

Later Ms. Garth said, "I'd like to talk about the answers you wrote and see if we can agree on what meteorologists mean when they state, 'The average temperature for the month of January is 35 degrees.'"

One of the students answered, "He means the overall temperature is such and such degrees. He added up all the temperatures and then divided by how many days are in January, and then he got the average."

Ms. Garth asked, "Where do these numbers come from? When do they take these temperatures?"

After some discussion, another student said, "They take it in one day: the highest temperature and the lowest of that day."

Ms. Garth replied, "So now we have the high and low. What good are those going to do us for that day? What else could we find?"

Some students answered together, "Find the average."

Ms. Garth responded: "All right. So now, how many Januarys do you think the weatherman is talking about when he says the average temperature is 35 degrees?" One student answered, "He means all the Januarys . . . ."

Although no one had yet been able to fit the pieces together to get the average January temperature, the students collectively had come up with all the pieces of a complicated method. They had found—

1. the average of the high and low temperatures for each day of the month;

2. the average of all the average daily temperatures in the month; and

3. the average of all the average January temperatures.

Ms. Garth then outlined how to fit the pieces together.

Then, Ms. Garth discussed the meaning of "the temperature for the month of January is usually five degrees lower than February." This discussion proceeded more smoothly than the previous discussion because the details were not so complicated. The important outcome was the students realized that average could be used to summarize a data set or compare two data sets.

Can You Solve It Another Way?

After her students had established a concrete model for calculating average using the leveling of tiles, Ms. Garth introduced the formal computational algorithm for calculating average. In her instruction, Ms. Garth ensured understanding of the concept of average by guiding students to solve contextually based, open-ended problems such as the food drive question discussed in the first class on averages, but she asked her students to solve it in different ways. This time, students used different strategies: the leveling strategy, the average algorithm, and guess-and-check. Figure 26.2 shows sample student responses.

When students used the leveling strategy, they

RESPONSE 1

Answer: 11

Explain how you found your answer.

7   2   3   4+7=11

Jason   Deon   Tonya   Essie   Deandr ?   7 Average

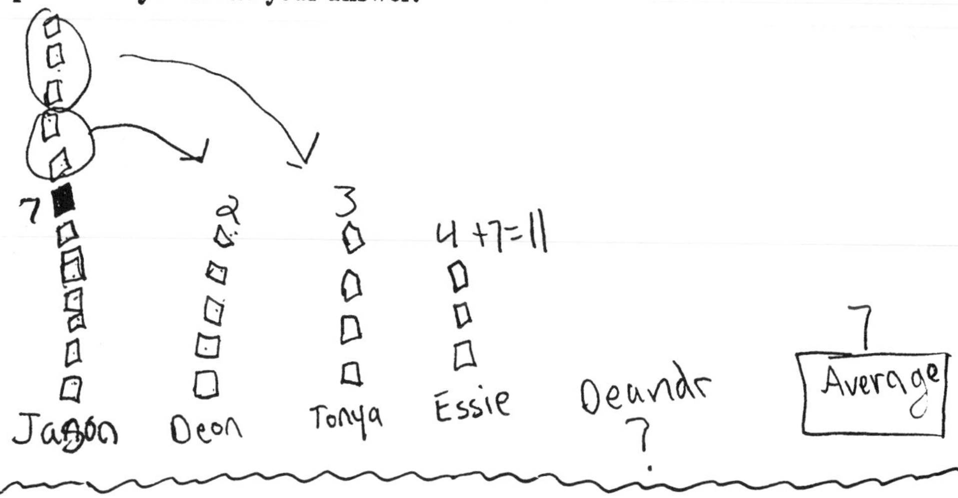

RESPONSE 2

Answer: 11

Explain how you found your answer.

First, I added all the cans together and got 24. I divided 24 by the 4 people and got 6. I made 4 rows of 6 then added another row of 6 for Deondre. Then I added 1 to each row. I added 6+5=11. (people)

RESPONSE 3

35
−24
11

fist I add all The canr it had 24 Then I 7×5= 35 -24 get

11 thet is my Answer.

Fig. 26.2. *Sample student responses*

either used a picture or written words to explain their solutions. When students employed the algorithm for average to solve the problem, they usually used symbolic representations. Ms. Garth took the opportunity to encourage students to use various representations to communicate mathematical ideas, as suggested in the NCTM *Standards* (National Council of Teachers of Mathematics 1989, 1991). Some students used an algebraic approach to solve the problem: "The number of cans that are Deandre's equals x. $5 \times 7 = 35$. $12 + 5 + 4 + 3 + x = 35$. $x = 11$."

Ms. Garth then discussed variables, equations, and equation solving, using the algebraic approach as a catalyst. Not all students were able to understand these algebraic ideas, but Ms. Garth planted the seeds. By using these problems, students made various connections within mathematics not only between various representations and solution strategies but also between algebra and statistics. Further, Ms. Garth consistently encouraged students to compare and discuss different approaches. For example, using the average formula or algorithm is more efficient than using the actual leveling approach in solving some problems.

To illustrate that point Ms. Garth presented the following problem to her students:

> The average of Ed's ten test scores is 87. The teacher throws out the top and bottom scores, which are 55 and 95. What is the average of the remaining set of eight scores?

Students were asked to explain their solution processes. A few students tried to use a leveling strategy to find the average for the remaining set of eight scores, but they failed. Students frequently used some variant of the average algorithm to solve the problem.

In explanations of their solution processes, they used either mathematical expressions or written words. For example, one student explained in words: "First I multiplied 87×10 and got 870. Then I subtracted 55 from 870 and got 815. Then I subtracted 95 and got 720. Then I divided 720 by 8 and got 90." Another student explained symbolically: "$87 \times 10 - (55 + 95) = 720$. $720 \div 8 = 90$."

One of the students used a unique strategy to solve the problem: First he determined that the average for the remaining eight scores must be between 55 and 95, then drew ten circles and put 95 on the first and 55 on the last, leaving eight empty circles in between. Using these two numbers, the average would be $[(95 + 55) \div 10 = 15]$. The student said, "Each of the eight blank spaces should get 15. But 15 is 72 less than 87" (the average for 10 scores). He then multiplied 72 by 10 and got 720; next, he divided 720 by 8 and got 90. Thus, 90 became the average of the remaining eight scores after the top and bottom scores were thrown away.

In this solution, the student viewed throwing away the top and bottom scores as taking 15 away from each circle. As the National Council of Teachers of Mathematics indicates, "[M]athematics is learned when learners engage in their own invention and impose their own sense of investigation and structure" (1991, p. 144). By inventing their own approaches, students demonstrated a deep understanding of the mathematical concepts (Cai, Moyer, and Laughlin 1998).

Conclusion

Ms. Garth used the leveling model in conjunction with an open-ended problem-solving approach to build foundations for her students' conceptual understanding of the concept of average. She also used instructional activities based on the need to make sense of real-life data. As part of the learning process, Ms. Garth guided the students to use hands-on, verbal, pictorial, and symbolic representations to communicate multiple solutions to open-ended problems.

References

Cai, Jinfa. "Exploring Students' Conceptual Understanding of the Averaging Algorithm." *School Science and Mathematics* 98, no. 2 (1998): 93–98.

Cai, Jinfa, John C. Moyer, and Connie Laughlin. "Algorithms for Solving Nonroutine Mathematical Problems." In *The Teaching and Learning of Algorithms in School Mathematics*, 1998 Yearbook of the National Council of Teachers of Mathematics, edited by Lorna J. Morrow, pp. 218–29. Reston, Va.: National Council of Teachers of Mathematics, 1998.

National Council of Teachers of Mathematics. *Curriculum and Evaluation Standards for School Mathematics*. Reston, Va.: National Council of Teachers of Mathematics, 1989.

———. *Professional Standards for Teaching School Mathematics*. Reston, Va.: National Council of Teacher of Mathematics, 1991.

Jinfa Cai, *University of Delaware, Newark, Delaware*

27

Developing Concepts in Probability: Designing and Analyzing Games

FRANCES R. CURCIO,
WITH BARBARA NIMEROFSKY,
ROSSANA PEREZ, AND
SHIREL YALOZ-FEMIA

We have been exploring ways of basing mathematics instruction on the interests and skills of our fifth- and sixth-grade students. Working in small, heterogenous groups, students develop and share mathematical ideas as they complete tasks designed to highlight specific objectives. In this article, we describe tasks that focus on developing concepts in probability. The tasks require students to design and analyze games that provide an exciting, challenging, and meaningful way to learn mathematics (Bright and Harvey 1982; Bright, Harvey, and Wheeler 1985; Sicklick, Turkel, and Curcio 1988). Further, observing students as they engage in the tasks and activities assists ongoing assessment and instructional decision making (Jones et al. 1997).

Three tasks are described: designing a game board, analyzing the outcomes of the sum of two dice, and analyzing and modifying the game board. Students work in pairs, sharing their ideas and discussing their work. Prior to assigning the tasks described, time is spent developing a classroom environment that promotes risk taking, inquiry, discourse, and mutual respect.

Task 1: Designing a Game Board

Children begin school with many informal notions of probability acquired as a result of playing games. By the time they reach middle school, they have had many experiences related to games of chance. We build on students' informal notions of probability by designing a series of tasks with multiple entry and exit levels. The tasks reflect two major student goals: (1) to determine which outcomes of the sums on two regular dice would be least likely to occur, and (2) to employ strategies to minimize the accumulation of points by their opponents. The tasks elicit a comparison of the theoretical probability of the outcomes of the sums on two regular dice and the experimental results of playing a game called "Take a Chance." The materials given to the students, who work in pairs to create a game board, are listed in figure 27.1.

As students play the game, we listen to their interactions and observe the sums on the dice they select to place on the game board as well as the number of points they assign to each sum. As early as fifth grade, some students are aware that a sum of 7 is expected to occur most frequently and a sum of 2 or 12 is expected to occur least frequently. They use this informal knowledge of theoretical probability in the design of their game boards. Although also aware of such information, other students do not use it in the design of their game boards. It is interesting to watch how the students decide whether to include the sum of 7 on the game board and how many points they assign to it.

206

OBJECT: *To create a game board so that your opponent accumulates fewer points than you.*

MATERIALS:

- Blank game board
- 2 dice
- 30 chips each worth 5 points, kept in a bank box or bag
- Writing tool

Rules for Two Players:

- Player ONE represents the bank. S/he labels each section of the board for player TWO by inserting EIGHT different possible sums that can be rolled using two regular dice.

- Next, assign point values of 5, 10, 15, 20, 25, and 30 to sections of the game board. Use each value AT LEAST once. Some values you will choose to use more than once.

- Player TWO rolls the two dice. If the sum is an outcome on the board, s/he collects the designated number of points in chips. If the sum is not an outcome on the board no points are allotted, but it counts as one of the eight rolls. This is repeated for a total number of EIGHT rolls.

- Keep a record of the total number of points awarded on each roll and calculate the sum. Return the chips back to the bank box or bag.

- *Players reverse roles.* Player TWO now creates a board for player ONE and the game continues as above.

- At the end of each player's EIGHT rolls, the winner is the player with the fewer number of points.

Questions for Thought:

1. Why did you choose the specific sums for your opponent's game board?

2. Why did you match certain point values with the sums?

3. How did all your choices affect the number of points that your opponent collected?

4. How can you improve your board so that your opponent will get fewer points?

5. How can you change this game?

Fig. 27.1. *"Take a Chance"—create a game board*

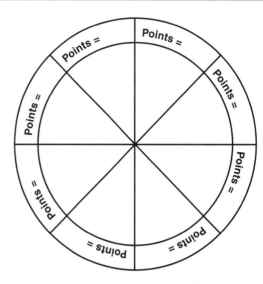

TAKE A CHANCE GAME BOARD

	Player One:			Player Two:	
Turn	Sum	# of Points	Turn	Sum	# of Points
1			1		
2			2		
3			3		
4			4		
5			5		
6			6		
7			7		
8			8		
	Total:			**Total:**	

We have students share their game boards and their responses to the "questions for thought." Two sample game boards and game outcomes are illustrated in figure 27.2.

George designed his game board first. Notice his selection of sums: 3, 5, 6, 7, 8, 9, 11, and 12. In response to the "questions for thought," George indicated that he wanted to use the odd sums, but he "ran out," so he picked some others. He did not have a plan for assigning points to the outcomes. The least likely outcomes among the eight he selected, 3 and 12, were assigned fewer points (i.e., 20 and 15, respectively) than the most likely outcome of 7 (i.e., 30 points). He was un-

able to describe how his choices of outcomes and points assigned to them affected Charlene's 110 points. George's game board and responses inform and guide us in directing him to the next task (see Task 2).

Charlene, however, realized she needed to select sums that are the least likely to occur (i.e., 2, 12, 3, and 11), but she included other sums with theoretically higher frequencies (i.e., 6 and 8) than others she could have selected (i.e., 4 and 5). She indicated that she was "looking for numbers that wouldn't come up too much," and she avoided "7 because it comes up a lot." She assigned 5 points to outcomes of 11 and 12, and she assigned points of 10 and 15 to outcomes of 2 and 3,

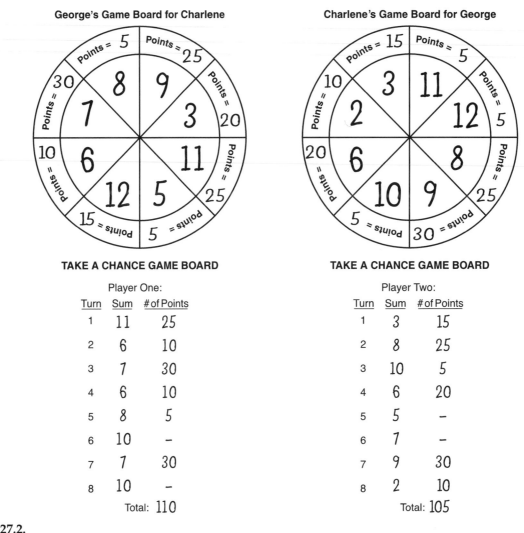

George's Game Board for Charlene

TAKE A CHANCE GAME BOARD

Player One:

Turn	Sum	# of Points
1	11	25
2	6	10
3	7	30
4	6	10
5	8	5
6	10	–
7	7	30
8	10	–
		Total: 110

Charlene's Game Board for George

TAKE A CHANCE GAME BOARD

Player Two:

Turn	Sum	# of Points
1	3	15
2	8	25
3	10	5
4	6	20
5	5	–
6	7	–
7	9	30
8	2	10
		Total: 105

Fig. 27.2.

respectively. This indicates that she did not realize the implications for assigning points to the sums she selected. She was also unable to describe how her choice of outcomes and points assigned to them affected George's 105 points, but she was happy that she was able to design a board that gave her opponent fewer points than the board he had designed for her. Charlene's game board and her responses convinced us that she would also be ready for Task 2.

Working in pairs, students put their game boards on overhead transparencies and shared their boards and results with the class. Students compared and contrasted the features of other students' game boards that were similar to, and different from, their own boards. Typical of the students in the class, neither George nor Charlene had thoughts about improving or changing the game board.

Task 2: Analyzing the Outcomes of the Sum of Two Dice

The next task was to have students collect some data. In the early stages of developing this task, we had students continue to work with their partners rolling two different-colored, regular dice one hundred times. As students collected the data, they recorded their results on graph paper and constructed a frequency graph of the outcomes. A giant master frequency graph for the class was compiled. As students worked, we walked around and listened to the discussion, making notes of which students were observing the number of ways various sums can occur and which children were not. We joined several groups to probe and elicit ideas related to the outcomes.

This approach was modified once we integrated

computers into our program. Students had the computer "roll" the dice, list the frequencies, and construct a frequency graph. The technology helped to expedite the task, allowing for a large number of trials.

When the pairs of students were finished collecting and analyzing their data, we discussed the results with the class. As the results of compiling a large number of trials were observed, students got a visual representation of the data and began to question and explore why a sum of 7 seems to occur so often and why sums of 2 and 12 seem to occur much less frequently. Students focused on the ways the different sums can occur, determining the theoretical probability of each outcome. At this point we called on selected students to list the possible ways to obtain various sums (see table 27.1).

Task 3: Analyzing and Modifying the Game Board

We then asked students to review their game boards and decide whether they wanted to make any changes. Many of them used the results of the data collection task to make adjustments in their boards. Then they played the game again. George's and Charlene's revised "ideal" game boards with outcomes are shown in figure 27.3.

George observed and articulated the chances of getting various outcomes when summing the results on two dice. He translated his understanding to his game board, selecting sums of 2, 12, 3, 11, 4, 5, 9, and 10. However, when examining the number of points he assigned to each outcome, he had some idea for minimizing points with more frequently expected outcomes (e.g.,

30 points for a sum of 2), but he was inconsistent in assigning 5 points to the sum of 12 and 20 points to the sum of 9. He wrote, "I wouldn't use 7, 8 but I would definetly [*sic*] use 2 because you can only get 2 by geting [*sic*] snake eyes. I think I made the ideal game board better because I used higher amounts of points on lower outcomes."

Examining Charlene's game board indicates that she refined her original board by systematically selecting the outcomes in pairs: 2 with 12, 3 with 11, 4 with 10, and 5 with 9. She assigned points to support her understanding of matching the least frequently expected outcome with the greatest number of points. She wrote, "I think to make an ideal game board for this game you should have numbers that have the least possible combinations. Put the least amount of points on the numbers you think will appear the most and use the most amount of points on the numbers you think will appear the least. And that's how I made my game board."

A comparison of George's game board and Charlene's outcome of 120 points with Charlene's game board and George's outcome of 40 points was quite revealing for George. He was overheard saying, "I think I need to put all the larger number of points on the numbers that are not most likely to appear."

Students' suggestions for changing the game included making fewer sections in the circular game board (e.g., six sections instead of eight), using products instead of sums for the outcomes on the dice, using other polyhedra dice (e.g., dodecahedral dice), and trying to get the opponent to accumulate the greater number of points rather than fewer points. We continued to explore these suggestions with other students.

One of the most important features of this type of activity is having students discuss the changes they make in their game boards and why they make them. The "big" mathematical ideas about probability are highlighted in the class discussions. In particular, we see students matching the greatest number of points with the least likely outcomes of the sum of the dice. When they play the game, however, they realize there are no guarantees their opponent will not end up with fewer points than before—but that's probability!

Closing Comments

"Take a Chance" is only one of the many game-related tasks that we use with our middle school students. Creating and playing mathematics games supports the social and intellectual development of the young adolescent learner. Opportunities to interact, explore, and discuss ideas foster the development of autonomous learners. Presenting students with interactive,

TABLE 27.1.

Ways to make sums on two dice

Sum	Ways to obtain sum	No. of ways
2	1 + 1	1
3	1 + 2; 2 + 1	2
4	1 + 3; 2 + 2; 3 + 1	3
5	1 + 4; 2 + 3; 3 + 2; 4 + 1	4
6	1 + 5; 2 + 4; 3 + 3; 4 + 2; 5 + 1	5
7	1 + 6; 2 + 5; 3 + 4; 4 + 3; 5 + 2; 6 + 1	6
8	2 + 6; 3 + 5; 4 + 4; 5 + 3; 6 + 2	5
9	3 + 6; 4 + 5; 5 + 4; 6 + 3	4
10	4 + 6; 5 + 5; 6 + 4	3
11	5 + 6; 6 + 5	2
12	6 + 6	1
	Total:	36

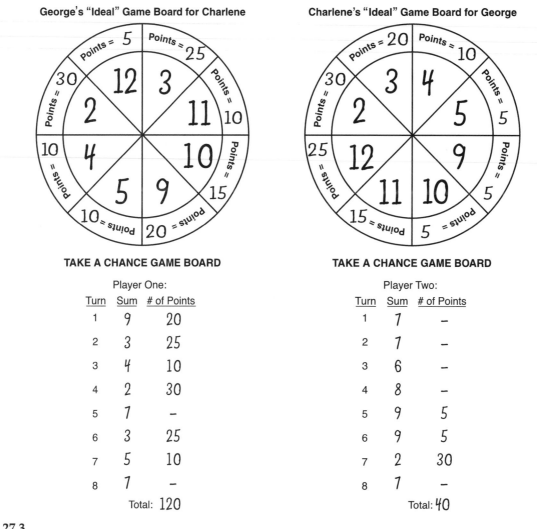

George's "Ideal" Game Board for Charlene

Charlene's "Ideal" Game Board for George

TAKE A CHANCE GAME BOARD

Player One:

Turn	Sum	# of Points
1	9	20
2	3	25
3	4	10
4	2	30
5	7	–
6	3	25
7	5	10
8	7	–
		Total: 120

TAKE A CHANCE GAME BOARD

Player Two:

Turn	Sum	# of Points
1	7	–
2	7	–
3	6	–
4	8	–
5	9	5
6	9	5
7	2	30
8	7	–
		Total: 40

Fig. 27.3.

challenging, and motivational activities builds confidence and bolsters achievement in mathematics. Whether the achievement measure is a traditional standardized test or a nontraditional, open-ended assessment task, we have found that our students excel on items and tasks that reflect the content of the games they have designed and analyzed.

Student-generated games provide a great source for eliciting mathematical understandings and provide a forum for developing discourse in mathematics. As they work in pairs or in small groups, students discuss and share ideas for games, talking about the mathematics embedded in the games as well as strategies to be employed. Student-student interactions are maximized and student-teacher interactions occur informally. After the games are created, students play them with one another, questioning the creator if rules are

not clear and informing the creator of any errors that exist. Students are very generous in offering ways to modify and improve games.

The mathematical ideas that we develop with our fifth and sixth graders through games and tasks are not trivial. We firmly believe that if we can capture students' interests, build on their strengths, and celebrate their achievements, everyone can be a winner!

References

Bright, George W., and John G. Harvey. "Using Games to Teach Fraction Concepts and Skills." In *Mathematics for the Middle Grades* (5–9), 1982 Yearbook of the National Council of Teachers of Mathematics, edited by Linda Silvey, pp. 205–16. Reston, Va.: National Council of Teachers of Mathematics, 1982.

Bright, George W., John G. Harvey, and Margariete Montague Wheeler. *Learning and Mathematics Games. Journal for Research in Mathematics Education*, Monograph no. 1. Reston, Va.: National Council of Teachers of Mathematics, 1985.

Jones, Graham A., Cynthia W. Langrall, Carol A. Thornton, and A. Timothy Mogill. "A Framework for Assessing and Nurturing Young Children's Thinking in Probability." *Educational Studies in Mathematics* 32 (February 1997): 101–25.

Sicklick, Francine, Susan B. Turkel, and Frances R. Curcio. "The 'Transformation Game.'" *Arithmetic Teacher* 36 (October 1988): 37–41.

Frances R. Curcio, *New York University, New York, New York;* Barbara Nimerofsky and Rossana Perez, *Louis Armstrong Middle School, East Elmhurst, New York;* and Shirel Yaloz-Femia, *Hunter College High School, New York, New York*

28

Promoting Mathematical Learning in the Middle School: PUMP Project Strategies

Carol A. Thornton,
Jane O. Swafford, Graham A. Jones,
Cynthia W. Langrall, Gladis Kersaint,
and Edward Mooney

The Peoria Urban Mathematics Plan (PUMP) algebra project is a systemic effort in a midsized urban city to increase the number of students, particularly minorities, who are algebra-ready and will remain in substantive mathematics classes at the high school level. The goal of the project is to use middle school mathematics as a pump, rather than as a filter, for the mathematics pipeline. The project title is both an acronym and a metaphor.

The project is systemic in that it involves forty-eight teachers representing all the district's fourteen middle schools and four high schools. Further, the district's administration is committed to using the project as a catalyst for improving mathematics instruction throughout Peoria. The project is also a collaborative effort involving teachers and administrators from the school district, faculty and graduate assistants from the university, representatives from business and industry, and staff and volunteers from the local Urban League.

Believing that improvement in mathematics begins in the classroom, the thrust of the project is a three-year teacher-enhancement program featuring three intensive summer sessions with follow-up academic year seminars and classroom visits. The summer sessions involve teachers *doing* mathematics and reflecting on mathematics teaching and learning. Topics for the

mathematics courses include rational numbers and proportional reasoning in the first year; algebraic thinking in the second year; and geometry, probability, and statistics in the third year. Materials from National Science Foundation–funded middle school curriculum projects have provided the springboard for studying content and analyzing new teaching approaches. Teachers are also given opportunities in the summer to rethink and reorganize their mathematics program to incorporate ideas and strategies from the project.

The PUMP project is driven by the philosophy that through enhanced forms of mathematics instruction, *all* students can learn a broad range of mathematics and develop their capacity not only to compute and to recall factual knowledge correctly but to think quantitatively, solve complex problems, and reason mathematically. This philosophy gives rise to four classroom strategies that serve to guide and unify the project:

- Emphasize that mathematics is for all students.
- Engage students in worthwhile mathematical tasks.
- Enhance levels of student discourse about mathematical ideas.
- Involve students in collaborative mathematical activities.

In what follows, we will illustrate how each of these strategies "plays in Peoria."

Emphasize that Mathematics Is for *All* Students.

As a way of preparing students to enter more meaningful mathematics classes in high school, the PUMP project is working with middle school teachers to raise their expectations of students' mathematical abilities. Too often, teachers have low expectations of students from economically disadvantaged and minority backgrounds, and they tend to accept mediocrity rather than stretching and elevating the students. The following vignette illustrates how believing "mathematics is for all students" is reflected in one PUMP classroom.

> While exploring linear equations, Ms. Glade realized that her students didn't really understand integer operations. To develop conceptual thinking about the operations, she introduced chips of two colors to model positive and negative numbers. After writing "11 + ⁻4 = _____" on the board, she had students use the chips to solve the problem individually at their desks. She then called for volunteers to show their solutions on the overhead. When no volunteer emerged, she asked Kamali to come up, having observed that he had correctly modeled the problem.
>
> KAMALI: I don't know how to do it.
> MS. GLADE: Come on, you can do it. Just show us what you did.
> KAMALI: I don't want to.
> MS. GLADE: Come on, Kamali, come on.
>
> Kamali reluctantly came to the overhead and correctly modeled the problem. This was the first time that Kamali had ever overtly participated in the class. He was clearly pleased with his success and seemed to gain self-confidence in that he volunteered later in the lesson to illustrate another problem.

The episode with Kamali is an example of how reluctant students will rise to meet higher teacher expectations. In the past, many PUMP teachers, including Ms. Glade, ignored students like Kamali. Part of believing that all students can learn is to include every student in the learning process, even those who are passive. In order to break the cycle of underachievement, the teachers must first break the cycle of failure by giving students opportunities to experience small successes. With reluctant students, one approach is to first help them individually and then, when they understand, give them an opportunity to explain their thinking to the group or class. Students who habitually experience failure are reluctant to take risks but, like

Photo credit: Jeff Saucek Photography

Kamali, once they experience a small success are more willing to share their mathematics thinking.

Having high expectations of all students involves not only expecting *all* students to do mathematics, but expecting students to do *all* kinds of mathematics. Teachers underestimate students' capabilities for learning higher-level mathematics and confine them to working in a narrow and deprived curriculum that is almost entirely computation driven (Elliott and Garnett 1995).

The irony of such limited expectations is that disadvantaged students often have few opportunities to learn mathematics through a broad-based curriculum that includes problem solving, reasoning, and communication (Stevens 1995). As a result, they fall behind their more advantaged peers in mathematics achievement (Burstein 1993). The following vignette illustrates how one PUMP teacher raised her expectations by broadening the curriculum.

> Prior to participating in PUMP, Ms. Edge had concentrated almost exclusively on whole-number computation with her fifth-grade students. In fact, mastering these computational skills was her only expectation of them. Ms. Edge's overriding belief in students' need to master computation precluded the inclusion of any other mathematical topics in her curriculum. As a result, she had never taught a geometry unit in her four years of teaching.
>
> During school visits, the PUMP staff emphasized the need for a broader curriculum and presented several demonstration lessons on the properties of polygons.

tional time to computation, she now has different expectations for her students than she did prior to PUMP.

Engage Students in Worthwhile Mathematical Tasks

Although PUMP teachers accepted the idea of engaging middle school students in worthwhile mathematical tasks (National Council of Teachers of Mathematics 1991), they had considerable difficulties generating appropriate tasks and implementing them in their instructional programs. During the academic year seminars and weekly site visits, PUMP staff worked with teachers to help them identify and use more worthwhile tasks.

For example, Mr. Dalton had asked for help in developing a more problem-focused and less procedural approach to the teaching of linear equations. In responding, the PUMP staff suggested that he use an instructional strategy in which the teacher provides the answer and asks the students to generate problems to fit. When Mr. Dalton asked for a demonstration lesson illustrating this instructional strategy, Mr. Mooney, a PUMP staff member, presented an activity from *Algebra for Everyone* (Glatzer and Choate 1992). In this activity, students are presented equations and asked to construct stories that could be represented by the equation.

> Starting with the equation "$11 + p = 20$," Mr. Mooney asked the class to think of situations that fit this equation. The students generated a diverse range of problem situations, such as the one given by Miranda: "Paul was training for a marathon. On Tuesday he jogged 11 miles. He also jogged on Wednesday. He jogged 20 miles in the two days. How many miles did he jog on Wednesday?"
>
> However, a few problems, like Cedrick's below, did not represent the equation, even though many students in the class thought it was appropriate: "Dane, the air time inventor, was MVP [most valuable player] for 11 years straight. No one could stop him but his mother. She told him he had to quit in 20 more years. So how many years did Dane have left to play?"
>
> As he had done with all the problems presented, Mr. Mooney opened up the discussion by asking Cedrick to explain how his story was represented by the equation.
>
> CEDRICK: 11 is there; 20 is there; and there's a question for the "p."
>
> TYRONNE: But the answer to your problem is 20. You say so right in it.
>
> LATOYA: And the answer should be 9 because 9 works in the equation.

Photo credit: Jeff Saucek Photography

Seeing how well students responded, Ms. Edge decided to continue the unit with the support of the PUMP staff. In one of her lessons from this unit, she asked students to construct four-sided shapes on their geoboards. She then called on pairs of students to show and name their shapes, and she challenged the class to tell how the two shapes were alike and how they were different. The first pair of students reported that they had constructed a square and a rectangle. The ensuing discussion focused on different properties of these shapes and raised questions like "When is a rectangle a square?" and "What happens when you put two squares together?"

What occurred in Ms. Edge's classroom represented an initial step toward broadening the mathematical experiences of her students. In contrast to her single-minded focus on whole-number computation, Ms. Edge now includes geometry, fractions, and other topics in her curriculum. The geometry lessons she designed also reflect her efforts to move toward a more problem-centered curriculum that fosters and challenges students' thinking. Although Ms. Edge continues to devote a considerable proportion of her instruc-

MR. MOONEY: In Cedrick's story, does Dane have 9 years left to play?

EMILY: No, he has 20 more years.

MR. MOONEY: Is there a way to change the story so that Dane has 9 years left to play?

CEDRICK: If he could play a total of 20 years.

MR. MOONEY: What do you mean?

CEDRICK: He's already played 11 years. If his mother told him he could only play basketball for a total of 20 years, then he would have 9 years left.

MR. MOONEY: Does that make sense to everyone?

TYRONNE: In Cedrick's problem, we don't know how long he'd played. Dane was MVP for 11 years, but he might have played for longer. I'd think it should be like this: "Dane, the air time inventor, was MVP for 11 years straight. The record for MVP is 20 years in a row. How many more years does Dane have to win the MVP to match the record?"

Cedrick's problem provoked meaningful classroom discussion and provided opportunity for the students to work together to modify it. In reflecting on the power of this worthwhile task, Mr. Dalton noted that his students took pride in presenting their problems and in grappling with the mathematical ideas the task incorporated. He also realized he had gained greater insight into his students' understanding of the mathematics and into situations and experiences that were relevant to his students.

Enhance Student Discourse and Involve Students in Collaborative Activities

Research has documented the effectiveness of discourse and collaboration with diverse student populations (Glaser and Silver 1994; Garcia 1991). For example, Garcia notes that collaboration and communication, two key strategies in the PUMP project, are essential elements of instructional practice with culturally diverse populations, especially when the curriculum contains a blend of challenging and basic material. The following vignette illustrates how a PUMP teacher, Ms. Cantrell, attempted to foster greater collaboration and discourse through a series of projects in which the students worked independently, in groups, and in whole-class settings. This was the first time that these students had engaged in any type of cooperative learning.

To open the school year, Ms. Cantrell designed a "Neighborhood Unit" to focus on rational numbers, measurement, and ratios. Initially, Ms. Cantrell challenged the students to design a six-block neighborhood to be con-

structed as part of an urban renewal grant. She had the students work in groups of three to produce a model diagram of the neighborhood, the relevant computations, and written commentaries on the advantages of their plans.

The students first worked independently to carry out the initial calculations and to sketch a preliminary plan. After comparing calculations and plans, each group had to reach consensus on a single plan and commentary and organize a group presentation.

Figure 28.1 shows the problem, the conditions relating to the problem, and the results computed by one group of students. Figure 28.2 presents a sketch and explanation of the group's six-block neighborhood.

Part of believing that all students can learn is to include every student in the learning process, even those who are passive.

After the class had succeeded with the six-block neighborhood, Ms. Cantrell developed a related problem involving a twelve-block plan. She also generated an extension problem in which the students examined architectural plans and then produced their own floor plans for five homes. Finally, they selected a favorite room, enlarged it by a factor of 2, and completed it with furniture to scale. As a challenge, some students enlarged another room by a factor of 3 1/2.

Throughout the year Ms. Cantrell used cooperative learning on a regular basis as she engaged students in units on number sense, data exploration, geometry, algebraic beginnings, and probability. The number sense unit integrated mathematics and science and focused on the solar system and bacteria. In this unit Ms. Cantrell and the science teacher, Mr. Bowman, worked in collaboration and began a partnership that extended to other units.

For Ms. Cantrell, the use of collaboration and enhanced discourse represented a substantial rethinking of her teaching. She discovered that the Neighborhood Unit provided an effective vehicle for initiating group work and class discussion with students who had little previous experience in working collaboratively. After Ms. Cantrell began using projects that incorporated group work and more student discourse, class achievement improved, with all but three students out of ninety being successful on the semester exam. Further, Ms. Cantrell found the rich tasks involved in projects provided an opportunity for all students to participate in mathematics.

NEIGHBORHOOD UNIT

NAMES Adam, Jacie & Charlene

Recently, Peoria was given an urban renewal grant from the government to clear six city blocks near our school and build a variety of buildings on the cleared land. The six blocks were located on either side of Orlando Boulevard, with Cantell Avenue and Bartlett Avenue running in between them.

Government regulations are as follows:

	How many lots are needed?	How many buildings?
Each block must be divided into ten equal lots.		
1/15 of the area must be designated for a park or parks.	4	
1/2 of the area must contain single family homes.	30	30 [H]
1/3 of the area must contain duplexes (two-family homes using two lots).	20	10 [DUP]
1/10 of the area must contain apartments (multiple-family homes using three lots).	6	2 [APT]

Fig. 28.1.

Conclusion

After only one year of participation in the PUMP algebra project, mathematics scores on the state-required mathematics achievement test have improved at *all* project grade levels; in addition, enrollments in first-year algebra have increased. Compared to baseline data gathered prior to the project, districtwide increases in student mathematics achievement have occurred in ten of the district's fourteen middle schools at the eighth-grade level. In addition, 50 percent of the middle schools have shown improvement in their sixth-grade mathematics scores. It is important to note that this growth in mathematics achievement has come at a time when many of these schools have also increased their enrollment of low-income students. Eighth-grade algebra enrollment has increased in eight of the fourteen middle schools, including a 7 percent increase in minority enrollments. Two of these schools, which also serve the most economically disadvantaged students, had never offered algebra. There has been a 12 percent increase in first-year algebra enrollments at the high school level, including a 10 percent increase in minority enrollment.

There have also been observable changes in instructional practices. During weekly classroom visits, PUMP staff have observed teachers breaking from their traditional forms of instruction and incorporating the four strategies advanced by the project. Moreover, there is evidence from principals and teachers that the project has made an impact on the district's mathematics program. In the words of one principal, "Project PUMP could not have arrived too soon for the students in my school. It is refreshing to see authentic, problem-based lessons happening on a regular basis in math classes. I see teachers enthusiastic about the new approaches . . . [and] students engaged in activities that allow them to discover, take risks, and find meaning."

These changes are also reflected in the comments of a PUMP teacher from a different school: "When students enter my class, they typically lack 'prior knowledge' required for problem solving. In the past, much of the class time was spent remediating computational skills for whole numbers and fractions. Now graphics calculators that have come about because of PUMP are used to enhance and reinforce basic math knowledge and develop higher level of understandings. All of my students this year are working at a more advanced level and understanding algebraic problems through graphs, tables, and written interpretation."

From our perspective, the four classroom strategies presented and illustrated in this article have been the impetus for teacher and student changes. These strategies, grounded in research and the NCTM *Stan-*

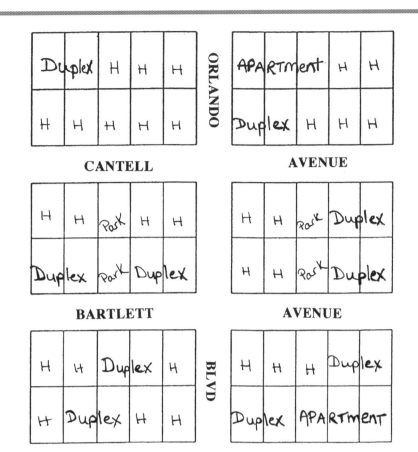

CANTELL   ORLANDO   **AVENUE**

BARTLETT   **AVENUE**

     BLVD

Parks are all over so everyone is near one. They are inside so all the people on other blocks won't take them over. Apartments are on outside so there will not be cars parking all over your street. Duplexes are not all in one place so there will be more even numbers of people all over. Parents can keep an eye on their kids in parks close to home.

Fig. 28.2.

dards (1989, 1991), have provided the common theme for PUMP teachers as they rethink mathematics teaching and learning in a midsized urban city.

References

Burstein, Leigh, ed. *The IEA Study of Mathematics III: Student Growth and Classroom Processes.* New York: Pergamon Press, 1993.

Elliott, Portia, and Cynthia Garnett. "Mathematics Power for All." In *Windows of Opportunity: Mathematics for Students with Special Needs,* edited by Carol A. Thornton and Nancy S. Bley, pp. 3–17. Reston, Va.: National Council of Teachers of Mathematics, 1994.

Garcia, Eugene. *Education of Linguistically and Culturally Diverse Students: Effective Instructional Practices.* Educational Practice Report 1. Santa Cruz, Calif.: University of California—Santa Cruz, National Center for Research on Cultural Diversity and Second Language Learning, 1991.

Glaser, Robert, and Edward A. Silver. "Assessment, Testing, and Instruction: Retrospect and Prospect." In *Review of Research in Education,* edited by Linda Darling-Hammond, pp. 393–419. Washington, D.C.: American Educational Research Association, 1994.

Glatzer, David J., and Stuart A. Choate. *Algebra for Everyone: In-Service Handbook.* Edited by Albert P. Shulte. Reston, Va.: National Council of Teachers of Mathematics, 1992.

National Council of Teachers of Mathematics. *Curriculum and Evaluation Standards for School Mathematics.* Reston, Va.: National Council of Teachers of Mathematics, 1989.

———. *Professional Standards for Teaching Mathematics.* Reston, Va.: National Council of Teachers of Mathematics, 1991.

Stevens, Floraline. "Closing the Achievement Gap: Opportunity to Learn, Standards, and Assessment." In *Closing the Urban Achievement Gap: A Vision to Guide Change in Beliefs and Practice,* edited by Belinda Williams, pp. 53–64. Philadelphia, Pa.: Research for Better Schools, 1995.

Carol A. Thornton, Jane O. Swafford, Graham A. Jones, Cynthia W. Langrall, Gladis Kersaint, and Edward Mooney, *Illinois State University, Normal, Illinois*